RESEA   **ATURE**
ANI   **TURE:**

                                      TURE

Researching Response to Literature and the Teaching of Literature:
Points of Departure

Charles R. Cooper, Editor
University of California, San Diego

Ablex Publishing Corporation
Norwood, New Jersey 07648

Library of Congress Cataloging in Publication Data
Main entry under title:

Researching response to literature and the teaching of
   literature.

   Includes index.
   1. Reading, Psychology of.   2. Literature—Study
and teaching.   I. Cooper, Charles Raymond, 1934–
BF456.R2R47   1983   153.6   83-11826
ISBN 0-89391-184-4

Ablex Publishing Corporation
355 Chestnut Street
Norwood, New Jersey 07468

CONTENTS

Acknowledgments

Most of the chapters in this book originate in a conference held at State University of New York in the fall of 1977. These papers were revised soon after the conference and then revised again and updated in the fall of 1982. Subsequently, I solicited three additional papers in order to fill particular gaps. Two of these papers were drafted in 1980, and both were just recently revised. The third was written in the fall of 1982. Though this book has been in preparation for some time, it is not in any way a dated collection. Indeed, all the authors believe their contributions now bring them much closer to their original aims at the time of the conference. As I point out in the Introduction which follows, recent developments in literary theory, cognitive psychology, and reading research make 1984 a propitious year for this collection to appear.

The conference was made possible by grants from the Research Foundation of the National Council of Teachers of English and the Division of Graduate and Professional Education, State University of New York at Buffalo. The staff of the University Learning Center at Buffalo and the staff of Third College Composition Program at San Diego provided valuable assistance with typing, duplicating, and mailing. Conference Secretary Roger Cherry and his assistant Michael Williamson provided conscientious, skillful coordination at all stages in organizing and administering the conference. My Buffalo colleague Lee Odell (now at Rensselaer Polytechnic Institute) helped me plan the conference and read the papers for the first round of revisions just after the conference.

At the very beginning I sought the advice of several knowledgeable people around the country. Some of them may not remember, but they were all especially helpful: Arthur Applebee, Richard Beach, Mary Beaven, Margaret Early, Norman Holland, Dianne Monson, Anthony Petrosky, and James Squire. Their broad knowledge of theory and research in response to literature was invaluable to me, although their mention here should not imply their endorsement of the plan for the conference or of this book. I had wanted a collection of papers that would provide a comprehensive introduction to research on response to literature and the teaching of literature. Even with the very best of advice and even after filling noticeable gaps in the collection after the conference, I still was not able to include every relevant theory and research methodology. Almost any knowledgeable reader will be able to think of a half dozen writers he or she would have wanted to see contribute a chapter. Still, for a first book of this kind, it covers a lot of ground and offers surprisingly wide-ranging possibilities for new research.

Charles R. Cooper

Introduction

The protagonist in Italo Calvino's novel *If on a Winter's Night a Traveler* goes to a great library, hoping at last to find and finish reading ten novels he has been unable to complete. None of the ten novels is immediately available and, while the library staff searches for them, he waits at a table with several intent readers. One of these readers suddenly begins explaining how he reads. Then others around the table in turn tell how they read:

> If a book truly interests me, I cannot follow it for more than a few lines before my mind, having seized on a thought that the text suggests to it, or a feeling, or a question, or an image, goes off on a tangent and springs from thought to thought, from image to image, in an itinerary of reasoning and fantasies that I feel the need to pursue to the end, moving away from the book until I have lost sight of it. (p. 254)

> My attention . . . cannot be detached from the written lines even for an instant. I must not be distracted if I do not wish to miss some valuable clue. Every time I come upon one of these clumps of meaning I must go on digging around to see if the nugget extends into a vein. (pp. 254, 255)

> The moment that counts most for me is the one that precedes reading. At times a title is enough to kindle in me the desire for a book that perhaps does not exist. At times it is the *incipit* of the book, the first sentences . . . In other words: if you need little to set the imagination going, I require even less: the promise of reading is enough. (p. 256)

> It is the end that counts . . . the goal to which the book wants to carry you . . . my gaze digs between the words to try to discern what is outlined in the distance, in the spaces that extend beyond the words "the end." (p. 256)

> Every new book I read comes to be a part of that overall and unitary book that is the sum of my readings. This does not come about without some effort; to compose that general book, each individual book must be transformed, enter into a relationship with the books I have read previously, become their corollary or development or confutation or gloss or reference text . . . I have done nothing but continue the reading of a single book. (pp. 255, 256)

> There is a story that for me comes before all other stories and of which all the stories I read seem to carry an echo, immediately lost. In my readings I do nothing but seek that book read in my childhood, but what I remember of it is too little to enable me to find it again. (p. 256)

Authors of chapters in *Researching Response to Literature and the Teaching of Literature* propose a variety of ways we can learn more about the surprising range of responses around Calvino's reading table in the great library. The main question we attempt to answer is this: What theories should guide our study of readers and what methodologies will enable us to learn more about readers? We explore a great many questions like these: What processes of thinking and feeling go on as readers read a text? What are the contributions of text, reader, and reading situation to these reading processes? Is reading a fictional text different from reading an informational text or from "reading" a movie? How can we describe and understand these differences? How do readers form memory representations of texts? What is remembered when we remember a text? How are those memories revealed in what we say or write about a text after one reading, after several immediate successive readings, a month later? How are they revealed in involuntary images, phrases, associations, ideas that may emerge in consciousness for days after we read a text?

While these questions provide a focus throughout the book, our chief purpose is to *stimulate further research* on response to literature and the teaching of literature.

We have written the book for those who would like to seriously and systematically study response to literature and the teaching of literature. We have attempted to present a comprehensive review of the major theories that might inform research on response as well as a catalogue of most, if not all, of the most promising techniques and methodologies for carrying out research. We have attempted here to say as clearly as we can to those outside our special fields what our work involves and how it might be useful to others. If we have succeeded, and we believe we have, then this book is an ideal starting place—a point of departure—for newcomers to research on response to literature and the teaching of literature.

The book is not primarily a review of research findings. It does not summarize everything we presently know about response to literature and its teaching. It is concerned less with what we know than with what we still need to learn.

This book will not provide direct assistance to teachers seeking new ways to teach literature. Nevertheless, we believe any teacher of literature will find the theorizing here challenging and compelling, for it raises basic questions about readers and their development.

Still another limitation of the book will be apparent to those who have followed the research on young readers: we have not dealt with studies of reader interest or preference. Our focus here is more narrowly on the basic processes of the reading act itself.

A special feature of the book is its concern with readers of all ages, backgrounds, and levels of sophistication. Researchers interested in very young children will find the book especially useful. Nearly all of the writers in this book raise developmental issues. Though all of us are presently teaching in colleges and universities, many of us have taught young children and adolescents and continue to do research with school-age readers and to train others to do such research. We believe, therefore, that the book will find an audience of readers with interests and backgrounds as varied as those of the authors: literary theory, teaching of literature, fiction writing, teacher training and supervision, curriculum and program evaluation, educational research, linguistics, rhetoric, discourse theory, aesthetics, computer science, cognitive psychology, developmental psychology, and pscyhoanalysis. We believe this variety reflects the complexity of the phenomenon to be studied.

Our use of the term "response" in the book title may require some discussion. We chose to identify our particular concern with the phrase "response to literature" rather than the phrase "reading of literature" for four main reasons:

1. For us, the term "response" suggests the full complexity of the reading process, from decoding to inference, as well as the particular demands of the uniquely aesthetic, globally contextualized reading which fictional literature requires.
2. Without necessarily displacing the centrality of the text in the reading process, the term suggests the importance of the reader's role, the reader's culture, reading experience, preferences and predispositions, and current state.
3. The term expands our view of the reading process to include not only the evocation and evaluation of the work during reading but the expressed response which follows the reading.
4. Finally, the term connects our particular concern with a long tradition of educational theory and research in literary studies in this country and in England, a tradition in which the term "response" has been useful in exactly the ways mentioned above.

This research tradition considerably predates the current interest in reader-response theory. While literary critics remained preoccupied with formalist issues, some psychologists and educational researchers were studying readers and readings. Though the major purpose of the research was the search for more effective ways to teach literature to children and adolescents and the assessment of their development as readers, the questions which guided the research were exactly those being asked now by reader-response theorists: What happens when someone reads a literary text? What are the possibilities of expressed response in remembered details from the text, as well as in associations, inferences, or interpretations? How can we interpret these responses? What is the status of the text? What is the role of the reader?

This research tradition actually can be traced at least as far back as Louise Rosenblatt's statement of her reader-response theory, *Literature as Exploration*, published in 1938 and reissued in 1968 and 1976. Over the years, studies have occasionally appeared in educational or psychological journals. But, beginning in the early 1960s, the number of studies increased. Students of David Russell and Walter Loban in the School of Education at Berkeley—Caroline Shrodes, James Squire, and James Wilson, for example—carried out important research which fostered a growing interest elsewhere. Alan Purves and his students at the University of Illinois were beginning to carry out notable studies. In Sweden, Gunnar Hansson explored readers' responses to poetry. In England, D. W. Harding and teachers in the Leeds Children as Readers Group published significant studies. (I have reviewed these studies [Cooper, 1976] as have Purves and Beach [1972].) The National Council of Teachers of English provided a critically important impetus for this new research by inaugurating a research monograph series in 1963 and a research journal

(*Research in the Teaching of English*) in 1965, both of which welcomed reports of research on readers.

In addition, a major revolution in reading theory was under way during the 1960s. Before that, studies of how we learn to read had been concerned mainly with word recognition. Studies of comprehension or interpretation had been limited by reductive assumptions from psychometrics. By the 1960s, however, new developments in psycholinguistics and cognitive psychology had made possible a new view of reading in which comprehension was approached through a study of the interaction of readers' knowledge and expectations with the constraints in connected discourse. Frank Smith was one of the first to summarize readably this new approach to reading (1971, 1978). By the mid-1970s, this new approach had stimulated a huge research effort into the nature of reading comprehension, learning to read, and children's development as readers. Early results of this effort have been presented by a research team at the Center for the Study of Reading at the University of Illinois (Spiro, Bruce, and Brewer, 1980). Researchers in response to literature and reader-response theorists would do well to follow this new work closely. Most of the authors in this book know this new research and consider it essential background for their discussions and recommendations.

By the early 1970s, a major revolution was also well under way in literary theory and criticism, one which overturned the dominance of the objective text as the chief object of study and instruction. The reader of texts achieved a new prominence. An ever larger number of highly regarded theorists argued that the results or effects of texts were worthy of serious study. They argued that meaning or interpretation in the act of reading is in the mind of the reader—or at least is the result of a transaction between the reader and a text—and not in the text alone. Reader-response theory is part of a gradual realization in the sciences, social sciences, and humanities that the observer effects the consequence of observations and that the focus of inquiry should be on the observer and the relation between observers and observations. The immediate result of this shift in focus for literary theory has been a very general redirection of theoretical concern since the early 1970s. (For a fine introduction and a perceptive historical essay see Tompkins, 1980; Suleiman and Crosman, 1980; and Harari, 1979.) In this redirection, theorists are concerned not just with a generalized reader but with particular, individual readers and readings. Some of the more prominent reader-response theorists are European phenomenologists Wolfgang Iser and Georges Poulet, American psychoanalytic psychologists Norman Holland and David Bleich, and three American theorists, Louise Rosenblatt, Stanley Fish, and Jonathan Culler.

Reader-response theory has meant not just a shift in theoretical perspective, but a new view of the moral values of literature, a new reason for reading literature. The theory also implies a necessity for a different approach to instruction and a new role for the teacher. Reader-response theory emphasizes the value of literature for self-knowledge and for understanding others. It insists on the importance of individual consciousness. In classroom teaching, it shifts emphasis away from critical authority and received knowledge toward elaboration and evaluation of personal responses and arbitration of responses in a classroom community of responders.

This shift in values and in teaching alone would connect current reader-response theory to the older tradition of educational research into response to literature, which was motivated in part by developmental and instructional concerns. But the fundamental and consequential connection among general reading theorists, educational researchers, and reader-response theorists is the acceptance of the reader's importance in studies of reading and theories about reading.

I review these three strands of research and theory not only to demonstrate their close relationship and their present strong convergence but also to place this book within the context of this lively current scene. Though reader-response theorists are represented among the authors, most of us are in the older tradition of educational and psychological research on reading and on response to literature. What we all share is a tolerance for empiricism: we are willing to examine closely not only our own readings but also the readings of other particular readers or groups of readers, and we are willing to systematically design studies and analyze results from them. We are willing to go further than constructing from the text itself some ideal or implied reader. We are eager to talk to real readers.

As I review briefly in the next few pages the major concerns in each chapter, it will be quite clear that the book offers an eclectic approach to research on response. Authors recommend a wide range of research modes, designs, and methodologies.

The book is organized into three parts: theories of response, ways to study response, and ways to study classroom instruction in literature. In Part I, authors take up the question of just what it is we should study when we study response to literature. Essentially the argument is over what weight should be given the text, the reader, and the context of the reading.

In the opening chapter, Norman Holland proposes a transactive model to explain response in terms of a reader's characteristic patterns of defense, expectation, fantasy, and transformation. His model is based on the concept of "identity theme" in current ego psychology. In order to test his model, and for continued research on response, he recommends holistic research, "closely examined case studies," where the researcher looks for themes and subthemes in extended associative responses. Such research has two stages: the researcher first uses a theory or a generalization as a guide to understanding the case study, and then uses the "better understood" case study to reach a stronger generalization or to find an improved way to do case studies. Holland's wide-ranging recommendations for research include further individual case studies of associative responses, studies of the relation of personal aspects of response to current critical consensus about a particular work, response to film and TV, group patterns of response, and the role of teachers in students' responses.

Contesting Holland's model of response, C. Barry Chabot proposes that our studies of response focus not on unique individual responses but on commonalities of response within communities of readers. He faults Holland for his inability to explain "how it comes about that several people can actually agree on the meaning of a piece of writing." He argues that we should study the "interpretive situation," the process by which different readers agree on the meaning of a text. Insisting that the interpretive situation "forms an irreducible totality," he claims we can never have an adequate model of response by looking at either texts or readers outside the context of a community of readers. Chabot's notion of the interpretive situation includes reader characteristics (expectations, reading interests, familiarity with the author's works or with similar works) and text characteristics (language accessible or arcane, discourse homogeneous or mixed, expectations fulfilled or frustrated, concern with characters or with something else). Studies of response must be concerned with the full interplay of reader and text characteristics. Chabot summarizes his position this way: "If we cannot meaningfully talk about any individual apart from considerations of his or her social context, it would seem to follow that the very nature of selfhood dictates that we consider interpretive situations, rather than isolated selves, as irreducible totalities."

Louise Rosenblatt, in presenting her transactional theory of literature, also questions Holland's model as too exclusively concerned with the personalities of readers. "In the reading situation," she writes, "the literary work that is evoked must be seen as a function of the two-way transaction of reader and text." The evoked work "is not an object but an event, a lived-through process or experience." For her this process is not so much a personal experience as an aesthetic experience, reflecting the particular nature of fictional works, as opposed to informational texts. In aesthetic reading, readers are concerned primarily with what they are getting from the reading experience as it occurs — the lived-through experience. By contrast, in informational reading (Rosenblatt calls it "efferent" reading) readers are concerned with what they will carry away, with facts or ideas which can be added to their information stores.

Rosenblatt makes a useful distinction between the *evocation* of the work during reading and the *response* to the evocation after reading. Her research recommendations are for a variety of studies of both evocation and response. In addition, she proposes a number of studies of the teaching of literature. Calling for a wide range of methodologies, she points out the potentialities of the ethnographic approach.

Alan Purves offers a theory of response which he claims should resolve the conflict between those who want to study the correctness of readings and those who want to study readers' responses. He proposes a comprehensive theory which is "responsive to theories of criticism and of literature as well as to the practice of readers and critics," a theory which takes as its basic premise "that a large number of readers share a response and that at the same time no two responses are alike." He points out that texts have objective existence in their words and syntax, and he argues — as does E. D. Hirsch — that any text has a discernible meaning for all readers as well as a personal significance for each particular reader. Purves' proposals for research would have us explore the causes of agreement among readers (the "central tendencies") as well as the causes of differences between readers (the "dispersion"). Particularly, he would like us to study the effects of schooling on response, the causes of difficulty in understanding certain texts, the variability among readers (especially the relation of age and liking to response), and the effects on response of the various contexts in which readers read.

Purves recommends integrated research plans in which case studies, surveys, and experiments may all play a part in answering a basic question about response to literature: "The case study is only effective when it is performed against a larger backdrop of many students . . . The backdrop only comes to make sense when it is tested against the individual case."

In the final chapter of this first section, Anthony Petrosky makes an ambitious claim: the attempt to understand how people read and respond to literature is only a special case of our attempt to learn about human understanding in general. Others in this first section of the book anticipate him: Chabot, that studying response will help us "understand understanding"; Holland, that it will reveal how an individual responds to all experience; Rosenblatt, that it will inform us about response to the other arts.

Petrosky reviews several basic issues in the study of reader response and then outlines the possibilities and limitations of three kinds of research. He argues that the three should be integrated into a comprehensive methodology to explore a single research question: surveys, to check initial impressions; case studies, to explore in depth the complex interactions inevitable in any response study; and correlation studies, for large-scale tests of informed, theory-based hypotheses. This integrated series of methodologies is Petrosky's version of what Piaget calls "interpretive research." Petrosky summarizes it this way: "An interpretive interdisciplinary approach begins with descriptive analysis and leads to systems-building to represent human processes. The methodology focuses on a specific phenomenon, like response, to describe, explain, and theorize about the phenomenon but, more importantly, to add to what we know about human understanding."

In Part II, authors continue to grapple with a wide range of theoretical issues, but their main concern is the exploration of research possibilities in various models of response and in different research methodologies. The question they ask insistently is the central question of this book: How can we learn more about how readers of all ages and backgrounds read fiction? Their proposals indicate the great variety of methods that researchers will be able to use and refine in the years ahead: surveys, interviews, discussions, oral and written responses to first readings as well as repeated rereadings, guided and free responses to real texts or to specially constructed texts, content analysis of response protocols, analysis or scoring of retellings, scoring of choices in constructed tasks, correlation of reading ability or cognitive style or self-concept with certain aspects of response, and the use of established techniques like the repertory grid, semantic differential, and Q-sort. Some authors discuss case studies of individuals while others discuss large-scale studies of groups. Many have a strong interest in developmental studies. All authors attempt to provide a sense of the possibilities and problems in research on response to literature.

In a wide-ranging discussion of research possibilities, Arthur Applebee begins by insisting on a distinction between spectator and participant roles in language use, a distinction similar to Louise Rosenblatt's between aesthetic and efferent readings. In researching response to literature, we study spectator role language use, a particular way of representing experience gained both from literature and from the world at large. Most of Applebee's discussion is concerned with ways we may learn about the development across the school-age years of one kind of spectator role—response to literature. One unique feature of his chapter is the proposal for research on reading interests with the repertory grid technique. Perhaps the most important conclusions of Applebee's chapter are that theoretical constructs (like the spectator-participant distinction) are required for good reserch and that researchers should be willing to look at data from a number of different perspectives.

Richard Beach begins his chapter with a careful discussion of speech acts theory and of discourse conventions. His intent is to suggest how readers use their knowledge of conversations to make inferences about dialogue in literature. After outlining a content-analysis system he has devised for analyzing readers' inferences about dialogue, he then explores several ways we might study the influence of readers' knowledge of discourse conventions (like conversations) on what they infer from literature. In the chapters by Applebee and Beach, as well as the following chapters by Rubin and Gardner and by Black, we see the influence of concepts like "representation," "schema," and "script," which are derived from emerging theory and research in cognitive psychology, especially research on memory.

Eugene Kintgen's interest is in how readers come to understand—to "perceive"— a poem. In his own research, he arranges for readers to record on audio tape as many of their thoughts as they can verbalize while they read and consider a new poem. From the typed transcripts of these recorded responses he studies both how groups of readers deal with a particular problem in a poem (say, ambiguous reference) and how individuals structure their full response. He outlines in detail a content-analysis system he has devised for the latter kind of study. In his discussion of future directions for research, he encourages us to rely on sophisticated adult readers for the study of reading processes.

The Beach and Kintgen chapters are more concerned with what we can learn from certain modes of response—answering questions orally about text features like dialogue, responding orally while reading and rereading a poem—than with particular methodologies, though both chapters mention a wide range of methodologies. By contrast, each of the remaining chapters in Part II advocates a very particular methodology and proposes certain questions which might be studied with the methodology.

Andrew Ortony discusses the importance of studying children's understanding of metaphor. He rejects definitions of metaphor as decoration or comparison, and argues for an understanding of metaphor as an interaction between its two terms, an interaction which produces new meaning. Later, in the context of a discussion of how readers comprehend any printed text, he distinguishes between discovery metaphors and recognition metaphors. The former lead to new insights, the latter only to recognition of what we already know. In his description of research he has conducted with young children and with college students, he illustrates the use of "artificially constructed metaphors in artificially constructed contexts," an approach he recommends in future studies.

The chapter by Shelly Rubin and Howard Gardner will be of particular interest to those who wish to study the development of narrative competence in young children. These authors describe a study they carried out with children in Grades 1, 3, and 6, and discuss some of the methodological problems in developmental research into the ways children come to understand and remember stories. Like Ortony, Rubin and Gardner propose research on arranged, rather than undirected, responses. These arrangements and constructions are for the purpose of controlling certain variables in the texts, of insuring that young readers "confront key problems posed by the story."

From a perspective similar to that of the Rubin and Gardner chapter, John Black's chapter will introduce many readers to a recent development in cognitive psychology: the use of brief narratives to study understanding and memory. Black describes some of his own research in order to illustrate how these studies are designed, and then he discusses possibilities for new research which will tell us more about how narratives are represented in memory. Researchers like Black are primarily interested in studying cognition, particularly the structure of memory. Nevertheless, their methodologies may be useful to researchers in response to literature, particularly those researchers concerned with young children.

Gunnar Hansson recommends the use of verbal scales (specifically, the semantic differential) to explore a wide range of questions in literary study. He specifically recommends their use in studies of response to literature because they make possible the direct study of response—especially the evaluative aspects—without the mediation of an expressed response. To demonstrate that what we learn from studying only expressed responses may be misleading, he reviews one of his own studies in which university students (age 20–25) and 16-year-olds wrote very different interpretive responses to a poem but had nearly identical patterns of response on a semantic differential verbal scale. A particularly valuable feature of Hansson's chapter is his review of recent Swedish and German research.

Like Hansson, William Stephenson has a very specific, well-refined research methodology to recommend. Stephenson insists that the way to study response is to study readers' responses to texts with an approach he has named Q-methodology. The reader sorts a series of self-referent statements (a Q-sort) in a prescribed way, and the results of each reader's Q-sort are analyzed by a statistical technique called factor analysis. The researcher then attempts to explain group patterns which emerge from the analysis. Like Hansson's verbal scales, Stephenson's Q-sorts enable a study of response which does not rely on expressed response.

In Part III, four authors move us directly to a consideration of what we might learn about literary instruction in school or college settings. They are concerned with obtaining new knowledge of response, as in the proposals for basic research in Parts I and II; but they are also concerned with implementing new programs of instruction in literature and evaluating the outcomes.

David Bleich views research on response as identical to the classroom study of literature. The heart of this teaching-learning-research process is the response statement, "a systematic means of authorizing knowledge of response." Bleich uses his own response to Kafka's "A Country Doctor" to introduce the possibilities of converting response statements into proposals for knowledge. In Bleich's proposal the teacher/ researcher helps students develop detailed subjective reactions to literature. These reactions or response statements become "documented acts of mentation which form an empirical basis for research." He shows how response statements might become the basis for studies of taste, literary form, authors, and literary types.

Though Agnes Webb would accept a much wider range of techniques and methodologies into her classroom research than Bleich, she agrees that the crucial questions about literary response can best be studied among a community of readers in school settings. Bleich's ideal school researcher is simply a member of the response community under study: this researcher submits his response statement for consideration with those of the other learners in the community. He or she is learner, teacher, and researcher simultaneously. Though Webb gives teachers a prominent place in her research plans—she calls her model "collaborative research"— she does see a place for a roving participant-observer, who remains closely involved with the ongoing research project but who also brings to the research site special insights, tools, and techniques—and even takes certain data away from the site for conventional analysis.

Webb's chapter is a case study of her own year-long research study in a high school. It is full of practical cautions and advice for those who plan to study literary instruction and response in school settings.

James Squire reminds us that certain questions of great interest to curriculum developers and policy makers can be answered only with status studies or surveys. Such studies attempt to inform us about the status of classroom literature instruction in American schools and colleges. They tell us what teachers are doing and saying, how students spend their time in the classroom, what materials are in use, how class time in literary study is patterned. They describe the way things are—as well as can be ascertained from observations, interviews, and questionnaires. Squire provides a comprehensive analysis of just what surveyors of practices in literary studies might look for in schools and colleges. From his own experience with major surveys of English teaching practices in this country and England, he is able to offer useful advice about procedures and instruments.

My own chapter is addressed mainly to school and college curriculum evaluators. My concern is to show how constructed tests and systematic descriptions of expressed responses may be used to evaluate certain limited short-range outcomes of classroom literary study. After arguing for the usefulness of such standardized procedures, I review what is presently available to evaluators and then call for further developmental work.

All of these chapters give us points of departure for important research to be carried out in the years ahead. Though there are already major contributions to the study of reader response and the teaching of literature—as these chapters illustrate—

we have barely begun the comprehensive, sustained research effort we will need. The rewards will be great for, in the end, a more adequate description of the reading and response process will enable us to teach literature better in school and college classrooms. Researchers joining this effort can be confident of making important contributions to education in literacy, humanities, and aesthetics.

Charles R. Cooper
La Jolla, California

REFERENCES

Calvino, I. *If on a winter's night a traveler.* (Translated from the Italian by William Weaver.) New York: Harcourt Brace Jovanovich, 1979.

Cooper, C. R. Empirical studies of response to literature: Review and suggestions. *Journal of Aesthetic Education,* 1976, *10,* 77–93.

Gibson, E. J., & Levin, H. *The psychology of reading.* Cambridge: MIT Press, 1975.

Harari, J. V. (Ed.). *Textual strategies: Perspectives in post-structuralist criticism.* Ithaca, New York: Cornell University Press, 1979.

Purves, A. C., & Beach, R. *Literature and the reader: Research in response to literature, reading interests, and the teaching of literature.* Urbana, IL: National Council of Teachers of English, 1972.

Rosenblatt, L. M. *Literature as exploration.* New York: Noble and Noble, 1968.

Smith, F. *Understanding reading: A psycholinguistic analysis of reading and learning to read* (2nd ed.). New York: Holt, Rinehart & Winston, 1978.

Spiro, R. J., Bruce, B. J., & Brewer, W. F. (Eds.). *Theoretical issues in reading comprehension: Perspectives from cognitive psychology, linguistics, artificial intelligence, and education.* Hillsdale, NJ: Lawrence Erlbaum, 1980.

Suleiman, S. R., & Crosman, I. (Eds.). *The reader in the text: Essays on audience and interpretation.* Princeton, NJ: Princeton University Press, 1980.

Tompkins, J. P. (Ed.). *Reader-response criticism: from formalism to post-structuralism.* Baltimore: Johns Hopkins University Press, 1980.

Part I:
What Do We Study?

Chapter 1
Reading Readers Reading

Norman N. Holland

Institute for Psychological Study of the Arts
University of Florida

We think in metaphors, I suppose. Some are explicit, some implicit, like that
"suppose" which metaphorically puts some support under the chapter which follows.
I want to suggest a metaphor (or model or theory) that one can carry about in one's
head for thinking through one's own and others' research into reading.

We typically think about reading in metaphors. "The first scene of *Hamlet* is
striking." "Shaw's dialogue has tremendous force." "A Dickinson poem invites
us to complete sentences." "Flashback technique adds a whole new dimension to
the story." "Do you really think Shakespeare put all this stuff in there?" Or, as I
often hear my colleagues say: "The meaning is right there! In the words on the
page!"

All these metaphors proceed from certain received ideas about the process of
reading: namely, that texts do something to people or invite people to do something;
that they coerce people; that a literary experience can be thought of in parts that
can be added or subtracted; or that literature is a kind of container or conduit into
which an author puts a meaning and out of which a reader gets (or should get) that
same meaning. All of these metaphors embody models or theories of reading, some
of which recent literary theory has challenged. I would like to examine some of
the common models we use to guide our thinking and research into reading and
point us toward a newer model that may initiate more successful research.

MODELS OF LITERARY RESPONSE

The root question for someone researching the reading or the teaching of literature
is: Why does this person read this text in this way in this context? For research
purposes, however, experimental psychologists want to convert one or more of the
singulars in that question into plurals. Their question is not just "Why does this
particular man prefer Shakespeare's *Hamlet* to the *Cliff's Notes* version?" but "Why
do just about all mature readers have the same preference?" Their question is not
just "Why does this particular woman read the ending of *King Lear* in this way?"
but "Why were five out of six women in a seminar on the catastrophe of *King Lear*
reminded of unsatisfactory relations with their own fathers, while all the men spoke
of their own helplessness or impotence?" Are there correlations of age or sex,
experimental psychologists might ask, to the different ways children respond to
Maurice Sendak's *Where the Wild Things Are*?

Experimental psychologists assume their research will uncover not just a singular description of a singular literary transaction in a singular context, but some general principle that will apply to many readers or *literents* (a broader word that applies to someone being read to or going to a play, that is, someone seeing or hearing literature as well as reading it). In the same way, English teachers would like to have general principles that are useful for improving teaching in many different settings. These are laudable aims, but they rest on certain theories about our responses to literature which are questionable.

Text-active and Bi-active Models of Response

Most people when they begin to think about general principles of literary response think in terms of a "text-active" model, in which the text determines the response. I tell someone a joke and he laughs. I instruct my seminar to read *King Lear* and the ending "does something" to them. There is something "*in*" *Hamlet* that makes literents prefer it to *Titus Andronicus*. There is something "in" the Gothic novel that addresses itself particularly to women, something "in" Sendak's work that especially appeals to children. The fact that we have not found these things "in" these texts after decades—even centuries—of search does not seem to discourage us. We nevertheless expect that the text, which looks so objective with its paper and ink and binding, will "do something" to its literent or at least serve as an independent variable. Then we can experiment with it by showing the same text to different people to discover what is constant and what is variable in their responses.

It is, of course, the variability of response that renders this simple model inadequate. A text-active model offers us no way of accounting for the often startlingly large variation in people's responses to a given text. For that reason, most scholars— after they have thought a little bit about response—sophisticate the one-way text-active model into what I call a "bi-active" model. The text "does something" to the literent, but the literent also "does something" to the text. Both are active. I bring to *Romeo and Juliet* schemata from other literary experiences, my knowledge of Shakespeare and Elizabethan drama, my critical and analytical strategies, my sense of language, my theories about human beings, my position in a socioeconomic class, my age, even my height or weight. I bring these things to bear on *Romeo and Juliet* but the tragedy also acts *on me*, ruling out some responses to the play as inappropriate or idiosyncratic.

The assumption that an objective text controls responses within certain limits is consistent with conventional experimental models. Given a number of literents— L_1, L_2, L_3—and a number of texts—T_1, T_2, T_3—I can present any given text, T_i, to L_1, L_2, L_3, and the rest. I can then correlate variables in the text with variables in their responses. For example, I could correlate fear with ghosts in the story. Finally, I could state these correlations in the neat if-then terms of a hypothetico-deductive system. "If the literent is a woman, and if the text is a Gothic novel, chances are nine out of ten she will feel the dangers described as though they were bodily threats." "If the literent is a woman, and if the text is *King Lear*, chances are four out of five she will speak of her own father in free associating to the ending."

Unfortunately, decades of this kind of experimentation have not led even to conclusions as uncertain as these, much less large-scale principles of literary response. Martin Lindauer's 1974 survey of properly "scientific" psychological research into literature quite innocently demonstrates the limitations of these results. Furthermore, a search for measurable and repeatable correlations and the claim to exclusive scientific validity of that one method rules out other lines of research that are more promising.

The survey approach is closely related to the experimental paradigm, but it differs in the degree to which the psychologist tries to control the situation: "If the poem is a rhyming, humorous narrative, 95% of 10-year-olds will prefer it to an unrhymed lyric." In this case, the psychologist is reporting on a "natural" situation, but—again—makes an assumption that, other variables aside, the text determines the outcome. I would say that the survey approach has proved more successful than the experimental. It has led to the conclusion, for example, that readers of Gothic novels are almost 100% women (Holland and Sherman, 1977). But why? The survey cannot tell us. We need a model of the literary process, and we can see the kind of model it must be by looking at the difficulties the conventional psychological experiment encounters when applied to reading.

First, the experimenter proceeds by operational definitions of the variables: laughter as measured by a laryngograph, tragic feelings as detected in a Thematic Apperception Test, changed opinion as measured by a semantic differential. Each new experiment results in new operational definitions. Hence, the experimental search for correlations "tends to produce a proliferation of variables and laws, many vaguely overlapping, rather than the single clear network of laws originally anticipated" (Diesing, 1971, p. 4).

Second, most numerical methods require categories from outside the reading transaction itself: diagnostic categories (compulsive, paranoid), psychoanalytic phases of child development (oral, anal), content categories (as from a content analysis computer program like the General Inquirer), categories in collected responses (like Purves' "reaction to content" or "perception of tone"), or literary categories (tragedy, comedy). All such categories, however, deal with individual reading transactions by lumping them together. The uniqueness of a given reader's response is lost or reduced to a special combination of categories (for example, an oedipal reaction to tragic content).

Such categories also suggest processes which are independent of the reader's personality. In effect, one assumes an isolable "oedipality" and a correlation between said oedipality and some impersonal definition of tragedy—surely a very doubtful assumption. Operational definitions and outside categories embody another doubtful assumption: that one can break up a human transaction such as reading into separable correlations derived from outside the transaction (for example, a relationship between oedipal feelings and tragedy). This is like dividing the Mona Lisa into a paint-by-numbers cartoon. I assume this is the mental "set" that persuades experimenters they can "control for" the literent's mood or, for that matter, the experimenter's.

My ultimate objection to a text-active or bi-active model for literary response is more personal. I tried it for two years, and I could not get it to work. I found that the differences among readers' responses were simply too great and too various to be bracketed within some limit imposed by the text. Close observation of readers reading showed that the notion of an active text is simply too rigid, and if the text-active model fails, the text-active half of the bi-active model fails, too. Text-active or bi-active models just do not fit the details of specific reading transactions. Fortunately, another model provides more telling feedback.

A Transactive Model of Response

In 1968, I began a simple—one might even say, obvious—experiment. I asked a group of students to read some short stories. Then I asked each reader questions designed to elicit his or her associations and feelings. I tape-recorded and transcribed these interviews in order to interpret them.

Naturally, I found certain similarities and certain differences in my readers' reading of the stories. At first, I tried to account for those similarities and differences by grouping several literents' readings of the same story together (T_i, and L_1, L_2, L_3, and so on). I attributed any sameness in the responses to the story and any differences to the different literents (L_1, and so on). In other words, I applied the usual bi-active model for psychological experiments: the story limits the literary response; each literent varies it within those limits.

After two years of experimentation, I found that I simply could not fit the responses to that model. Then I tried grouping all the readings by a given literent together, L_i and T_1, T_2, T_3 . . . T_{10}. Eureka! I found I was able to understand the responses by attributing the sameness that ran through all of them to the literent and the differences to the different stories. In other words, I could explain what the literents said about the stories they had read by making the literent the active, causal one instead of the story. (I have since described this "experiment" and my interpretation of the results many times—see Holland, 1973a, 1973b, 1975a, 1975c, 1975d, 1976.)

The literent determines the story. If I choose to read *Romeo and Juliet* as a spiritualist tragedy (a forerunner of Menotti's *The Medium*), the text can neither stop me nor advance me in my enterprise. All the text can do is provide or not provide evidence for my view. It is I who decide what is evidence and how to apply it. I may follow the guidelines of some interpretive community or I may simply be idiosyncratic. If I read Mercutio's threat to "raise a spirit" in Romeo's "mistress' circle," ("Letting it there stand / Till she had laid it and conjured it down") as central, and I define the play, therefore, as a spiritualist tragedy, you or any jury of literary critics may ridicule me, but *the text* cannot stop me, if for no other reason than that words do not exert physical force, but I do. I can close the book or refuse to peruse this or that part of it. I always control the text, not vice versa. I even decide where it begins and ends and what parts will be included (Title? Author's name? Footnotes?). As a result, it is I who actively, constructively make the physical object—the book entitled *Romeo and Juliet*—into a literary experience called *Romeo and Juliet*, and I can choose to follow approved procedures for doing so, or I can be as wacky as I please.

Though it may seem simple, this one assertion about literary transaction matches what cognitive scientists who study memory, knowledge, and the senses tell us about other perceptions of experience (Holland, 1978b). Reality does not simply act on us. Rather, we bring perceptual schemata to bear on the information our senses give us so as to yield a coherent picture of the world (Neisser, 1967). Perception is a constructive act, and so is reading (Smith, 1978).

A story does not "cause" or even "limit" the responses to it. The response comes from the literent. A literent sets up a feedback loop. In reading, I bring to a text schemata from previous literary experiences, from my historical or critical knowledge, my sense of human nature, my values, my preferences in language, my politics, my metabolism—I bring all these things to bear on the text, and the text feeds back to me what I bring to it either positively or not at all. It rewards my hypotheses or, so to speak, ignores them. That is all the text does, for always it is I who am in control. It is I who ask questions of the text and I who hear and interpret its answers. The text may change the payoffs on the various fantasies, defenses, themes, or expectations I bring to it, but that is all it does (and even then I decide what is a good payoff and what is not).

We cannot read without actively constructing the text before us, and that is why actual readings vary so much from one person to another. Reading is permeated with the uniqueness of your personality or mine (Gibson and Levin, 1975, p. 465).

I should have expected, then, difficulty in trying to deduce from actual readers the sort of thing a psychological experimenter usually looks for: a predictive, quantifiable, if-then sort of conclusion correlating a dependent variable (response) with an independent variable (text). I would have to break up a continuous, highly personal transaction into discrete segments, necessarily arbitrary: potency, relationship with father—and how am I to define those? I would have to assume that *King Lear*, which has no more power to impose its "meaning" or "content" on me than a Basque epic, controls my transacting of *King Lear* as much as I do. The underlying problem is that experimental psychology of the correlation-of-variables or if-then kind has no successful way of dealing with the singular and organically continuous acts of unique individuals.

We need a way of talking rigorously about uniqueness and individuality. We need to begin, not with a set of impersonal procedures designed to make our inquiry "scientific," but with immediate, personal data about (and, I would claim, a more telling model for) the dynamics of literary response.

Some of us at Buffalo's Center for the Psychological Study of the Arts found that rigor in Heinz Lichtenstein's concept of identity (1961, 1977). By identity, Lichtenstein means the pattern of sameness and difference that you or I can discover in another human being's actions. I understand that continuity in you by seeing what does not change in you or your actions against a background of what does change. Conversely, I understand changes in you by seeing them against a background of what does not change.

That dialectic of sameness and difference I can comprehend by thinking of someone's choices and actions as variations on that person's identity theme. The variations are the changes, the newness, or the difference. The theme is what I interpret as the sameness. Yet I never see the theme by itself, but only as I read it in one or another variation—just as in a piece of music, I can never hear the theme as such, only this or that particular orchestration of it.

The general principle, then, is that you *can* understand how I transact poems and fictions: I experience them so as to add to my identity, that is, to develop a new variation on my identity theme, as I do with every other new experience. Each literary response is unique, but you *can* conceptualize that uniqueness and relate it to other unique acts by me through the concept of my identity as a theme and variations.

Consider *laughing* as a prototype of literary response. The physical stimulus — the text, the joke, the cartoon—is the same for everyone. There is an emotion and even physical response: the feeling of being amused, the act of laughing. These are more or less the same in all of us and in all cultures. But each of us has a highly personal sense of humor, and each culture has a different sense of humor. No joke is funny to everybody, and anything can be funny to somebody. In that sense, there is no such thing as a joke. It is an identity that laughs.

We can imagine laughing in, as it were, three components, which correspond to a famous maxim of Clyde Kluckhohn and Henry Murray: "Everyone is in certain respects (a) like all other men, (b) like some other men and (c) like no other man" (1948, p. 53). An individual, with an identity like no other person's, finds this or that event funny and feels amused or laughs. To do so, the individual *uses* a bodily equipment more or less the same (so far as laughing is concerned) for everyone: eyes, ears, or the zygomatic and cricothyroid muscles with which we laugh are like all other people's. Similarly, the individual *uses* cultural and semiotic codes that are like some other people's.

When I am reading a joke, it is virtually impossible for me not to see a *b* as a *b* or, if listening to someone tell a joke, to hear "we am" as grammatical. If I am looking at a cartoon it is almost impossible for me to see a certain network of 90° and 45° angles as other than a perspective view of a box. Of these things, one could say, "No normal member of this culture could perceive this in any other way." In that sense, some cultural codes are as stringent in limiting or expanding our sensibilities as our bodies.

Other codes are more variable. Mothers-in-law nag. Women are terrible drivers. Professors are unrealistic. These are the stock materials of American cartoon art, but they would be incomprehensible to the average Nepalese or Bengali. In that sense, they are cultural codes, but not with the same strength as the perception of letters or grammar or systems of perspective. One might believe these codes or not and therefore use or not use them to find something funny. A feminist might not laugh at jokes about women drivers, as I do not laugh at jokes about impractical professors. These codes, unlike the others, are flexible—take it or leave it—and they are limited to this or that interpretive community.

We might imagine the different codes an individual identity uses to perceive a joke as several feedback or information-processing loops. When confronted with an experience (like a joke), an identity tries out this or that hypothesis, according to the ideas that unique person shares with a community—or perhaps just for a whim. Mothers-in-law nag—that would be a high-level hypothesis. To try out that hypothesis on the cartoon, however, one has to use fixed lower-level cultural codes about, for example, the letters and the words in the caption. Those cultural codes, in turn, use bodily systems related to eyes and ears. Imagine, then, a hierarchy of feedback loops. The lowest level is physical and physiological. One level up, cultural codes set the guidelines for physical feedbacks—what will feel right. Finally, personal identity sets the standards for the cultural codes—again what will feel like good feedback.

Within this hierarchy, what will I find funny? On seeing a certain cartoon, I try out some communal hypotheses (about mothers-in-law, for example) but not others (about impractical professors). If one of the hypotheses I try out on the cartoon feels right to me—gives me good feedback—I adjust the standards for the various feedbacks accordingly. If the feedback suddenly and playfully confirms my identity, I find the cartoon funny. If not, I do not. A similar model would apply to all literary experiences—not just to amusement, but to all experiences, literary and non-literary. (Psychologists will recognize the similarity of this model to George Kelly's personal construct theory. For a more detailed development, see Holland, 1982, Part II.)

This *transactive* model combines the re-creation of personal identity through an experience with cultural and physiological processes of feedback. It thus describes situations which combine a shared stimulus, a personal reaction, and a community of response. Using a transactive model, we can talk about an experience which is, in some respects, like *all* other people's experience, in some respects like *some* other people's experience, and in some respects like *no* other person's experience. The next question is how to translate that model into research.

RESEARCH WITH A TRANSACTIVE MODEL: HOLISTIC METHOD

We can interpret a unique event like a child's description of its response to the ending of Sendak's *Where the Wild Things Are* by a process of tracing textual themes through the details of the child's wording. A theme in holistic research, as philosopher Paul Diesing explains the term, "asserts simply that a certain uniformity exists in the data, that some sort of clustering or syndrome exists in the system being studied." Women reading *King Lear* talk about their fathers. The theme "is tested by seeing whether further instances do appear." If not, or if there are many negative instances (women who don't talk about their fathers), one tries another theme. "A theme is the lowest level of interpretive statement in a case study; it is like a pawn, easily gotten and easily discarded" (1971, p. 229). A theme in holistic research is thus similar to what a literary critic might call a motif. It is a category, but one closely derived from the unique transaction being studied. A literary critic will recognize in this concept a familiar method of analyzing a text for its unity, as in the widely used techniques of the Brooks and Warren textbooks.

Having construed several small themes or motifs, one organizes them into larger themes, then a configuration or a model or what I, as a literary critic, would call a central (or "centering") theme. For example, suppose that I have arrived at the following large themes for *Macbeth*: kingship; the supernatural; parents and children; ghosts, hallucinations, and uncertainties of perception; clothing. I can pull all these together into a centering theme for the whole play: *Macbeth* focuses on the way supernature penetrates nature and thence breeds outward through men's bodies, families, and nation. (This example of a thematic study of *Macbeth* is developed in great detail in Holland, 1964, pp. 43–71.)

Testing such a configuration, says Diesing, "involves three elements: first, how many themes [or motifs] are included in the configuration and how many are left out; second, how coherent or well-organized the themes are; and third, whether new themes fit into the model as well" (1971, p. 230). For example, will the central theme connect the play's recurring references to birds to the other themes? Birds build homes for their progeny as the Macduffs and Banquo do. Birds hover between heaven and earth as do the characters of *Macbeth*.

In such a way, one can shape a unique "event" such as *Macbeth* into a configuration of details grouped into motifs or subthemes, larger themes, and one large overall centering theme. The technique, however, is used by not only literary critics but anthropologists, clinical psychologists, galactic astronomers, geologists, and many other scientists. All of them gather data which they then must organize into a coherent pattern, in order to explain a given feature by placing it within the pattern of the whole (Holland, 1977a, 1978b).

To study reading, one might use the same procedure. One gathers details about the ways different literents transact different literary works. To study them holistically, one converts those responses or transactions into a text that one can then study as subthemes, themes, and central theme. Mostly that means simply listening to what the literents say or listening and then studying a transcription of what they said during a recorded interview.

Listen to a child's comments on *Where the Wild Things Are* and construe subthemes and themes from what he or she says; the comments will reveal the dynamics of that child's particular transaction of the story. In the same way, listen to people— both male and female—as they speak freely about their responses to the deaths of King Lear and Cordelia. Put aside for the moment the datum that women read Gothic novels and men do not, and just listen to what each says about them.

Notice particularly that they are not saying these things in an abstract way. They are saying them *to you* in a particular interpersonal situation. You are the participant-observer. You are construing what your informant is saying. Yet you are not a variable that can be factored out or controlled for. You and the literent and Sendak's book are all in this transaction together. You are, in fact, the vital center of the study and should be included and taken into account at all times, as your informant transacts with you, the setting, and *Wild Things* all at once (Holland, 1978).

The situation is the same in the study of educational settings or teaching styles. What kind of statement by a teacher seems to make *Hamlet* come alive to a group of adolescent literents? Ask them to talk freely and at length about their responses to different statements the teacher has made, or different kinds of classrooms.

One must establish an open-ended way of gathering data, not one truncated by outside categories or fixed hypotheses. Simply listen to what students say about teaching style or classroom design and organize it by subtheme, theme, and central theme. Holistic, participant-observer method serves beautifully, notes Diesing, "to describe the individual in its individuality, as a system of rules, goals, values, techniques, defense or boundary-maintaining mechanisms, exchange or boundary-crossing mechanisms, socialization procedures, and decision procedures." In short, "its primary subject matter is a single, self-maintained social system" (1971, pp. 5–6), and that would include the unique system of observer and subject.

Holistic method is, however, less suited to deal with the regularities across such individual, self-maintaining systems. Those regularities, unfortunately, include precisely the questions we began with: Why do mature literents prefer Shakespeare's *Hamlet* to the *Cliff's Notes* version? Why do many women but few men read Gothics? Why is Sendak's work or Dr. Seuss' so popular? Why did the women in my seminar on *King Lear* free associate to their fathers and the men associate to feelings of helplessness?

We are in a quandary. We have a holistic, case study, participant-observer method that will discover why one individual prefers *Hamlet* to *Titus Andronicus*, but will not tell us why 95% of readers do. Therefore, our problem is this: How can we use a holistic method to investigate and perhaps explain regularities in response? To put it another way, how can we sum up holistic accounts of individual transactions into an analysis of many readings?

Combining Holistic Studies

This kind of research would have to begin by collecting a large number of individual responses to a certain text, from both naive readers and trained critics or scholars. Such research establishes actual *and therefore possible* responses, not abstract categories of response, but a personal sense of responsive possibilities. One gains wisdom about one's fellow humans rather than the kind of hard-edged knowledge psychological experiments are designed to provide.

It is possible to publish this summary of individual responses as a psuedo- or quasi-impersonal conclusion. Thus, researchers have been able to use analyses of the texts of individual responses to study a variety of phenomena: the reactions of undergraduates to short stories (Holland, 1975a; Grant, 1982); the reactions of graduate students to a poem (State University of New York) and to the ending of *King Lear* (Holland, 1977b); the reactions of schoolchildren to various kinds of literature and to their teachers (Petrosky, 1975, 1976, 1977a, 1982; Webb, 1980, 1982); the teaching of writing (Samuels, 1978; Petrosky, 1982); reactions to the popular arts (Rollin, 1975; Paramathan, 1978); the difference in reaction between a man and a woman to Gothic novels (Holland and Sherman, 1977); a person's sense of humor—why one finds something amusing or laughs (Holland, 1982); and a person's political style (Little, 1973, 1978, 1980). No doubt, research of this sort—the close analysis of an open-ended response to a text or other stimulus—has just begun.

The treatment of actual responses as possibilities rather than as categories leads to an open-ended kind of knowledge. For example, the knowledge that fifty different people responded to the appearance of the ghost in *Hamlet* in fifty different ways does not rule out the possibility of a fifty-first response—certainly not when one remembers the volume upon volume of idiosyncratic readings of Shakespeare even a small library provides. Suppose that forty-nine of those fifty people were frightened by the ghost. Could we then conclude that in a larger sample, approximately 98% would feel fear? No, because each new transaction of *Hamlet* is an individual act. Therefore, our fifty people or even fifty thousand do not represent a sample, unless we have some reason to believe that the first fifty identities somehow typify the next fifty thousand. For the same reason we cannot predict, from any pattern of responses by one group of people, a pattern of responses for another group. The whole correlation procedure of the experimental or the survey approach has, in this identity model, very limited usefulness. On the other hand, the identity model throws us back again and again to the individual case.

Nevertheless, I think it is possible to use holistic research to study more than one person. In 1975, I proposed consideration of a tribe, a village, a corporation, a street gang, or even a nation as a "macroperson" (Holland, 1975a, pp. 233–245). In effect, you draw a line of definition around the group to be considered. Then you can treat all the thoughts, words, and actions from that group as though they were one text from one organism. You can then look for a centering unity in this text "written" by a "macroperson" and so—perhaps—arrive at a group identity.

I have been able to try out this hypothesis in a seminar, using Lawrence Wylie's fine anthropological and sociological study of the French village of Rousillon (1974). We treated his book as the record of a self-sustaining organism that would admit our search for a "character" or "identity" for the whole village. The seminar concluded that an "identity theme" for the village might be as follows: the balance of a heavy commitment to realism with a romantic, unreal longing for escape. I felt we indeed gained a useful perspective by treating the whole social group as a "macroperson." We found we could even comprehend the village's response to outside changes as Wylie chronicled Rousillon's adaptations and maladaptations in successive editions of his book.

I think it is possible to analyze a class, a program, or a school the same way. One would define the "single person," the undivided "individual" who provides the basis for case study as a classroom of students with a teacher, a program within a school, indeed, the whole school or university, or just one student with one teacher in a one-on-one teaching setting.

Even if we were to use holistic research this way to study more than one individual, however, we would still be studying uniqueness. We would not have tried to explain regularities in response which are applicable from individual to individual or group to group.

What does holistic research yield, then? It serves us in the same way that a case history serves the medical profession. Each response we collect is a past actuality that represents a future possibility. Each response is a hypothesis to try out on the next response. Gathering responses does not lead to knowledge in the abstract, but to active interpretation of new responses which must then be gathered. Holistic research does not yield the quantified knowledge we expect from a psychological experiment, but it does lead to new bases for relationship between the researcher and the people and texts the researcher is working with.

Researchers would nevertheless like case studies to help us arrive at generalizations that deal with the regularities in response. Can we never explain why people prefer *Hamlet* to *Titus Andronicus*? Or why children like Sendak's books? Are there distinctively female and male responses? Why do many women but few men read Gothic novels?

The Two Stages of Holistic Research

Holistic or case-study methods do lead to general principles, but they are principles of a special kind. I am thinking of Piaget's sequence: modes of cognition that progress from sensorimotor explorations in infancy to the logical thought of the adult. This is a general principle that is supposed to apply to all human beings, just as the assertion "Humans have two legs" applies universally.

Such universalizations have a special status in our store of scientific knowledge. They cannot be disproved by counter-example, because they deal with the type rather than the actuality. For example, I do not disprove the principle *as a principle* that humans have two legs by pointing to amputees or Siamese twins. Thus, these universalizations are peculiarly powerful, because we can treat them either as claims to truths about the world or about types in the world (which they are) or—more usefully—as principles for guiding further inquiries into experience.

Piaget's studies of cognitive development are holistic, and they lead to universalizations of this kind. Recent work by T. G. R. Bower or Daniel Stern with very young infants traces out a similar cognitive development for the first year of life by combining the close observation of particular cases with experimentation with a logical structuring of propositions, as Piaget did. For example, Bower shows that a child has to learn that one object can be inside another before it can realize that a ball inside a cup shares the movements of the cup (1974). Similarly, Stern shows how mother and child interact by videotaping particular mothers and children and analyzing those nonverbal texts holistically for patterns and themes of inter-action (1977).

Chomsky asserts that language is an innate capability that will mature to adult functioning just as the liver does, or the eye. In saying so, he engages in the same kind of universalization from listening to particular children and adults as Piaget or Bower or Stern. Some recent work in cognitive psychology involves the same universalizing of carefully studied cases, even of introspections. For example,

William T. Powers uses introspections to model the mind as nine hierarchical levels of feedback networks (1973). Cognitive scientists like Donald Norman et al. can show how individuals use widely-shared schemata for perception and cognition (1975).

Psychoanalysis, of course, is full of this kind of universalization: Everyone— theoretically—has an id, ego, and superego. Individuals develop through oral, anal, urethral, phallic, and oedipal stages. All behavior is adaptive. All behavior is part of a genetic series (Rapaport and Gill, 1959). Again, these guiding principles are not refuted by pointing to the counter-examples of, for instance, a child who died before reaching the oedipal stage or developing a superego. These principles describe the human as a type.

In the same way, the principles that I believe explain the reading transaction combine the close observation of individual cases with universalizations from psychoanalytic psychology. We read, as we perceive other events, so as to achieve a new variation on our identity theme. Within that re-creative relationship, I believe, one can trace four modalities.

We perceive a literary work in terms of the *expectations* we bring to this particular text (our notions about Dickens, for example, or romanticism or tragedy or whatever we are required to read in school). We also bring our characteristic expectations toward any other entity (our degree of trust in others, for example), As we admit the text to our mental processes, we shape and filter it through our characteristic patterns of *defense* and adaptation (projection, repression, identification, and the like). As part of those mental processes, we imbue the story with our characteristic clusters of wishes—our *fantasies*. As another part of those mental processes, we *transform* the text and the fantasy with which we have endowed it into an experience of moral, intellectual, social, or aesthetic coherence. In short, we DEFT the text, re-creating our identities through our own characteristic patterns of *d*efense, *e*xpectation, *f*antasy, and *t*ransformation (Holland, 1975a, 1975d, 1976, 1978b). I believe this DEFT principle is, like Lichtenstein's principle of identity re-creation, a universalization, a description of the human type. One arrives at such a principle by combining close observation of individual cases with an awareness of the logical necessities (Holland, 1975a, pp. 123–127), like the universalizations of Piaget, Chomsky, the psychoanalysts, or the cognitive psychologists.

Nevertheless, it would be a falsification of the idea of DEFTing literature if one were to treat defense, expectation, fantasy, or transformation as abstract categories— little boxes into which one could sort this or that part of what a literent said about a story. On the contrary, any given statement about a text is likely to function as two or more of these modes of relationship. One should use these four modes not as labels or pigeonholes, but as ways of discovering how a literary response (both in its details and in its overall strategy) functions multiply in the literent's psychic economy.

Similarly, one would use any psychoanalytic generalization as a way of seeing how a given transaction combines many different purposes (is "overdetermined"). The transaction will typically function at several levels in the developmental sequence described by classical psychoanalysis (oral, anal, oedipal), it will serve all three structures (id, ego, superego), and it will act simultaneously as defense, adaptation, and gratification. All these terms are universalizations.

If such universalizations were offered as statements about reality, they would fail, because it is obvious that they have exceptions. There are amputees who do not have two legs, there are retarded children who have not developed language in Chomsky's sense, there are autistic children who do not develop in the psychoanalytic sequence, and there are responses to literature that have nothing to do with identity (for example, my not knowing any Basque poetry).

When universalizations are posed as questions, however, they give us a way of transferring easily from one case study to the next. They become modes of inquiry, possibilities for new relations to the subject of study, ways of beginning a dialectic search from the unique case study to regularities among responses.

Then, using universalizations as guiding principles—hunches—I can combine holistic studies. For example, I can use the principle that all humans have two legs to realize that something odd has happened to the amputee and the Siamese twins and to guide an inquiry into their exceptionality. I can use Chomsky's assertion that language is an innate, universal human capability to study children who lack that capacity. I can use the psychoanalytic statement of an immutable oral-anal-phallic sequence to inquire into the pathology of autistic children who seem not to have passed through such a sequence. I evaluate the universalization by its payoff or—more properly—by the subtlety and success of the inquiry I can structure from it. In the same way, I can use psychoanalytic universalizations about identity in the transacting of literature as guides to inquiry in each new case study rather than as conclusions to be reached after many observations of individual cases.

In other words, these guiding universalizations are not the end-product of the research project—they lead us further into it. We can do better research by treating id, ego, and superego as questions than as structures. The same is true with identity and DEFTing—these terms are ways of asking, bases for a new relationship with the people and events under study. The construction of a new relationship between researcher and subject fits Clifford Geertz's well-known recommendations for anthropological research (1973). An anthropologist living in a hut in Africa must recognize his or her own involvement with the people he or she is studying. The anthropologist must accept as an aim of research into culture, not abstract principles but more and better talk about and with other cultures. Our aim in studying reading is the same.

I see, then—as a general method in holistic research—two interacting stages. In one, we collect data in a rather unstructured, uncritical way, by free association, for example, as opposed to a questionnaire. We use one or more of these large universalizations as guides for inquiring into and structuring that unstructured data, for tracing themes and patterns in it. For this purpose, we use universalizations like the psychoanalyst's oral stage or the cognitive scientist's perceptual schemata or the reading theorist's principle of identity re-creation. These universalizations serve as ways for better interpreting the case study, and then the better understood case study can lead to an improved way of gathering data or perhaps to a better universalization.

We DEFT research the same way we DEFT literature. By bringing our personal strategies to bear on the data, we can judge their effectiveness by the replies we get. The successful reply leads to more complex strategies we can bring to the data, and so on and around into a continuing feedback or dialectic or dialogue.

Among the strategies we can bring to this kind of holistic data are the correlative studies of experimental psychologists, but, in case study research, I would use them differently than experimentalists do. I would not treat a correlation between a dependent and an independent variable as a conclusion. For me, such a correlation would be useful primarily to read back into the case data, to see if one could find themes, and themes of themes, guided by the correlation from the experiment. Once again, holistic research opens a feedback or dialectic relation between the generalization and the individual case, and to stop that dialectic once it has started is to falsify the situation.

These psychological generalizations correspond to what I called above "hypotheses" in describing feedback loops. They are different from the cultural codes that limit and expand our perceptions, and they are different from the mechanisms of our bodies or the physical reality that is the same for all humans. In effect, we try out these generalizations as hypotheses and get feedback from the case study. We then use the case study to frame new hypotheses. All this takes place within the general framework of a personal identity—the researcher's, who seeks good feedback from the world "out there."

Now, the problem is how to translate this dialectic of case study with guiding principles into holistic research into the teaching of literature.

Teaching Literature

In my own work with readers, once I got over treating the text as a dominant force, I found I could understand my readers' readings by formulating unifying themes for their responses, according to these hypotheses and universalizations about identity. Once I received satisfying answers to the questions I asked of the data, I could then see the transaction in still more detail. I could trace out patterns of defense, expectation, fantasy, and transformation in the tape-recorded responses: a second universalization. I could conceptualize the whole process as a hierarchy of feedbacks: a third universalization.

The most urgent next step, I think, would be to see if identity theory and the DEFT model are satisfactory as they stand, or if they need to be further modified. Are there other universalizations we can add to the feedback metaphor or the DEFT model of defenses, fantasies, expectations, and transformations? Can we refine those terms? Can we trace still subtler modes in perception?

Obviously, what we need immediately for any such research program is simply more information about actual literents. We need to collect many, many more associative responses to texts. The identity-DEFT-feedback model then gives us familiar questions to ask. What expectations do people bring to texts? With what fantasies do they endow the text? With what transformations do they give their reading a more than transient significance?

As I speak here and there about identity and DEFT, I am asked two questions over and over. First, what relation is there (or should there be) between the kind of free response used in *5 Readers Reading* (Holland, 1975a) or generally in applying the identity-DEFT model and a "right," "valid," or "correct" reading? I would like to see, in the next few years research that inquires into the way individual literents feel about the relationship between the more personal aspects of their responses and what is accepted as "valid" by teachers, the community of literary scholars or critics, the people who grade examinations, and so on. I think this knowledge is particularly important for educators to have. So does Alan Purves, to judge from his 1979 Modern Language Association (MLA) paper in which he suggests that a literature curriculum can not only acknowledge the individuality of response but can also provide schemata for perceiving literature both efficiently and sensitively. These aims are by no means inconsistent.

So far, we have been using psychoanalytic psychology to understand reading. I would like to see the study of reading enrich psychology, and I think one way of doing this would be to treat the familiar categories set out by Purves and Rippere (1968) not as categories but as universalizations. Instead of sorting or scoring different parts of a given literent's response into these categories, I wonder what would happen if we proceeded on the assumption that everyone at every moment in the literary transaction engages and becomes involved (the *f*antasy in DEFT?), everyone perceives (the E and D in DEFT?), everyone interprets (the *t*ransformation in DEFT?), and everyone evaluates (the overall effect of DEFT). What kind of feedback would we get if we were to bring these universalizations to bear on responses?

The extension into the media of the identity-DEFT-feedback model for reading is, I think, more socially urgent. A relatively easy—yet very important—project would be to bring the identity principle and the DEFT hypothesis to bear on both adults' and children's free responses to television in general and to particular programs. Less urgent, but equally interesting and important, would be the application of this model of reading to arts that border on the purely verbal (cinema, comics, or children's illustrated books and song, musical comedy, or opera). They resemble television in that they are partially verbal, and they thus provide a relevant contrast. These semiverbal arts also offer a path from our understanding of literary experiences toward the visual arts and music.

There is another, more difficult question to research that is of great importance to psychology. Can I find patterns of identity or even simply of defense or fantasy that apply to particular groups, for example, to certain age groups or certain regions? (This question is particularly important to research with children of elementary-school age.) Can I discover a pattern of defense or an identity which is more common in America than elsewhere? Do I encounter responses which are distinctively male or female? I have suggested above that—since identities are unique—there may be no way to consider any one group of identities as a sample of any other group. Nevertheless, the question nags: Is there some way of generalizing about identities in a particular historical place and moment? To begin to answer it, we need more data, more recorded responses to texts.

Another line of research might look at the special relationship of literature to schools. For example, a psychoanalyst would say that people in general, but adolescents in particular, are likely to endow some other person with the characteristics of a superego. Can we trace this action in student statements about their work? What persons do students cast in the superego role? Teachers? Authors of literary works? Authors of textbooks? School administrators? Furthermore, how do students' relations with their peers enter into their readings of poems and fictions? In general, how do the special issues of adolescence enter into responses to literature? (See Petrosky, 1977b.) Here again the method I suggest is to gather free associations and study them carefully. I wish I could tell you what to expect, but it is characteristic of holistic research that, although you may know the universalizations you bring to the case, you cannot know ahead of time what other universalizations you might take from it.

In that spirit, one might inquire into the role of teaching and criticism in students' readings. My own work with reading convinced me that literents relate to statements about a text through the same DEFT transaction by which they relate to the text itself (Holland, 1973b, pp. 128–131; 1975a, pp. 209–221; 1978k). Yet surely there are some differences, particularly with statements that claim authority, and again, we should be able to find them by closely examining associative responses to texts and statements about texts. One would hope for some generalization about the types of statement that students feel open up the text for them as compared to those that seem to close it down. What statements about a text does a student remember? Do students treat statements by teachers the same way they treat statements in textbooks? Do school environments or administrative strategies play the same role in student reading as statements about a text? How do students relate the compulsory aspect of school to what they are reading? Here again, I am sure the general principles of the identity-DEFT-feedback model apply, but I do not know ahead of time what other principles one might discover.

A particularly intriguing line of research has to do with optimizing. In Piaget's theory, for example, if an input is precisely congruent with a child's existing cognitive structure, no new learning takes place. At the other extreme, if the input does not match the child's cognitive structure at all, it is simply not assimilated. Evidently, then, learning occurs best when there is some optimum degree of mismatch between the task and the child's capacities, that is, when the task almost, but not quite, matches. This, then, is a universalization or guiding principle.

Something similar must be true in identity theory. I cannot take in at all something that I cannot relate to my identity, yet I do not grow if what I relate to matches my habitual mental strategies too easily. Perhaps there is some way of describing a match that is optimal for growth. If so, then we could apply that strategy to school environments, administrative tactics, teaching methods, or the choice of texts and of statements about texts. I do not expect such an optimization to be quantitative, nor do I expect that one person's optimum will be the same as another's. Again we can arrive at an answer, if indeed an answer is possible, by universalizations derived from closely examined case studies.

I return to that phrase, "closely examined case studies"—that is, the bringing of universalizations to data and the learning of universalizations from data, which are the two stages of holistic research. Holistic interpretation is the Ariadne's thread that has guided this somewhat tortuous exploration of research methods; it is the centering theme, in fact, of the transaction which is my writing of this paper and perhaps your reading of it.

Together, the responding person and the stimulus form a feedback system—or, to be more literary, a dialogue—and we can study that unique system holistically, as a theme and variations. Such study should lead to universalizations. We will beget guiding principles that can serve as new hypotheses which one can bring to new theme-and-variations analyses of new data. By such an analysis, both new and old gatherings of data can yield still other universalizations, which in turn become new guiding principles. Round and round goes the feedback loop which is research.

I urge that we no longer let preconceived ideas of literary or scientific responsibility distract us. By combining different sorts of generalizations with holistic, theme-and-variations studies, we can achieve a psychological research that does not evade our own uniqueness as human beings.

REFERENCES

Bower, T. G. R. *Development in infancy*. San Francisco: W. H. Freeman, 1974.

Diesing, P. *Patterns of discovery in the social sciences*. Chicago: Aldine-Atherton, 1971.

Geertz, C. *The interpretation of cultures*. New York: Basic Books, 1973.

Gibson, E. J., & Levin, H. *The psychology of reading*. Cambridge, MA: MIT Press, 1975.

Grant, A. N. Young readers reading: A study of personal response to the reading of fiction based on five case studies of students at the upper secondary school level. Unpublished Ph.D. dissertation, Department of Education, University of Melbourne, Australia, 1982.

Holland, N. N. *The Shakespearean imagination*. New York: Macmillan, 1964.

Holland, N. N. *Poems in persons: An introduction to the psychoanalysis of literature*. New York: Norton, 1973. (a)

Holland, N. N. "English" and identities. *The CEA Critic*, 1973, *35*, 4–11. (b)

Holland, N. N. *5 readers reading*. New Haven and London: Yale University Press, 1975. (a)

Holland, N. N. Unity   identity   text   self. *PMLA*, 1975, *90*, 813–22. (b)

Holland, N. N. *The psychoanalytic study of literature*. (Module No. 9–140.) Educational Materials Distribution Center, Empire State College, Saratoga Springs, NY, 1975. (c)

Holland, N. N. *Hamlet—My greatest creation*. *Journal of the American Academy of Psychoanalysis*, 1975, *3*, 419–27. (d)

Holland, N. N. Transactive criticism: Re-creation through identity. *Criticism*, 1976, *18*, 334–352.

Holland, N. N. Identity: an interrogation at the border of psychology. *Language and Style*, 1977, *10*, 199–209. (a)

Holland, N. N. Transactive teaching: Cordelia's death. *College English*, 1977, *38*, 276–85. (b)

Holland, N. N. How can Dr. Johnson's remarks on the death of Cordelia add to my own response? In G. H. Hartman (Ed.), *Psychoanalysis and the question of the text*. (Selected Papers from the English Institute, 1976–1977.) Baltimore and London: Johns Hopkins University Press, 1978, pp. 18–44. (a)

Holland, N. N. What can a concept of identity add to psycholinguistics? *Psychiatry and the Humanities*, 1978, *3*, 171–234. (b)

Holland, N. N. *Laughing: a psychology of humor*. Ithaca: Cornell University Press, 1982.

Holland, N. N., & Sherman, L. F. Gothic possibilities. *New Literary History*, 1977, *8*, 270–94.

Kluckhohn, C., & Murray, H. A. Personality formation: The determinants. In C. Kluckhohn & H. A. Murray (Eds.), *Personality: In nature, society, and culture*. New York: Knopf, 1961. (Originally published, 1948.)

Kuhn, T. S. *The structure of scientific revolutions* (2nd ed.). Chicago: University of Chicago Press, 1970.

Lichtenstein, H. Identity and sexuality: A study of their interrelationship in man. *Journal of the American Psychoanalytic Association*, 1961, *9*, 170–260.

Lichtenstein, H. *The dilemma of human identity*. New York: Jason Aronson, 1977.

Lindauer, M. S. *The psychological study of literature: Limitations, possibilities and accomplishments*. Chicago: Nelson-Hall, 1974.

Little, G. *Politics and personal style*. Melbourne: Thomas Nelson, 1973.

Little, G. Theory and the individual case-study: An illustration. Paper presented at the first annual conference of the International Society of Political Psychology, New York, September 2–4, 1978.

Little, G. Leaders and followers: A psychosocial prospectus. *Melbourne Journal of Politics*, 1980, *12*, 3–29.

Neisser, U. *Cognitive psychology*. New York: Appleton-Century-Crofts, 1967.

Norman, D., Rumelhart, D. E., & the LNR Research Group. *Explorations in cognition*. San Francisco: W. H. Freeman, 1975.

Paramathan, N. Television themes and styles—an application of N. Holland's transformation theory. *Melbourne Journal of Politics*, 1978 *10*, 51–64.

Petrosky, A. R. Individual and group responses of fourteen and fifteen year olds to short stories, novels, poems, and Thematic Apperception Tests: Case studies based on Piagetian genetic epistemology and Freudian psychoanalytic ego psychology. Doctoral dissertation, State University of New York at Buffalo, 1975. (Ann Arbor, MI: University Microfilms No. 75–16,956).

Petrosky, A. R. The effects of reality perceptions and fantasy on response to literature: Two case studies. *Research in the Teaching of English*, 1976, *10*, 239–258.

Petrosky, A. R. Response to literature: Research roundup. *English Journal*, 1977, *66*, 86–88. (a)

Petrosky, A. R. Genetic epistemology and psychoanalytic ego psychology: Clinical support for the study of response to literature. *Research in the Teaching of English*, 1977, *11*, 28–38. (b)

Petrosky, A. R. From story to essay: Reading and writing. *College Composition and Communication*, 1982, *33*, 19–36.

Powers, W. T. *Behavior: The control of perception*. Chicago: Aldine, 1973.

Purves, A. C. *Putting readers in their places: Some alternatives to cloning Stanley Fish*. Paper presented at the annual meeting of the Modern Language Association, San Francisco, December 27–30, 1979. (ERIC Document Reproduction Service No. ED 179 974)

Purves, A. C., & Rippere, V. *Elements of writing about a literary work*. (Research report 9.) Champaign, IL: National Council of Teachers of English, 1968.

Rapaport, D., & Gill, M. M. The points of view and assumptions of metapsychology. *International Journal of Psycho-Analysis*, 1959, *40*, 153–162.

Rollin, R. B. Against evaluation: the role of the critic in popular literature. *Journal of Popular Culture*, 1975, *9*, 355–365.

Samuels, M. S. Norman Holland's "New Paradigm" and the teaching of writing. *Journal of Basic Writing*, 1978, *2*, 52–61.

Schwartz, M. M. Shakespeare in the light of modern psychoanalytic theory. *Hebrew University Studies in English Literature*, 1977, *5*, 182–98.

Smith, F. *Understanding reading: A psycholinguistic analysis of reading and learning to read* (2nd ed.). New York: Holt, Rinehart, and Winston, 1978.

State University of New York at Buffalo, English Department, Seminar 692 (1975). Poem opening: An invitation to transactive criticism. *College English*, 1978, *40*, 2–16.

Stern, D. *The first relationship: Mother and infant*. Cambridge: Harvard University Press, 1977.

Webb, A. J. Introducing the transactive paradigm for literary response into the high school literature program: A study of the efforts on curriculum, teachers, and students. Research prepared at the State University of New York at Buffalo, 1980. (Available through ERIC).

Webb, A. J. Transactions with literary texts: Conversations in classrooms. *English Journal*, 1982, *71*, 56–60.

Wylie, L. *Village in the Vaucluse* (3rd ed.). Cambridge: Harvard University Press, 1974.

Chapter 2
Understanding Interpretive Situations

C. Barry Chabot

Department of English
Miami University

> Whereas, rightly understood, truth is objective, and ought so to regulate the conviction of every one, that the conviction of the individual is stamped as wrong when it does not agree with this rule. Modern views, on the contrary, put great value on the mere fact of conviction, and hold that to be convinced is good for its own sake, whatever be the burden of our convictions—there being no standard by which we can measure its truth. (Hegel, 1975)

INTRODUCTION

What follows is a contribution to the line of inquiry into the reading process initiated by Norman Holland and David Bleich. Three traits seem to characterize this line. First, it relies upon psychoanalysis as the only discipline sufficiently flexible to offer an adequate account of the processes involved in the reading and teaching of literature. Second, it denies that reading can be adequately conceptualized as an innocent process in which the reader simply appropriates strings of words; rather, it insists that reading must be recognized as a constitutive activity. Finally, it claims or assumes that the processes it finds central to reading—whether they be termed "the subjective paradigm" or "DEFT"—are, in fact, definitive of human cognition in general. Despite such basic agreements, however, this is a new and still highly variegated line of inquiry and, as yet, there is little stable agreement upon terms and final conceptualizations (Bleich, 1976; Holland, 1976).

Although my own thinking about the reading and teaching of literature is heavily indebted to Bleich and Holland, for some time now I have been troubled by two interrelated problems in their work: their varying definitions of "self," "identity," and "subjectivity", and their apparent inability to understand how several people can actually agree on the meaning of a piece of writing (or anything else). Not only are these problems related, but it seems to me as well that the latter is the consequence of the former; that is, I sense that inadequate conceptualizations of subjectivity account for their common difficulties in grasping the grounds for interpretive agreement. Such, at any rate, is the thesis I propose to explore. Moreover, while I would hope that I am working within the psychoanalytic tradition, I propose to do so from the outside, without explicit reference to its literature, in an attempt to begin development of a notion of the *interpretive situation* which might help us grasp both the nature and the terms of human individuality and the grounds for the agreement to which readers do occasionally arrive.

I begin with an assumption: nothing that we know or perceive is simply given; all we know or perceive derives from a process of interpretation. Thus whenever we read—be it Hegel or Dickens, a letter from a friend, or an opinion by Justice Holmes—we are constantly presented with the problem of discerning meaning. That problem is always with us, whether we are conscious of it or not. Most of the time we are not aware of what we are, in fact, doing; the meaning seems so clear and obvious that our derivation or construction of it is rendered covert, as if it never occurred, as if meaning were simply there, waiting patiently to be appropriated by the casual passer-by. If we wish to understand the processes through which we always construct meanings, therefore, it seems that moments of puzzlement, times at which, try as we might, we cannot bring a passage or event to meaning, are privileged, for they occasion our self-reflexive awareness of the processes we wish to forward.

Suppose for the moment that I sit in my study reading Dostoyevsky's *Notes from Underground*. After reading 20 pages more or less successfully I come upon a passage on page 21 that simply eludes me. Either it contradicts my reading of the first 20 pages, perhaps therefore suggesting I reconsider my understanding of those pages, or it remains a tangled know I can neither assimilate to what I have read thus far nor even make grammatically meaningful. I assume that all of us have had such experiences; the quetion they suggest are deceptively simple. What do we in fact do when confronted by passages, like that on page 21 of *Notes from Underground*, which initially only puzzle us? Or even: what was I doing when I thought I understood the previous twenty pages? What interpretive moves was I then making unconsciously that I must now make consciously?

These are the questions to which this collection of articles is dedicated, but at this level they can seem to begrudge answers. Let me suggest a comparable but more mundane situation. Suppose that I am a visitor to Buffalo walking along Main Street, but I come from some all but unimaginable corner of this country and have never been exposed to traffic signals. As I approach the intersection of Hertel Street, I am puzzled by the oblong box hanging from a telephone pole on the far corner. I assume that it has something to do with regulating traffic, but do not know in what way, or what each of the three lights means. However, traffic is sparse and since other pedestrians cross with the red light, so do I. As I approach the next intersection the traffic is heavier and I am the lone pedestrian. On the basis of my experience at Main and Hertel, I assume that I can cross on the red light. I step off the curb and immediately find myself dangerously encircled by honking cars. This experience suggests that I have been interpreting the situation incorrectly. At the next intersection I try crossing with the yellow light and essentially repeat the experience. At the next I repeat the experience with the green light and cross unimpeded. At each of the succeeding intersections, I cross on the green light and do so more or less unthreatened. I now assume, on basis of my experiences during this morning's walk, that green means cross, or more correctly that I then have the right of way.

As humans we interpret constantly; the fact that my example concerns a much less complex system of signs than language should not diminish its relevance to the task at hand. Understanding the process of reading or interpreting is, in the final analysis, understanding understanding. Let me call your attention to some of the characteristics of the situation I have briefly sketched. First, although I interpret all the time, I am coerced into doing so consciously by an inability to do so unreflectively; that is, a break or moment of rupture "tells" me that some hitherto foreign phenomenon has entered my field. In this example, as so often occurs in reading, a lack of familiarity with a social convention occasions the break. Secondly, I try to understand this phenomenon on the basis of my understanding of previous experiences. In the example, this happens several times; first, when I assume that the oblong box has something to do with regulating traffic and then again when, on the basis of trial and error, I reason that neither the red nor the yellow are signals that I have the right of way. This historicity of understanding, I shall argue, is a constant feature of interpretation: we always seek understanding of the new by assimilating it to what we already know (or infer or guess) to be the case. (We might note in passing that these two characteristics of interpreting stand in a complementary relationship to one another; that is, we need to interpret reflectively precisely because something is new to us, yet we can only do so by modeling that reading on our present understanding of our previous experience.) Thirdly, each time I attempted to interpret the situation, I did so by taking into consideration its many diverse features, by *totalizing* the situation: consideration of my previous experiences, my objectives (here, crossing safely), the actions of the drivers and other pedestrians, and so on. Finally, when honking cars endangered my crossing on two occasions I presumed that I had interpreted inadequately; since the signal seemed designed to regulate the right of way, and since when I tried crossing with the red and yellow lights that right seemed very much in question, I must have erred. The traffic surrounding me in the street on those occasions served to disabuse me of my interpretive error; the momentary danger I was in was a consequence of that error. Now of course I have deliberately presented an extreme example, but I shall presently argue that interpretation (reading, if you will) always and necessarily entails comparable consequences.

INTERPRETIVE SITUATIONS

Using the above examples as recurrent points of reference, I want now to begin developing a model that I hope can assist us in understanding the subtle processes through which we come to understand a text, or for that matter anything else. First, I think it is necessary to ground understanding of the reading or interpretive process in a conception of the entire *interpretive situation*, that is, in the full interplay between reader and book, between any subject and its object. What sort of expectations from his or her previous reading does the reader bring to this text? Is he or she familiar with the author? With the genre? With contemporaneous works? Do such acquaintances make much difference? If so, how? What sort of expectancies does the reader bring from situations not so directly similar to the reading of this particular book? (Of course this opens up a potentially endless series of questions.) As for the book, is its language now, at the time of the reading, generally accessible or has it become arcane? Does it sustain a relatively homogenous line of discourse or does it mix several? Would one say that it focuses on characters? Does it contain long discursive descriptions of setting, and so on? Who ostensibly narrates the story? Does the story fulfill or frustrate the expectations to which it itself may be said to give rise? All of these questions, and many more like them, must in principle be addressed by any model of the reading process. Therefore, it is essential to consider the interpretive situation as the grounding concept. It is finally irreducible to terms growing solely from either of its poles. The play between reader and text goes both ways, and each partially defines the other, just as is the case in any interpretive situation.

The previous scholarship suggests that to remain with either pole of this exchange produces a regrettable loss. If one generates a model of the reading process solely from the book—its language, conventions, and the like—one comes finally, I think necessarily, to a simple form of behaviorism. One then says that the book emits some complex stimuli to which the reader answers; reading becomes a secondary, passive adjustment to a governing stream of external stimuli. While their number and variety is legion, such models cannot carry us far, because they completely occlude the constitutive activity of the reader. Moreover, we know that reading cannot be this sort of activity; the plurality of readings cannot be accounted for within such a model. One might say that the ill-prepared reader does not respond appropriately because he or she does not yet recognize the "stimulus," that once the reader recognizes it the response will be corrected. However, that only displaces the problem, for "recognition" is precisely what is at issue. Indeed, one might say that such models represent finally futile attempts to get around the problem of interpretation, but they banish it at one place only to have it re-emerge—still unaccounted for—elsewhere (Loewenberg, 1950).

It would seem, therefore, that models which begin with the reader—as do Bleich's and Holland's—are inherently superior. Both honor the constitutive activity of the reader; neither evades the problem of interpretation. To this extent, their common work represents a substantial contribution to our understanding of the reading process. However, precisely to the extent that they valorize the reader's active contribution to the reading process, Bleich and Holland minimize the role off the text itself. With Bleich, the danger is more immediate; his reader seems the sole measure of all things. For Holland, the self must still negotiate with an occasionally recalcitrant text. Thus he talks about "transactions" between the reader and the text, but in his work the latter always is viewed as a poor bargainer; the terms of the transactions are always thrust upon it and passively received. I suspect that this tendency in their work derives from their finally inadequate accounts of the concept into which they subsume the reader, be it called "self," "identity," or "subjectivity."

As Holland and Bleich set about describing any particular reading situation, the self soon comes to seem an irreducible given, at once imperial and impermeable. While such conceptions allow us access to the reader's constitutive role in the reading process, I doubt they can get the terms of that activity quite right, for they suggest a reader essentially impervious to new experience. Their "self" is an irreducible atom, a given, an entity always prior to its engagement with others, who are likewise given; it necessarily follows from such a position that the social world seems simply an aggregation of these atoms, a mere collection of irreducible selves. But such conceptions do not tally with what we know about the ways in which selves are formed through a process of interaction with others and through a sort of social encoding which leaves traces even at the very core of the presumably unique individual. Since they lack notions which account for these general processes through which the self is constituted, neither Bleich nor Holland are able to account for any consensus or agreement which may be reached by a group of readers; given their models of "self" or "subjectivity," such an outcome can only appear fortuitous, a piece of dumb luck. As I see it, the self is not only, as Bleich and Holland rightly insist, constitutive, but constituted as well; it has no substantive existence apart from the transactions in which it is both defined and defining. If I am right—if we cannot meaningfully talk about any individual apart from considerations of his or her social context—it would seem to follow that the very nature of selfhood dictates that we consider interpretive situations, rather than isolated selves, as irreducible totalities.

READING AS TOTALIZING

Reading or interpreting is *always and necessarily a totalizing activity*. We do not understand first this passage and then the next—and so forth—and simply summarize our understandings at the end, calling the resultant package our "reading" of the text. Whether we are aware of it or not, we constantly strive for an understanding that lends provisional meaning to the entire text at once. Moreover, this meaning of the whole takes precedence over those of this or that particular passage, even though, in one sense, the meaning obviously derives from such local understandings, and may undergo dramatic revisions several times while we read. The process I am briefly sketching is what others have termed the hermeneutical circle (Palmer, 1969; Hirsch, 1967; Hirsch, 1976). This notion has been developed most fully in a certain strain of continental philosophy which is ostensibly inimical to empirical testing; nevertheless, I find empirical confirmation in the results of various "cloze" experiments (Hirsch, 1977), and in the principles of reading deduced by Gibson and Levin (1975) from a consideration of the experimental literature. These experimental results suggest that totalization, or the hermeneutical circle, characterizes a reader's activity in all interpretive situations, literary or not, in those which proceed smoothly and in those that do not.

Common sense might suggest otherwise. Do we not proceed incrementally, move from knowing first this, then this and that, and so on? Such often seems the case;

I at least frequently find myself striving for understandings in this fashion. In this instance, however, I believe that our intuitive sense of interpretive procedures is incorrect. Even when we seem to be understanding incrementally, if we reflect back on the experience we notice that our first, local knowings have most often been radically transformed when we approach the whole. What we witness at such times are pure instances of the hermeneutic circle: a detail leading to a projection of a whole, that whole reshaping the contours of the detail and so on, around and around, with local understandings always containing within them, grounding them, anticipations of the whole in which they partake.

Thus one sense in which reading is a totalizing activity has to do with the attempt to understand the text at once. There are other senses in which I believe this is true; let me mention only two. We necessarily constitute these totalizations along the lines of our previous experiences; that is, we invariably pattern them after previous totalizations, since all new situations are construed analogously. An especially problematic passage, like that on page 21 of *Notes from Underground*, necessitates— if I am not simply to pass it by—that I try consciously what I have been unable to accomplish without thinking: I must construe the role of that passage within the whole I conceive the text as constituting, and I can only imagine that role (or that totality) in terms of my previous experiences of books, of people, and so on. A passage that resists assimilation immediately calls into question far more than my acknowledged dissatisfaction with my renderings of its possible meaning. At the same time such a passage calls into question my hitherto confident interpretation of the previous 20 pages; beyond them, it implicitly suggests a possible inadequacy in my entire way of interpreting the world. In a very real sense, therefore, if our understanding of the past serves as a constant resource in understanding any new text, that *total* understanding is at stake at all moments of apparent interpretive impasse: the reader necessarily commits his or her understanding of his or her experience through time in any interpretive situation (Britton, 1970).

Finally, at some moment in the interpretive process, the reader should totalize the interpretive situation in which he or she is presently engaged. That is, a self-reflexive moment seems an inescapable characteristic of the reading process; the reader must incorporate himself within the developing circle of his or her understanding of the text at hand. Why am I reading this book and not another? How am I reading it? To what am I primarily attending? Why? Do I find the experience satisfying or not? The list of such questions could be extended interminably, but their purpose should already be clear: a text cannot be understood pared from the reader's self-understanding. It is not a question of logical or chronological derivation—my self-understanding does not stand behind and quietly dictate a reading of this or that text; rather, they constitute one another, are born each out of the other. Since reading is never disinterested, it would seem to follow that the conscientious reader would reflect upon the nature of his or her stake in understanding the text at hand.

In at least three senses, therefore, a reader's activity in any interpretive situation is (or should be) characterized by totalization: (a) the text itself must be totalized, assumed cohesive at some high level, as more than the aggregation of its parts; (b) at stake in any interpretive situation is far more than the understanding of the text at hand, but is in fact the reader's understanding of his entire experience to this point; and (c) at some moment in any interpretive process the reader should incorporate himself within the circle of understanding, that is, should totalize the present in-interpretive situation.

INTERPRETIVE CONSEQUENCES

Despite the manifest differences in conceptualization, until now I have more or less reproduced the model of the reading process developed by Bleich and Holland. In any event, I have, like them, focused largely on the reader's active role in the transaction. However, I think it is necessary to extend the model by recognizing the perhaps more passive, resistant, but nonetheless crucial role played by the text itself. I want to discuss that role by developing the commonsensical notion of *consequences*. All interpretations entail consequences; they are most easy to recognize, however, both outside the literary situation and in instances of interpretive inadequacy. If in crossing the street I decide that a red light means "go," I might very well find myself dodging cars; or if, after listening to a friend recount some recent misfortune, I offer some suggestion, he or she might reply, "That is not what I mean at all. That is not it, at all." In these instances, I would say that my friend's disclaimer and the honking cars are consequences of interpretive inadequacies. Both force me to rethink the situation (assuming of course, that I want to understand it) and, most likely, to reinterpret it. Beyond the immediate situation, both suggest that I might need to revise my understandings of previous experiences as well—other occasions I have talked with this friend, other times I have crossed the street.

I believe that the reading and interpreting of books entail consequences too. The problem, however, is that they occur so far down the line, or apparently have so little immediate force, that we think them of no account, if indeed we recognize them at all. No author, after all, is going to speak back to me, much less run me over. Of course for students in an educational setting the consequences of interpretive success and inadequacy are often only too apparent. They must deal not only with the text at hand but also with the instructor, who may mediate the book for them. However, they occupy a different interpretive situation, one transformed by the presence of the instructor. Here I want to confine myself to the simpler case: a reader, on his or her own initative, along with a book. In these circumstances, the consequences of interpretation can seem remote indeed. So what if I cannot understand that passage on page 21 of *Notes from Underground*? I may momentarily damage my self-esteem, but I shall not endanger my job, my marriage, or the like.

The most immediate and pressing consequence of misinterpreting a book is the inability to totalize our interpretation of it. Unfortunately, this does not have the force it should, because too few recognize that that is exactly what we do when we understand anything, or what we should attempt in an interpretive impasse. While reading the first 20 pages of *Notes from Underground*, for instance, we may have anticipated that the novel would form such and such a whole. However, the passage on page 21 has no place in such a totality; at this point we must choose between two alternatives. We can either continue to assume that the novel forms such a whole, thereby necessitating that we leave out of our consideration that passage and any subsequent ones like it (perhaps terming them aberrant and the book ill-formed); or we can reconsider the nature of the totality formed by *Notes*, which permits us to acount for the presence of the passage on page 21, and in the process perhaps radically transforms our understanding of other images, characters, situations and the like. The first alternative seems self-defeating: the modesty with which it freely admits the partiality of its understanding mistakes the very nature of understanding. Again, understanding is not a piecemeal, cumulative process in which we summarize the aggregation of our local decipherings, but the very nature of reading demands that we understand the totality of a text at once, as if we could already know the final words as we read the first sentences.

The initial presumption off the nature of the whole we project in reading the initial lines, a presumption informed by our previous experience and the nature of the lines we now read, is subject to revision continually in the course of reading. Whenever we project an inaccurate image of the whole, we inevitably bump into some remainder, some residue we cannot assimilate to our projection. Each time we come upon something like this, it should prompt our reinterpretation of the text at hand. If part I of *Notes from Underground* seems irremediably at odds with Part II, we can be confident that we have erred. In saying this, I am not denying the fact that texts can, at some level, appear internally at odds with themselves; such an assertion is too obviously false as regards a novel like *Notes from Underground*. I would insist, however, that to grasp these internal tensions properly we must be able to conceptualize them in terms of a larger totality in which they participate. Nor am I arguing that it is the nature of literary texts to form some organic unity. My claim is larger: I want to insist that it is the nature of understanding to form such totalities, that we do so all the time, no more in grasping texts than in understanding the social circumstances in which we live.

As the reader strives for understanding, certain passages or aspects of the text can take on the quality of recalcitrance; they stand as stubborn witnesses to the partiality, and hence falsity, of our present efforts. If we can relegate the impasse to some lesser status, think it local, we lessen its force (but not its irresistable effect upon the adequacy of our understanding). But in any event, the relative force of a recalcitrant passage depends on our awareness of its resistance; that is, although any unassimilated residue always falsifies our interpretation, it only has force in any interpretive situation insofar as we are aware of it. Thus while we might say that reading (or interpretation generally) is inherently a self-correcting activity, one in which remainders repeatedly necessitate that we revise our projections of the totality the text forms as we read, it is such only insofar as we recognize its necessarily totalizing character. To put it another way, ignorance of the interpretive process has consequences also: it cannot only lead us into inadequacy, but insure that we remain there as well.

THE COMMUNITY OF READERS

Before considering some of the research implications of this model of the reading process, let me briefly summarize the argument. I have argued that we can only grasp the movement toward understanding if we recognize that the interpretive situation forms an irreducible totality. Thus we cannot generate an adequate model exclusively from either of its poles, be it text or reader; to attempt the former necessarily occludes the constitutive activity of the reader, and to attempt the latter precludes the possibility of understanding how, in fact, readers can come to agreements about the meaning of texts. Secondly, for the reader's part, reading or understanding is necessarily a totalizing activity. At every step of the way, our understanding of a text we read depends upon our projection or anticipation of the totality it constitutes. This projection may undergo revision any number of times, but at all times our understanding of this or that passage depends upon it. Moreover, each time we read a text we necessarily and always commit our total understanding of the world we inhabit; since we can only understand the new in terms of the familiar, the meanings of the text and of our experience must finally cohere. Totalizing also characterizes the reader's activity in a third sense. At some moment in any interpretive situation the reader must reflect not only upon the totality of the text but also upon the totality he or she forms with the text. Finally, I have tried to introduce the text's activity in the reading process from the other side. I look not to the inherent characteristics of texts but to how they manifest themselves as the reader tries to bring them to meaning. I suggest that as we struggle to bring the text to meaning, portions of it can take on the characteristic of recalcitrance, of mulish resistance; these are always signs of interpretive inadequacy. Thus one consequence of interpretive inadequacy is precisely the inability to totalize the text at hand. Finally, however, this consequence can only have a compelling force in any interpretive situation if the reader knows that understanding only proceeds through the sort of totalizations that elude him or her at this moment.

Thus far I have concerned myself exclusively with the individual reader alone with his or her book. Implicit in my discussion is the possibility that if the reader stays with it long enough, conscientiously enough, he or she will eventually arrive at an adequate understanding of the text. In principle I think this is always a possibility; in practice, however, it is rarely true. There are a variety of psychological reasons why this is the case, but I do not want to go into them here; Holland's 5 Readers Reading (1975) considers them in some detail. Rather, I want to suggest a quite different reason, one that by now should surprise no one: readers fail so often because they do not know what they do at the best of times and hence what they should do at moments of interpretive impasse. Without that knowledge, we flounder; reading becomes chancy, a hit-or-miss phenomenon. If we seriously wish to lessen the arbitrary character of much reading, then, we need a formalized method appropriate to the task, and I have argued that that method should be based on an understanding of what we do when we read successfully.

The vagaries of individual psychology, however, make any individual's reading, no matter how methodological, problematic. If we are to arrive at a body of adequate readings, we need a community of readers, all of whom are committed to an appropriate methodology and to the production of adequate readings. If that community of readers reads well enough, long enough, they should reach a consensus as to the meaning of this or that text, even though at no point in that communal process can we predict beforehand the final nature of that consensual reading. As some of you no doubt already recognize, I have appropriated ideas first put forward by Charles Peirce (1868; 1877; Smith, 1965). Thus, if for Peirce the real is something that will emerge or be constituted if the community of inquirers pursues methodological investigation long enough, I suggest that the most adequate reading of a text will emerge if the community of readers persists long enough in the totalizing process which is reading.

At present our classrooms, professional colloquia and journals rarely provide such a securing community. They fail in this regard precisely because we lack any shared criteria of what constitute adequate interpretive procedures and acts. Lacking such agreements we talk past one another. The ways in which we do so are legion, but I suspect two factors are especially at play—a basic failure to recognize that knowing is a totalizing activity, and a failure to agree on the kinds of totalizations we produce. In the first instance, we knowingly offer one another partial readings— decipherings of this image, that series of episodes—in the belief that we are contributing our bit to some cumulative reading. The belief is misplaced. Each piece furtively harbors within an anticipation of a particular whole, and the pieces can never be joined together unless they project the same totality. Such a procedure transforms the community of inquirers into a mere aggregation, one bound only externally, like too many classrooms. The second failing is rather different. We may recognize that reading is a totalizing activity, but then fail to agree on appropriate boundaries. Do we—must we—totalize only the string of words which comprise the text? The text plus author? Plus canon? Plus genre? Plus social circumstances? This is not the occasion to argue the relative merits of these varying interpretive strategies. I do want to insist, however, that we constitute quite distinct objects for study in each case. Furthermore, the failure to recognize these differences too often results in our talking at cross-purposes. It would seem, therefore, that effective reading, at both the individual and communal levels, can be best insured by a prior understanding of the totalizing nature of the reading process, and by the communal establishment of appropriate interpretive strategies.

RESEARCH IMPLICATIONS

Though I believe it is essential to establish a community of inquirers who are internally bound by a commitment to appropriate interpretive strategies, it remains a task for the future. More immediately, this conception of the interpretive situation seems to issue in three calls to future work. At present the model is altogether too abstract; while coherent, that coherence is achieved at the cost of specificity. Thus the model must be fleshed, a process which could result in substantial reformulations. Second, it would seem appropriate to test empirically what here remains frankly speculative, if no less serious for that. Two complementary experimental procedures suggest themselves. Since the various forms of the "cloze" tests gauge the ways in which readers can successfully supply deleted information, such tests might give empirical confirmation to the notion that reading is an inherently totalizing process. Cloze tests designed in stages could test whether or not subjects alter their initial conceptions of a whole passage when presented with new information. Alternatively, one could employ the case study methods described in Eugene Kintgen's chapter in this book. Kintgen's method would seem suited to providing not only further confirmation of the totalizing character of reading, but also, if one focused upon moments of hesitation and doubt, for confirming the self-corrective role of resistant passages, and therefore the notion of interpretive consequences. Finally, if such empirical confirmations are forthcoming, it would seem desirable to underscore its totalizing nature in the teaching of reading at all levels. Others know better how this might be most effectively accomplished, whether through initial exercises divorced from reading itself, a graduated series of experiences with texts (perhaps even utilizing cloze procedures), or some other means. The crucial point, however, seems clear: only knowledge about the nature of the reading process can assist the reader in an interpretive impasse, or in evaluating the adequacy of any act of reading.

REFERENCES

Bleich, D. The subjective paradigm in science, psychology, and criticism. *New Literary History*, 1976, 7, 313–34.

Britton, J. *Language and learning*. Coral Gables: University of Miami Press, 1970.

Gibson, E. J., & Levin, H. *The psychology of reading*. Cambridge: MIT Press, 1975.

Hegel, G.F.W. *[Hegel's logic]* (William Wallace, trans.) Oxford: Clarendon Press, 1975.

Hirsch, E.D. *Validity in interpretation*. New Haven: Yale University Press, 1967.

Hirsch, E.D. *The aims of interpretation*. Chicago: University of Chicago Press, 1976.

Hirsch, E.D. *The philosophy of composition*. Chicago: University of Chicago Press, 1977.

Holland, N. N. *5 Readers Reading*. New Haven: Yale University Press, 1975.

Holland, N. N. The new paradigm: Subjective or transactive? *New Literary History*, 1976, 7, 335–46.

Loewenberg, J. The futile flight from interpretation. In *Meaning and Interpretation*, University of California Publications in Philosophy, No. 25. Berkeley: University of California Press, 1950.

Palmer, R. *Hermeneutics: Interpretation theory in Schleiermacher, Dilthey, Heidegger, and Gadamer*. Evanston: Northwestern University Press, 1969.

Peirce, C. S. Some consequences of four incapacities. In Philip P. Wiener (Ed.), *Selected writings*. New York: Dover, 1966. (Originally published, 1868.)

Peirce, C. S. The fixation of belief. In Philip P. Weiner (Ed.), *Selected writings*. New York: Dover, 1966. (Originally published, 1877.)

Smith J. E. Community and reality. In Richard J. Bernstein (Ed.), *Perspectives on Peirce*. New Haven: Yale University Press, 1965.

Chapter 3
The Transactional Theory
of the Literary Work: Implications
for Research

Louise M. Rosenblatt

Department of English Education
New York University

For at least a decade, an outpouring of books and articles has dealt with what has come to be called "reader-response" or "reader-oriented" criticism. By 1980, the multiplicity of such writings led to the publication of two anthologies on the theory of literature. I mention these collections not only as evidence of the current interest in the field, but also for a personal reason: The authors of each of these anthologies make brief statements about my work. One refers to *Literature as Exploration*, published in 1938 (republished in 1968, 1976, and 1983) as a "pioneering work in the field of subjective criticism, challenging the objectivist assumptions of the New Criticism" (Suleiman and Crosman, 1980, p. 45). The other writes:

> Rosenblatt deserves to be recognized as the first among the present generation
> of critics in this country to describe empirically the way the reader's reactions
> to a poem are responsible for any subsequent interpretation of it. Her work . . .
> raises issues central to the debates that have arisen since. (Tompkins, 1980, p.
> xxvi)

Each also cites my 1978 book, *The Reader, the Text, the Poem: The Transactional Theory of the Literary Work*.

If it were simply a matter of asserting priority in having set forth a "reader-oriented" theory of literature four decades ago, I should not have quoted these comments. However, though many of the current publications on literary theory recognize the reader, many seem ultimately counterproductive. The very terms "reader-oriented" and "reader-response" become problematic. They sometimes imply a fixation on the reader's personality as all-important, to the virtual exclusion of the text. Sometimes, on the contrary, the reader becomes merely a locus for the convergence of literary conventions, with the text the major real concern. From the beginning, while affirming the importance of the neglected reader, I have insisted on the contribution of both reader and text. Moreover, I find lacking in current theories a satisfactory differentiation between the reading process that results in poems, stories, or plays and the process that characterizes other kinds of reading. The strength of any research design depends ultimately on the strength of its underlying model of the reading process. Hence it seems necessary to present a brief review of major aspects of my transactional theory, as the basis for suggesting questions for further research, with some remarks on methodology.

Just to boggle the minds of the young and inspire the middle-aged, I shall point out that *Literature as Exploration* was not my first book. In 1931, I published a study of the art for art's sake movement, *L'Idée de l'art pour l'art*, my dissertation for the doctorate in comparative literature at the University of Paris. This work treated the theories developed by nineteenth-century writers who sought to free themselves from the social, moral, and aesthetic constraints imposed by an uncomprehending society. In the concluding pages, I asked whether the solution was not to raise the level of the reading public "so that readers might participate fully in the poetic experience" and hence learn to appreciate the distinction between aesthetic and other modes of experience. I also referred to a recently published work, *Practical Criticism* (1929), by I. A. Richards.

Purves and Beach, in their 1972 survey of research, *Literature and the Reader*, cite Richards' major pioneering contribution, and then state that *Literature as Exploration* added two emphases: first, on the process of interaction between reader and text that results in the interpretation, and second, on the teaching process. "This provided the theoretical frameworks or hypotheses for a number of the studies of response, bibliotherapy, and teaching methods" (p. 2). They report that the studies of response surveyed "tend to support the transactional theory" (p. 35).

Literature as Exploration appeared in the same year as Brooks and Warren's *Understanding Poetry* (1938), which reflected Richards' analysis of the inadequacy of his students' readings by their "New Criticism" emphasis on the importance of normative "close" readings. The theories of the New Critics—which treated the poem as a hypostatized object to be analyzed—led to the neglect of the author and the reader. I was—I cannot help phrasing it thus—saved from that development by my interest in both the "autonomy" of literary experience and the place of art in human society. On completion of my doctorate, I had done two years of graduate work in anthropology with Franz Boas and Ruth Benedict at Columbia University, where I was teaching English at Barnard College. After immersion in the philosophic origins of English, French, and German romantic theory, I was influenced by John Dewey, especially his *Experience and Nature* (1925) and his *Art as Experience* (1934). By the time I came to write *Literature as Exploration*, in which I presented a theory of literature as the basis for a philosophy of teaching, I was able to avoid the extremes of both aestheticism and moralism. It was possible to affirm the reader's contribution, the uniqueness of the literary experience, and yet recognize its social origins and potential social effects.

THE LITERARY TRANSACTION

The Reading Process
Transaction vs. Interaction. My use of the term *transaction* stems from Dewey and Bentley's *Knowing and the Known* (1949). They selected this word in order to

eliminate the dualistic overtones carried by the term *interaction*, which suggests a relation between two separate and distinct entities. As early as 1896, in his "Reflex Arc" article, Dewey had rejected the dualistic stimulus-response concept and had set forth his view of the two-way process by which the live creature selects out stimuli from the environment, thus creating it to some extent while responding to it. Dewey had sometimes used the term *situation* to suggest the reciprocal relationship that the term *transaction* makes explicit. A *known*, for example, implies a *knower*, and vice versa. Within the past fifty years, both in America and in Europe, the old dualism has been progressively challenged by philosophers and scientists: the observer has come to be more and more generally viewed as entering into his observation. Adelbert Ames (1955) and Hadley Cantril (1963), in their "distorted room" and other perception experiments, demonstrated how much perception is dependent on the perceiver's contribution. They found Dewey's conceptual framework so congenial that they called themselves transactional psychologists. Current ecological concerns are another expression of the spread of the transactional mode of conceptualizing human life (Bateson, 1972).

The transactional terminology seemed especially pertinent to the view of the relation between reader and text that I had been espousing. An element of the environment (the marks on a page) becomes a text by virtue of its particular relationship with the reader, who in turn is a reader by virtue of his relationship to the text. And at the same time the term *transaction*, as I use it, implies that the reader brings to the text a network of past experiences in literature and in life. (The author's text also is seen as resulting from a personal and social transaction, but that is a question for another discussion.) In the reading situation, the poem—the literary work—is evoked during the transaction between reader and text.

Post-Sputnik intellectualism and the dominant New Critical orthodoxy led me to write "The Poem as Event" (1964), which attacked the New Critics' focus on normative readings of "the poem itself " as a hypostatized entity, and also rejected Northrop Frye's relegation of literary experience to the realm of history of "taste," as distinct from supposedly objective "criticism." The tendency to think of "the work" as an object, an entity, existing somewhere apart from author and reader, has seemed to me the greatest stumbling block in literary criticism and the teaching of literature. The New Critic, intent on impersonal analysis of that hypostatized object, the poem, was not interested in the reader's response.

Moreover, there has been a confusion between the poem and the text: for example, teachers ask their pupils to "read the poem"; critics analyze the text and present it as analysis of "the poem." I have urged, and in this paper follow, the distinction in usage between *the text*, the set of signs capable of being interpreted as verbal symbols, and *the poem*, or *work* which a reader elicits in a transaction with the text. *The poem*—which here stands for any literary work of art—is not an object but an event, a lived-through process or experience.

The transactional theory, by its insistence on both elements of the transaction— the author and the text, or the reader and the text—avoids the formalist's neglect of author and reader, but at the same time does not swing the pendulum to the other extreme of seeing "the poem" as a function only of the reader. As I pointed out in 1938, "The reading of any work of literature is, of necessity, an individual and unique occurrence involving the mind and emotions of some particular reader," and a particular text at a particular time under particular circumstances (p. 32). While insisting on the "poem as event," I underlined the importance of the personal, social, and cultural context, recognizing that "our own reactions, like the author's work of art, are the organic expression not only of a particular individual, but also of a particular cultural setting" (1938, p. 139ff).

The same text may give rise to different works in transactions with different readers, or with the same reader at different times. This leads to rejection of the notion that there is a single "correct" reading of the text of a literary work of art (Rosenblatt, 1978, chap. 5). Some have feared that admission of this would lead to critical chaos. Yet, in any specific situation, *given agreed-upon criteria*, it is possible to decide that some readings are more defensible than others. Criteria of completeness, consistency, and coherence, for example, would permit us to decide that one evocation "did greater justice to the text" than another reading of it: the work evoked by a reader may not account for all of the text, or may include elements not referable to the text. But, of course, various interpretations might be equally acceptable. Similarly, the transactional theory provides for the differences in texts, which vary greatly in the potentialities for evocation that they offer. Both text and reader must be taken into consideration, if one seeks to understand the factors that either permit or block the reader's attention to elements of the text, or that permit or block an organization or synthesis of the reader's responses to the pattern of words.

Reaction against the impersonality of the New Criticism has generated a rediscovery of the reader, but sometimes with an overemphasis on the reader's personality. Unfortunately, some who seem open to that criticsm have adopted a terminology similar to mine, referring to the literary "transaction" and to reading as "transactive"; others have co-opted me under the heading of "subjective criticism." Since they treat the text as "passive" (Holland in Conference on Researching Response to Literature, State University of New York at Buffalo, October 28, 1977) or "secondary" (Bleich, 1975), their view does not do justice to the two-way interfusion required to produce a literary work of art.

Like the Rorschach inkblot, a verbal text may be used to stimulate personal, "free" associations and memories of childhood traumas. But this makes the text simply a passive tool in the psychological study of personality. The emphasis is then on free association, whereas—when the text is read aesthetically—emphasis is on selective attention, guided by cues provided by the text. The whole matter cannot be dealt with here, but it should be recognized that an overemphasis on personality moves the discussion out of the realm of a primary concern for the *literary* transaction and the teaching of literature.

The text, as an active element in the reading process that produces a literary work of art, offers guidance and constraint, yet it is also open, requiring the creative contributions of the reader (Rosenblatt, 1978, chaps. 4, 5). No metaphor or comparison does justice to this unique character of verbal art. A musical score suggests something of this combination of openness and constraint. Reading, when it is an *aesthetic* transaction, can be called a "performing art."

Efferent and Aesthetic Transactions

The transactional paradigm applies to all reading-events. The reader actively creates meaning under guidance of the printed symbols, no matter whether in a newspaper or the text of Virginia Woolf's *To the Lighthouse*. From the beginning, I have emphasized the difference between reading, for example, a novel and a social science text, and I have been concerned with the development of an explanation which differentiates the aesthetic transaction—the evocation of a poem, a novel, a play— from other kinds of reading (Rosenblatt, 1938, 1969, 1978). Aestheticians have, of course, expressed this general distinction in a variety of ways, some more acceptable than others, yet the heart of the matter for reading—what the reader *does* in these kinds of reading—seems to have been glossed over or at best only tacitly admitted.

In general, most weight has been placed on the text, the set of verbal symbols. The essence of the poetic or aesthetic is often attributed to the author's "poetic" or expressive language, to such linguistic details as the deviations from normal syntax, or to imagery. Sometimes the essentially poetic is found in the content, such as Poe's ideal subject, the death of a beautiful woman. Obviously, as I have insisted, the text is important. A Keats text will reward an aesthetic reading more than, say, a legal text. Yet the pop poets have been reminding us that the seemingly most mundane and refractory texts may become materials for poetry. The difficulty in looking only at the text, we must recall, is that any text—no matter what its author's intention—can be read either aesthetically or efferently, to use the term that, as I shall explain below, I apply to the nonaesthetic.

Those who emphasize literature's remoteness from "real life," (often designated as fictionality or "aesthetic distance"), also fail to isolate what is special to the verbal work of art. To express the contrast, for example, in terms of an opposition between "participation" in actual life and the "spectator role" in literature (Britton, 1970) is to use a metaphor that obscures the directly-experienced, dynamic character of the literary work. Moreover, the contrast with actual life applies to all kinds of reading; a scientific formula or an historical account is as much a way of *looking on* at actual life as is a story or a poem.

The Two Stances. The difference between these kinds of reading lies elsewhere— in what the reader *does*, where he or she turns his or her attention during the transaction with the text.

In *efferent* (nonaesthetic) reading, the reader's attention is centered on what should be retained as a residue *after* the actual reading-event—the information to be acquired, for example, from the label on a medicine bottle; or the operations to be carried out, as in a scientific experiment; the conclusion to be reached, as in a legal brief; or the actions to be performed, as in a recipe. I have sometimes thought of this as "instrumental" reading, but this criterion of practical purpose also breaks down. Hence I have chosen to call this kind of reading *efferent*, from the Latin *efferre*, to carry away. The reader's attention is focused mainly on what the words refer to, on what is to be taken away from the transaction.

In the *aesthetic transaction*, the reader's attention is focused on *what he is living through during the reading-event*. He is attending *both* to what the verbal signs designate *and* to the qualitative overtones of the ideas, images, situations, and characters that he is evoking under guidance of the text. The literary work of art comes into being through the reader's attention to what the text activates within him.[1]

Any literary transaction will fall somewhere in the continuum between the aesthetic and the efferent poles.

The transaction between a reader and a text involves the reader in a highly complex ongoing process of selection and organization. We need not pause here to deal with the primary level of recognition of the printed signs. As soon as we turn to the matter of their lexical or semantic interpretation as symbols, we find ourselves involved in consideration of "what the reader brings" to the text—a fund of past linguistic, literary, and life experiences. The reader must select out from the multiple meanings and associations activated by the verbal signs. Extrinsic or intrinsic cues suggest the general stance to adopt—whether primarily efferent or aesthetic—since this provides the basic principle for selecting what to pay attention to. Drawing on past experience, the reader must also sense some organizing principle or framework suggested by the opening verbal cues. This will guide interpretation and organization of the further cues as the text unrolls. If elements appear that cannot be synthesized into the earlier framework, there may be revision or even a complete reversal and rereading.

For the efferent reading of, for example, a newspaper or a scientific work, another text, a paraphrase or restatement, or a summary by another reader may serve. But for an aesthetic transaction, no one else can substitute and no other text can serve. The reader must personally select out and synthesize the ideas, feelings, and images that have been aroused within by that particular set of verbal signs. Throughout, in the evocation of the poem or novel or play, there is a to-and-fro movement of attention between the words and the experienced, felt, meanings being elicited, organized, and reorganized. The literary work "happens" during the aesthetic transaction. Recognition of the importance of the reader's stance, or focus of attention, in the aesthetic transaction is unfortunately lacking even in theoretical treatments

---

[1] Where I use *efferent*, Britton (1970) uses *transaction* and *transactional*. Britton's association is evidently with practical "real life" affairs, as in "commercial transaction." He obviously is not thinking of the two-way process (a buyer implies a seller, and vice versa) as the reason for calling it a transaction. When I use transaction or transactional, I am indicating the reciprocal relationship in all reading events.

Where Britton uses *spectator role*, I use *aesthetic stance*. It is regrettable that in this field, as in others, terminological problems have arisen, especially since in many ways Britton reinforces and supports much that I have been saying since 1938. Britton seems to derive his terminology mainly from the point of view of the *speaker* and *writer*, which is another reason why his terminology does not fully take care of the aesthetic *reading* transaction.

that seem to emphasize the reader but still seek the aesthetic factor entirely in the text.

The reader, then, is not passively receiving the imprint of an already-formed "object" encased in the text. Nor is the reader merely a distanced spectator. Readers' feeling that they are looking on at the characters and situations of a novel does not contradict the fact that they have themselves called forth those scenes during the transaction with the text. They have had to draw on their individual past experiences of language and of life to provide the raw materials for this new experience. Hence, even when we feel ourselves as onlookers at the characters and situations of a novel we are also *participants*, having ourselves created the scenes that unroll before us. The aesthetic transaction is not vicarious experience, not 'virtual' experience, but a special kind of experience in its own right.

The transactional concept of "the evocation" should save us from the fallacy of reducing the poem to a set of theoretical categories. The tendency is to turn away from the lived-through experience and to efferently apply a ready-made system of analysis to the reading. The structuralists draw on the analogy with Saussurian linguistics to see the text as manifesting a particular set of codes, for example, social, moral, literary. The linguists analyze the text as a set of phonemic, morphemic, syntactic patterns, as do some analysts of style. The Freudians would reduce the work to particular defense mechanisms or symbols of postulated unconscious drives underlying a reading. The Marxists apply a similarly reductive type of analysis. Such analysts are perhaps psychologists, bibliotherapists, semiologists, social or economic analysts and historians, or linguists. They are doing something different from analysis of response to the poem or story or play *as evocation*.

The literary transaction, as a form of human behavior, can be fruitfully studied from the point of view of any discipline (Rosenblatt, 1976, Pt. 3; 1978, chap. 7). But from a literary point of view, such analysis is useful only if it illuminates, places in a context, and does not destroy or ignore the lived-through structured evocation which the reader sees as the work of art corresponding to the text and which is the "object" responded to both during and after the reading. Keeping the reader's active process of evocation of the work central—keeping the aesthetic transaction central—will have important implications for questions raised and methods used in both teaching and research.

Evocation and Response. It is now possible to refine our understanding of "response to literature." To what, in fact, do we respond? Often the term is used rather loosely to cover two processes—both the aesthetic relationship to the text and our response to the work that we are evoking. Hence, I prefer to speak of, first, *the evocation*—what we sense as the structured experience corresponding to the text—and second, *the response* to the evocation. In our transaction with Dickens' text, *Great Expectations*, for example, we evoke the characters of Pip and Joe. We participate in their relationship and, at the same time, we respond with approval or disapproval to their words and actions. We see parallels in our own lives; perhaps we savor the vividness of imagery or linguistic exuberance. All of these processes may be going on at the same time. Later reflections on the transaction can be seen as an effort (a) to recapture, to reenact the evocation, and (b) to organize and elaborate our ongoing responses to it. I shall return to these topics in considering specific problems for research.

Transactional Concepts

Concern with research on response to literature and the teaching of literature requires clarification of the underlying theoretical model, since that model influences the questions we ask, the formulation of hypotheses, and the research methods used to test them. It affects the teaching situations we study and the criteria of evaluation we apply. Hence the importance of the distinctions I have been sketching:

- The concept of reading as an event involving a particular reader, a particular text, at a particular time, under particular circumstances.
- The concept of the *transaction* between reader and text as a reciprocal *process*, in contrast to notions of the passive reader acted on by the text, or the passive text acted on by the reader.
- The concept of *stance* or focus of attention, which leads the reader to select from a broader or narrower range of the elements of consciousness activated in transaction with the text.
- The concept of the *efferent transaction* in which the reader's selective attention during the reading is focused mainly on the public referents of the words, on the ideas being developed for retention after the reading.
- The concept of the *aesthetic transaction* in which the reader's attention during the reading is focused on his or her lived-through evocation of the literary work.
- The concept of *the evocation*: the aesthetic transaction with the text is a process in which the reader selects out ideas, sensations, feelings, and images drawn from his past linguistic, literary, and life experience, and synthesizes them into a new experience, the evocation—the poem, story, novel, or play.
- The concept of the *response to the evocation*, generated during and after the aesthetic transaction.

It has not been possible to do justice to these matters here, but merely to suggest some major themes of the transactional theory and to hope that answers to questions raised will be sought in my fuller presentations.

IMPLICATIONS FOR RESEARCH

Even research in the natural sciences, we have seen, recognizes that "the observer is part of his observation" (Bohr, 1949, p. 210). Many who are now researching response to literature have been subjected to teaching that assumed the literary work to be an "object" for analysis and categorization, with a single "correct" interpretation to be assimilated. Such assumptions lie deep. Hence, researchers in this field should approach it, I believe, with self-critical concern for the full implications of the transactional theory for both research and teaching.

In an earlier statement concerning needed development of research in our field, I used the analogy with research in the physical sciences to set forth the need for both "basic" research, for example, in such areas as language acquisition, and "applied" research, centered on the effectiveness of teaching methods in the classroom (Rosenblatt, 1963, pp. 11–37). Many of the research problems cited in that earlier monograph remain to be treated. The declining dominance of natural science research methodology favors the development of effective research designs.

Basic Problems of Language Development
As we come to understand the complexity of both the efferent and aesthetic reading transactions, we realize the relevance and importance of basic research in language development. We need to understand more fully the individual's development of the capacity for selective attention to the various components of meaning. As psychologists emerge from the constrictions of behaviorism, the Piagetian emphasis on the mathematical and logical and on the child's decontextualization of language is giving way to interest in the affective and the qualitative (e.g., Deese, 1973; Drucker, 1979; Izard, 1977; Lewis and Rosenblum, 1978). Recent studies reinforce the view that the child's earliest "words" represent "a peculiar fusion of processes which will later branch off into referential, emotive, and associative part processes" (Rommetveit, 1968, p. 167). Following William James (1890), Vygotsky (1962) saw language as "a dynamic system of meaning in which the affective and the intellectual unite" (p. 146). Werner and Kaplan (1963) demonstrate that a word and its referent acquire meaning when they are linked to the same organismic state. Thus the child's early vocables "are expressive not only of reference to an event external to the child" but also of "the child's attitudes, states, reactions, etc." (p. 141). Bates similarly sees the emergence of decontextualized linguistic symbols as a "selection process" (1979, p. 65–66). Both efferent and aesthetic reading are made possible by the reader's awareness of the different dimensions of the inner states that the verbal signs activate. Whether the reading will be predominantly efferent or aesthetic, and whether at the extreme or near the middle of the continuum, will depend on what "mix" of referential and associative elements will be admitted into consciousness. The adult capacity to engage in the tremendously complex reading process depends ultimately on the child's development of habits of selective attention. Thus a better understanding of how children "learn to mean" in specific contexts should yield signals for those involved in all aspects of reading, especially research on response to literature and the teaching of literature.

Factors Which Affect Aesthetic Capabilities
A scholar who wished to stress the need for suspended judgment told about an eight-year-old who objected, "But rabbits don't carry watches!" The scholar had replied, "Shut up! In this story they do," and had continued reading. The boy was simply listening efferently, and his critical thinking was entirely appropriate for that kind of stance. He had somehow not learned, or had lost, or had been given

the wrong cue as to the appropriate (aesthetic) stance. He should have been living in the experience evoked from Lewis Carroll's words, perhaps even delightedly savoring the unorthodoxy of this rabbit. The scholar was depending entirely on the text to force the aesthetic stance. That, we have seen, cannot be taken for granted, but is precisely the question to be explored: How does the child learn to adopt the aesthetic stance toward the spoken or printed word? What happens as the child moves from the early, undifferentiated phase to the use of "decontextualized" language? To what extent do environmental pressures—in home, school, community— lead the child to focus on the efferent, practical function of language and to push into the fringes of consciousness the rich affective aura that no one doubts does subliminally persist?

More specifically, do language activities in the schools—speaking as well as writing and reading—push the child mainly in this nonaesthetic direction? My favorite illustration is a reading workbook that prefaced the first poem presented in its pages (a poem about a cow) with the question: "What facts does this poem teach you?" The reader was clearly being asked to adopt a nonaesthetic stance, to pay attention to what was to be retained *after* the reading. This would not permit the kind of experienced meaning that derives from attention to a synthesis of sound, image, and ideas. How many potentially aesthetic texts—poems, stories—are used in this way in basal texts for the purpose of teaching efferent reading? How often does the preliminary emphasis, when a presumably "literary" text is introduced, foster neglect of all but the information that will be required at the end of the reading?

The kinds of questions that teachers ask have been a subject for study for some time. But, so far as I know, little has been done to test my view that most questions in classrooms, in literature anthologies, and also in many research projects, turn the young reader's attention away from the lived-through poem or story toward an efferent reading and analysis of the text.

It becomes important to inquire about the kinds of situations (home, classroom, social climate), the kinds of strategies (teaching methods, nonverbal activities such as painting, dramatizations, writing), and the kinds of texts (those meeting the reader's needs and interests) that can contribute to the child's development of the habit of attention to the qualitative character of what the text triggers within him. At what point can the young reader be helped to adopt either the efferent or the aesthetic stance toward what he elicits from a text? When and how can the young reader learn the circumstances, the "purpose," of the reading that makes one or the other stance appropriate? When and how can the young reader be helped to respond to the cues offered by the text for one or another stance?

We are finally receiving experimental support for the importance of "prior knowledge" (not simply "skills" or vocabulary) for reading comprehension. Although the research thus far deals mainly with efferent reading, the importance of the context of the reading act is being demonstrated (Harste and Carey, 1979). In aesthetic reading, prior knowledge cannot be limited simply to abstract information. "Prior experience" is a better term. My remarks on the child's early language point up the importance of the richness of the sensuous, personal, and social experiences provided by the environment; these are the contexts for developing what is generally phrased as sensitivity to the nuances of the spoken and written word. Many teachers, realizing that the new experience, the story or poem, must be built out of the elements of past experience, have sought texts with some linkage with the child's background and interests. These should not be understood too narrowly, however (Rosenblatt, 1976, p. 283–284). We should study in greater depth the relationship between, on the one hand, the range of experiences that the young readers bring to the page and, on the other, the types of imagery, social assumptions, and basic emotional structures, as well as linguistic patterns, offered by specific texts.

A more rounded concept of comprehension in both efferent and aesthetic reading is needed, with attention to experiential, affective, and cognitive components of meaning. The efferent stance—the kind of reading appropriate to an economics text—has generally been the concern of reading teachers, theorists, and researchers. Yet even the strategies of critical efferent reading—the discounting of irrelevant personal associations, the role of inference, the testing of logical connections— has not been sufficiently stressed. Even less has been done to help the student to assimilate also the aesthetic mode of relating to a text. As we have seen, students need to learn to select out and handle both the referents of the verbal signs *and* their inner matrix. They need to be encouraged to savor the sound of words in the inner ear, and to attend to the qualitative overtones of the ideas and situations evoked. They need, not to explicate or translate figurative language, but to be aware of its sensuous and emotional reverberations. They need, we have seen, to focus attention on, and organize—to apprehend in order to comprehend—the structure of image, idea, feelings, and attitudes that each of them constitutes as the poem or story or play.

I have suggested negative factors that probably inhibit the aesthetic stance and foster efferent approaches to even "literary" texts. We need to study the positive factors that reinforce children's sensorimotor explorations of their worlds and their acquisition of the habits of linguistic performance required for the evocation of a poem or story or play from transactions with a text. Research is needed to accumulate some systematic understanding of favorable and unfavorable environmental factors, and the relation of cognitive and emotional development to the growth of aesthetic capabilities.

Psycholinguists have underlined the extent to which the child intuitively derives from the environment command of the basic structure of the language, in contrast to the traditional fixation on direct teaching of "formal grammar." Recent structuralist and post-structuralist revivals of emphasis on the essentiality of linguistic and literary conventions (Culler, 1981) may lead to a similar fixation on abstracted patterns as against the realities of literary and linguistic activities and experiences. Studies of the child's entrance into the realm of the literary arts can be hampered by dependence on the—until recently dominant—formalistic identification of literary art with product rather than process. Experimental designs which seek to deal with the development of the ability to handle some aspect of literary art often use methodologies and experimental tasks that actually serve rather to test the children's efferent, metalinguistic capacities. For example, levels of ability to elucidate metaphor may not reflect children's actual sensing or experiencing of metaphors so much as their capacity to efferently abstract or categorize (Verbrugge, 1979). Children's ability to retell or summarize or comment on the "grammar" of story may reflect their cognitive development more than their aesthetic growth, or it may reflect simply the effect of schooling in what is the appropriate way to talk about a story. It is important to make sure that research techniques do indeed reveal aesthetic sensitivities and that research designs take into account the processes of evocation and response.

The problem of the development of aesthetic capabilities is extremely complex, even when delimited to the verbal arts. Both short-range and longitudinal studies are needed. Howard Gardner (1973) has made a brave beginning, but in his effort to cover all the arts he has created a general model that seems very unsatisfactory so far as aesthetic reading is concerned. Because it is not a transactional model, he does not recognize that the reader—that is, the evoker—of a poem from a text is not simply an "audience" but much more a "performer" (Rosenblatt, 1976; Scruton, 1977).

Research on the Process of Evocation
As Purves and Beach (1972), Purves (1973), Cooper (1976), and others point out, the data in research on response are always in some form indirect. The response is always being reported by the reader, and usually after the reading event. In much criticism and research, the term "response" covers both the work-as-experienced (the evocation) and the current of accompanying attitudes and ideas (the response). Hence it becomes especially important to make clear precisely what is being studied. In any research design or report on "response to literature," it is necessary to clarify what concept of "the literary work" is embedded in the study. Some studies purportedly dealing with literature would be as applicable, or perhaps more applicable, to efferent reading. What evidence is there that the reading has been aesthetic? That a literary work of art, as compared to a piece of information, or an act of classification, has resulted? To what are the responses directed? Different readers of the same text are not necessarily responding to the same "work."

We need to delve more deeply than has thus far been done into the processes by which the reader creates the poem or story or play in transaction with the cues offered by the text. James R. Squire's study (1964) is notable not only as a pioneering work on response to stories but also because it deals with activities going on *during* the actual reading, the actual evocation of the story. His method was to interrupt the reader at set intervals to allow free responses. Instead of accepting the reader's production of the work as a *fait accompli* and concentrating on his or her later reflections on it, we need many more studies centered on the actual literary transaction or reading-event.

From 1948 to 1972, I was able to carry on quite systematic study of students' transactions with texts, presenting some texts year after year to finally hundreds of students, and utilizing various ways of learning about their thoughts and feelings. Sometimes the reader simply started to make jottings as soon as possible after encountering the text and wrote whenever there was a pause, a break, a hesitation, a need to look back, to synthesize, and so on. On other occasions, there were oral comments as the transaction unfolded. Sometimes records were kept of repeated readings. Interchange among readers, who tended to point to parts of the text in support of different evocations or different judgments, revealed much about the linguistic habits, literary expectations, and social assumptions brought to transactions with the same text. My 1964 article on "The Poem as Event" developed some of the results of my observations. Using as illustrations the jottings of one group as they encountered a quatrain by Robert Frost, I outlined the process of organizing the ideas, feelings, and associations elicited in the to-and-fro relationship with the text. "Towards a Transactional Theory of Reading" followed in 1969. *The Reader, the Text, the Poem* (1978) elaborates this model.

Joanna Williams (1971, pp. 7–158), commenting on implications for the reading teacher and reading research of various models of the reading process, reported that practically all recent model building has focused on the cognitive aspects of learning to read, with little attempt to incorporate affective features. She differentiated my "transactional model" from the others, e.g., the "linguistic" and the "information processing" models. She indicated that the Goodman "linguistic" model does not provide for "miscue analysis" of aesthetic reading.

Here, again, we return to the need for research on the differences between aesthetic and efferent reading, at all levels. Studies might be made of the strategies involved in aesthetic and efferent transactions with the same text. The effect of varied cues, visual and verbal, that lead to the adoption of one or the other stance should be analyzed. We recognize the importance of visual cues for signaling the aesthetic stance, for example, when a newspaper item is segmented as a piece of "found poetry." We have many analyses of the complex verbal patterns embodied in literary texts, but we know little about how readers attend to them or how they organize their reactions to the verbal cues (Rosenblatt, 1978, pp. 162–171). The use of simple, fairly brief texts seems indicated, because of the complexity of the processes involved.

Such studies of evocation would lead to analysis of the role of what the reader brings to the text, in terms of past linguistic, literary, and life experiences, assumptions, and expectations, and of present preoccupations. The cumulative effect of earlier instruction in reading and literature especially should be recognized. Research designs should provide for consideration of this factor, since it is possible to attribute to the reader's personality or stage of development patterns of organization and response that are actually the residue of earlier instruction.

Recognizing that each reading is an event in time, we cannot limit ourselves to study of reader and text. We must take into account the context, the pressures to which the reader may be subjected, the social tensions that may affect the character of the transaction. I have already mentioned some potential contextual factors, and later I shall deal more fully with this important research consideration.

Research on Response

I have stressed the importance of devising strategies for studying the actual process of organizing a sense of "the work" because our "response" to it begins and continues during the reading (Rosenblatt, 1978, chap. 4). *We respond to the work that we are evoking.* Further reflection on our response after the transaction involves a reexperiencing, a reenacting of the evocation and an elaborating and ordering of our responses to it during and after the reading-event.

Alan Purves has made perhaps the major contribution to research on response, through his direction and report on the international investigation into responses of students (1973), his survey of research on literature and the reader (Purves & Beach, 1972), and his editing of the journal and *Research in the Teaching of English*, to mention only a few of the major items. The publication of *The Elements of Writing about a Literary Work* (Purves and Rippere, 1968) undoubtedly was an important contribution to the increasing research on literary response. It provided a coherent system of analysis of students' written (or oral) reports of their reading of literary texts. Its usefulness is demonstrated by the number of research projects that utilize it, and it will surely continue to provide a common framework for various types of analysis.

More Emphasis on Process Needed. As Odell and Cooper (1976, p. 204) have pointed out, the Purves categories for content analysis need further refinement, to provide a basis for moving into research which focuses on "the *processes* by which students formulate their responses." Cooper (1976, p. 80) suggests subgroupings of the main categories. There could be further functional groupings of the coded elements, it seems to me, to reveal aspects of the relationship between reader and text. Just as I indicated earlier the need to study the strategies of the reader as he or she evokes a "work" from the text, so processes of handling and organizing his or her response to that evocation should be studied.

Part of the strength of Purves' work lies in the care with which he frames his findings and clarifies the lacks as well as the important gains made by him and others in the field. Thus he points out the need to study "the relationships among the various aspects of response" (Purves and Beach, 1972, p. 178). Squire (1964) found a correlation between expressions of personal involvement and literary judgment, for example, in response to stories. We need to understand more clearly the relationship between involvement and perception, or involvement and technical analysis.

Studies should be made of the kinds of elements in a written or oral response that can be judged to reflect the inward-looking synthesizing activities which lead to the crystallization of a sense of "the work." We need clarification of what the reader perceives as the existential "work," as distinguished from analytic references to, say, the sonnet form or recurrent imagery. It makes a great difference if such references result from—or to phrase it operationally, occur in the context of—for example, an effort to understand the sources of an ambivalent feeling generated by the reading. Such concern for context would result in what might be called functional groupings of the coded elements. Coding of indications of aesthetic as compared to efferent activities would probably cut across some of the Purves categories, such as "Perception." Perhaps a category such as "Evocation" might be set up to code responses which reflect a qualitative sense of the lived-through work.

Work in propaganda analysis between 1942 and 1945 gave me a sense of the limitations as well as the possibilities of both content analysis and "intuitive" study as ways of eliciting meaning and "intelligence" or information from texts. Hence the importance, increasingly recognized, of combining both types of approach. Research designs for study of response have tended to be excessively restricted to conventional experimental designs derived from the physical sciences. Fortunately, the dominance of the behaviorist "paradigm" is being eroded. Systematic analysis of multiple elements present in the responses of appropriately-selected groups need not rule out intuitive study in depth of full individual responses.

Increasingly sophisticated statistical techniques have reinforced work in content analysis. The tendency is to think of statistical findings as a check on intuitive observations. The checking of the statistical by intuitively-acquired knowledge should be even more important, involving as much as possible whole responses or protocols, the personality, and the conditions or situation that provide the impetus and manner of the responses. The simplest checking, of course, would involve interpreting the statistical content-analysis findings in the light of an intuitive reading of appropriately-selected whole written or oral responses. "Case studies" offer another dimension, sometimes providing hypotheses for broader investigation or the opportunity to test the insights derived from other methodologies. Even more important than methodological cross-checking is the bringing of the fullest possible sense of factors in the total human situation that may feed into the literary transactions. Ethnographic research methods are relevant here (see p. 50).

Factors That Affect Expressed Responses

In both content analysis and intuitive study of responses, it seems very important to recognize that various factors will have affected what is expressed as a response. As I have watched succeeding generations of freshmen enter college—or for that matter, succeeding generations of English majors as beginning teachers—I have been struck by changes in their assumptions about what in the literary transaction should be attended to. These shifts reflected changes in teaching methods in the earlier grades, changes in the dominant theories of literature in the universities, and changes in the social climate. It becomes essential that any research on response take into account the fact that the reader will reflect earlier indoctrination about what to note and talk about.

It also is essential that the researcher on response become aware of any theoretical bias on his or her own part that might exert pressure on the character of the reader's response, or that might lead to emphasis on one aspect and neglect of others. The most obvious illustration is the New Criticism's overemphasis on analytic skills and its neglect of the reader's response. The current reaction against the supposed objectivity of the New Criticism may be leading to an equally biased overemphasis on feeling, on the search for childhood memories, and so on. We need also to keep in mind the danger of a certain circularity in any research approach based on acceptance of, rather than a testing of, a particular closed or imputed explanatory system, whether psychological, social, or economic. In research, as in teaching, the danger is that the investigator will indoctrinate the subject with the very concepts—or elicit the very activities—that should constitute the hypotheses to be tested.

Investigations that are dependent on psychoanalytic doctrine—for example, assumptions concerning the defense mechanism or the role of fantasy—may tend to be self-fulfilling and fail to do justice to the aesthetic aspect (Crews, 1975). I can do no more here than suggest the presence of such dangers. Hence my espousal of the relatively open transactional view of the human creature, who shapes and is shaped in a two-way relationship with the environment—choosing and rejecting, as well as assimilating (Dewey, 1931; Piaget, 1970). Such a theoretical base, it seems to me, offers much more opportunity for discovery of the many facets of the literary transaction. (This does not imply that we should ignore the potential contributions that depth psychology, for example, offers, so long as we recognize that there are various ways of envisaging the dynamics of human personality.)

A narrow focus on the personality of the reader viewed in terms of a formula obscures the total literary transaction in its cultural context. The difficulty that the psychoanalytic observer has in finding a way to move from the "holistic" study of individuals to generalizations about literary transactions evidently results from this lack. Just as language is socially developed and individually internalized, so the evocation of a literary work of art must be seen both in its social and its personal aspects. The uniqueness of each transaction—the uniqueness of each reader and of each evocation—need not obscure the role of language as communication or the literary transaction as a link between reader and author, on the one hand, and as a link between reader and reader on the other (Rosenblatt, 1938, 1978). The literary transaction in itself may become a self-liberating process, and the sharing of our responses may be an even greater means of overcoming our limitations of personality and experience. Therefore, it is important that research keep the transactional model open to the whole range of possible psychological and cultural hypotheses.[2]

RESEARCH ON TEACHING

Relation Between Aims and Teaching Methods

Implications of the transactional theory for teaching generate hypotheses for research on the teaching of literature. The aim is no longer primarily the imparting of accepted interpretations and analyses of a traditional canon of works. Therefore, many research

---

[2] Although my approach is sometimes cited in support of research on bibliotherapeutic uses of literary works, I see this use as primarily clinical, dealing with a level of personality that can be handled only in a most superficial way in schools as we know them and by teachers who are not trained therapists. It would be unfortunate if teachers were given the impression that recognition of the reader necessarily requires them to engage in such probing. Research on students' responses during and after their transactions with texts involves the personality, but it can be on a different level, more relevant to the teaching situation, and for the study of different, continuing, developmental patterns (Rosenblatt, 1976, chaps. 7, 8, and passim).

designs that evaluate different "treatments" by tests of "correct" results become irrelevant. Concern with correctness of product gives way to interest in the process by which the student arrives at a personal evocation and response. Attention turns to the attitudes of the teacher, the classroom atmosphere, the selection of texts, and the procedures that will encourage students to participate freely and honestly—and ultimately, self-critically—in transactions with texts.

The individual's personal transaction with the text becomes the basis for growth in the ability to engage in increasingly complex and demanding literary transactions. To foster such growth, the classroom must provide the opportunity for spontaneous interchange among students concerning the works evoked and their responses to them. Self-awareness and self-criticism develop from students' discovery of diversities in attention to various elements of the text, differences in social and moral assumptions embedded in the evoked works, and the ways in which those assumptions confirm or contradict beliefs held by the readers. The teacher's function is less to impart information than to help students reflect on their experience, clarify its significance for themselves, become aware of alternative emphases, discover their own blind spots, or reinforce their own insights. Much research on response thus far has centered on analysis of, and generalizations about, students' expressed responses. Statistical analysis has led to inferences about the relative importance of various factors. Much remains to be done through study of classroom dynamics to discover how the teacher's guidance (without domination) of group discussion can contribute to growth in students' ability to handle and reflect on their transactions with texts. One factor deserves particular study: the effect of the teacher's own understanding of the theoretical basis for the fact that—although there is no single "correct" interpretation—there can be developed criteria of validity of interpretation. Clarification of the criteria that are being applied—not necessarily consensus—is the basis for critical communication.

I have alluded above to the danger that the current interest of some theorists (e.g., Fish, 1976; Culler, 1981) in interpretive conventions may lead to preoccupation with abstractions. This could lead to an analytic approach to the text even more extreme than the New Criticism. Of course, conventions enter into all language and all reading, not only literary. In fact, we might phrase the individual's development as a member of a society or culture in terms of the assimilation of conventions, viewed as ways or patterns of behaving and feeling and thinking. Our disappointment with teaching of formal grammar has led to inquiries into how the basic patterns or conventions of a language are acquired. Some questions to be investigated, then, are: What are these "interpretive conventions," operationally defined? How flexible or prescriptive? How are they to be assimilated, intuitively or through direct indoctrination? And again, we need to elucidate the differences in "interpretive strategies" related to differences in stance: Is there a difference between the way we read a metaphor in a scientific report and in a lyric poem?

The relationship among the linguistic processes involved in speaking, writing, and reading constitute another important area of research. It is my belief that the concept of the efferent-aesthetic continuum applies to speech and writing as well as to reading. The writer, I have pointed out, is the text's first reader. The interplay between writing and reading—and the hypothesis is that the influence tends to be reciprocal—offers another area of research, especially for those interested in the teaching of literature.

Teachers brought up in the traditional modes especially are at a loss to understand how they can evaluate students' work in literature classes once the security of "correct" answers is lost. Here, research could do much to elucidate the kinds of evidence that might signal growth in quality of transactions with texts, for example, relating response to evocation and to elements of the text, clarifying underlying attitudes and assumptions, or placing the evocation in broader contexts (cf. Rosenblatt, 1976, 1978).

Obviously, we must seek insight at whatever point research is feasible. But the time has come to hope for longitudinal studies of various aspects of linguistic development, covering the range from the beginning to adulthood. I have emphasized the need to study the acquisition of habits of aesthetic attention. Given the complexity of our problems, interrelated group studies could make an important contribution. The assumption is that everyone engaged in research on literary transactions would bring to it a rich literary experience and a feeling for its role in individual lives. Each investigator might approach the problem from a particular angle or at a particular academic or age level. Another basis for the division of labor might be further specialized expertise—sociological, psychological, linguistic. Such group cooperation would permit the study of the total situation in which the literary transactions take place, and of developmental sequences.

The Ethnographic Approach

The emphasis on context in the preceding pages perhaps stems from my early interest in anthropology, which contributed from the outset recognition that the reader's "reactions, like the work of art itself, are the organic expression not only of a particular individual but also of a particular cultural setting" (Rosenblatt, 1938, p. 139 and passim; 1978, pp. 128–160 and passim). Any encounter between readers, teachers, and texts in a classroom has as its setting the society, the community, the ethos of the school, the total curriculum, the cumulative social concepts embodied in the works presented to the pupil over the years, and the earlier experiences with literature at home and in school. The dynamics of the particular classroom, in turn, provide a context for the individual students' evocations and responses. The restrictions of conventional experimental design have made it difficult and often impossible to deal with many of these facets of the total situation, in research on either individual readings or classroom teaching and discussion.

The "ethnographic" approach, which utilizes the techniques of the anthropologist and the sociologist rather than the natural scientist, seems especially congenial to research problems involving the transactional view of language and literature. The growing interest in ethnographic studies is confirmed by the publication of an entire issue of *Research in the Teaching of English* devoted to this trend. The authors of the lead article (Kantor, Kirby, and Goetz, 1981, pp. 293–309) discuss the appropriateness of ethnographic methods for language and literature studies. The anthropologist's "thick description" (Geertz, 1973) calls for the careful account of particular events, which yield, but are not submerged in, theoretical constructs. Ethnographic field notes and recorded or transcribed interviews provide the basis for explicit descriptions organized in terms of observed recurring patterns (and their exceptions). The view of the researcher as participant especially opens the way for informal interviews, with recognition that the researcher's presuppositions and relationship to the reader or situation must be taken into account. The systematic examination of affective and emotive responses becomes a disciplined strategy. At the same time, the researcher must guard against the pitfalls of such methods, which are to be distinguished from simple personal accounts or descriptions. Corroborative procedures (such as "triangulation," the recourse to different points of view) constitute an essential part of such research.

Ethnographic methods can be applied frutifully to the study of classroom dynamics such as I have suggested above. Perhaps one reason for this is that the teaching process postulated is a collaborative process "in which teachers and students engage in a speculative and interpretive enterprise, building a perspective as they proceed" (Kantor et al., p. 295). Among the examples of ethnographic research published in this issue of the journal, the article by Hickman (1981, pp. 343–354) demonstrates the value of this approach to the study of the classroom. Stretching the term "response" to cover "any events that revealed some connection between children and literature," she acted for four months as a participant-observer in three elementary school classrooms (kindergarten through grade 5). Her report is rich in evidence concerning children's spontaneous verbal and nonverbal reactions to, and uses of, literary experiences (heard and read). At the same time, the study points to the influence of teachers' strategies and the importance of the context and setting. Many questions are opened for further inquiry.

The questions we raise, our research designs, and our interpretations of our findings will benefit from a cultural perspective. We need to reflect on where a problem fits into broader questions about the development of individual human capacities and the role of verbal arts in our society and in other human cultures. Such considerations will produce research conducive to the development of the kinds of teaching that will foster the capacity for more and more rewarding transactions between readers and texts.

REFERENCES

Ames, A. *The nature of our perceptions, prehensions, and behavior*. Princeton, NJ: Princeton University Press, 1955.

Bates, E. *The emergence of symbols*. New York: Academic Press, 1979.

Bateson, G. *Towards an ecology of mind*. New York: Ballantine, 1972.

Bleich, D. The subjective character of critical interpretation, *College English*, March 1975, *36*, 739–755.

Bohr, N. Discussion with Einstein. In P. A. Schilpp (Ed.), *Albert Einstein, philosopher-scientist*. New York: Harper, 1959.

Britton, J. *Language and learning*. Coral Gables, FL: University of Miami Press, 1970.

Brooks, C., & Warren, R. P. *Understanding poetry*. New York: Henry Holt, 1938.

Cantril, H., & Livingston, W. K. The concept of transaction in psychology and neurology. *Journal of Individual Psychology*, 1963, *19*, 3–16.

Cooper, C. R. Empirical studies of response to literature. *Journal of Aesthetic Education*, 1976, *10*, 77–93.

Crews, F. *Out of my system: Psychoanalysis, ideology and critical method.* New York: Oxford University Press, 1975.

Culler, J. *The pursuit of signs.* Ithaca: Cornell University Press, 1981.

Deese, J. Cognitive structure and affect in language. In P. Pliner, L. Krames, & T. Alloway (Eds.), *Communication and affect.* New York: Academic Press, 1973.

Dewey, J. The reflex arc concept in psychology, *Psychological review*, July 1896, *3*, 357–70.

Dewey, J. *Experience and nature.* New York: W. W. Norton, 1925.

Dewey, J. *Philosophy and civilization.* New York: Minton Balch, 1931.

Dewey, J. *Art as experience.* New York: Minton Balch, 1934.

Dewey, J., & Bentley, A. F. *Knowing and the known.* Boston: Beacon Press, 1949.

Drucker, J. The affective context and psychodynamics of first symbolization. In Nancy R. Smith & Margery B. Franklin (Eds.), *Symbolic functioning in childhood.* New York: Halstead Press, 1979.

Fish, S. Interpreting the *Variorum. Critical Inquiry*, Spring 1976, *2*, 465–85.

Gardner, H. *The arts and human development.* New York: John Wiley, 1973.

Gardner, H., & Wolf, D. (Eds.). *Early symbolization.* San Francisco: Jossey-Bass, 1979.

Geertz, C. *The interpretation of cultures.* New York: Basic Books, 1973.

Goodman, K. S. Reading: A psycholinguistic guessing game. In H. Singer & R. B. Ruddell (Eds.), *Theoretical models and processes of reading.* Newark, DE: International Reading Association, 1970.

Halliday, M. A. K. *Learning how to mean.* New York: Elsevier, 1975.

Harste, J. C., & Carey, R. F. Comprehension and setting. *Monographs in Language and Reading*, October 1979, No. 3, Indiana University.

Hickman, J. A. A new perspective on response to literature: Research in an elementary school setting. *Research in the teaching of English*, 1981, *15*, 343–354.

Izard, C. E. *Human emotions.* New York: Plenum Press, 1977.

James, W. *The principles of psychology.* New York: Henry Holt, 1890.

Kantor, K. J., Kirby, D. R., & Goetz, J. P. Research in context: Ethnographic studies in English education. *Research in the teaching of English*, 1981, *15*, 293–309.

Lewis, M., & Rosenblum, L. *The development of affect.* New York: Plenum Press, 1978.

Odell, L., & Cooper, C. R. Describing responses to works of fiction. *Research in the teaching of English*, 1976, *3*, 203–225.

Piaget, J. *Thought and language of the child* (M. Gabain, trans.) New York: Humanities Press, 1959.

Piaget, J. *Genetic epistemology* (E. Duckworth, trans.) New York: Columbia University Press, 1970.

Purves, A. C. *Literature education in ten countries.* New York: John Wiley, 1973.

Purves, A. C., & Beach, R. *Literature and the reader: Research in response to literature, reading interests, and the teaching of literature.* Urbana, IL: National Council of Teachers of English, 1972.

Purves, A. C., & Rippere, V. *Elements of writing about a literary work: A study of response to literature.* Urbana, IL: National Council of Teachers of English, 1968.

Richards, I. A. *Practical criticism.* New York: Harcourt, Brace & World, 1929.

Rommetveit, R. *Words, meanings, and messages.* New York: Academic Press, 1968.

Rosenblatt, L. M. *L'Idée de l'art pour l'art.* Paris: Champion, 1931; New York: AMR Press, 1977.

Rosenblatt, L. M. *Literature as exploration.* New York: Appleton-Century, 1938; revised ed., New York: Noble & Noble, 1968; London: Heinemann, 1970; 3rd ed. New York: Noble & Noble, 1976; reprinted New York: Modern Language Association, 1983.

Rosenblatt, L. M. *Research development in the teaching of English.* (Project #G-009.) Cooperative Research Branch of the Office of Education, U.S. Department of Health, Education, and Welfare, 1963.

Rosenblatt, L. M. The poem as event. *College English*, 1964, *26*, 123–133.

Rosenblatt, L. M. A way of happening. *Educational Record*, 1968, *49*, 339–346.

Rosenblatt, L. M. Towards a transactional theory of reading. *Journal of Reading Behavior*, 1969, *1*, 31–49.

Rosenblatt, L. M. *The reader, the text, the poem: The transactional theory of the literary work*. Carbondale: Southern Illinois University Press, 1978.

Scruton, R. Attaching words to the world. *Times Literary Supplement*, August 12, 1977, p. 963.

Squire, J. R. *The responses of adolescents while reading four short stories*. Urbana, IL: National Council of Teachers of English, 1964.

Suleiman, S. R., & Crosman, I. (Eds.). *The reader in the text*. Princeton: Princeton University Press, 1980.

Tompkins, J. P. (Ed.). *Reader-response criticism*. Baltimore: Johns Hopkins University Press, 1980.

Verbrugge, R. R. The primacy of metaphor in development. In E. Winner & H. Gardner (Eds.), *Fact, fiction, and fantasy in childhood*. San Francisco: Jossey-Bass, 1979.

Vygotsky, L. Thought and language (F. Hanfmann & G. Vakar, Eds. and trans.) Cambridge: MIT Press, 1962.

Werner, H., & Kaplan, B. *Symbol formation*. New York: John Wiley, 1963.

Williams, J. P. Learning to read: A review of theories and models. In F. B. Davis, (Ed.), *The literature of research in reading with emphasis on models*. New Brunswick: Rutgers University Graduate School of Education, 1971.

Winner, E., & Gardner, H. (Eds.). *Fact, fiction, and fantasy in childhood*. San Francisco: Jossey-Bass, 1979.

Chapter 4
That Sunny Dome:
Those Caves of Ice*

Alan C. Purves

The Curriculum Laboratory
University of Illinois at Urbana-Champaign

It is evident that research in response to literature needs a theoretical base, yet in much of the research such a base is lacking. Early research was based on I. A. Richards' *Practical Criticism* (1929) which, while not explicitly theoretical, nevertheless tended to follow from the premise of hermeneutics that the literary text contained a verifiable essence. The plain sense of meaning of the text could be determined, as could its feeling, tone, and the intention of the writer. If a reader made some sort of outlandish interpretation or some sort of uncommon judgment, the reader strayed from the paths of proper criticism. Later theorists of literature, like René Wellek and Austin Warren (1956), modified Richards's seeming dogmatism somewhat, asserting that the poem is a "structure" of norms which can be approximated by a reader-critic, although not fully apprehended. They tended to reject the possibility that an author's intention could be known or even that it had any importance for the reader or critic.

This semi-Platonic stance was counterposed by certain of the Freudians who first, like Ernest Jones (1949), sought to go through the work to the mind of the writer, treating the text as if it were an account of a fantasy. Later Freudians, like Norman Holland (1968), shifted their attention to the reader, taking the text as a relatively neutral phenomenon, a Rorschach blot to which the reader reacted according to the reader's ego-structure. The extreme of their approach would support the theory of Berkeley's *Siris* that the literary text—like all phenomena—exists only through the mind of the reader; one can, then, examine the reader, know the reader, but one cannot know the text.

One may speculate as to why the reader has come to replace the text as the central figure in the literary enterprise. Perhaps it is because the growth of psychological criticism which found itself confronted by the Heisenberg principle of uncertainty of knowledge and could do little else than observe the reader. Perhaps the reason

---

*Portions of this chapter were published in two articles: *That Sunny Dome: Those Caves of Ice*: A Model for Research in Reader Response. *College English* 40 (March, 1979), 802–812; *Putting Readers in Their Places*; *Some Alternatives to Cloning Stanley Fish. College English* 42 (November, 1980), 228–236.

is that critic-teachers were losing the students who did not want to deny their own personalities. Perhaps the reason lies in the growth of interest in communication theory; perhaps it is resurgent romanticism, or distrust of the dogmatism of the critics. Additional reasons might occur to others, but the fact remains: The reader reigns. But who is the reader? The critic Stanley E. Fish writes: "It is the structure of the reader's experience rather than the structures available on the page that should be the object of description" (Fish, 1980). Who is this reader that we should look at?

One can find a number of partial identifications. Some people claim to be the reader. Norman Holland in *5 Readers Reading* (1975) suggests it is he or his students, many of whom resemble him in their awareness of their "identity themes." The structuralists and the semiologists would suggest that the reader is that person who is well aware that the literary text has no direct referent but is an interplay of language that can be toyed with but not fully interpreted. It can be deconstructed, but such deconstruction, the reader finds, still misses the essence of the text. The reader realizes that his or her status is always that of the outsider (Said, 1975; Eco, 1976; Lewis, 1979; Nelson, 1976). Louise M. Rosenblatt (1978) disagrees and goes further, I think, for she claims that the reader enters into an aesthetic transaction with the text to create a poem. Stanley Fish would appear to agree when he says that the "intention, form, and shape of the reader's experience are simply different ways of referring to (different perspectives on) the same interpretive act" (Fish, 1978, p. 479). Rosenblatt would agree with the deconstructionists that the text is not message-bearing, but something to be experienced and contemplated; she would agree with Eco (1976) that to take the text as having a referent, to read it *efferently* (her term) is a mistake if one seeks to read aesthetically. All would seem to agree that the reader brings a great deal to the text and is no passive recipient nor is the reader one who can "crack" a text as one cracks a code.

Obviously, these two positions tend to produce quite different approaches to research. If one starts from Richards' theory, then research issues deal with the degree to which individuals or groups approximate the correct reading of the text. One examines the reader with Richards, perhaps pathologically as he did, but certainly with an eye to the distance of the approximation from the correct response and to the direction of that approximation away from the correct response. One is, in sum, examining error and its causes: readers may err in different ways—from ignorance, from prejudice, from the inability to use the appropriate procedures. Certainly the researcher is warranted in looking not singly at individuals, but at groups, for if a correct reading exists, then any number of people may share certain types of deviances or deficiencies. Given that the approach assumes a criterion— the correct response—researchers may legitimately use such techniques as the rating of papers or interviews or multiple-choice tests on a text, and the attendant criterion-based modes of analysis.

From the Berkeleyan perspective, the response is individual and implies that one must first examine individuals, seeing them as particular cases. Little may connect one reader to another and the fragility of a text is such that it becomes the personal property of a reader. Few generalizations about readers may be made common because of the idiosyncratic world of each reader. Each reader is a case, not necessarily a pathological one, because normalcy is indeterminable. The research may gather written or oral responses, but is limited to description of their content or form. Each reader forms a discrete case; perhaps to the purist, each reading or each text read must be viewed discretely, although most Freudians consider the individual person to have consistency. Criteria disappear, and tests become impossible.

These, then, are the two positions, and the two modes of research; they seem incompatible because they are antipodal. How can one undertake meaningful research in response to literature without being damned by the adherents of one position or the other? One might say that reconciliation is impossible. Either one takes the test as the norm, or one takes the individual as the norm. It seems to me that both positions are overly dogmatic and that, while both contain elements of value, neither provides a fully comprehensive theory to explain much of what we know from the hisotry of literature and of literary taste. One problem with the conflicting theories is that they are only parts of a more comprehensive theory of response to literature. Such a theory needs to be responsive to theories of criticism and of literature as well as to the practice of readers and critics. As we shall see, this theory must account for the elements common to the responses of large groups as well as for individual differences. It does so primarily by taking as its very premise that a large number of readers share a response and that at the same time no two responses are alike.

Let us begin with a text, so that we can help this theory come alive.

Wild Iron

Sea go dark, dark with wind,
Feet go heavy, heavy with sand,
Thoughts go wild, wild with sound
of iron on the old shed, swinging, clanging:
Go dark, go heavy, go wild, go round,
     Dark with the wind,
     Heavy with the sand,
Wild with the iron that tears at the nail
And the foundering shriek of the gale.

               —Allen Curnow[1]

THE EXISTENCE OF THE POEM

I shall not undertake an exegesis of the poem nor will I say much about my response to it, except as these bear upon the elaboration of a theory. First of all, the poem exists, as Northrop Frye (1957) would say—it does not act as a direct communication

---

[1] Allen Curnow, *Collected Poems 1933–1973* (Wellington, New Zealand: A. H. and A. W. Reed, 1974), p. 107. Reprinted by permission of publisher.

from Allen Curnow to me or to anyone else. It is a collection of phonemes and morphemes, arranged syntactically and rhythmically. It does not communicate, in part because it communicates too much. It uses and calls to our attention all the devices of language: sound, sight, syntax, morphology, semantics. It becomes an artifact that we perceive and in perceiving, see, hear, and take in as a highly complex utterance.

A nonliterary communication, such as the sentence from a newspaper—"The prison is to get a four-bed infectious diseases ward to isolate the increasing numbers of cases of leprosy, infectious hepatitis, and tuberculosis."—also uses phonemes, morphemes, and sememes in a syntactic arrangement, but one might say that the semantic weighting predominates and that sound and visual impression play a secondary role. We might argue, as have many critics, that the difference between the two kinds of writing is a difference in the writer's intention. James Britton (1975) has established a continuum of writing from the transactional—such as the newspaper article where the writer primarily intends to convey information—through the expressive to the poetic, in which the writer is primarily interested in exploring language for its own sake. The writer is seeking through language to set forth an experience. He has an eye on the reader, to be sure, but the reader is not seen as the recipient of information or exhortation. The writer also explores language as a possibility of expression. To be sure, even the newspaper article can be treated as literature or poetic language by the reader who so chooses, but for the most part readers would consider it as a newspaper article and "Wild Iron" as a poem. As Louise Rosenblatt points out, the reader makes this choice as an act of will, in deciding whether to read aesthetically or efferently, but the reader is partially led to the choice by certain features of the text, as we shall see.

Considered as a poem, the poem is mute, and role of the critic is, as Frye says, to speak.[2] In speaking about the poem, however, the critic does not have absolute freedom. The writer has an intention which directs the poem and, through the poem, the reader and the critic. Curnow's intention, we might say, is to express his experience of a story, a seashore, and a swinging piece of iron, and to evoke a particular set of emotions about that experience. The precise nature of that experience is captured in language, words ricocheting off words, sounds off sounds, images off images.

MEANING AND SIGNIFICANCE

As readers we may ascertain the work's intentionality as it is expressed in that language. That which we ascertain is the meaning of the text, as E. D. Hirsch, Jr. would have it:

---

[2] Louise Rosenblatt (1976) says that each reader recreates the poem, that reading is not a passive act. There is a close relationship between Frye's critic and Rosenblatt's reader; in fact, they differ only in that the critic has frequently read more and considered his or her responses to the variety of poems. I shall use the term *critic* and *reader* almost interchangeably, reserving only the distinction that the critic is the one who articulates (discourses about) what he or she has read.

"Meaning" is not restricted to conceptual meaning. It is not even restricted to mental "content," since, on my description, it embraces not only any content of mind represented by written speech but also the effects and values that are necessarily correlative to such a content. Defined in Husserl's terms, "meaning" embraces not only intentional objects but also the species of intentional acts which sponsor those intentional objects. . . . The reader should understand that an intentional object cannot be dissevered from a species of intentional act, that subjective feeling, tone, mood, and value, are constitutive of meaning in its fullest sense. One cannot *have* a meaning without having its necessarily correlative effect or value. (1976, pp. 8–9)

This meaning, the *cor cordium* of the poem, survives different printings, different recitals. Hirsch argues that even a word or two might be changed and the meaning would remain, much as the deep structure of a sentence lies constant within a variety of surface structures. I am not sure I accept this point fully, since I am too much of an organicist to think that stylistic changes are inconsequential. There may be an aspect of meaning that persists, but, as a work like Raymond Queneau's *Exercises in Style* (1981) with its hundred versions of a banal story attests, each version sets forth a different tone, if not a different meaning and intention. Each version might be paraphrased in the same way—thus supporting Hirsch—but a shift in point of view, of emphasis, or imagery, modifies the paraphrase.

Meaning is not narrowly circumscribed; rather it acts through the articulation of words into sentences and rhetorical patterns to form a complex pattern. The first word of the poem, *sea*, contains a variety of potential meanings—a calm sea, a broad sea, a sea full of monsters, a sea like the Dead Sea, and so forth. As each successive word is added, the sea in this poem becomes limited to a particular "set" of meaning. So too with each of the other words in the text, which, by virtue of their interaction with each other become a semantic whole. Context builds and, in building, directs the meaning of the poem.

But there is more to a text than its meaning. Hirsch differentiates meaning and significance, that which a reader attaches to a text, whether it was intended or not. When I read the Curnow text, I associate with it a sense of loneliness, desperation, and despondency. I see in it a comment on the interrelationship of object and feeling—the objective correlative—and I also can see a comment on the war between nature and the fragile creations of humanity. The wildness is more than potency for me. As I read the poem, the images it establishes raise allied images of the eastern coast of the United States, as well as images from films and other books and poems. These allied images constitute an aspect of the poem's significance to me. Other aspects of that significance besides the images include certain intellective associations: to tenets of romanticism, and to artistic antagonism to technology. Whether these form a part of Curnow's intention, I am not sure. It is probable that "Wild Iron" has a significance, personal and poetic, for Curnow that it does not have for me.

Parts of this significance I suspect I share with other readers of my culture and education; parts belong to me alone. To take another example, *Hamlet* deals, in part, with the relationship of a son to his mother, father, and stepfather. The importance of that relationship pervades the play. Since the work of Freud, and of course Ernest Jones, a modern reader can hardly read the play without thinking of the Oedipal situation. Earlier critics like Johnson, Coleridge, and Hazlitt tended to emphasize other aspects of the play. The Oedipal significance did not loom as large for them, as did the significance of reason and emotion or of the reconciliation of opposites. Neither the pre- nor post-Freudians can be called mistaken or even partial; they simply differ in their perception of the texts' significance.

As an aspect of deriving meaning, readers grasp the emotionality and tone of what they read. In effect, they make decisions about emotion as they make decisions about sense, and it can be said that there is a distinction between emotional meaning and emotional significance. One might go so far as to say that emotion, like form, is an aspect of meaning. Curnow's "Wild Iron" tells us something about the writer's experience of wind, shore, sea, and feeling; it also evokes a set of emotions in us which, in fact, form part of that meaning. In part, the poem does so because its language provides us with a set of images. At a general level, these images are common, although each person who reads it particularizes and limits the images to a certain extent, by virtue of the fact that each has had a set of experiences, virtual and vicarious, that provide each with the particular image, and —accompanying the image—an emotion.

It is also true that each person has an idiosyncratic association with any given work in the text: *wild*, *gate*, *dark*, *sea*. What controls these idiosyncratic associations is the combination of words that is the whole text. The poem's combination of images tends to produce a central image pattern that comes to dominate any of the idiosyncratic images of a given reader and to subordinate them to the totality of the pattern. The combination of images and emotions, like the combination of meaningful words, leads to a central imagic and emotional meaning. The individual and personal images and emotions are only held in abeyance, however, and personal emotions like significance also exist.

THE READER AS PART OF A COGNITIVE COMMUNITY

Recent psychological research has focused on the concept of schemata, a kind of mental outline one has when one perceives something. It is close to an expectation, or a prediction that the phenomenon is to be understood in a particular way. Recent research in reading comprehension suggests that, when we read, we project a schema upon the text. Even a young child begins a sentence or story with the expectation that it will have certain features. Reading, then, appears to follow a pattern of prediction followed by confirmation; it is not a purely inductive process. A group of cognitive psychologists says: "Text understanding proceeds by progressive re-finement from an initial model to more and more refined models of the text . . . The initial model is a partial model, constructed from schemas triggered by the beginning elements of the text" (Collins, Brown, and Lakin, 1980; p. 387).[3] The work of these researchers appears to be confirmed by the developmental psychologists and others. In a particularly cogent essay on metaphor, Andrew Ortony (1979) shows how schemata enabled one to define metaphor more sharply. In fact, Rand J. Spiro (1979) has even argued against a reader's overreliance on the text and distrust of the schemata that the reader possesses, a clear support of the role of the reader. It is suggested that the readers acquire schemata in a variety of ways— from apprehension of the phenomenal world, from hearing various kinds of discourse, and from prior reading, to name the most obvious. Different readers acquire different schemata, which is why one student can interpret Emily Dickinson's "I never lost as much before/And that was in the sod" as having to do with golf, another as having to do with horse races, and a third as having to do with death and burial. (I am not inventing the first two readings; they appeared in Advanced Placement papers in the 1960s.)

Schemata, then, are perceptual bases for reading texts; they constitute the "clouds of glory" each reader trails in entering the act of reading, not unlike Holland's "identity theme," but perhaps more encompassing. It would appear that they are also modes of perceiving discourse, which is to say, choices as to what to attend to as one reads. In a recent informal study, I asked a group of undergraduates to tell me what the theme of a story was and how they arrived at it. About half related the theme to one set of characters, the parents; another half related it to the child. This, one might say, was an instance of schema theory at work. Equally interesting, perhaps, were the reports of how these students derived theme, or meaning: from a specific phrase or sentence, a repeated word, phrase, or event; from a perceived parallelism of objects or events, or a perceived contrast of objects and events; from comparison to another work or to a genre; from concentration on and analysis of one character; and from a perceived pattern of words, objects, or events. There may be means other than the ones they report, and they did not report why they chose the method they did; perhaps they did not know. Their reports, nonetheless, suggest that these methods of reading have the characteristics of schemata: acquired, dependent on the reader, determined by the reader.

Now, that readers have schemata raises an epistemological question: How are they acquired and how do they relate to a text? It would appear that people acquire schemata through experience, as Shelley Rubin and Howard Gardner show in another chapter in this volume. To a great extent, they acquire literary schemata through hearing or reading texts. Texts, then, help produce readers who read texts in a particular way. Texts also help produce "communities" of readers and writers. *Community* is the word Stanley Fish uses in *Is There a Text in This Class?* (1980,

---

[3] Schema theory dates back to the 1930s and is related to both Gestalt psychology and George Kelly's psychology of personal constructs. Schemata also resembles the semiologists' "code." R. P. Abelson (1973) suggests six levels of schemata: elements, atoms, molecules, plans, themes, and scripts, each defined in terms of the lower ones. Whether these levels may also be seen developmentally remains to be determined, but they do appear to have linguistic analogues.

p. 468); he follows Coleridge, Northrop Frye, and Louise Rosenblatt, and is supported by linguists such as Edward Sapir and Benjamin Lee Whorf, and by schema psychologists. This position maintains that individuals are held together in communities which are, to a great extent, bound by language, and particularly by a common semantic space. Groups of people hold similar meanings for words and sentences when those words and sentences are placed in a common context. For a rather familiar example, let us look at Shakespeare's lines from *Cymbeline*:

> Golden lads and girls, all must,
> As chimney-sweepers come to dust.

One group of readers would assume that Shakespeare belongs to a Renaissance community that held certain beliefs about morality, and so would interpret the lines as *meaning* that death comes to young and old, rich and poor, noble and commoner. That assumption seems reasonable, since we know when Shakespeare lived and we know that "dust" could hold in the seventeenth century, as it can today, the connotation of death ("dust thou art and to dust thou shall return"). At the same time, other readers know that in seventeenth-century English, a spent dandelion was called a chimney-sweeper and the young blossom a golden lad. These readers assume that they, along with Shakespeare, inhabit a floral community and that the lines are much less serious in their portrayal of the inevitability of change and perhaps death.

Which community did Shakespeare inhabit? Which does the text really mean? Or does it mean something completely different? Fish asserts that we cannot know and that the questions are, indeed, the wrong ones—the text cannot be used to answer the question, for the text is a human production viewed by humans who may or may not be members of the same community as the writer. But one can go to the writer through the text in a general sense; Shakespeare was probably not referring to dust from atomic bombs.

The notion of community supports the idea of meaning and significance as constructs, for it asserts that communities can be as broad as a language group or as narrow as one reader. *Meaning* might be defined as the large interpretive community—educated users of the language. *Significance* might be defined as the small interpretive community.

THE ACTIVITIES OF THE CRITIC

There are other aspects to the act of reading and criticizing literature which must be noted, in addition to the derivation of meaning and significance. Frye's *Anatomy of Criticism* (1957) or Wellek and Warren's *Theory of Literature* (1956) account for these aspects to a great extent. The latter indicates aspects of a poem—diction, image, metaphor, prosody—that the reader may focus upon analytically in order to make a statement about the construction of the text and how it leads the reader to meaning or possibly to significance. Frye sees this activity as only one of four modes of criticism—what he calls *ethical criticism*. Another is *historical criticism*, which seeks to relate works to one another as parts of a complex cycle of relationships between the writer and the world he or she inhabits, as seen in the writer's view of the subject matter and his or her place in society. *Archetypal criticism* relates works to one another within a large mythic pattern, that corresponds to the succession of the seasons. *Rhetorical criticism* sees the works in relation to their use of the aural or optical or logical patterns of language.

In terms of Frye, criticism of "Wild Iron" can deal with a variety of matters: what is Curnow's place in the spectrum of poets? What is his relation to society? Where does "Wild Iron" fit in the larger mythopoetic picture? Frye might also ask questions about the symbolic structure of the poem, the relationship between words, images, and symbols, and the relationship of these symbols to conventional symbols. Thus, the wave and the storm are related to other poetic manipulations of wave and storm. The poem is vested in other poems and poetry like a Chinese puzzle. Morris Weitz (1964) would add two other questions: Is it a poem? and Is it a good poem? Frye would assert that these questions are not critical; Weitz would remark that they are nonetheless asked, just as the question as to whether *Hamlet* is a tragedy has been asked.

How does this excursion through theory help us to deal with the matter of response and criticism? I think that it indicates a set of relationships (Figure 4-1). First come the relationships of writer, text, and reader; the writer does not simply put words down at random and depart from the scene. We can say that the writer inhabits a world and, in the writing, expresses the experience of it. The world is not simply a world of external reality; it is also a world of artifacts called literature, and the

Figure 4-1.   A model of literary understanding

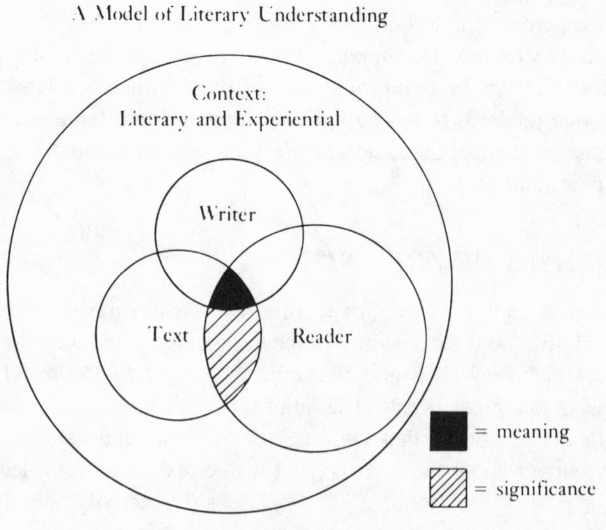

writer is aware of tradition and convention. Out of this awareness, and from the expressive and poetic impulse, comes the poem. The reader approaches the poem, aware that it is such an expression and aware, too, that the poem is part of a larger poetic body. Some readers have more experience of that poetic body than others. All readers have experiences of the world and of aspects of that which the poem is treating. When readers read, they retain partial consciousness of the various relationships between the text and these experiences.

When people read, they seek to ascertain meaning which is guided by their belief in the intentionality of the writer, and they find significance which has an experiential base and a critical one. The experiential base expresses itself in what is often called the response of the reader, but the critical base exists too, even for the "untrained" reader who nonetheless has derived a set of expectations about poems which is either satisfied or denied by the poem in question.

The model in Figure 4-1 is, however, not quite complete. The reader's relation to the text may be seen in terms of meaning and significance: the first is shared with other readers and the writer, and the second is personal; the first is convergent, the second divergent. One must add to this model, however, one other element— the audience to whom critical discourse (an articulated response) is directed, which is to say Fish's smaller communities. I might say one thing about "Wild Iron" to my wife if I wanted to share it with her; I might say something quite different to a graduate seminar. The audience may enter into a reader's consciousness even at first reading, and the audience may serve to determine what aspects of a response may be uttered. Students in a psychologically oriented group might talk more about significance; students in a course in prosody, about meaning. We might call this audience the culture of the reader, or the reader's community, and we might make a second figure to represent it (Figure 4-2) to see another way in which response and criticism are convergent and divergent. In fact, as we look at the diagram, we can see that groups of readers bound by a single culture can share significances as well as meanings, which explains something of the shifts in *Hamlet* criticism noted earlier. Culture, like the intention of the writer, can bring about a centripetal response within it; cultures, like individuals, can bring about centrifugal responses.

The reader's response, then, is both a centripetal and centrifugal one, and it is this combination which Coleridge so aptly describes in *Biographia Literaria*.

> The poet, described in *ideal* perfection, brings the whole soul of man into activity, with the subordination of its faculties to each other, according to their relative worth and dignity. He diffuses a tone, and spirit of unity, that blends, and (as it were) *fuses*, each into each, by that synthetic and magical power, to which we have exclusively appropriated the name of imagination. This power, first put in action by the will and understanding, and retained under their irremissive, though gentle and unnoticed, control (*laxis effertur habenis*) reveals itself in the balance or reconciliation of opposite or discordant qualities: of sameness, with difference; of the general, with the concrete; the idea, with the image; the individual, with the representative; the sense of novelty and freshness, with old and familiar objects; a more than usual state of emotion, with more

Figure 4-2.   An augmented model of literary understanding

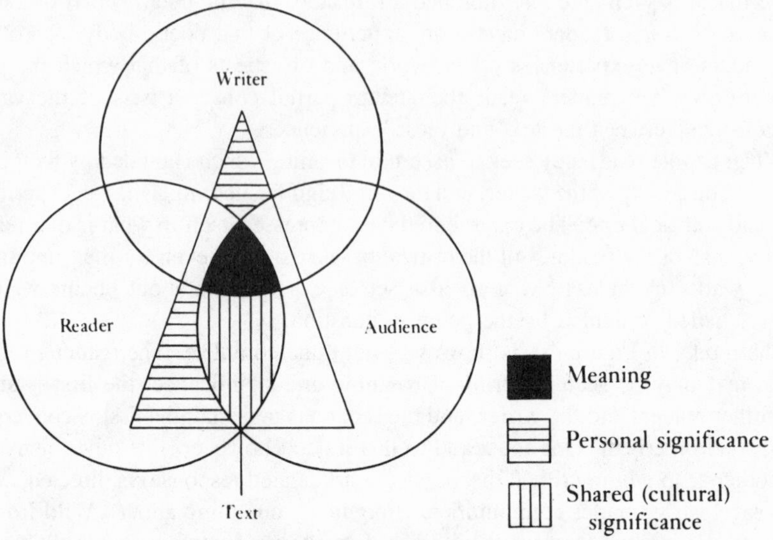

than usual order; judgement ever awake and steady self-possession, with enthu-
siasm and feeling profound or vehement; and while it blends and harmonizes
the natural and the artificial, still subordinates art to nature; the manner to the
matter; and our admiration of the poet to our sympathy and the poetry . . .
Finally, GOOD SENSE is the BODY of poetic genius, FANCY its DRAPERY,
MOTION its LIFE, and IMAGINATION the SOUL that is everywhere, and in
each; and forms all into one graceful and intelligent whole.

IMPLICATIONS FOR RESEARCH

The organic fusion of meaning, image, and emotion through language is the poem
and the reader's response to it. For that reason, Gunnar Hansson's research in *Dikt
i Profil* (1964) is of immense importance. Using the semantic differential with a
variety of readers from all walks of life, he showed that there was a central tendency
in the response to a poem. Only when the readers began to articulate their response
did diversity enter, for then readers began to focus on different aspects of the poem,
and began to make critical statements (see Hansson's chapter in this volume).

The twin ideas of central tendency and dispersion are important to a theory of
response and to research in response. The central tendencies occur in the sense of
meaning, image, and emotion that readers have; the dispersion occurs in the significances both intellectual and emotional that they derive, and in their critical
approaches. One cannot really have one without the other, for such is the nature
of language and of poetry. Even criticism, the conscious decision to consider certain
aspects of a poem and to consider the poem in certain relationships to poetry, has

central and dispersive tendencies. Research questions begin to emerge: what are the central tendencies of a group of readers and how are these tendencies to be viewed? As aspects of meaning influenced by the text? As aspects of cultural significance resulting from a sense of audience? What are the major causes of dispersion? A set of random changes of significance? A coherent individual perception? Is meaning culturally determined, so that an American cannot truly understand an English text, let alone a French one? When does significance most diverge from meaning—at the emotional value plane or the content-ideational plane?

Certainly a central focus of research can be on both the development of the child and the educational system. Why is it that as people grow up they tend to move from emotional to intellectual talk, from the immediate impact of the individual work to its various ramifications and to its interpretation? The educational system tends to channel criticism into certain set modes, asking for an increasingly complex discussion of the work in its structuring of language and experience and in its relation to other literary works, whether historically, thematically, or stylistically. Yet as the individual progresses through the educational system, particularly at the university level, the possibilities of critical approaches enlarge and dispersion takes place, so that at the end of university training there can emerge diverse critical schools. What is the power of this apparent curriculum? What if it were to be changed?

In a sense, one cannot examine response to literature without consideration of the effects of school. There are few "untrained" responses, if any. Through school, children are taught to read and, in school, literature has traditionally played a large part in the process of leading people to literacy. One might argue that film or television elicit untrained responses in that they are not part of the curriculum, and there has been little attention paid to what to look for and how to criticize. This argument has some merit, and one can note differences between response to print and response to television, but television is a literary medium to a certain extent, and the effects of education are there. One might say that school forms a centripetal institution; it leads people from individuality to consensus, whether in terms of sense, feeling, or criticism. Even those curricula that seek to encourage critical diversity have a centralizing focus, one that seeks to bring students to the awareness of the interrelatedness of responses and of critical positions. The principles of convergence and dispersion are at work even in the best of formal education and, I would add, should be at work, for the two principles cannot be separated.

RESEARCH ON TEXTS AND RESPONSES

How does research examine the interrelationships of these principles? First, I think, by noting the important variables: the text, the reader, the audience. That the text forms a variable almost goes without saying. The International Association for the Evaluation of Educational Achievement (IEA) study, *Literature Education in Ten Countries* (Purves, 1973; Purves, 1981), clearly indicated that each text is unique, not simply in its meaning and emotion, but in the critical perspective that it elicited from the students across a broad spectrum of cultures and educational systems. The study examined the most frequently chosen critical questions of students to draw a "response profile." One story provoked more questions about its worth, another more questions about its meaning, a third more questions about its emotional and personal aspects. One set of issues that this finding raises deals with the differences among texts. What aspects of a literary text lead most clearly to different responses? Researchers like Holland (1968) and Petrosky (1976) seem to argue that the major differences lie in the fantasy of the selection, in its content. That conclusion would seem plausible, certainly, but what of the other aspects of a text—its point-of-view, its language, its structure? Certainly the difficulty of the text seems to play a part. In a reanalysis of the IEA data (Purves, 1981) we found different response patterns depending on the degree to which individuals understood the selection; if one does not understand it, one tends to be less concerned with probing its meaning and more with finding it. If we can take understanding—getting the meaning—as an aspect of response, we need to examine that which is difficult about a text. The dimensions of difficulty are several—certainly in the language of the text, in the structure in the text, in the tone expressed by the author, and in the nature of the experience portrayed. We must be concerned, then, with the texts that are being used in any research into response.

At the same time, we must beware of looking for differences within a reader across texts without noting the possibility of similarity. That is to say, a reader writing about three different texts might make an analytic discussion about one, an interpretation of another, and a personal evaluation of a third, but in all these cases he or she is writing about the characters. In each case, the reader has focused on the same aspect of the text; what is significant about that aspect may vary, and may depend on variations among texts. In such a way, professional critics vary and are the same. A case study of a reader should not leap to conclusions about textual differences that mask similarities of approach.

RESEARCH ON READERS AND RESPONSES

If the text plays an important part in the research, so too does the reader. The variations among readers are several, to be sure, but certainly age looms large, as do sex and culture. If we take, as an example, the responses of two groups of people to a selection, there may be diversity hidden within the commonality such as that which Hansson identified. In a pilot study I conducted, two groups of readers—one aged about 12, the other about 25—read the same story, one in which a father tells about an encounter between his son and another family. The younger readers discussed the son and saw the story as the son's story; the older readers focused much more directly on the narrator. In part, the difference lay in experience with literature, in part with the probability that the younger readers could more readily identify with the children in the story and so considered them more important. Another example of the influence of age in relation to the derivation of meaning can be seen in the differing responses to a set of questions about a text. In a pilot study for the IEA survey involving students ranging in age from 12 to 18, we found that the younger children answered the questions in terms of specific details; at about 15, they began to generalize or to consolidate their answers; at about 17, they began to answer in terms of the larger meaning of the text. Do sex and culture play roles similar to that of age? Such a question deserves study.

A second variation among readers may lie in whether they like the selection or not. The reanalysis of the IEA data (Purves, 1981) using the seventeen-year-old group in the United States showed that those who liked a story differed in their response patterns from those who did not like it. Those who liked a story tended to be more concerned with the organization of the story, with the emotions it aroused, and with its success in arousing those emotions. Those who disliked it tended to be more concerned with the appropriateness of the story and with whether the characters resembled anyone they knew. One might conclude that the search for some link between the story and the reader is a key to liking and becoming involved in the story. Certainly the interplay validates many of the points made by Norman Holland in *The Dynamics of Literary Response* (1968). One might even go so far as to say that Holland's statements could not be generalized until they had been tested through a method like this; they remain an introspective conjecture that both the hypotheses and interpretations of research must emerge. Certainly one must realize that the variability within readers is matched by the variation among readers. But each reader is not truly unique, nor is each response truly unique, nor each text. Some variations appear systematic, and one must seek to note the variations and their systematic natures.

RESEARCH ON AUDIENCES AND RESPONSES

The third area of variability lies in the audience, or the situation in which an individual is asked to respond to a text. The response may vary within one individual across several texts; it may vary over individuals dealing with the same text; it may vary within or between individuals and text or texts dependent on the audience. The audience may be the classroom or the examination or a talk among friends. As the audience changes, so might the focus of the expressed or articulated response. Richad Beach's dissertation (1973) clearly demonstrated this phenomenon when he compared solitary responses made into a tape recoder with classroom discussion and found differences between the two that suggested that having done the solitary response, a student is now ready to engage in other concerns, particularly impressing fellow students and a teacher. Although the underlying response and understanding may be the same, the audience may determine what is talked about. The context of school, for example, or the context of an examination like the University Entrance Examination in New Zealand with its set books and set papers, does much to inhibit variability in the expressed response. Just as the Freudian teacher may elicit Freudian responses, so the formal teacher may elicit formal responses. Even the "neutral" question might appear to the student as "leading" and thus channel response. It may even have an impact on the response that is expressed in other contexts. The nature of context, in fact, may even preclude the expressed responses being the most accurate depiction of what is going on in a reader's head. The researcher must live with that fact and must take it into account when drawing conclusions. In various studies I have conducted, I have found that when students realize they are not writing for a grade they tend to diverge from what might have been written for a teacher or an examiner. They may, for example, turn from meaning to significance. One must, I think, realize that, in Britton's (1975) terms, the spectator of the work becomes a participant in a dialogue with a teacher or an interviewer.

CONCLUSION—THE INTERPLAY OF RESEARCH STYLE

The three sources of variation—among texts, among readers, among contexts— have individual and systematic differences, and lead to points of convergence and points of individuation. These are related to the differences between meaning and significance and the uniformity and diversity of the critical act. This whole web of connectedness and dispersion needs to be the province of research in response to literature. One cannot examine variation except in reference to a central tendency; one cannot regard the individual except in relation to the groups, nor the group except in relation to the individual. One response by one individual to one text in one situation tells us little; it is an isomorph. There must be a second response, a second person, a second text, a second situation—even a third—in order for a pattern to emerge. It has become fashionable of late to do the case study; the glamour of the anthropologist or the psychiatrist has replaced that of the sociologist. But the case study is only effective when it is performed against a larger backdrop of many students. The backdrop only makes sense when it is tested against the individual case. Similarly, significance can only be seen against the backdrop of meaning, as Richards demonstrated, and private emotional significance against the central emotional tenor of the text. As I read Curnow's "Wild Iron" in order to write about it, I have to reconcile a tension between my personal experience of the text with the need to communicate—to be a member of an interpretive community. The tension between individuality and community, between centrality and diversity, that exists in a theory of literary response must also inform research into that response. Coleridge's definition of poetry as the reconciliation of opposites must be the ends and means of theory and research. As he said in "Kubla Khan":

> Could I revive within me
> Her symphony and song;
> To such a deep delight 'twould win me
> That with music loud and long
> I would build that dome in air
> That sunny dome, those caves of ice. . .

He was, of course, referring to inspiration and the resultant poem which would harmonize the opposites of sun and ice. That harmony, which necessarily contains tension, lives at the heart of literature and of research into the tension that is response to literature.

REFERENCES

Abelson, R. P. Structure of belief systems. In R. C. Shank & K. M. Colby (Eds.), *Computer models of thought and language.* San Francisco: Freeman, 1973.

Beach, R. The literary response process of college students while reading and discussing three poems. (Doctoral dissertation, University of Illinois, 1972). *Dissertation Abstracts International*, 1973, *34* 656A. (University Microfilms No. 73-17112)

Britton, J. *The development of writing abilities, 11–18.* London: Macmillan, 1975.

Collins, A., Brown, J. S., & Larkin, K. M. *Inference in text understanding.* In R. J. Spiro, B. C. Bruce, & W. F. Brewer (Eds.), *Theoretical issues in reading comprehension.* Hillside, NJ: Lawrence Erlbaum Associates, 1980, pp. 385–410.

Eco, U. *A theory of semiotics.* Bloomington: Indiana University Press, 1976.

Fish, S. *Is there a text in this class? The authority of interpretive communities.* Cambridge: Harvard University Press, 1980.

Frye, N. *The anatomy of criticism.* Princeton: Princeton University Press, 1957.

Hansson, G. *Dikt i profil.* Gothenburg: Scandinavian University Books, 1964.

Hirsch, E. D. Jr. *The aims of interpretation.* Chicago: University of Chicago Press, 1976.

Holland, N. *The dynamics of literary response.* New York: Oxford University Press, 1968.

Jones, E. *Hamlet and Oedipus.* New York: W. W. Norton, 1949.

Lewis, T. E. Notes toward a theory of the referent. *PMLA*, 1979, *94*, 459–475.

Nelson, C. Reading criticism. *PLMA*, 1976, *91*, 801–815.

Ortony A. W. Beyond literal similarity. *Psychological Review* 1979, *86*, 178.

Petrosky, A. R. The effects of reality perception and fantasy on response to literature: Two case studies. *Research in the Teaching of English*, 1976, *10*, 239–258.

Purves, A. C. *Literature education in ten countries: An empirical study.* Stockholm: Almqvist and Wiksell, 1973.

Queneau, R. *[Exercises in style]* 2nd ed. (Barbara Wright, trans.) New York: New Directions, 1981.

Richards, I. A. *Practical criticism.* New York: Harcourt, Brace, 1929.

Rosenblatt, L. *Literature as exploration.* 3rd ed. New York: Noble and Noble, 1976.

Said, E. *Beginnings: Intention and method.* New York: Basic Books, 1975.

Spiro, R. J. *Etiology of reading comprehension style.* Technical Report No. 124. Center for the Study of Reading, Urbana, IL 1979.

Weitz, M. *Hamlet and the philosophy of literary criticism.* Chicago: University of Chicago Press, 1964.

Wellek, R. A. *Theory of literature.* New York: Harcourt, Brace & World, 1956.

Chapter 5
Response: A Way of Knowing

Anthony R. Petrosky

School of Education
University of Pittsburgh
and
The Division of Curriculum
The Pittsburgh Public Schools

INTRODUCTION

In this chapter I discuss, first, some of the more bothersome problems facing researchers who study complex activities like reading, responding, and composing. I also outline some of the basic unresolved issues in the area of reader response, including curriculum evaluation, and argue for explanatory observational studies and an approach to curriculum evaluation called *causal modeling* (instead of traditional comparison group studies) as the most productive ways to evaluate the network of factors that influence students' achievements. Next, I briefly review the accomplishments and inadequacies of three approaches to the study of reader response: surveys, case studies, and correlation studies. And, finally, I present a description of and an argument for an interpretive, interdisciplinary approach to the study of reader response that begins with descriptive analysis and leads to theory (or model) building. The methodology, as I would have it, focuses first on the description and explanation of reader response, then on the theorizing (or modeling) of it, and finally on the analysis of the theory to establish its plausibility and to add to what we already know about human understanding.

GENERAL PROBLEMS

Activities like reading, responding, and composing involve the mind and its interactions with the world. When we set out to study how readers respond to texts, we confront the same kinds of problems faced by psychologists and sociologists who set out to explain why people behave the way they do. Whenever we study psychological and sociological phenomena, like reader response, we use our collective intellectual tools (Toulmin, 1972) to make inferences about what, for example, a pattern of behaviors might mean in terms of people acting as individuals and as members of groups. These intellectual tools, that is, summary, classification, analysis, synthesis, and so on, derive their authority, finally, from our collective understanding of them, and we use them with certainty to study individuals and groups because many people agree on their application and usefulness. When we study understanding through reader response, we focus, consequently, on the summary, classification, analysis, synthesis, and so on, of peoples' recollections of and reactions to their readings. This focus is, I think, one of the most revealing and accessible reflections of the ways our minds work.

Clearly, then, the problems researchers face in studying reader response are related to the difficulties encountered by those who study human understanding. Responses to texts, like responses to people, situations, and objects, are influenced by many things. Personality, mental abilities, past experiences, expectations, symbolizing, and language all play major roles in readers' responses just as they do in our responses to the people, situations, and objects in our lives. We can, though, for the sake of explanation, divide these major features that influence readers' responses into two broad categories, internal (inside readers) and external (outside readers), to come to grips with the range and variation of the features that might affect readers' responses. Internal features like personality, developmental characteristics, expectations, and past experiences continually interact with external features like culture, texts, and instruction to produce a general process we refer to as *interactive*; that is, these influences on readers' responses act in conjunction with each other in ways that are not always predictable. While these many features and their subsequent unpredictability pose an initial problem for researchers who must take them into account when they study readers' responses, the second kind of problem that researchers in this field face is, perhaps, even more confounding. Not only do these features of readers' responses interact with each other, but they also, finally, become more than the sum of their parts. In other words, readers' responses, like understanding or reading itself (Cooper and Petrosky, 1976), are not the sum of component skills like recall, interpretation, and evaluation; instead, they are the results of component skills (including reader, text, and contextual features) acting reciprocally with each other, giving and taking, so to speak, in ways that reflect our thinking and feeling.

Some researchers think that some of these features, like personality or mental characteristics, are genetically determined and invariant or unchanging, while others argue that they are malleable, especially through interactions with the environment (including instruction). The notions of genetically inherited mental characteristics are only theory, but we would do well to consider, however casually or formally, whether our explanations and theories about readers' responses assume that invariant mental characteristics or structures determine their responses. If we prematurely predispose our thinking to assume that there are unchanging aspects of our minds, there is always the danger that we will not give the fundamental notion of invariability the kind of scrutiny and testing it demands.

This brings me to the third problem that researchers in this field face. We must take developmental characteristics into consideration when we study how readers respond. Nine-year-olds respond differently than 13-year-olds, and 13-year-olds respond differently than 17-year-olds. Good teachers have known this for a long time, but the major questions remain: How do we characterize these differences, and what accounts for them? There is evidence from the research of Alan Purves

(1973), Arthur Applebee (1978), myself (Petrosky, 1976), and others that developmental traits in mental abilities and personality play weighty roles in readers' responses; researchers in other fields—Jean Piaget (1937, 1951), and Inhelder and Piaget (1958) in psychology, Anna Freud (1973) in psychoanalysis, Evelyn Goodenough Pitcher and Ernst Prelinger (1963) in language development, and Therese Gouin Decarie (1965) in early childhood development, among others—have built a compelling body of research on developmental traits that bears directly on reader response and continues to grow and show itself as one of the most valuable resources for research in reader response.

Longitudinal studies that follow the same students through all grades, much like Walter Loban's (1976) study of language development from kindergarten to twelfth grade, should hold a high priority among research approaches so that we can paint a picture of reader response along the developmental continuum. Clearly, longitudinal studies represent a commitment, like Loban's, over the course of a researcher's career. Not everyone can or should make this kind of commitment. There are alternatives. Cross-sectional studies, for example, that look at different readers at different ages certainly have a value in charting developmental traits; but, on the other hand, they cannot address issues like the consistency of personality over time. Developmental issues like the consistency of personality over time gives us a sense of the complexity of the response process, and it is this complexity with its many facets that makes the thorough study of reader response a longitudinal issue, especially if we are interested in characterizing developmental differences and what accounts for them.

The fourth problem facing researchers in response can best be presented, I think, as a rule-of-thumb that can help us retain the complexities of reader response while playing off of the interactive nature of the response process in the theory or model building stage of our research. We need to be sure that our attempts at model building to portray the response process will consider the features of the process not in isolation as, say, only psychological, but as parts of the whole working in conjunction with each other (Koestler and Smythies, 1969). And while it is true that our models of the response process can be constructed of numerous subsets of features (like psychological ones), these subsets need to be thought of and presented as clusters of related features—in the sense that a psychological subset, for example, is composed of many attributes like identity and imagination—that are related to other clusters of related features like, for instance, a sociological subset. Our explanation of how readers respond to texts and the models we build to portray the explanations will be, therefore, conditional and predicated on those features such as personality, developmental traits, the nature of the texts, and the contexts for reading and responding that affect readers' reactions, and on the forms—oral free association, guided discussions, essays, multiple choice questions—the responses take. Our interpretations, in other words, need to consider as many relevant features as possible, including what we already know about these features (such as developmental traits) from other areas of research in order to formulate more and more complete theories of reader response and, finally, human understanding.

Ancillary to these issues that face researchers is the question of what to do with research once it is completed. Do we continue to do more research to achieve a sophisticated understanding of response for the sake of understanding, or do we want to direct some of our efforts into translating our research into pedagogy? Pedagogical implications are important. If we do not refine pedagogy through research, then we stand little chance of building sophisticated curricula on anything other than trial and error. Our research and theory should, I think, inform the decisions we make about what we do in the classroom where the lecture/critical analysis approach to teaching literature, for example, still dominates. Attempts to apply response-centered approaches where the emphasis is on what students have to say about their readings meet with problems ranging from teacher insecurity to logistical difficulties involved in arranging for students to write about their readings as well as disuss them. These problems can be solved, but we need the people who know—teachers, researchers, and, especially, teachers who are researchers—to tell us how to go about solving them. Consequently, we need research to document and study instructional approaches; we need to know, for example, to what degree teachers implement instructional approaches, and we need to know how these various approaches influence students' readings and responses. Indeed, we need research to examine the effects of response-centered instruction if we want to make the case for this kind of pedagogy.

Traditionally, this kind of research, curriculum evaluation, has been fraught with problems. So many factors intervene in studies of instruction that much of the research in this area renders the findings useless. But good solid curriculum evaluation research can be designed, and it does not need to be the traditional comparison group kind where the effects of two treatments are compared. Instead, it can focus in detail on a single treatment and the elements that influence the implementation and outcomes of that treatment. The recent work of William Cooley (1978) and Gaea Leinhardt (1980) in explanatory observational studies and the modeling and measuring of educational treatments can help us better understand the elements that affect learning and that, therefore, should be considered in an evaluation of instruction. They propose that researchers use explanatory observational studies which involve the specification and testing of causal hypotheses to explain why students in some programs achieve more than students in others rather than traditional experimental or quasi-experimental studies where the focus is on comparing the outcomes from two or more tightly controlled instructional treatments on students randomly assigned to the treatments. They suggest that we begin to shift our thinking about instructional treatments as multidimensional domains that are affected by the various ways in which teachers implement programs, by students' characteristics, and by the outcomes we seek, and not as discrete, homogeneous treatments that warrant the direct comparisons of experimental or quasi-experimental studies.

If we approached program evaluation in this way, we would not be concerned with the outcomes of treatments on randomly assigned students. We would be concerned with modeling (theoretically specifying) the elements of the instructional domain—including our observations of how the treatment (in this case a response-centered curriculum) is implemented, students' characteristics and entering abilities, and the types of outcomes we seek (achievement, rate of learning, affective)—to hypothesize and, eventually, determine how these elements interact and influence students' achievements. What we end up with on paper are structural equations that express the elements of the instructional domain and our hypotheses about their relationships, as well as diagrams that graphically represent the equations. We get the equations and the diagrams from what we already know about the elements that influence learning in specific subjects, like reader response, and from our thinking about how they might be related. Once we build our model, we then construct measures and scales of the elements in it, administer the measures and use the scales, and, finally, statistically analyze the model using a program like LISREL (Jöreskog and Sörbom, 1978)—a program that can even take into account the effects of multiple, unmeasured factors known as latent traits—to establish its plausibility in terms of what accounts for students' achievements. If we could design curriculum evaluation programs as explanatory observational studies, we would be, I think, on the way to establishing a responsible body of empirical evidence on the outcomes of response-centered curriculum.

BASIC ISSUES

Before discussing surveys, case studies, and correlation studies, I want to briefly outline some of the intriguing issues in reader response that remain unresolved or, at the very best, hardly resolved. First, the notion of the effects of developmental traits—stage specific operations as Piaget refers to them (Inhelder and Piaget, 1958)—on reader response needs further close attention. We need single and multiple case research to simultaneously look at mental operations like mathematical and language performance in the same people to determine whether universal concepts or abilities function across these different mental operations. We also need longitudinal studies examining the nature of response at various stages of development and, perhaps more importantly, inquiring into the nature of the transition from stage to stage. We know little about the development of shared traits in individuals or what accounts for group differences and similarities in transactions with texts. We need, in short, to know the characteristics of both idiosyncratic and shared responses; and furthermore, we need to know how instruction, including testing and the widespread use of reading series, influences readers' responses.

One virtually unexplored area of reader response is rereading. Why do people reread? What happens when readers reread texts at different times in their lives? Given what we know about the development of temporal connectedness (Cottle and Klineberg, 1974), the changing sense of time people experience throughout their lives, and the effects of maturation on memories and interpretations of the past, we would do well to examine rereading in light of our changing senses of time, especially since we know that what we seek to become, what we become, and how we see ourselves in relation to time gone and time available, determine how we remember and interpret the past. If our remembrances and interpretations interpenetrate and shape each other—change each other—then we need to ask questions about the effects of memory on interpretations. We need to know how change—changing senses of time, goals, self-images, and so on—influences our reading at different times in our lives. Since we already know, for instance, that time is not perceived as a continuum until around the ages of 13 or 14, and that future time spans become longer, more realistic, and integrated with the present as logical thought processes develop, we can study readers' interpretations of texts to see if they change to reflect these changing perceptions of time and whether readers key on issues of time future more readily when they are older or on issues of time present more readily when they are younger.

Other areas in need of examination include the influences of enculturation, especially for people new to a culture, on reader response at different stages of development. We might also ask, for instance, whether subcultures within larger cultures teach preferred ways of responding to texts through such things as oral tradition and social values. Or we might study the classroom as if it were a culture or community that sets limits and expectations on its members in much the same way that David Bleich theorizes that it does in his book *Subjective Criticism* (1978). Another important area of research has to do with instructional materials and the ways they influence the development of readers' responses, especially of younger students who are taught reading with basal reading series. In this area we might ask, for example, how the nature and breadth of reading selections in basals influence students' expectations for response, or we could examine the suggested questions and activities in these series, as others have done for reading comprehension (Beck, McKeown, McCaslin and Burkes, 1979; Durkin, 1981), to determine how they define and limit students' early experiences with response. Finally, we have a pressing need to know how response to fiction and nonfiction differ; we need to ask, in other words, whether what we know about response to stories, poems, and films also applies to readers responding to expository prose.

SURVEYS

Surveys provide us with descriptive information about large groups of people. We rely on them to assess a field in broad ways and to assess trends, knowledge, and behavior, including change, across and within whole populations before beginning more concentrated research. Survey questions are generally posed in the form of forced-choice formats, although open-ended questions can be used in surveys even though they pose scoring problems.

The National Assessment of Educational Progress' (NAEP) first assessment of literature (1973) and third assessment of reading and literature (Applebee, Barrow, Brown, Cooper, Mullis, and Petrosky, 1981) make use of open-ended questions for all three age groups they survey (9-, 13-, and 17-year-olds) and have come to grips, in some clever ways, with the use of open-ended data. The NAEP third assessment of reading and literature, especially, is one of the most sophisticated descriptive studies on reading, and it cuts across the domain of surveys by using both multiple choice and open-ended questions for the same reading passages. By looking at students' performance on similar tasks posed in multiple choice and open-ended formats, its developers were able to conclude that American schools have been reasonably successful in teaching students to recall textual information and make preliminary inferences in the multiple choice format, but have failed to teach more than 5% or 10% of all students to move beyond initial readings of texts. As a result, the NAEP researchers conclude that responses to items which require written explanations of comprehension or judgments or points of view were disappointing and, in general, superficial. Simply put, this national assessment gives us, by using both multiple choice and open-ended measures for the same passages and similar tasks, the far-reaching information that students have not learned the response skills that would allow them to make written interpretations and look for evidence to support their interpretations by referring to the reading selections or their own ideas and values. This is a good example of what we can learn from national assessment type descriptive studies that define a domain, like reading, thinking, and writing, and then measure students' performance with multiple measures.

The NAEP assessments, other sophisticated objective-referenced surveys, and the International Education Association's (IEA) study of *Literature Education in Ten Countries* (Purves, Foshay, and Hansson, 1973) are the best examples of large scale surveys of reader response. Not all surveys can or should be as ambitious as these. Valuable information, for instance, can be collected from cross-sectional surveys of school-age readers within a school or, better yet, within a school district or state. Surveys are widely used to assess reading interests at various grade levels, and although we only need a few carefully executed interest surveys every ten years or so, we certainly do need surveys of other areas of reader response, like teaching practices, where research is only beginning. Descriptive surveys designed to reveal national or statewide curriculum trends, teaching practices, and teacher preparation in response-centered instruction would certainly be useful for the profession, especially for teacher trainers who are concerned with the state of reading, writing, and literature instruction. Finally, large-scale descriptive surveys are valuable because they add to and clarify what we know about the elements in instructional domains, just as the NAEP third assessment of reading and literature helped to clarify the relationship of reading and writing. This addition to and clarification of specific content knowledge can then help us better specify and hypothesize about the elements and their relationships in the causal models we build in the later stages of our research, especially in our curriculum evaluation studies.

One of the problems with surveys is also one of the strengths: They provide information about whole populations and can only be used to paint sweeping pictures. When surveys do yield information about individuals instead of groups, the profiles that emerge are superficial compared to the detail of case studies; in addition, most surveys rely on a self-report type of response—a format considered weak by psychometricians. In comparison to explanatory observational studies, surveys rely on experts from the profession for data explanation and interpretation and lack the explanatory power of model building and analysis that is part-and-parcel of explanatory observational studies. Researchers interested, then, in detailed analyses of readers' responses will want to direct their attention away from surveys once they have, if needed, collected initial information on the area they are studying. After new, relatively unresearched aspects of a phenomenon have been explored with surveys, researchers can turn their attention to case studies.

CASE STUDIES

Educational research, including reader response research, is replete with large-scale studies of many people examined in superficial ways. Large-scale statistical studies abound while detailed case studies are almost nonexistent. There are many reasons for the paucity of case studies in educational research. Most researchers are not trained in case study methodology (graduate students typically receive most of their training in experimental methodologies based on correlation statistics), and the large-scale experimental model has long been the major way of studying educational phenomena. On the other hand, research in anthropology, psychology, psychoanalysis, medicine, sociology, and pharmacology attests to the usefulness of case study methodology for describing and explaining complex human phenomena in detailed ways.

Hedda Bolgar in *A Handbook of Clinical Psychology* (1965) reviews and summarizes case study methodology, including a sharp, coherent history of the case study. Like other researchers (Erikson, 1964; Henry, 1972; LaBarre, 1969), she points to the need for case studies concentrating on on a few subjects when the phenomenon being studied is complex and interactive. This analytic approach lends itself particularly well to describing and explaining phenomena we know little about or have hardly studied. Virginal areas of research like the study of the relationship of reading, response, and writing (Petrosky, 1982) defy large-scale statistical analysis because, simply, we do not know enough about the major features involved in the relationship. Even if we did know the features, large-scale analysis would be hard pressed to describe and explain the interaction of the features in detail within a few subjects. To get close to the relationship of these processes we need to spend time talking with the people we are studying. We need to interview them, administer individual-sensitive tests, and tease out information by carefully constructed tasks and questions.

Case studies, then, allow us to obtain detailed information on individuals by using historical data, interviews, and pre-/post-test tasks. The power of methodology comes into play when we analyze the data and construct descriptive explanations of what we observe, infer, and theorize (Diesing, 1971, pp. 142–168). If we need additional information, we can usually go back to the individuals we are working with and reinterview or retest. We can look at the same aspect of a phenomenon across a few individuals with the depth and precision unattainable by any other approach. We can even analyze the data we obtain from case studies using statistical programs designed for small samples (Davidson and Costello, 1969).

Additionally, if analysis of readers' responses is to yield insight into the mental and emotional workings of readers, it must consider that not only are people subject to developmental traits, but that they are also symbol-creating and symbol-using beings. We communicate through an intricate system of symbolic language. The acquisition and use of symbolic language is a far-reaching proposition that is beyond the scope of stimulus-response or cognitive psychology. When we deal with these sophisticated language abilities in readers, we need a methodology that allows us specificity yet tentativeness throughout our analysis and, finally, synthesis. Detailed examination of a few longitudinal or cross-sectional cases can yield the kinds of information we need to study readers making meaning in ways that take into account our symbolic use of language. This is one of the strengths of case study methodology. The difficulty of generalizing beyond the sample being studied is the main weakness of case studies, although even this point is arguable (Davidson and Costello, 1969). Even though case studies do not do what large-scale studies do—represent whole populations—they do compliment large-scale studies by providing the basis for identifying, defining, and analyzing factors. Case studies can, in other words, provide the basis for statistical analysis with large samples. We can isolate factors, form hypotheses, and generate models of behavior that can, in turn, be analyzed in powerful ways with larger samples of people.

Another general objection to using case study methodology is that it lends itself too readily to subjectivism (Diesing, 1971, pp. 277–285). Jules Henry (1972) and Erik Erikson (1964)—two psychologists who have used case studies frequently— argue most persuasively against this objection, and both point out that a real weakness of the case study approach comes about when researchers attempt to use it without proper training and experience. Like any other observational procedure, it requires training and practice. Most often the best way to acquire this expertise is in formal courses on case methodology and projective testing.

CORRELATION STUDIES

I have purposely left this approach for last because I want to argue that it is the final step in a continuum of methodologies for the study of complex, interactive phenomena like reader response. To construct this argument, I am going to use myself as an observer to an event, event X, that is, for the sake of my argument, totally new to me and, at the same time, quite intriguing. As I stand off in the distance observing X take place, my curiosity is aroused, and I immediately want to know more about X. I want to know if what I think I saw actually exists. I could ask one or two or a handful of people participating in the event whether they saw what I saw, but this approach has too many built-in problems: What if they are not aware of what I saw? What if I pick the few who saw it differently, or did not see it at all while everyone else did see it? Even if the people I could ask were outside observers like myself, I would not want to trust my initial curiosity to a few people. I want to ask a lot of people the same general questions to determine if there is something out there to study. I want to survey.

Let us say that event X is the reading of a poem, and that I have noticed almost everyone who reads it responds differently. One of the first questions I might want to ask as many people as possible could be: How do you respond to this poem? I would want to check my initial impressions against a fairly large sample in a gross way to see if the event I observed is occurring with some regularity and reality. There would certainly be many other questions I would want to ask about event X, but my initial purpose remains the same: to survey the event and to narrow down the area that I want to study in detail. I would survey first and then do some detailed longitudinal or cross-sectional studies of selected individuals to get a more specific description of the event (response to the poem) and its possible causes before going on to generate explanations, hypotheses, and theories about response to the poem. I would need to feel fairly confident about my explanations and hypotheses before going through the expense and time involved in subjecting them to large-scale correlation studies where I would, for example, attempt to find out whether what a group of readers says about this poem is strongly or weakly related and correlated to, say, personality or age or schooling.

Correlation studies used this way—as the final step in a series of investigative methods—can provide useful large-scale tests of hypotheses and theories. In contrast, when researchers plug factors into the programs most likely to pay off, correlation studies are little more than technical guessing games that yield ludicrous results.

A serious weakness with many correlation studies is that they are seldom controlled by informed, multidimensional hypotheses or theoretical models of the phenomena being studied. Most correlation studies begin by asking researchers to treat students' performance, for example, as the direct outcome of one or two factors that are, more often than not, treated as homogenous, unlike causal modeling, for instance, which asks researchers to first build a theoretical model of, for example, the factors that account for students' performance in response, and then asks that they treat the elements of the model and their relationships as a multidimensional domain composed of multiple hypotheses. Causal modeling asks researchers to begin by building an explanatory model—a model meant to explain the causes, for instance, of students' achievement—while correlation studies do not provide us with causal relationships, but only with relationships that should not be interpreted as causal. The explanatory power of correlation studies comes from the people who interpret the data and the models or theories that they bring with them, which are perhaps even unknown to themselves; while, on the other hand, in causal modeling the explanatory power is built into the model and tested in the statistical program that analyzes it with actual data.

Clearly, reader response still needs a great deal more work through descriptive surveys and case studies before we are ready to subject theories regarding it to large-scale correlation studies. We want to avoid premature correlation studies because they can steer decades of research in the wrong direction. We can end up talking about the forest when we do not know much about the trees. There is an extremely limited number of accurate statements we can make about individuals when looking only at groups.

INTERPRETIVE RESEARCH

The system that I have proposed in the preceding sections—the movement of research from surveys to case studies to correlation studies—forms the core of my rendition of a very systematic approach to research proposed by Piaget in 1973. Interpretive research, as Piaget calls it, brings together various kinds of research by relating elements in an explanation of one phenomenon to elements from other explanations of other phenomena. Piaget writes that interpretive research "involves distinguishing between many scales of phenomena, both in the organism or nervous system and in behavior or conduct, and discerning the interaction or feedback between processes of different scales, so that there is no longer a reduction from the higher to the lower" (1973, p. 19). To put it another way, Piaget claims that activities like learning or reading are the results of many systems, some of seemingly greater or lesser magnitude than others, working together. He is interested in portraying the activities as systems and subsystems acting together, rather than as a hierarchy of systems. He approaches behavior from a perspective very much akin to causal modeling where a wide range of knowledge can be brought to bear on our understanding of a specific phenomenon, like reader response, acting in concert with other phenomena like personality, growth, cultural values, instruction, and experience.

Piaget claims that we can see the whole human system as the continual assimilation and accommodation of events, information, and other feedback from other aspects of the system to produce behavior or conduct that cannot be explained by simply reducing it to one aspect of the system. Once we see behavior this way, he argues, we can concentrate our efforts on describing, explaining, and theorizing about how these aspects interact with each other and, in the process, change each other. He is particularly concerned about integrating biological and psychological explanations of the same phenomena, especially learning and maturation. He believes, like other researchers (Eccles, 1973; Pribram, 1971) that we cannot talk about aspects of a phenomenon, like response or learning, from only one perspective and understand it in either theoretical or operational ways. All we get from studying one aspect, or scale, of a phenomenon is one perspective, unless, of course, we integrate what we know from other areas of study into our approach to and explanation of the phenomenon. Although fields like psychology, sociology, and education abound with various interpretive approaches to research, few have made attempts at integrating knowledge across disciplines or even within disciplines. A good example of this lack of integration is the separation of reading, responding, and composing in both the research and pedagogy of professionals who see themselves as either reading, literature, or composition specialists. Few people have crossed the boundaries of their disciplines to examine the relationships among these activities. Consequently, the research in these three areas of language development remains unintegrated, and we continue to study them as if they were discrete phenomena when, in fact, they are all related, at the very least, under the umbrella of human understanding.

My version of interpretive research adds to Piaget's the notion of moving research through a sequence of surveys, case studies, and correlation studies. This kind of approach leads to model or theory building and is flexible enough to lend itself to tentativeness. Interpretive research, then, according to Piaget, generally proceeds through three stages:

1. Description of general facts, patterns, relations; the listing and classifying of what we observe;
2. Coordination of facts, patterns, relations, and so on, into a system of distinctions where laws are derived from observations and other laws or hypotheses;
3. Model or theory building to represent processes, to explain and to theorize about their workings.

Piaget claims that only through integrative approaches to research based on the interpretive model can we understand the links between mental life and biological life. "There is no mental life," he says, "without organic life, while the opposite is not necessarily true; and there is no behavior without functioning of the nervous system, the former going further than the nervous system" (1973, p.17). His point is that we cannot explain mental life from only a psychological perspective, nor can we explain it from only a biological or neurophysiological perspective. We need to come to understand mental life as the result of many elements. The same is true, I think, of reading, responding, and composing.

The interpretive scheme calls for a great deal of synthesis. Once we have coordinated the numerous studies of reader response, we will then be faced with the task of coordinating these with other work in human understanding. Although we are only beginning to understand how to coordinate our data, researchers are developing procedures in the hopes of summarizing whole fields of inquiry for a kind of meta-analysis that takes into account diverse kinds of research.

We do not want, finally, a model of reader response. We want a model of understanding. Reading, responding, and writing are important parts of this model. What we say about reader response must be coordinated with what we say about reading and writing. We want to know not only what the world, including texts, does to us, but also what we do to the world as we attempt to understand it.

REFERENCES

Applebee, A.N. *The child's concept of story.* Chicago: University of Chicago Press, 1978.
Applebee, A.N., Barrow, K., Brown, R., Cooper, C.R., Mullis, I.A., & Petrosky, A.R. *Reading, thinking, and writing: Results of the third national assessment of reading and literature.* Denver: The National Assessment of Educational Progress, 1981.
Beck, I.L., McKeown, M.G., McCaslin, E.S., & Burkes, A.M. Instructional dimensions that may affect reading comprehension: Examples from two commercial reading programs. Learning Research and Development Center, University of Pittsburgh, 1979.
Bleich, D. *Subjective criticism.* Baltimore: Johns Hopkins University Press, 1978.
Bolgar, H. The case study method. In B. Wolman (Ed.), *Handbook of clinical psychology.* New York: McGraw-Hill, 1965.
Cooley, W.W. Explanatory observational studies. *Educational Researcher,* 1978, 7, 9–15.

Cooley, W.W. & Leinhardt, G. The instructional dimensions study. *Educational Evaluation and Policy Analysis*, 1980, *2*, 7–25.

Cooper, C.R., & Petrosky, A.R. A psycholinguistic view of the fluent reading process. *Journal of Reading*, 1976, *20*, 184–207.

Cottle, T.J. *Perceiving time: A psychological investigation with men and women*. Boston: The Free Press, 1976.

Cottle, T.J. & Klineberg, S.L. *The present of things future*. New York: The Free Press, 1974.

Davidson, P.O. & Costello, C.G. (Eds.). *N = 1: Experimental studies of single cases*. New York: Van Nostrand Reinhold Company, 1969.

Decarie, T.G. [*Intelligence and affectivity in early childhood: An experimental study of Jean Piaget's object concept and object relations*] (E.P. Brandt & L.W. Brandt, trans.). New York: International Universities Press, 1965.

Diesing, P. *Patterns of discovery in the social sciences*. Chicago: Aldine-Atherton, 1971.

Durkin, D. Reading comprehension instruction in five basal reader series. *Reading Research Quarterly*, 1981, *16*, 515–544.

Eccles, J.C. *The understanding of the brain*. New York: McGraw-Hill, Inc., 1973.

Erikson, E. *Insight and responsibility*. New York: W.W. Norton and Company, Inc., 1964.

Freud, A. [The ego and the mechanisms of defense] (Rev. ed., C. Bainse, trans.). In *The writings of Anna Freud* (Vol. 2). New York: International Universities Press, 1973. (Originally published, 1937.)

Henry, J. *Pathways to madness*. New York: Random House, 1972.

Holland, N.N. *Poems in persons: An introduction to the psychoanalysis of literature*. New York: W.W. Norton, Inc., 1973.

Holland, N.N. *5 Readers reading*. New Haven: Yale University Press, 1975.

Inhelder, B., & Piaget, J. [*The growth of logical thinking from childhood to adolescence*] (A. Parsons & S. Milgram, trans.). New York: Basic Books, 1958.

Jöreskog, K. & Sörbom, D. *LISREL IV: Analysis of linear structural relationships by the method of maximum likelihood*. National Education Resources, Inc., 1978.

Koestler, A. & Smythies, F.R. (Eds.). *Beyond reductionism: New perspectives in the life sciences*. Boston: Beacon Press, 1969.

LaBarre, M. The case for case studies in research. Address presented at the AAPCC meeting in Boston, November, 1969.

Leinhardt, G. Modeling and measuring educational treatment in evaluation. *Review of Educational Research*, 1980, *50*, 393–420.

Loban, W. *The development of language abilities, k-12*. Urbana: National Council of Teachers of English, 1976.

National Assessment of Educational Progress. *Responding to literature* (Volume B). Report 02-L-02. Washington D.C.: U.S. Government Printing Office, for the Education Commission of the States, 1973.

Petrosky, A.R. The effects of reality perceptions and fantasy on response to literature: Two case studies. *Research in the Teaching of English*, 1976, *10*, 239–258.

Petrosky, A.R. Genetic epistemology and psychoanalytic ego psychology: Clinical support for the study of response to literature. *Research in the Teaching of English*, 1977, *11*, 28–38.

Petrosky, A.R. From story to essay: Reading and writing. *College Composition and Communication*, 1982, *33*, 19–36.

Piaget, J. [Principal factors determining intellectual evolution from childhood to adult life.] In D. Rapaport (ed. & trans.), *Organization and pathology of thought*. New York: Columbia University Press, 1951. (Reprinted from *Factors determining human behavior*, Harvard Tercentenary Publication, 1937.)

Piaget, J. [*The psychology of intelligence*] (C.K. Ogden, ed., M. Piercy & D.E. Berlyne, trans.). London: Routledge and Kegan Paul, 1951.

Piaget, J. Main trends in inter-disciplinary research. New York: Harper Torchbooks, 1973. (Reprinted from *Main trends of research in the social and human sciences*, Part I. Mouten/Unesco, 1970.)

Pitcher, E.G., & Prelinger, E. *Children tell stories: An analysis of fantasy*. New York: International Universities Press, 1963.

Pribram, K.H. *Languages of the brain: Experimental paradoxes and principles in neuropsychology*. Englewood Cliffs: Prentice-Hall, 1971.

Purves, A. C., Foshay, A. W., & Hansson, G. *Literature education in ten countries*. Stockholm: Almquist and Wiksell, 1973.

Rosenblatt, L.M. *Literature as exploration*. New York: Appleton-Century, 1938, (3rd ed.) New York: Nobel and Nobel, 1976. (Distributed by the National Council of Teachers of English.)

Rosenblatt, L.M. *The Reader, the text, the poem*. Carbondale: Southern Illinois University Press, 1978. (Distributed by The National Council of Teachers of English.)

Toulmin, S. *Human understanding*. Princeton: Princeton University Press, 1972.

Part II:
How Do We Study?

Chapter 6
Studies in the Spectator Role: An Approach to Response to Literature

Arthur N. Applebee

School of Education
Stanford University

INTRODUCTION

The nature and function of the arts is an ancient philosophical, and more recently a psychological, question. Though the commentators who have considered it are many and distinguished, there has been little consensus in the specification of either the nature of artistic experience, or the particular role that it plays in the life of the individual. The most promising explanations of the arts have been those which recognize artistic expression as part of our general tendency to construct symbolic representations of experience, a tendency which manifests itself on levels as diverse as science and mathematics, architecture and poetry, myth and ritual. Yet these approaches have suffered from a tendency to treat the arts one at a time, in isolation from one another as well as from other modes of representation.

In the first part of this chapter, we will draw upon recent reconceptualizations in fields such as psychology, philosophy, and linguistics, to propose a more general model of symbolic representation. Within that model, Britton's (1970) notion of spectator role experience will provide a framework for our explorations of response to literature. In the second part of the chapter, we will examine a series of seemingly disparate studies, arguing that they gain their unity and interest from the ways in which they relate to the general framework. As part of this exploration, we will find that the production and use of "literary" materials are complementary aspects of the general process of building and sharing symbolic representations of our experience. Rather than studying literary understanding in separation from the process of creating literary works, parallel explorations of production and comprehension will increase our knowledge of both.

MODES OF REPRESENTATION

The model from which we will work in this chapter begins with a relatively conventional distinction between "literary" or "artistic" representation on the one hand, and "scientific" or "discursive" representation on the other hand. The distinction is often made on purely formal grounds: literary discourse relies on such devices as rhythm, repetition, and the sound of language; while scientific discourse relies on such devices as explicit definition of terms and the rules of formal logic.

A distinction based on purely formal criteria quickly becomes difficult, however; there are too many "well-written" (and in that sense literary) scientific treatises, and too many shifting conventions of form and style governing the shape of various literary genres. Rather than beginning with form, we want to ground our distinction between modes of representation in the purposes these modes serve, their functions in our lives.

Langer's (1967, 1972) analyses of the nature of mind provide a good starting point. In a wide-ranging examination of phenomena as diverse as cognition, perception, sensation, and emotion, Langer argues that we ordinarily are aware of two broad classes of phenomena: we perceive things which seem to come from outside of us as "objective," and things that arise from internal processes and activities as "subjective." In general, we seem to think of our experiences in these two domains as distinct from one another; they reflect the worlds of self and not-self, of personal and public, of affective and cognitive, of emotional and rational.

These analyses of the nature of objective and subjective experience provide a background for understanding the differing modes of representation that we have evolved for these two types of experience. In the next section, we will work from Langer's framework to explain the purposes underlying some of the formal techniques that separate artistic from scientific modes of representation.

Representation of Objective Experience

The most important characteristics of "objective" experience is that it seems to have an existence independent of any one individual. In symbolic systems such as language, such independence or externality is achieved most fully by *stating the rules* underlying the system. In an abstract logical system, for example, relationships between symbols and referents are defined, axioms are stated, and permissible operations and transformations are specified. Chomsky (1957), for example, relied heavily upon such a system of abstract representation of the English language to argue the limitations of earlier phrase structure grammars, and to propose in their place a theory of transformational grammar. Though highly abstract and distant from commonsense experience, such representations seem "objective"; we judge Chomsky's derivations against the system of rules itself, and test the "truth" of the argument against the "evidence" provided by our knowledge of English. Such representations rely on *transactional* techniques to convey a "meaning" on which we as individuals have little influence.

Fully formalized logical systems are rare, but there are many common modes of discourse that obtain a similar objectivity from an *implicit* formalization provided by the context in which the system is used. Kuhn (1970) has given detailed attention to the contexts that validate such writings within the various fields of science, treating the contexts as underlying "paradigms" governing inquiry in a particular field. These paradigms change over time and are rarely fully explicit; they reflect instead the combined "commonsense wisdom" of professionals within the field. Such paradigms specify rules of evidence, methods of study, relevant questions, and to some extent even the results which will be treated as valid evidence rather than inexplicable anomalies. Such contexts, though lacking the axiomatic rigor of formal logic, similarly externalize discussion, increasing the sense of objectivity by insuring that individuals bring similar frames-of-reference to bear in their judgments and interpretations. Though Kuhn's analyses focused on the natural sciences, they provide a model for understanding techniques used to achieve "objectivity" in professional discourse in all fields, including literary criticism.

Representations of Subjective Experience

If we try to represent subjective experience through the techniques we have been describing, that experience also becomes external and objective; we can analyze and describe it, but in doing so we fail to share the experience itself. (The difference is similar to that of knowing that a friend has a toothache, and perhaps even knowing its cause, as opposed to having a toothache oneself.) The representation of subjective experience thus requires a different approach, one which invites viewers to recreate the experience for themselves. The essential process becomes one of synthesis rather than of analysis — the synthesis and re-creation of real or imagined experiences.

Langer (1953) has gone further than most in analyzing the *presentational* techniques through which subjective experience can be represented. Discussing artistic systems as diverse as architecture and poetry, she finds that each system has characteristic formal patterns that establish systems of interrelationships from which the audience can "read back" the artist's idea, whatever the medium.

Whereas the symbolic structures in a transactional work are essentially linear and deductive, the relevant patterns in a presentational system occur at many different levels. The phonemic, semantic, syntactic, and thematic structures of a poem, for example, will be inextricably interwoven to produce an "import" that will always be much richer than any transactional paraphrase. It is this import which is a part of subjective experience in Langer's sense, a result of the working of the individual mind as it assimilates and makes sense of the presented experience.

Essentially, an audience is asked to "live through" or "experience" a presentational work, in contrast to "following the argument" in a transactional piece. The import that we take from a presentational work is personal but not arbitrary. The interrelationships expressed in the work result from the activity of the artist, and are shaped by the consistencies which the artist sees in the world. In a sense, the presentational symbol is an artifact, the tangible record of a particular way of looking at experience. As readers or viewers, we are faced with a constructive task; we seek to build our own interpretation of the parts of the piece. No two readers will take exactly the same meaning because the process of understanding is an internal, personal one. The meaning will arise out of the patterns that are perceived, just as the meaning we take from any new experience arises out of the patterns we choose to impose upon it. Nonetheless, most readers of a common age in a common culture will make sense of a work in a similar way, because they will be making sense of the text through a similar screen of linguistic and cultural conventions and presuppositions.

These internal, personal responses are controlled by the desire to "make sense" of the work: the interpretations we build must be adequate to explain both the detail and the broad pattern of what we are reading. Similar reactions from different readers are obtained not by the analytic unraveling of meaning characteristic of transactional technique, but by the weaving of elements in an ever-tighter system of interrelationships, thus reducing the number of adequate alternative interpretations. Readers can and sometimes do ignore this constraint, building totally unique personal interpretations of what they have read, but in doing so they are violating an underlying convention governing presentational discourse.

Spectator and Participant Roles

Any written text usually relies to some extent on both transactional and presentational techniques. A novelist will describe a character or set a scene using a straightforward transactional description; an essayist will use a range of "subjective" presentational techniques for rhetorical effect in carrying an argument forward. Such mixtures rely upon establishing a congruence between objective and subjective experience; when all of the parts "fit," the text is strengthened.

James Britton (1970) has carried the argument a step further, in his recognition that in addition to responding to such blends of techniques, both reader and writer take an overall stance toward any given work. We treat the work as a whole either as a presentational symbol or as a transactional argument, and we judge it accordingly. Britton points out that the meaning of a literary work emerges from a global perception of the whole, and he has labeled the stance we adopt toward literature the "spectator role." In this role we are removed from the demands of direct involvement; indeed, to rush onstage to stop the villain would be a fundamental violation of the conventions of spectator role discourse. At the same time, as Holland (1968) has noted, the more effectively a work is distanced from the world of immediate concerns, the freer we are to let ourselves become involved in the work. In a sense, to establish ourselves in the spectator role is to establish the conviction that we do not have to act as the result of our experience, and thus to allow ourselves to be caught up in it without fear of the consequences.

In contrast, Britton argues that with expository text we adopt a participant role, accepting or rejecting the evidence as it is presented to us. This is the language of action in everyday life as well as the medium of most professional dialogue (this chapter included). Rather than validating a text against the subjective reaction it evokes, we begin by verifying the "truth" of its claims and the accuracy of its logic.

Like other aspects of symbolization, the choice of spectator or participant roles is not arbitrary; it is governed by conventions or rules-of-use which indicate the intended role for author and audience. Britton (1970; Britton et al., 1975) explores the implications of this choice in detail, arguing that the choice shapes our whole experience of a work. It determines our conventions for understanding the work, our criteria for evaluation, and the effect the work will have upon our own view of the world.

RESEARCH QUESTIONS

Within the context of the framework outlined above, my own studies of literary understanding have had several related focuses:

1. What is the origin of children's spectator role experience? Does it develop early, as a fundamental part of their interaction with the world? Or does it emerge later, as a differentiation out of other modes of understanding?

2. What conventions do authors and readers use to signal that a particular text should be construed as a representation of spectator role experience? When do children learn both to recognize these conventions and to manipulate them to their own ends?

3. What organizing principles underlie presentational discourse? What techniques are used to create a "structured whole" or "verbal artifact?"

4. What is the relationship of discussion, using transactional techniques, to our understanding of presentational discourse?

5. What factors govern our evaluations of particular spectator-role works? What makes us like some and dislike others? Are their similarities as well as differences among individuals' reactions to the same or similar pieces?

The sections that follow will illustrate a variety of approaches that can be taken in addressing such questions. Some of the data are quite typical of studies of literary response, but others are at the borderline of what has traditionally been considered to fall within the scope of studies of response to literature. They have been chosen both to illustrate how the framework outlined above can extend our insight into the processes that underlie the spectator role, and to suggest the areas where further research would be most helpful.

The Origin of the Spectator Role

For our first question, concerning the origins of children's spectator role experience, we have some interesting preliminary evidence but lack careful, systematic studies. Ruth Weir (1962), describing the presleep monologues of her son Anthony at the age of two-and-a-half, provides many examples of language the child is using to structure his experiences for himself. Since language is a new and central experience for a child of this age, many of the examples involve play with language, but there are also attempts to deal through language with other important events in the child's life. These range from the unfairness of the fact that the family dog, but not the child, is allowed to cross the street, to the competition for attention among mother, father, and son.

Michael Halliday (1977) finds similar evidence of early use of the "imaginative function" in his studies of his son Nigel. Halliday provides an excellent summary of one line of development in the use of presentational forms:

> the child also uses languge for creating a universe of his own, a world literally
> of pure sound, but which gradually turns into one of story and make-believe
> and let's pretend, and ultimately into the realm of poetry and imaginative
> writing. (p. 20)

Halliday claims that Nigel has begun this progression by 15 months, at a stage which precedes the acquisition of the lexico-grammatical system that is usually identified as the beginning of speech.

Halliday and Weir are lingusits, and neither was primarily concerned with the origins of literary experience. Their evidence is also tentative in that each relies upon the experience of a single child. Their analyses gain power from the theoretical perspectives that each brings to bear, and, for our purposes, from the convergence of views in an area which was, for them, of only peripheral concern.

While such studies give us a good starting point, careful study of the differentiation of spectator role (or presentational) uses of language remains as an interesting task for other investigators.

Learning the Conventions: A Sense of Story

One aspect of spectator role experience involves learning the variety of conventions which govern discourse in this mode, within the cultural group of which the child is a part. We can see some of these processes at work in studies of children's early storytelling (Applebee, 1978). In telling stories, children as young as two-and-a-half begin to adopt such simple aspects of conventional form as the use of a title or "Once upon a time," a consistent past tense, and a formal ending such as "the end" or "and they lived happily ever after." In analyses based on stories told by children in preschool settings in the New Haven, Connecticut area, the use of such conventions rose steadily with age, appearing almost universally in the stories of five-year-olds. These devices are usually accompanied by the adoption of other presentational conventions, such as a special pitch or tone of voice for storytelling, and an expectation of being allowed to tell through to the end without interruption. Such changes are easily-noticed indices of assimilation of the conventions of storytelling, as it finds expression in mainstream Western culture.

Children also develop expectations about the actions and events that will appear in stories. In another series of studies, six- and nine-year-olds were asked how certain common character-types are likely to behave in a story (Applebee, 1978). We found that most children have quite firm expectations that witches will be wicked, fairies good, and lions brave.

Because the particular expectations examined in these studies are specific to the genre and the cultural group which we were studying, further studies are needed both of other genres and of the conventions governing storytelling in a wider range of cultural contexts.

Storytelling is only one side of a child's experience with stories: the expectations that shape the stories they tell must come primarily from the stories they have heard. Our best data about very young children's responses to stories are, again, case studies, particularly Dorothy White's (1954) diary-chronicle of her daughter Carol's experiences before the age of five. As a librarian, White is a sensitive both to books and to children and provides many intriguing insights into the changing needs and interests which books can satisfy in these first years. Among the developments which can be traced using the diary entries are a gradual complication in the child's concept of what a story is. Initially interpreted as a true *history*, for example, it gradually becomes a representation or "copy" of present experience. ("Not real England," Carol asserts at about the age of four, "just paper England.") (White,

1954, p. 127.) Other conventions with which the child becomes familiar during the years before age five include an enjoyment of nonsense verse, a concern with the origin of stories, and a lack of concern until a relatively late age with the fictional element in most spectator role narrative.

Case studies such as White's provide a wealth of hypotheses to explore with other and larger groups of children. How much of Carol's development is the result of the fact that she is unusually bright, comes from an unusually literary home, and is observed unusually closely?

In a study of six- and nine-year-old children in London, England, we pursued White's finding that children are late in becoming aware that most stories are fictional. (With school-age children, it is possible to ask quite directly about their expectations and responses to stories, as long as one remembers that the particular wording of a question can have a very strong influence on the response. Preadolescents in particular are likely to respond to the most literal interpretation of a question rather than to the underlying intent.)

With the London children, we found that beliefs among the six-year-olds were wavering. Most of the children interviewed would defend at length the reality of one or another favored story character, but were less sure about whether all characters were similarly real. (It was not uncommon for a child to believe in Cinderella but not in Red Riding Hood—or vice versa.) Joseph, discussing giants, is typical of many in his unquestioning acceptance of giants as a part of the world, and also in the way in which he uses more general frames of reference to make sense of his literary experiences:

> Have you ever seen a giant?—*David saw one when he was a little boy.*—Have you ever seen one?—*No*—Why do you think you've never seen one?—*One was made, only David picked, . . . fired stones up and he fell to the ground and he was killed and he's in heaven.*—Do you think there ever used to be giants?—*Yes.*—Do you think there are any now?—*No, they were all killed by the police.* (Applebee, 1978, p. 44)

Joseph has obviously had a thorough introduction to the biblical narratives. In another part of the interview, he uses the story of Noah and the flood to explain the disappearance of witches, though he dates it all to "A long time ago when I was a baby."

By age nine, such belief in the existence of fictional characters has for the most part disappeared. Though some children initially treated our interview questions as an invitation to indulge in some storytelling, when they realized that the questions were being asked in earnest, their immediate reaction was to conclude the investigator was singularly stupid.

Findings such as these shed considerable light on children's growing knowledge of the conventions of the spectator role, as well as on the ways in which their experiences may differ from those of older children and adults. It is very likely, however, that many of these patterns of development are unique to the cultural groups that we were studying, and will show a different pattern in other social groups (cf. Heath, 1982; Scollon and Scollon, 1981). We need further studies to explore the roles that storytelling may play in other cultures, and children's expectations as they learn these roles.

Learning to Organize the Whole
One problem that we all face in telling stories is a structural one: how can we bring all of the pieces together into a coherent whole? The relative simplicity of the stories children tell makes them particularly amenable to analysis; the principles that emerge from such studies can in turn be generalized as hypotheses about the structure of more mature forms.

Vygotsky's (1962) studies of concept development offer one very productive way to approach the structure of children's stories. Vygotsky was concerned with the ways in which children link various examples of a concept together into a unified "whole." Similarly, children telling stories have to link the various parts (characters, actions, setting, mood) into a "structured whole" or "presentational symbol."

Figure 6-1 presents a schematic summary of the various types of organization that we found in a study of stories told by children between the ages of two and five. The simplest form of organization illustrated is the "heap," which takes its name directly from Vygotsky's studies. Vygotsky found that, at this stage in concept formation, children would reach out and heap together objects within their reach when asked to indicate what "went together." In storytelling, children at this stage build *heaps* of story-characters or events from their immediate perceptual field, with little beyond their immediate presence to link the parts of the story together.

The five other types of organization illustrated in Figure 6-1 also have direct parallels in Vygotsky's studies. The details of the relationships are elaborated in Applebee (1978). Of more immediate interest is that the six stages result from the development and eventual integration of two basic structuring principles, centering and chaining. *Centering* involves the addition of new parts to the story on the basis of characteristics shared with a fixed "center"—a main character, a particular setting, or (in more sophisticated works) a theme or point of view. In the simplest versions of centering, the "shared" attributes are in fact identical, repeated from one scene or episode to another; in more mature versions, the links to the fixed center become ones of complementarity—elaborating and expanding rather than remaining fixed and constrained.

Chaining involves the linking of incidents or episodes one to another in a long "chain-of-events," so that each part is related to its nearest neighbors, if not to other parts of the story as a whole. Though centering and chaining develop separately in children's stories, they gain their greatest power when they are brought together in a single story. At that point, the stories take on a true narrative form, with a chain of events developing around a common center and leading toward a final resolution.

The power of centering and chaining as analytic devices is that they can be generalized both to more sophisticated literary forms and to a variety of levels of analysis. The simple narratives that represent the most mature forms from five-year-olds can themselves become parts to be bound together (with centering and

Figure 6-1.   The structure of children's stories. (From Applebee, 1978, p. 58)

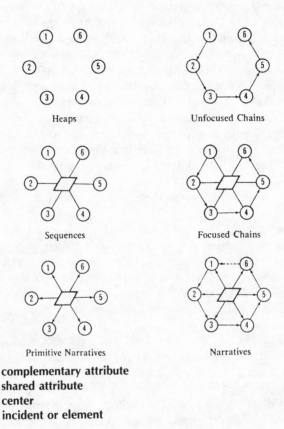

Key: ←   **complementary attribute**
       —   **shared attribute**
       ▱   **center**
       ①   **incident or element**

chaining) as incidents or episodes in more complex stories. Or, shifting genres, we can recognize that adult poetry could be analyzed into series of chains and centers at levels as diverse as sounds, images, and themes. B. H. Smith's (1968) analyses of adult poetry in fact reveal a number of organizational structures that parallel those summarized in Figure 6-1.

As with other aspects of storytelling, these descriptions of organizing principles need to be extended in other studies to a variety of genre, as well as to story structures of other cultural groups. The descriptions also need extension to other levels of analysis. The nature of the links among elements of the plot should be spelled out in greater detail (as story grammar analyses begin to do), and patterns of centering and chaining involving other layers of story structure (e.g., relationships among characters) need to be explored.

The organizational patterns underlying children's stories serve a number of functions, including that of simplification of increasingly complex experience. There is a sense in which any given event in the more sophisticated plot structures is more predictable than an event taken from the less sophisticated structures, because it is bound more fully to the other parts of the story. Though in analyzing these stories we have been looking at children's productions rather than their responses to literature, a number of hypotheses about response also emerge for further study. We would predict, for example, that the child who is capable of producing a story with a simple narrative structure would also be able to use such a structure as a kind of scaffolding for memories of stories heard; this should be reflected in retellings of unfamiliar stories. We would also predict that stories that make use of more sophisticated modes of organization would be easier to retell than those with less sophisticated organizing principles, again because of the scaffolding the organizational pattern would provide. Finally, we would predict that for any given child, the use of these organizational patterns would develop first in responding to stories and would later be evident in telling stories. (There is an analogy here to adult experience: most of us respond to novels that we could not begin to write.)

All of these predictions remain as hypotheses for other investigators to explore.

Discussing Stories

Discussion tasks are a more traditional method of examining response to literature. Here, we are not looking at spectator role language directly. Instead, we are asking readers to use transactional techniques to tell us what they can about spectator role experiences they have had. Thus one of our tasks (in both design and interpretation) is to look *through* what they say, to the subjective and personal response they are describing for us.

Applebee (1978) presents data from a series of such tasks used with six-, nine-, 13-, and 17-year-old students. The tasks were relatively traditional ones in this area of research: asking students to discuss stories they know, to retell unfamiliar material, to explain proverbs, to give reasons for liking or not liking particular texts, and the like. The variety of tasks is essential, because each task produces its own characteristic and different response. A question such as "What do you think about this story?" produces a virtually universal "It's nice" or "I liked it." "What was the story about?" produces, at least with preadolescents, a tendency to give a long list of characters. "Tell me about the story" prompts some children to give an extended retelling. What saves the situation from disintegrating into chaos is the fact that there remain broad and discernible patterns which apply to the full range of responses. It is those broader patterns that we will focus on here.

The underlying patterns in children's discussions of stories parallel findings in other areas of psychological study, in particular Piaget's investigations of the development of various scientific concepts (see, for example, Inhelder and Piaget, 1958). Piaget's preoperational, concrete operational, and early and later formal operational stages provide a convenient way of organizing and interpreting the results.

During the earliest stages we studied, the child's representations of literary experience take a very simple form: a one-to-one correspondence between the story and its mental representation. There is little or no evidence of recoding at this age; there is virtually no summarization or categorization, though with a story that has not been thoroughly learned there may be a good deal of fragmentation and disorganization. The basic representational principle is an enactive one, in which the parts of a story seem to be linked sequentially one to another (in much the same way that most of us memorize the alphabet). This may explain two phenomena with which parents and teachers are familiar: the child's pleasure in hearing a story again and again (a process necessary to establish a complete enactive representation of it), and the word-by-word exactness of any retelling.

The familiar phenomena of centration, syncretism, and egocentrism are very evident at this stage, in tasks for which the enactive retelling of a story is obviously not appropriate. (This is the case, for example, in a request for reasons for liking a favorite story.) Such tasks yield very little evidence of any further logical structure underlying the child's representation of a story. In general, these characteristics are very similar to those Piaget has labeled "preoperational" in studying children's responses to other phenomena.

At the next stage in their discussion of stories, children represent a story in terms of the characteristics which it shares with other literary experiences: it may be an "adventure," for example, or a "happy story," or "about trains." For the first time, the child begins to give systematic reasons for liking or disliking stories, showing an ability to integrate various aspects of response through the categories into which the work has been classified. A favorite story will be liked, for example, because it is "funny" and "about clowns." These aspects of children's discussions of stories parallel Piaget's descriptions of concrete operational thought in other areas of conceptual development.

It is only at this stage that children begin to engage in relatively extended transactional (participant role) discussions of a story; at the earlier stage, the child "discussing" a story relies on presentational techniques, reexperiencing the story in the process of retelling it.

Piaget's stage of formal operational thought brings with it a number of changes, summed up most simply as an ability to look "beyond the information given" (Bruner, 1974). In children's discussion of stories, this aspect of development finds expression in two stages. During the first, the predominant approach to discussing literature is one of analysis. Everything becomes a legitimate topic of inquiry: the motives of characters, the structure of the work, reasons for personal reactions of pleasure or distaste. Paralleling and seemingly distinct from this analytic approach is a movement away from the exacting literalism of the preadolescent. Where a nine-year-old will explain a saying such as "When the cat is away, the mice will play" in terms of pets and rodents, a 13-year-old will see an analogy with a wider class of experiences: "It is like when the teacher goes out, the children shout." This is a major step toward the recognition that literature is, in Denys Harding's (1962) words, "an accepted technique for discussing the chances of life."

The final step toward Harding's goal is characterized by an explicit concern with generalized meanings. Students' earlier focus on analysis becomes somewhat secondary, as a part of the explanatory framework supporting broader generalizations. Works are discussed in terms of their theme or point of view, and the effects of

Table 6-1.   Developmental Stages in the Formulation of Response

	Characteristic response	
Mode of thinking	Objective	Subjective
Preoperational (ages 2 to 6)	*Narration,* in whole or part	*Syncretism,* lacks integration
Concrete operational (ages 7 to 11)	*Summarization* and categorization	*Categorization,* attributed to the work
Formal operational stage I (ages 12 to 15)	*Analysis* of the structure of the work or the motives of the characters; understanding through analogy	*Identification* or perception of involvement in the work
Formal operational stage II (age 16 to adult)	*Generalization* about the work; consideration of its theme or point of view	*Understanding* gained or not gained through the work; its effect on the reader's own views

the work upon the reader begin to be formulated in terms of understanding gained (or not gained) through the experience of the work.

Table 6-1 provides a schematization of the trends we have been discussing, and illustrates one further aspect of this line of development: there is a parallel evolution. in the ways children formulate their response to the objective characteristics of the work, and the ways they describe the effect this objective construct has upon them (their subjective response).

There are two constraints on the model presented in Table 6-1 that need to be made explicit, for they reflect both its limitations and a number of directions for further research. First, the model is a summary of children's preferred way of responding—of what they do when they have a choice about what to say and how to say it. The model says nothing about what children can do if placed in a position where this preferred mode of response is rejected as inadequate or inappropriate. It also says nothing about the possibilities for response that might emerge in inter-action with a teacher or peer.

Second, the model is based on those aspects of response which children are able to verbalize, and quite likely obscures some developments which are occurring at a less conscious level.

Thus we need further studies testing the limits of students' understanding and response when "anything goes" will no longer do.

Likes and Dislikes

It is easy to criticize the typical study of reading interests for concentrating on superficial aspects of response: to learn that boys like adventure stories and girls prefer romance says very little about the processes that have led them to those preferences. It is nonetheless true that our evaluation of an experience is an important aspect of our encounter with it. We usually remember if we liked or disliked a book or an author long after our memory of the details of the story have faded.

In a series of studies, we asked six-, nine-, 13-, and 17-year-old students to compare stories they knew on a variety of dimensions (Applebee, 1975, 1976a, 1976b). We were interested both in their general attitudes toward the selections they knew, and in the features that were most important in differentiating one selection from another. Analyses revealed three major dimensions of response underlying the students' ratings: an overall evaluation of a story, a judgment about how easy or difficult it was to comprehend, and a concern with the realism of the events depicted. Responses of even the six-year-olds studied reflected these major patterns, though consensus about the components of each dimension increased with age. (Students at each of the ages we studied provided an evaluation of the stories they discussed, for example, but 17-year-olds were more likely to agree about the specific features that were important in their evaluations.)

There were also some interesting changes with age in the features characterizing the three major dimensions of response. Among the features related to evaluation, for example, both "ends happily" and "works out as you would expect in the end" shifted from positive characteristics at nine to negative ones at 17, while "disturbing" shifted from a negative to a positive characteristic during the same time period. Each of these changes can be interpreted as reflecting an increasing interest in adult literature employing more sophisticated and mature themes.

Features related to the "simplicity" of stories showed a different sort of change. The youngest children studied were primarily concerned with reading difficulty and age-appropriateness; the older ones with the contrast between simple and complex books, all of which are adult. (*1984* versus *Far from the Madding Crowd* illustrated this contrast for one 17-year-old; *Ice Station Zebra* versus *The Go-Between* illustrated it in the responses of another.) Concern with realism also showed some evolution, from the six-year-olds' distinction between real and make-believe to a later concern with the distance between the world of the story and that of the reader's own life.

Such findings provide a starting place for more detailed explorations of the factors which shape individual readers' judgments of the books they encounter. In future studies, we need to examine how perceptions of particular works change over time, as well as how individual students' tastes and interests expand and develop. Does an overfascination with simple books lead to stagnation, or serve as a necessary step in the eventual development of more sophisticated taste? Do early encounters with difficult texts provide challenge and stimulation, or generate frustration and distaste? How do interactions with other spectator role forms — art and architecture, as well as television and comic books — interact with students' literary interests and enthusiasms? The questions remaining for study are various, and their implications for the materials we recommend and the selections we teach are obvious and direct.

CONCLUSION

The studies discussed in this paper are ones in which theoretical constructs played an important role. They shaped the questions which were asked and the ways in which particular sets of data were interpreted. At this stage of our knowledge, at least, the most productive focus for our work seems to be with building up a coherent and consistent portrait of literary and artistic experience, a portrait structured around such general theoretical constructs as presentational and transactional, spectator and participant, subjective and objective. All of these are probably oversimplifications, but useful ones which further rather than constrict our understanding.

Given that research funds and energies are limited, we gain more from a variety of carefully constructed experimental tasks, each utilizing a limited number of subjects, than from a smaller number of tasks completed by larger numbers of people. Like other aspects of language use, literary response is a complex phenomenon, with many differing dimensions of interest in our studies. No one study is likely to be able to address itself to all of these dimensions, but by using a variety of tasks which approach the phenomenon from different directions, we can add considerably to our overall understanding. Most of the studies reviewed in the preceding sections, for example, were based on relatively small samples (60 to 100 children per task), but were part of one larger research undertaking that was eventually reported in a single volume (Applebee, 1978). In contrast, the international studies of achievement in literature (Purves et al., 1973) and the studies sponsored by the National Assessment of Educational Progress (NAEP, 1972, 1973) needed very large samples in order to provide valid and precise estimates of achievement levels in subpopulations of interest to the sponsoring organizations. But as studies of literary response, the same tasks used with smaller samples would have been equally informative. As it is, we are left in the national and international achievement results with "significant" correlations and "significant" differences which (though real enough) are too small to be worth the effort needed to explain them. Yet their very presence invites interpretation and diverts attention from larger differences that may reflect the operation of more powerful and pervasive dimensions of response.

Given the usefulness of a set of theoretical concepts to guide our work, it is also necessary that our approach to any given set of data be open-minded. There are many useful lines of evidence that can be drawn from literary critics, linguists, psychologists, anthropologists, sociologists, media researchers, and the national and international studies of achievement. We would lose a great deal if we allowed our interests to be restricted to the findings of those who shared our own presuppositions.

Suggestions for further research on specific topics have been embedded in the earlier discussion. There are, however, also a number of ways in which the general framework outlined here awaits further development. One of the most interesting involves the generalization of the spectator role and the structures that underlie it to other modes of discourse. There are obvious unities in our experience in the several arts, which Langer (1953) and Gardner (1973), among others, have noted. Many of the lines of development discussed in this paper have direct parallels in the other arts.

A second, perhaps more practically relevant, dimension in need of amplification concerns the effects of a literary text on the reader—particularly the process of learning the conventions and techniques of the spectator role through our involvement in it. In some sense, every story we hear or tell both reflects and extends our understanding of the conventions and possibilities of storytelling. The changes that result are hard to study except at a distance because they are slow; the effective change from any given experience is usually minimal and the ways of measuring it limited. Nonetheless, it is the cumulative effect of such experiences, however minimal any one of them may be, that is our major concern as teachers, scholars, and readers of literature.

REFERENCES

Applebee, A. N. Developmental changes in consensus in construing within a specified domain. *British Journal of Psychology*, 1975, *66*, 473–480.

Applebee, A. N. The development of children's responses to repertory grids. *British Journal of Social and Clinical Psychology*, 1976, *15*, 101–102. (a)

Applebee, A. N. Children's construal of stories and related genres as measured with repertory grid techniques. *Research in the Teaching of English*, 1976, *10*, 226–238. (b)

Applebee, A. N. *The child's concept of story: Ages two to seventeen*. Chicago: University of Chicago Press, 1978.

Britton, J. *Language and learning*. London: Allen Lane The Penguin Press, 1970.

Britton, J., Burgess, T., Martin, N., McLeod, A., & Rosen, H. *The development of writing abilities (11–18)*. London: Macmillan Education Ltd., for the Schools Council, 1975. Distributed in the U.S. by the National Council of Teachers of English, Urbana, Illinois.

Bruner, J. S. *Beyond the information given*. Edited by J. M. Anglin. London: George Allen and Unwin, 1974.

Chomsky, N. *Syntactic structures*. The Hague: Mouton & Co., 1957.

Gardner, H. *The arts and human development*. New York: John Wiley and Sons, 1973.

Halliday, M. A. K. *Learning how to mean*. New York: Elsevier, 1977.

Harding, D. W. Psychological processes in the reading of fiction. *British Journal of Aesthetics*, 1962, *2*, 133–147.

Heath, S. B. What no bedtime story means: Narrative skills at home and school. *Language in Society*, 1982, *11*, 49–76.

Holland, N. *The dynamics of literary response*. New York: Oxford University Press, 1968.

Inhelder, B. & Piaget, J. *The growth of logical thinking from childhood to adolescence*. London: Routledge & Kegan Paul, 1958.

Kuhn, T. S. *The structure of scientific revolutions* (2nd ed.). Chicago: University of Chicago Press, 1970.

Langer, S. K. *Feeling and form*. London: Routledge & Kegan Paul, 1953.

Langer, S. K. *Mind: An essay on human feeling*. (Vols. I and II.). Baltimore: Johns Hopkins University Press, 1967, 1972.

National Assessment of Educational Progress. *Reading and literature: General information yearbook* (Report 02-GIY). Washington, D.C.: U.S. Government Printing Office, for the Education Commission of the States, 1972.

National Assessment of Educational Progress. *Responding to literature* (Report 02-L-02). Washington, D.C.: Government Printing Office, for the Education Commission of the States, 1973.

Purves, A. C., Foshay, A. W., & Hansson, G. *Literature education in ten countries*. Stockholm: Almquist and Wiksell, 1973.

Scollon, R. & Scollon, S. B. K. *Narrative, literacy and face in interethnic communication*. Norwood, NJ: Ablex Publishing, 1981.

Smith, B. H. *Poetic closure*. Chicago: University of Chicago Press, 1968.
Vygotsky, L. S. *Thought and language*. Cambridge: MIT Press, 1962.
Weir, R. H. *Language in the crib*. The Hague: Mouton & Co., 1962.
White, D. *Books before five*. London: Oxford University Press, 1954.

Chapter 7
Discourse Conventions and Researching Response to Literary Dialogue

Richard Beach

Department of Curriculum and Instruction
University of Minnesota

A reader glances at the two opening lines of a short story. One character, John, says to Mary, "There's a really good movie coming to town this Friday." Mary responds, "That's nice."

Right from the start some questions come to the reader's mind:

What is John doing? Is he making an assertion about the fact that the movie is coming to town? Is he inviting Mary to the movie? What are John's intentions? Is he interested in Mary? Does he believe that Mary is interested in him? If she believes that John is inviting her, is she accepting or rejecting the invitation? What are Mary's intentions? What do these lines have to do with the development of the story?

In order to understand those two lines of dialogue, a reader may consider some or all of these questions. Most readers know that there is more to the meaning of the dialogue than simply the literal meaning of each utterance. They know that the dialogue is functioning symbolically to imply meanings about the nature of the characters, their intentions, their beliefs, their goals—all of the elements that contribute to the development of a story.

How do readers learn to make these inferences about dialogue? This is an important research question because drama and much of narrative fiction revolves around conflicts developed through dialogue. Unpacking the implied meanings of dialogue is an essential element in response to literature.

Readers differ in their ability to make these inferences because they bring different background knowledge of discourse conventions to their reading. While eight-year-olds can decode the words, "There's a really good movie coming to town this Friday," and "That's nice," they are not able to make the same inferences as an older reader—the fact that John could be either simply describing the fact that a movie is coming or inviting Mary to go to the movie, while Mary (if she took John's words as an invitation) could either be accepting or rejecting the invitation. Because older readers are more familiar with the speech act conventions which constitute these acts or the social conventions which constitute the social relationships between John and Mary, they can make inferences about these acts along with other inferences about John's and Mary's traits, beliefs about each other, goals, feelings, and plans.

Much of recent reading research has demonstrated that readers use their prior knowledge to make inferences (Spiro, Bruce, and Brewer, 1980). Less attention has been devoted to examining *how* readers use their prior knowledge to make these inferences, more particularly, inferences about dialogue in literary texts.

This chapter suggests some strategies for conducting research on readers' inferences about characters' speech acts, intentions, beliefs, traits, and goals. It also suggests ways to examine the influence of differences in readers' prior knowledge of discourse conventions on their ability to make these inferences.

Authors create dialogue according to certain conventions that readers then use to make inferences. In order to explain differences in readers' inferences, I am proposing a model of the inference process based on three different types of discourse conventions: speech act, social, and literary conventions. Conventions are "decisions or agreements by humans to behave under certain conditions in certain ways" (Steinmann and Brown, 1977, p. 6). These conventions both constitute and regulate characters' dialogue by defining those conditions that must be followed for characters to perform certain speech acts (requesting, inviting, ordering, promising). If, for example, a gangster boss tells his "hit man," "I want you to knock off the guy who's been giving us trouble," a reader, inferring this utterance as a request, also infers that certain conditions have been fulfilled that constitute an order—that the boss is sincere in issuing his order, that he has the power to issue such an order, that he believes that the hit man will take his utterance as an order and that the boss believes that the hit man is capable of fulfilling the order.

However, simply making inferences about these speech act conditions does not provide a complete understanding of speech acts. Readers also use knowledge of social conventions which constitute appropriate behavior in certain social contexts to make inferences about the appropriateness of characters' behavior. Readers who are familiar with the social conventions of, for example, legal trials, are able to make inferences about a courtroom drama that readers who do not know courtroom conventions will not be able to make. Similarly, readers use their knowledge of the conventions which constitute literary texts to make inferences about character types and storyline development. For example, the readers who are familiar with the prototypical gangster novels or movies use this knowledge to infer certain traits, beliefs, or goals such as those implied by the boss's order.

Thus, our prior knowledge of discourse conventions determines the inferences we make about speakers' or characters' behavior. For example, one evening, an encyclopedia salesman stopped by and gave his spiel to my wife and me. He began by trying to sell us a child's version, expounding on how much our child would learn from these volumes and how important all that learning was for the child's future. He formulated these ideas as requests for information, questions for which he already had the answers. Because it was difficult to disagree with these ideas, he got the affirmative answers he wanted. Delighted with his initial success, he continued with his questions about the attractiveness of the pictures, the readability of the text, and the importance of knowing things like the different insects. By then, his strategy was wearing thin. Despite our assertions that, as teachers, we were painfully aware of the things he was talking about, he continued on, oblivious to his audience's waning attention. Sticking to his well-rehearsed script, he then began to talk about the adult version. At that point, my wife left. Continuing to play the role of a cooperative audience, I listened politely. When his spiel finally came to an end, he left, probably assuming that he had made a positive impression.

In our post-session analysis of this living-room drama, my wife and I made a number of inferences about the salesman's successes and failures, the sequential development of his learned script, the roles, the rhetorical appeals, and so on. Having placed it in a conceptual frame of sales-talk conventions, we could detach ourselves from the context, recognizing that our own and the salesman's speech and roles had momentarily been constituted by a set of social conventions. The salesman remained naively oblivious to our reactions because he could not alter his script; he was locked into a convention about which he had little understanding.

Our tacit knowledge of these conventions carries over to our experience with similar discourse situations in literary works. Knowing the social conventions of sales talk helps us in making inferences about such characters as Willy Loman or the Bible salesman in Flannery O'Conner's "Good Country People." We understand that O'Conner's Bible salesman is a con artist who, unlike the encyclopedia salesman, plays on the conventions and is acutely aware of the nonsense of it all.

One does not acquire a tacit knowledge of these conventions overnight. As suggested by sociolinguists, social psychologists, ethnographers, and now writing researchers and others, one learns or gains "competence" in particular types of discourse conventions through discourse experiences (Britton, 1977, pp. 1–38; Bates, 1976). The fact that the readers are continually acquiring discourse and literary experiences suggests that the potential or capacity for the "fullest response" or understanding of a work is related to a reader's level of development in these experiences.

One of the important contributions of the developmentalist perspectives on research in literary response is the finding that the response process is best undestood as relative to a subject's personality and psycholinguistic or cognitive level of development.

THEORY: DISCOURSE CONVENTIONS

The Development of Tacit Knowledge
The developmentalist is interested in how readers acquire a tacit knowledge of literature, assuming that each new reading builds on prior knowledge. By knowledge, I am referring less to "knowing-that," or theoretical knowledge, about literature, and more to readers' "knowing-how" or "knowing-with" competence (Broudy, 1977, pp. 1–18) in both producing and understanding discourse.

Knowing-how consists of:

> one's implicit, unformulated, *practical* knowledge of rules or laws. It is knowing
> how to use rules or laws, how to do something with them—how to speak

English, for example, or how to write well. Knowing-that, on the other hand, is explicit, formulated, *theoretical* knowledge of rules or laws. It is knowing that they are such and such, knowing how to formulate or describe them. (Steinmann and Brown, 1977, p. 5)

For example, students know how to write grammatical sentences because they have an implicit knowledge of grammatical rules. They may not be able to explicitly state any of these rules. Similarly, readers develop a knowing-how competence in the ability to predict the outcomes of stories or the ability to combine disparate behavioral cues to make inferences about a character. They know how to write or tell stories and create characters using behavioral cues. This knowing-how competence develops from experiences with reading, writing, or telling stories.

Acquiring knowing-how competence could be thought of as acquiring schema or conceptual frames for understanding the world. Schema theory posits that people determine meaning by cognitively organizing information or experience according to various schema or conceptual frames that range from simple concepts to high level abstracts or complex scenarios or paradigms (Anderson, Spiro, and Montague, 1976; Bobrow and Collins, 1975; Bruce, 1977). One of the important tenets of schema theory is that the meaning of discourse is not contained within an utterance or text, but that the auditor or reader reconstructs the meaning according to his or her own schema. As Richard Anderson notes, "A schema is a cryptic recipe that can guide a person in constructing a message . . . a text is gobbledygook unless the reader possesses an interpretative framework to breathe meaning into it" (Anderson, 1977, pp. 422–423).

It is important to recognize that knowledge is not a general, coherent, and consistent picture of reality, but is an activity specific to certain contexts; it is selective and limited by what is appropriate for a particular task or experience (Olson, 1977, pp. 19–30). Readers learn to employ the knowledge that is most useful for understanding a particular work. As they develop a more complex repertoire of schema, they learn how to select the most useful schema for understanding particular bits of dialogue.

Learning or growth in understanding literature, therefore, involves a "remodeling of one's perspective that enables one to 'see' differently. Such remodeling involves developing a more global, abstract framework that one acts in terms of and that sets the stage for providing concrete particulars with their distinct significance and place" (Bransford, Nitsch, and Franks, 1977, p. 51).

We use conventions as schema to give meaning to experience, often in the form of "if-then" relationships between context, behavior, conditions, time, and consequence—if you swing three times at a ball in baseball, then you are out; if you want to convince someone, then they need to believe that what you say is true.

In order to explain response to dialogue, it is often useful to examine the extent to which a reader or readers are able to apply their "multiple competencies" (Steinmann and Brown, 1977) to the work—meshing the three types of conventions in intricate ways to make inferences.

I will now further elucidate these different types of conventions with examples of how readers use their knowledge of these conventions to make inferences.

Speech Act Conventions

Speech act theorists (Austin, 1962; Searle, 1969, 1975; Grice, 1975; Labov and Fanshel, 1977; Bach and Harnish, 1979; Stiles, 1981) define certain conditions which are involved in the performance of certain speech acts. These conditions refer to speakers' beliefs, traits, status, goals, or attitudes that are necessary and/ or sufficient for successful performance of certain acts.

Speech act theory assumes that words have meaning in the context of a sentence which can be imagined as part of an authentic language act. If a sentence does not occur in an acutal speech context, which is the case with discourse acts embedded in fiction, readers create a speech context using their knowledge of speech act rules (Brown, 1975).

Searle (1969) argues that an utterance involves three essential acts: the utterance act, the illocutionary act, and the perlocutionary effect. The *utterance act* is simply the act of uttering words which conform to grammatical rules. However, such acts by themselves lack intentions which provide a meaning for the utterance. A parrot can perform utterance acts, but these acts are not part of authentic language use because the parrot's utterances lack intention.

In making an utterance, a speaker is also performing an *illocutionary act*. Illocutionary acts are those acts performed *in making* an utterance. If an audience or reader knows that certain conditions have been satisfied, then that audience or reader can infer that a particular utterance counts as a particular type of illocutionary act.

Different speech act theorists define these conditions in different ways. For example, Labov and Fanshel's (1977) definitions of conditions emphasize the speaker and the audience's beliefs about each other's intentions, needs, obligations, rights, or sincerity.

Labov and Fanshel define the conditions for performing a requesting act as follows:

> If A addresses to B an imperative specifying an action X at a time T_1, and B believes that A believes that
>
> 1a. X should be done (for a purpose Y) (*need for the action*)
>   b. B would not do X in the absence of the request (*need for the request*)
> 2. B has the *ability* to do X (with an instrument Z)
> 3. B has the *obligation* to do X or is willing to do it.
> 4. A has the *right* to tell B to do X,
>
> then A is heard as making a valid request for action (p. 78).

Thus, if speaker A says to B, "Would you close the door?" a reader could infer that A's utterance constitutes a request because the conditions stated above have been met. A reader therefore explains the success or failure of an act in terms of particular conditions: the request to close the door may fail because the speaker wasn't sincere, the door did not need to be closed, the speaker did not have the power to make such a request, and so on.

Readers use their knowledge of these speech act conditions to make inferences about characters' traits, beliefs, and goals. The mere fact that a character performs certain acts implies certain character traits or status. The fact that character *A* orders character *B* to do something and character *B* obeys implies that character *A* has the power or status to successfully issue an order.

Readers can also infer that characters' beliefs about each other's traits, status, goals, or beliefs may or may not be valid. If character *A* requests certain information from *B*, *A* must believe that *B* has that information. However, a reader may know that *B* does not have the information, inferring that *A* is mistaken in her belief.

By tracing a pattern in a character's acts, a reader infers that a character is using acts to achieve certain goals. Acts often function to "save face" (Brown and Levinson, 1978) by preserving relationships or maintaining privacy. In some cases a character may employ acts that are more mitigating than aggravating in order to achieve these goals. (Labov and Fanshel, 1977).

Speech acts also have certain *perlocutionary effects* that are not governed by conventions. Through performing certain acts, speakers achieve certain effects. By asserting, a speaker informs; by ordering, a speaker gets someone to obey. Readers use the effects to infer whether or not an act has succeeded or failed. If the character refuses to obey, then a reader knows that there is a problem—the audience may not believe that the speaker has the authority to issue an order, or the speaker may not have been sincere, and so on.

Theorists have also grouped specific illocutionary acts into larger composite clusters or family resemblances (Searle, 1969; Ohmann, 1972; Hancher, 1979; Stiles, 1981). As an example, I will discuss Stiles' categories, particularly because Stiles has developed a manual for using his categories for content analysis research (Stiles, 1978). Based on differences in speakers' knowledge of, and perspective on, their own and audience's experience, Stiles proposes eight basic categories: disclosure, advisement, question, interpretation (which use speaker's frame of reference), edification, confirmation, acknowledgement, and reflection (which uses a shared frame of reference). One advantage of this taxonomy over other systems is that it is not limited to illocutionary verbs.

Each of these categories represents different levels of social distance and power. Research studies (Stiles, 1981) of conversations indicates that speakers who are intimate (as opposed to distant) or of high status (as opposed to low status) use more acts of advisement, interpretation, confirmation, and reflection which require a certain presumptuousness about one's intimacy or power. Thus, if a character gives advice or interprets another, then a reader may infer that the speaker presumes a certain degree of social distance and relative power. Moreover, certain conditions are particularly appropriate for judging the success of certain acts. In judging a character's act of disclosure, a reader is concerned about the character's sincerity, whereas with acts of advising or ordering, a reader focuses on a character's beliefs about feasibility—whether an audience can perform a certain act.

The fact that a reader knows the conditions for a particular act means that he or she can infer a wider range of implied meanings than a reader who is less familiar with these conditions. For example, one set of conditions for making assertions which are intended to impart information has been defined by Paul Grice (1975). Grice proposes a *cooperative principle* which he believes governs the exchange of information in conversation.

The cooperative principle states that, in speaking, you should "make your conversational contribution such as is required, at the state at which it occurs, by the accepted purpose or direction of the talk exchange in which you are engaged." For this principle, Grice derives a series of maxims:

Quantity: 1. Make your contribution as informative as is required (for the current purposes of the exchange).
2. Do not make your contribution more informative than is required.

Quality: 1. Do not say what you believe to be false.
2. Do not say that for which you lack adequate evidence.

Relative: 1. Be relevant.

Manner: 1. Avoid obscurity of expression.
2. Avoid ambiguity.
3. Be brief.
4. Be orderly. (pp. 45–46)

Grice also suggests that a speaker, by intentionally (and in some cases, unintentionally) violating one or more of these maxims implies meanings beyond the meanings of explicit statements. Grice notes that speakers flout the maxims to draw the listener's attention.

For example, speaker A may deliberately engage in a lot of irrelevant digressions; both speaker A and the listener B know that the speaker has something important to communicate. A's intentional or unintentional violation of the maxim, "Be relevant," could imply any number of possible meanings—that A is deliberately trying to avoid discussing another, more pressing matter ("beating around the bush"); that A is oblivious to the listener's needs; or that A has difficulty in coming to the point.

A reader could make these inferences by understanding that a particular maxim has been violated. A reader who recognizes that a character is being deliberately indirect or dealing with topics not relevant to a particular topic or issue—and is, therefore, violating certain maxims—is able to infer certain meanings implied by those violations (Cooper, 1977). For example, the fact that characters opt for more indirect forms implies certain attitudes or intentions—that they are uneasy with the situation or their audience. The character never states these meanings; the reader infers them as implied by the dialogue.

Pratt's (1981) critique of Grice—that his cooperative principle waxes over the emotional and nonverbal conflicts that pervade conversation—suggests that characters' emotional and nonverbal cues also imply meaning.

Social Conventions

Readers also draw on knowledge of social conventions that define appropriate versus inappropriate behavior within certain social, cultural, or historical contexts. For example, in the nineteenth century, it was often considered inappropriate for women to be assertive or to perform those acts necessitated by status or power. Women who violated these conventions were often ostracized.

Often social conventions concern behavior that is appropriate to social class distinctions. Within the social or hierarchical structure, a reader infers that certain speech acts are appropriate to certain roles. For example, a viewer watching *Upstairs, Downstairs* infers the following pattern of behavior:

1. Hudson, the butler, requests that the parlor maid, Daisy, "stop being so uppity." She reluctantly obeys.
2. Bellamy, head of the household, requests that Hudson bring in his dinner. Hudson obeys immediately.
3. Bellamy requests that his son, James, be more careful in his relationships with women. James tells his father that his relationships with women are none of his father's business.

Certain factors are consistently more crucial to the success or failure of requests than other factors. In the case of *Upstairs, Downstairs*, the social status or role seems to be more important than, for example, sincerity or needs.

Thus, readers who are familiar with certain social conventions may differ in their inferences from those readers who are not familiar with certain conventions. Readers may also differ in their social attitudes (not to be confused with knowledge of conventions). Readers who espouse feminist attitudes will respond negatively to traditional sex-role portrayals.

In order to make dialogue inferences, readers mesh knowledge of social conventions which define prototypical character traits, beliefs, and goals with knowledge of speech act conventions. Knowledge that a character has certain typical "teacher" traits and presumably holds certain prototypical beliefs about students or is engaged in certain prototypical teachers' acts, is useful for fleshing out the speech act conditions of beliefs, intention, ability, or status. If a character/teacher openly ridicules a student in front of a class, a reader may infer that, as a teacher, that character is violating certain social conventions.

Readers who are familiar with the social conventions which constitute appropriate teacher/student relationships can then make inferences about a teacher/character's intentions, beliefs, and traits more readily than readers who are less familiar with these conventions.

For example, I compared how college education majors and high school students responded to a short story, "Tomorrow and Tomorrow and So Forth" (Updike, 1967, pp. 175-185): The story portrays a well-meaning, disgruntled English teacher's attempt to teach Macbeth to a group of uninterested eleventh-grade students (Beach, 1983). I selected these subjects with the assumption that, because the education majors knew more about the social conventions of teaching and—as determined by an attitude scale towards literature teaching (Gallo, 1968)—held less traditional attitudes towards literature instruction, they would differ from the high school students in their inferences about the teacher's speech acts. On three selected acts in the story—lecturing about Macbeth, requesting students to recite a memorized passage, and posing a sarcastic question—the college students made inferences that reflected more understanding of the teacher's pedagogical goals than did the high school students. For example, in response to the teacher's sarcastic question to a student, 58% of the high school students simply made a positive judgment (reflecting their more traditional attitudes toward teaching). In contrast, 40% of the college students (compared to 10% of the high school students) inferred that the question was being used as a put-down or punishment of the student, a perception of the inappropriateness of the teacher's behavior.

Literary Conventions

Readers also draw on their knowledge of literary conventions to make inferences about dialogue. Reading a text as a literary text means that a reader perceives the dialogue as more than simply a transcript of people conversing.

One of the most important literary conventions is that of "intentionality." A reader knows that an author is deliberately using the dialogue for symbolic purposes to imply meanings. This impels a reader to go beyond simply decoding the speech act to infer character traits, beliefs, and goals, as well as thematic meanings. A reader also expects that the parts of a text conjoin according to some larger composite purpose; that, for example, a character's initial dialogue acts differ from later dialogue acts, implying a change in the character.

As with social conventions, readers also apply their knowledge of certain literary genres—romance, science fiction, detective, comedy, tragedy, and so on—that define certain prototypical character acts or story development. Readers who are familiar with the romance novel formula know that a male character's initial requests will often be rejected, only to later be accepted. When they read a comedy, readers know that the negative consequences of certain acts will ultimately be mitigated. Thus, reading a text *as* a certain genre-type helps a reader apply those genre-schema which are useful for that particular genre.

Summary of the Model

In summary, I have suggested the following:

1. In responding to dialogue, readers go beyond inferring only characters' utterances to inferring characters' intentions, goals, beliefs, needs, traits, and so on, that are implied by the utterances. Understanding a text has much to do with inferring these implied meanings.
2. As illustrated in Figure 7-1 below, readers employ certain schema in the form of tacit knowledge of discourse conventions to make these inferences. Because readers already know the conventions which constitute successful performance of certain acts, or the conventions which determine appropriate or typical

Figure 7-1.   Readers' use of discourse conventions

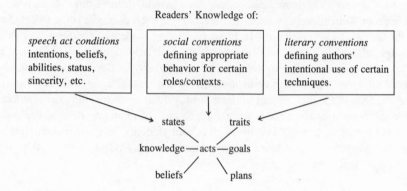

Readers' Knowledge of:

| *speech act conditions* intentions, beliefs, abilities, status, sincerity, etc. | *social conventions* defining appropriate behavior for certain roles/contexts. | *literary conventions* defining authors' intentional use of certain techniques. |

states   traits

knowledge — acts —goals

beliefs   plans

behavior in a certain context, they can infer various meanings implied by dialogue.

3. Differences in students' tacit knowledge of these discourse conventions, due to the extent or nature of their background experiences, result in differences in their inferences about dialogue.

CONTENT ANALYSIS CATEGORIES

Based on my model, I believe that readers often follow a certain sequence in making inferences. They first make inferences about the types of acts, inferring either an illocutionary verb (request, order, invite, assert) or a larger composite category, for example, Stiles's "disclosure" or "interpretation," as well as perlocutionary effects. Readers also draw on knowledge of conditions for performing acts to make inferences about characters' beliefs, knowledge, ability, power, status, and intentions. Because characters' acts often succeed or fail because they follow or violate certain conditions, readers then try to explain these successes or failures by giving reasons based on the characters' adherence to or violation of certain conventions. At this point, a reader is drawing on speech act as well as social and literary conventions. For example, a reader may explain Mrs. Bennet's tendency to irritate Mr. Bennet in Jane Austen's *Pride and Prejudice*, inferring that she violates Grice's quantity maxim—she blathers on needlessly, in contrast to the laconic Mr. Bennet. The reader may then infer that, socially, Mrs. Bennet's blathering on has unfortunate social consequences.

Based on my model, I have derived a set of categories listed below that can be used to analyze readers' inferences. This content analysis category system is designed simply to determine inference types—the extent to which readers infer illocutionary acts or perlocutionary effects or give a reason or cite an assumption. Within each of these inferences types, it is also possible to categorize the content of the inference, a technique I will discuss later in this chapter.

These categories can simply guide a descriptive, anecdotal discussion of responses, or they can be used to derive the number and/or percentage of response "statements" falling within each category. It may then be possible to compare two age groups' inferences. One might find, for example, that older readers are more likely to infer reasons for violations than are younger readers.

For advice on conducting content analysis of literary response, I refer the reader to discussions of applications of a range of category systems by Purves and Riperre (1968), Odell and Cooper (1976), and Cooper and Michalak (1981). An essential first step is breaking up the responses into discrete units or chunks (often called T-units or clauses) so that judges will be rating the same units. Then, judges (ideally three or four for this type of analysis) must be trained so that they can achieve relatively high interjudge agreement (measured crudely by percentage of agreement, or better, correlations or Cronbach's alpha—an SPSS program). If agreement is not high, judges may need more training until they all share the same perceptions or assumptions, or the categories may need to be modified. In some cases, judges may be reading beneath the surface to impute intentions, breaking the shared objectivity among judges. Once the responses have been categorized, the number of responses or percentages within each category can be determined for individuals or for groups. The appropriate statistical analysis may then be applied to determine if differences between or among groups are statistically significant.

A Sample Category System
The following is a sample set of categories that builds on three basic types of inferences: (a) inferred descriptions, (b) inferred reasons, and (c) implications/predictions. Under each category, I suggest some ways to group inferences according to content and cite some examples of inferences.

1. Inferred descriptions of a character's, narrator's, or author's acts, goals, plans, beliefs, preconditions (Bruce, 1977).

- Illocutionary acts: *She ordered him to leave.*
- Intended perlocutionary effects: *She didn't want him around anymore.*
- Actual perlocutionary effects: *He refused to leave.* (Inferences about acts and/or effects could be grouped according to inferences about nature, complexity, or importance of the acts; judgments of the success or failure of the acts; judgments of the appropriateness of the acts relative to the social context; inferences about other characters' inferences/conceptions of the acts.)
- Characters' goals or purposes: *She wanted to get even with him.*
- Characters' beliefs or knowledge about other characters: *He believes that she really cares about him. She knew that he didn't have any right to say things like that.*
- Characters' ability, power, status: *He could order them around because he was the boss.*

2. Inferred reasons which imply knowledge of speech act or conventions (reasons given for a character's, narrator's, or author's acts, effects, success/failure, or conversational behavior.) Reasons could be grouped according to the implied conventions.

- Inferences could be grouped according to the implied conversational or contextual conventions followed or violated. For example, *She droned on and on*: violation of Grice's quantity maxim of the cooperative principle. *Once the initial questioning was out of the way, he started to drive home his proposal*: inference based on knowledge of negotiations. *He failed to get him to obey because he lacked the power*: implies speech act convention—ability to perform an order. *He answered the phone in an impersonal manner because he was only a telephone operator*: implies a discourse type convention—professional role related to telephone service.
- Reasons may reflect knowledge of literary conventions. For example, *He failed to obey the order because the author wanted to show his resistance. She was able to get them to agree because she was the main character.*

3. Implications/predictions, or inferences as to what the discourse acts imply or will lead to. These are grouped according to what the implication/prediction refers to.

- Character: *His going on and on suggests that he is strange.*
- Storyline: *The fact that she rejected him means that he will probably go out and kill himself.*
- Thematic/Values: *Their constant game of one-upmanship means that they lived in a cut-throat world.*

THE MODEL APPLIED: SAMPLE RESPONSES

Let me illustrate what a researcher initially may go through in applying the model. Consider first a brief fictional vignette to which readers might respond:

> It was late Friday afternoon. Mary and Bill were alone in the teaching assistants' office going over Bill's paper. Mary looked at her watch.
> "Bill, this paper could use a little work."
> "Well, what do I need to do about it?"
> "You ought to work on it this weekend; maybe some more work will improve it."
> "But what do I need to do to improve it?"
> Mary began to wonder.
> "Do I really need to tell you?"
> Bill smiled, "Yes, Mary, I wish that you would."

In responding to this "story," there are a number of speech act rules or conditions important for making inferences about the assertion and request acts. In making a request, a speaker must believe that his or her audience is able to perform the requested act or knows certain information. The audience must also believe that the speaker is sincere in making a request, or has the status or right to make a request. In making an indirect request (using an assertion to imply a request for action or information, for example, "Is that the salt next to your glass?"), a speaker must believe that his or her audience infers the intention. If a speaker has to repeat a request, that repetition can be taken as a criticism of the speaker's competence (Labov and Fanshel, 1977).

One Reader's Response

In order to illustrate the use of prior knowledge in responding to this story, I will discuss one reader's response. Susan is a college senior whose responses are on a relatively sophisticated level. She was asked to respond to each line of the vignette separately.

1. *It was late Friday afternoon.*

The weekend is approaching. The work week is over. Something is going to happen during the last few hours of the week. It's nearing dusk. There is a note of desperation and ominousness in the sentence, or is it just tired? The drab language probably means it's just a tired time, after a long week. If there was anything shady going on the language would have been more colorful.

Susan draws on her knowledge of literary conventions to infer that the language of this opening line connotes potential conflict. She will then be particularly attentive to conflict in the dialogue.

2. *Mary and Bill were alone in the teaching assistants' office going over Bill's paper.*

Mary is a T.A. and Bill has turned in a paper to the T.A. for help. It's really late, but for some reason (highly unusual) Mary has decided to stay and help Bill. Mary knows more about writing papers than Bill does. Bill looks to Mary for help. Mary's is the helping role.

3. *Mary looked at her watch.*

Mary is anxious to get home. She is not happy in her helping role at this time of the day. Mary is hungry and tired. She is wishing he had learned to write in high school so she wouldn't have to spend her Friday nights like this. There are other people Mary would rather be with than Bill. Perhaps Bill is not a quick learner. Perhaps Bill just turned in a bad paper and expects Mary to do rewriting that he should be doing.

Susan initially infers that a teacher/learner relationship involves certain obligations: that Mary, the teacher, has the ability and obligation to help Bill and that Bill believes that Mary can help him. She also infers that Mary believes that the time is inappropriate and that Bill lacks the ability or obligations consistent with the learner role. Susan then begins to define a goal for Mary based on Mary's needs or desires.

4. *"Bill, this paper could use a little work."*

Mary has decided to make a move to close this session. She is tired of looking at Bill's paper. Yes, his paper is bad and he should be home rewriting it.

5. *"Well, what do I need to do about it?"*

Bill needs help. He doesn't know how to rewrite papers. Perhaps he does know how to rewrite papers but is stalling to try to get Mary to spend time with him. Bill is showing unusual interest in writing at this late hour of the week. Perhaps Bill has plans for the weekend that include Mary.

6. *"You ought to work on it this weekend; maybe some more work will improve it."*

Mary is trying to press the point that he has two days to work on it. She does not want to be included in his weekend plans.

Susan infers that line four is an indirect request to end the conference, an inference consistent with her perception of Mary's goal of terminating the conference. She then suggests thoughts that Mary might have expressed had she opted for a more indirect, polite form. She infers that Bill puts off her request with a request for information. She then considers several options. One option, based on a condition about audience belief, is that Bill is violating a sincerity condition—that he is not really interested in the information. She now speculates that Bill may have a different goal or plan which is more consistent with courtship conventions than the teacher/learner conventions.

By inferring that Mary is reiterating the request in line 6, Susan recognizes that Mary's reference now to obligation and consequences implies a more direct approach in Mary's relationship with Bill. Susan now infers that Mary believes that Bill has a different goal in mind.

7. *"But what do I need to do to improve it?"*

Bill is still stalling. He will not take no for an answer. Mary has given her cues to close the interview and Bill is ignoring them.

8. *Mary began to wonder.*

Mary is beginning to think Bill is a complete loser. She is wondering what it will take to get rid of him. She can't throw him out because she is a dedicated T.A. who never turns away a student who needs help with his work. But she is beginning to wonder what Bill's real motives are.

9. *"Do I really need to tell you?"*

Mary feels Bill should take some more of the responsibility of this paper onto himself. She is making the last ditch effort to get rid of him.

10. *Bill smiled. "Yes, Mary, I wish that you would."*

Bill is definitely more interested in Mary than his paper. He is trying to play on her sympathies and is trying to butter her up with his smiles.

Susan now infers that Bill continues to reject Mary's indirect requests; the fact that Bill is repeating the request for information further implies that he has a different set of plans. Susan relies on knowledge of interviewing conventions in inferring that Bill refuses to recognize that Mary is terminating the conference.

She then infers a conflict between Mary's goals or motives as defined by teacher/learner conventions and her beliefs about Bill's own perceptions of the situation. She infers that in repeating her request, Mary is challenging Bill's competence as a student; she continues to conceive of Mary's acts in terms of her goals of terminating the conference.

In my analysis of Susan's responses, I do not want to imply that Susan has any theoretical knowledge of speech act rules. However, she is able to make a number of inferences that reflect some understanding of those intentions, acts, beliefs, and abilities involved in making requests. She also uses conventions constituting teacher/ learner relationships, interviewing, and flirtation.

Another Reader's Response

I now want to give an example of a reader's responses to a longer selection, the first chapter of Jane Austen's *Pride and Prejudice*. The reader, Diane, a former English teacher in her mid-thirties, was asked to respond to a series of open-ended questions. Her responses reflect her ability to combine knowledge of speech act conventions, nineteenth-century courtship conventions, and literary conventions constituting Austen's comic techniques in making inferences about the dialogue.

Much of the dialogue in the first chapter between Mr. and Mrs. Bennet regards the arrival of a wealthy, eligible bachelor as their new neighbor. Diane infers that Mrs. Bennet's goal is marrying off her five daughters. Diane notes that the conventions of the time dictate that Mr. Bennet must visit their new neighbor in order to invite him over to the Bennets', which means that Mrs. Bennet's acts are indirectly and directly designed to convince her husband to pay a call.

Diane infers that—when Mrs. Bennet says to her husband, "My dear Mr. Bennet, have you heard that Netherfield Park is let at last?", and Mr. Bennet replies that he had not—"she is excited about this situation and he is deliberately unresponsive to her excitement; he has a kind of droll, dry wit; he's teasing her." Diane infers all of this because she senses the intended comic irony—that Austen is parodying the courtship conventions through Mrs. Bennet. Diane then infers that Mrs. Bennet's assertions misfire because Mrs. Bennet believes that Mr. Bennet doesn't know the information she is conveying, information he already knows. Moreover, she infers that in order for Mr. Bennet to cooperate, Mrs. Bennet must shift from assertions and indirect requests to more direct requests. Having defined Mrs. Bennet's plan, she infers Mr. Bennet's counterplan: "to force her to state in plain words all the things she is just hinting at." She can then infer, as in the following responses, that Mr. Bennet's questions are insincere but that, given the comic tone of the novel, his insincerity is not malicious.

How do you know that Mr. Bennet's misunderstanding is deliberate?

Well, it's possible that it isn't. It's possible that he really doesn't understand but I think just the tone that was set in the beginning of a kind of humorous irony leads you to conclude that he does understand, that he is simply being humorous, and in fact, as it goes on, one of the things that gives the clue is that the kind of questions are really so dense, that they're too dumb to be true. For example, when she says, "I'm thinking of him marrying one of our girls," and he says, "Is that his design in settling here?" Well, nobody would really be that dumb; and in fact, it's his wife that doesn't get it, because she takes him seriously in this obviously leading or stupid question, so that the impression you get is that she's the one who's misunderstanding and he really understands it all very well and is just playing a game.

How would you describe that game?

Well, it's one of knowing her so well, and knowing the kinds of things she'll come up with and knowing exactly what will frustrate her in a playful way, not in any serious way, but just irritate her or force her to state in plain words all the things she is just hinting at . . . It forces her to bring to the surface all of her assumptions and spell them right out. As it goes on, he's also pretending not only to be stupid about the assumptions she has about this rich man who may marry one of their daughters; but also he's pretending to not understand the social conventions which exist, because she says to him, "You must visit him as soon as he comes," and he says, "I see no occasion for that; you and the girls may go." Well, it's very clear that in those days, in those times, this would not be acceptable that a woman and her daughters would make the first social call on the new neighbor who happened to be a single man. The man in the family would be the one who would make the first contact.

Can you think of any reasons why he is teasing her?

Probably for his own amusement. He lives with this rather silly woman, and it's the way he gets his kicks; because obviously she's not very much company for him. They seem, he seems to be pretty well above her in mental abilities, so he gets his laughs by teasing her in ways that she isn't even aware of. He goes on to take what he has teased out of her, that is the laying out on the table of all of the assumptions that she has made, and he takes those and he pretends that it's perfectly okay to simply state those desires, the desire that this new Mr. Bingley will marry one of the daughters. He says, "I'll send a few lines by you to assure him of my hearty consent to his marrying whichever he chooses of the girls, but I must throw in a good word for my little Lizzy." And his wife gets all upset and thinks that he really will do that, and here again it's just continuing the game and really elaborating on it. Also, it's a continuation of flouting social conventions. One would never, it just simply isn't done, to approach a single man and say, "You have my consent to marry any of my daughters," even though everybody understands that families with unmarried daughters would be trying to get this single wealthy man to favor one of their daughters. And the young man would certainly understand that too; so it's all part of the social game that everybody plays that these things simply must not be stated, and Mr. Bennet is flouting all that by bringing them right to the surface and stating them.

Diane's use of tacit knowledge of conventions is reflected in her own inferences and generalizations about behavior. For example, she describes Mr. Bennet's questions as "so dense, that they're too dumb to be true," that "nobody would really be that dumb." The reference to "nobody" implies some understanding of conditions for requests for information: if one already knows the information, one violates the conventions for requests for information. She then uses her inference based on requesting conditions to infer that Mrs. Bennet is "the one who's misunderstanding" because she fails to recognize Mr. Bennet's violation of the conventions. As she notes, "he's pretending to not understand the social conventions which exist," in response to Mr. Bennet's saying, "I see no occasion for that; you and the girls may go." She conceives of Mr. Bennet's goal as flouting courtship conventions by doing such things as stating that he would give Bingley his consent to marry his daughter.

In response to a question as to why Mr. Bennet picks out Lizzy, Diane infers that Mr. Bennet's praising of Lizzy implies Lizzy's function as a character within the novel—that Lizzy is an important character and is similar to Mr. Bennet. This reflects her understanding of narrative conventions—that Austen is deliberately highlighting certain information in the beginning of the novel in order to foreshadow later developments.

Diane's own attitudes toward social discourse, particularly the courtship conventions, are apparent in her judgments of Mrs. Bennet as "silly" and dull and Mr. Bennet as a "witty and bright and droll sort of person." She looks favorably on Mr. Bennet's attempt to "bring to the surface all of (Mrs. Bennet's) assumptions and spell them right out," suggesting that she conceives of Mrs. Bennet as someone whose role is limited by these conventions. She seems to view Mr. Bennet's "game" favorably because it constitutes a rejection of courtship conventions. At the same time, she infers that the "game" is all part of a "playful relationship" in which any serious problems in their relationship are mitigated, reflecting her understanding of the novel's comic conventions.

There are certainly other things one could say about Diane's rather complex inference strategies. I have focused primarily on the processes of "contextualizing"—her ability to conceive of behavior as embedded within various types of conventions. This ability to consider and apply appropriate schema may be one characteristic of relatively sophisticated readers.

A Study of Group Response

It is possible, as we did with Susan and Diane, to discuss individual readers' responses as a reflection of certain levels of prior knowledge. However, it is difficult to define the level of knowledge presented by Susan's or Diane's responses without some comparison to responses of other readers who possess different background knowledge.

Another option is to study different groups' response to dialogue. By comparing two or more groups' responses to the same dialogue and by making assumptions about differences between these groups' knowledge, it may then be possible to attribute differences in responses to differences in presumed prior knowledge. I say presumed prior knowledge because it is difficult, if not impossible, to develop a valid measure of tacit knowledge of conventions. Any test of theoretical knowledge, one's "knowing-that" competence, must bear little relationship to one's "knowing-how" competence, the capacity to employ tacit knowledge in making inferences about texts. Many readers who can make inferences about speech acts are not able to articulate speech act rules.

An optional approach is to assume that readers of comparable cultural background but different age levels will, within each age-level group, make inferences similar in content that will differ from another group's inferences. While much of response research highlights differences in response, I am suggesting that the similarity in the content of response is equally intriguing, particularly if this similarity reflects a common background knowledge.

The difficulty in all of this is in determining what constitutes similarity. Let me report on one exploratory attempt. As part of a larger recall study, I developed a technique for determining similarity in the content of the inferences.

This study compared the responses of high school and college students' responses to a one-act play. Sixty tenth-grade students and 60 freshmen at the University of Minnesota were administered the Gates-McGinitie Comprehension Test, Form F. At each grade level, 15 subjects scoring above the median for that grade level and 15 subjects scoring below the median were randomly selected, resulting in 30 subjects at each grade level. The play selected, *Here We Are* by Dorothy Parker, is a comic play about a newlywed couple on the afternoon of their wedding. This play was selected because I assumed that college students would be more familiar with the social conventions constituting the behavior of newlywed couples than would high school students.

The play was divided into sections of approximately 1500 words in each section. Subjects were interviewed separately and asked to read each section of the play silently as many times as they needed. Subjects were then asked to recall everything they could remember from a section. Analysis of the recall, using the "inferred descriptions" categories for types of inferences (see pages 113–114 for the content analysis categories)—in addition to a category known as literal restatement—indicated that about 75 percent of the recall for both groups consisted of literal restatement. There were no statistically significant differences between the groups in the number of illocutionary act inferences; the college students did make significantly more trait inferences than the high school students.

Students were also asked to describe and give reasons for characters' use of 16 specific acts in the play. Our analysis of the content of those reasons illustrates one technique that can be used for determining similarity of readers' responses. I call this technique the *clustering technique* (Beach, 1979).

Students' reasons for each targeted act were written on index cards; if no reason was given, then that was noted. Two judges then sorted these cards into piles according to similarity of content. Reasons of the same general type were grouped together and given a title that best described the composite group. Two to four categories were produced for each section, including a category, "no reason."

Once the different composite categories were determined, the percentage of reasons for each category out of the total number of reasons given by each group was determined. To take a hypothetical example, judges determined that in responding to a character's utterance, "You certainly look nice today," readers either inferred that the character is "complimenting her" or that the character was "trying to get her to do a favor." It can then be determined, for example, that 60 percent of the readers in a group inferred that the character was complimenting her and 40 percent inferred that the character was trying to get her to do a favor.

I then compared the high school and college students' reasons for characters' acts in terms of whether their inferences referred to characters' overall goals and long-range effects or immediate or short-term goals and effects. In the above example, the response "trying to get her to do a favor," reflects a more acute sense of that character's long-range goal than the inference, "complimenting her." I assumed that readers with more knowledge of the social or literary conventions are better able to infer a character's long-range goals.

Three judges then read over the category titles and ranked the categories according to the extent to which the inferences explained acts in terms of long-range versus short-range goals or effects. The agreement for the three judges was .74 (using Kendall's Coefficient of Concordance Test).

In 12 of the 16 acts, the college students had higher percentages for categories ranked higher by the judges than did the high school students.

To give specific examples of the groups' inferences, let me discuss their responses to one exchange from the play. The couple—"He" and "She"—are on the train and She asks He if he likes her hat. He responds: "Looks good on you." The groups' inferences were similar; more than 60% of both groups inferred that He was trying "to make her feel good," or "to get her in a better mood," an inferred perlocutionary effect of what they presumably inferred was an act of praise. These inferences refer more to He's short-term than long-term goals. Another set of inferences, "to avoid the question and a fight," reflect a different perspective: that He failed to respond to She's question, "Do you like it, sweetheart?" which was read as more than simply a request for information, but rather as an attempt by She to test He's loyalty. These subjects inferred that He really doesn't answer the question to She's satisfaction. Furthermore, it may be the case that He is being insincere or is deliberately flouting Grice's quantity maxim by cooperating (in answering the question) by giving no more of an answer than is necessary.

"She: No, but I mean, do you really like it?" A large percentage of subjects in both groups inferred that She is trying to "probe his response" or to "get the truth," inferring a request for information. The college students were more likely to infer that She was doing more than making a request for information about the hat. About 40 percent of the college students as opposed to 10 percent of the high school students inferred that She wants "to seek praise," an inference that reflects an explicit awareness of She's long-range goal or motives—that she is testing his loyalty by determining if He is sincerely willing to praise her. They, therefore, go beyond the request/probe inference to consider She's motives.

"He: Well, I'll tell you, I know this is the new style and everything like that, and it's probably great. I don't know anything about things like that. Only I like the kind of hat like that blue hat you had. Gee, I like that hat."

Most students inferred these different utterances in terms of one act. A number of students imputed certain traits: that He's being "defensive or nervous" or "honest." One explanation of this inference is that in going on at length, He violates the quantity maxim, implying that he is unsure of himself or that he is deliberately flouting the maxim and therefore is being "honest." However, more college students than high school students inferred underlying motives or goals—that he was "trying to please her" or that he was "being neutral or diplomatic," an indication of their sense of He's long-range goal—to avoid conflict.

These results suggest that the college students were more attuned to the strategies and motives underlying these characters' acts than the high school students.

RESPONSE STUDIES: SOME PRACTICAL SUGGESTIONS

After assigning and reading over five-hundred informal response studies conducted by students in my classes, I can offer some practical suggestions for conducting small-scale descriptive response studies. Because most of my students had little or no background in research, they found these suggestions both necessary and useful. These studies are generally limited to examination of two or three readers' open-ended responses to a test.

Selection of a Topic
Students who formulate a clear question or questions they want to explore are often better able to develop procedures and techniques for eliciting responses than students who have no idea why they are conducting a study. The formulation of questions in advance does not preclude the discovery of certain unexpected phenomena that may have little to do with their original question.

Because the question guides decisions for setting up the study, I often recommend that the question include specific components: reader characteristics; text characteristics; response strategies (or types and methods of eliciting or analyzing response); and a basis for comparison—for example, a contrast of two or more readers with different characteristics, or readers' responses to different texts. Comparison often helps students focus and sharpen their analysis of subjects' responses. One question, for example: "How and why do readers of the same age with different prior experiences in reading literature differ in their ability to predict story outcomes in reading formulaic and nonformulaic stories?" Note that the question addresses all four components. Note also the emphasis on *how* and *why*. Simple determination that readers' predictions will differ does not shed light on response processes. I also ask students to limit their questions to some relatively simple relationship or phenomenon but, again, I stress that they need to be open to unexpected phenomenon.

The other chapters in this book suggest a range of different topics or questions. In discussing the four components involved in a response study, I will propose some other possible topics.

Readers' Characteristics
As this and other chapters amply demonstrate, differences in age, reading ability, prior knowledge, social experiences, attitudes, personality, "identity style," needs, purpose for reading, level of cognitive development, cognitive flexibility, level of moral purpose for reading *all* influence response. Some of these phenomena can be determined by paper-and-pencil measures for which, ideally, there is some established validity and reliability. Students could compare subjects who represent different levels or extremes for any of these characteristics. Take, for example,

cognitive flexibility. Perry (1981) has defined a number of stages in the development of cognitive flexibility or reflective judgment.

People at the lower end of his scale, whom he defines as "dualists," conceive of the world in absolute, rigid "black and white" categories, believing that whatever an authority says is the "gospel truth." In contrast, persons at higher stages are more flexible; they are able to espouse or understand two different perspectives or ideas simultaneously, and, at a higher level, they are able to test the validity of competing ideas. (King, 1982, has developed a paper-and-pencil measure, the Reflective Judgment Questionnaire, that can be used to determine readers' stage of reflective judgment). By comparing readers at different levels, a student may find that readers who are rigid "dualists" are less apt to explore optional responses or to question the validity of a character's or narrator's assertion because they assume that there is a "one right answer."

Because most students won't be using paper-and-pencil measures, they can simply ask subjects to talk about their own previous reading experiences, attitudes, or beliefs. By selecting friends, relatives, and spouses as subjects, students can draw on what they know about the subjects in explaining their responses. Friends are also more willing to cooperate with the student.

Characteristics of Texts

Differences in texts' difficulty, complexity, depth, quality, predictability, evocativeness, subject matter, tone, attitude, and historical period *all* influence response. Students joften select texts with contrasting features in order to compare the same reader's responses to these different texts. However, I caution students not to assume that the text is an autonomous, independent force. I ask them to consider how text features mesh with what the reader brings to the text. For example, a reader's ability to make inferences about dialogue may have much more to do with his or her knowledge of social and literary conventions than with the difficulty of the dialogue per se. Even though the vocabulary of a proposing scene in a romance novel may be quite difficult, a knowledgeable reader of romance novels may readily understand the characters' acts, beliefs, and goals. In contrast, while the vocabulary of a Beckett play may be quite simple, a reader may experience difficulty in inferring actions, beliefs, and goals because they have had little experience with experimental drama. Students could study the interplay between text and reader by examining how readers alter their expectations or prototypical schema as they move through the text. For example, in responding to the Mary/John exchange in the teaching assistants' office, Susan shifts from a teacher/student schema to what could be called a "romance" schema. Students can then focus on how cues in the text trigger shifts in schema, or how schema shape or guide the cues readers attend to. When subjects reread texts, particularly poems, it is possible to study how readers recognize that their initial hypotheses were inadequate to carry them through from one reading to the next.

Students could also study shifts in response types, or strategies with different texts. As Jacobsen (1982) found, some texts that provide more "reader cues" invite more engagement response than less accessible texts.

Elicitation of Response

The most challenging aspect of conducting a response study is eliciting open-ended responses so that a subject responds in a comfortable, uninhibited manner. Students often learn that they "got what they asked for." A series of literal level convergent questions simply yields a series of one-word answers. Certain types of response formats generate certain types of responses. My own research comparing written and taped/oral responses (Beach, 1973) indicated that a written format fosters more interpretative responses and a taped/oral format fosters more engagement/autobiographical responses.

My own recommendation for collecting open-ended responses is to have a reader respond on tape or in writing *while* reading a text, followed by an interview. Because a student then has both "private" and interview responses, he or she is not left with an analysis of just interview responses that may have been shaped by the interviewer. An interviewer can not only elicit further responses, but, by going back over the taped or written responses, ask subjects to describe or explain their own responses.

As every teacher knows, the quality of the questions developed for an interview affects the quality of response elicited. While it is important to carefully prepare a set of questions—particularly if a student is making comparisons of different subjects' answers—it is equally important not to be bound solely to those questions. One benefit of the interview is that a student can probe responses, asking subjects to cite examples from a text, clarify their response, infer relationships to similar texts or experiences, and so on.

Students try to base their questions or probes on the types of responses or heuristic strategies they are interested in studying. Responses to questions about reasons for characters' speech acts can therefore be analyzed according to the nature or depth of that reason. As previously noted, if a student is interested in subjects' assumptions or attitudes, he or she can probe their reasons in order to tease out assumptions (see Ennis, 1969, for a discussion of "gap-filling" probes in explanation). Or subjects could be asked to identify problems or difficulties in understanding texts; then reasons for those problems and information from the text that could clarify their misunderstandings. Responses to these questions could then be analyzed according to a problem-solving analysis or "protocol analysis" used in composition research (Swarts, Flower and Hayes, in press).

Students can also ask subjects to write literary texts, for example, containing dialogue, and then ask subjects to respond to their own writing (Vardell, 1982). The dialogue or dialogue revisions can then be analyzed according to the extent to which students intentionally use dialogue to portray character or theme. Similarly, subjects could role-play texts which would require them to translate their understanding of characters or story conflict into their own dialogue. Follow-up interviews could ask subjects to explain how and why they employed their own dialogue.

Analysis of Response

I have already discussed strategies for conducting content analysis of responses using categories or the "clustering technique." If students are interested in developing categories for analyzing quality, I refer them to the primary trait scoring systems developed by the National Assessment of Educational Progress for use in the Reading/ Literature Assessment (Education Commission of the States, 1981). Many students do not use categories because they require the use of more than one judge as a check on agreement. They can also, as Bleich and others argue, limit understanding of the complexities of response. However, if students do not simply impose categories and are skillful in interpreting the category results, categories can be useful, particularly in making comparisons.

If students are simply not using categories, I urge them to read over the elicited responses numerous times from a range of different perspectives. They can then inductively intuit certain consistent patterns or strategies (see, for example, Jacobsen's, 1981 discussion of differences in readers' ability to "enter" the world of the text). For example, students could trace the way subjects link separate bits of dialogue according to characters' goals or plans. Students can also chart the evolution of subjects' responses across time, comparing their responses from beginning to the end of a course (Petrosky, 1982).

In trying to explain response phenomena, students find it useful to fall back on one or more theories of the response process espoused in this volume (see also Tompkins, 1980). On the other hand, students need to recognize the limitation of a rigid application of any theoretical perspective.

SUMMARY

In summary, I argue that readers differ in their tacit knowledge of speech-act, social, and literary conventions; these differences are reflected in readers' responses to literary dialogue. My analysis of Susan's and Diane's responses illustrate relatively advanced readers' ability to infer characters' beliefs, traits, and goals from dialogue.

I also compared college and high school student response to a one-act play. The fact that the college students made more inferences about characters' long-range goals than did high school students reflects a difference in their prior knowledge of conventions. I concluded with some practical suggestions for conducting small-scale descriptive response studies which could further illuminate the unique complexities of a reader's response to literature.

REFERENCES

Anderson, R., Spiro, R., & Montague, W. (Eds.). *Schooling and the acquisition of knowledge*. Hillsdale, NJ: Lawrence Erlbaum, 1977.

Anderson, R. The notion of schemata and education: General discussion of the conference. In R. Anderson et al., *Schooling*. 1977.

Austin, J.L. *How to do things with words*. J. Urmson, Ed. Cambridge: Harvard University Press, 1962.

Bates, E. *Language and context: The acquisition of pragmatics*. New York: Academic Press, 1976.

Bach, K., & Harnish, R. *Linguistic communication and speech acts*. Cambridge, MA: MIT Press, 1979.

Beach, R. The literary response process of college students. *The English Record*, 1973, *14*, 32–39.

Beach, R. Differences between high school and college students' inferences about literary dialogue. Paper presented at Annual Meeting of American Educational Research Association, San Fransico, 1979.

Beach, R. Attitudes, social conventions and response to literature. *Journal of Research and Development in Education*, 1983, *16*, 47–54.

Bransford, J., Nitsch, K., & Franks, J. Schooling and facilitation of knowing. In R. Anderson et al., *Schooling*. 1977.

Britton, J. Language and the nature of learning: An individual perspective. In J. Squire (Ed.), *The teaching of English: The seventy-sixth yearbook of the national society for the study of education*. Chicago: University of Chicago Press, 1977.

Bobrow, D., & Collins, A. (Eds.). *Representation and understanding: Studies in cognitive science*. New York: Academic Press, 1975.

Broudy, H. Types of knowledge and purposes of education. In R. Anderson et al., *Schooling*. 1977.

Brown, R. How readers understand fiction. Paper presented at the Minnesota Center for Advanced Studies in Language, Style, and Literary Theory, University of Minnesota, 1975.

Brown, P., & Levinson, S. Universals in language usage: Politeness phenomena. In E. Goody (Ed.), *Questions and politeness: Strategies in social interaction*. London: Cambridge University Press, 1978.

Bruce, B. *Plans and social actions*. (Technical Report No. 34.) Urbana, IL: Center for the Study of Reading, 1977.

Cooper M. Implications in fictional conversations from *Days of Our Lives* and *Mary Hartman, Mary Hartman*. *Centrum*, 1977, *5*, 5–19.

Cooper, C., & Michalak, D. A note on determining response styles in research on response to literature. *Research in the Teaching of English*, 1981, *15*, 163–169.

Education Commission of the States. *Reading, thinking, and writing: Results for the 1979–80 national assessment of reading and literature*. Denver, CO, 1981.

Ennis, R. *Logic in teaching*. Englewood Cliffs, NJ: Prentice-Hall, 1969.

Gallo, D. Toward a more effective assessment of poetry teaching methods. *Research in the Teaching of English*, 1968, *2*, 125–141.

Grice, P. Logic and conversation. In P. Cole & J. Morgan (Eds.), *Syntax and semantics, III: Speech acts*. New York: Academic Press, 1975.

Hancher, M. The classification of cooperative illocutionary acts. *Language in Society*, 1979, *8*, 1–14.

Jacobsen, M. Looking for literary space in the willing suspension of disbelief revisited. *Research in the Teaching of English*, 1982, *16*, 21–38.

King, P. Reflective judgment questionnaire. Unpublished manuscript, 1982. (Available from Department of College Student Personnel, Education Building, Bowling Green State University, Bowling Green, OH 43403.)

Labov, W. & Fanshel, D. *Therapeutic discourse, psychotherapy as conversation*. New York: Academic Press, 1977.

Odell, L., & Cooper, C. Describing responses to works of fiction. *Research in the teaching of English*, 1976, *10*, 203–225.

Ohmann, R. Instrumental style: Notes on the theory of speech as action. In B. Kachra & H. Stahlke (Eds.), *Current trends in stylistics*. Edmonton, Alberta: Linguistic Research, Inc., 1972.

Olson, D. The language of instruction: On the literate bias of schooling. In R. Anderson et al., *Schooling*. 1977.

Perry, W. Cognitive and ethical growth: The making of meaning. In A. Chickering (Eds.), *The modern American college*. San Francisco: Jossey-Bass Publishers, 1981.

Petrosky, A. From story to essay: Reading and writing. *College Composition and Communication*, 1982, *23*, 19–36.

Pratt, M. The ideology of speech-act theory. *Centrum New Series*, 1981, *1*, 5–18.

Purves, A., & Rippere, V. *Elements of writing about a literary work: A study of response to literature*. Urbana, IL: National Council of Teachers of English, 1968.

Searle, J. *Speech acts*. Cambridge, England: Cambridge University Press, 1969.

Searle, J. A taxonomy of illocutionary acts. In K. Gunderson (Ed.), *Minnesota studies in the philosophy of language*. Minneapolis: University of Minnesota Press, 1975.

Spiro, R., Bruce, B., & Brewer, W. (Eds.). *Theoretical issues in reading comprehension*. Lawrence Erlbaum Associates: Hillsdale, New Jersey, 1980.

Steinmann, M. Competence in writing. In R. Beach, & D. Pearson (Eds.), *Perspectives on literary*. Urbana, IL: National Council of Teachers of English, 1978.

Steinmann, M., & Brown, R. Multiple competencies. Paper presented at the 4th Annual Conference on New Ways of Analyzing Variation, Georgetown University, Washington, D.C., 1977.

Stiles, W. *Manual for a taxonomy of verbal response modes*. Chapel Hill: Institute for Research in Social Science, University of North Carolina, 1978.

Stiles, W. Intersubjective illocutionary acts. *Language in Society*, 1981, *10*, 227–249.

Swarts, H., Flower, L. & Hayes, J. Designing protocol analysis: An introduction. In R. Beach and L. Bridwell (Eds.), *New directions in composition research*. New York: Guilford Press (in press).

Tompkins, J. *Reader-response criticism*. Baltimore: Johns Hopkins University Press, 1980.

Updike, J. Tomorrow and tomorrow and so forth. In R. Gold (Ed.), *Point of departure*. New York: Dell, 1967.

Vardell, S. The development in use and understanding of literary conventions in children's reading and writing of stories. Unpublished doctoral dissertation, University of Minnesota, 1982.

Chapter 8
Studying the Perception of Poetry

Eugene R. Kintgen

Department of English
Indiana University

The study of literary response has a long and distinguished history which stretches from I. A. Richards's seminal *Practical Criticism* to a host of current practitioners (Purves and Beach, 1972; Cooper, 1976). Most of this research has dealt with the expressed response to the literary work rather than with the evocation of the work during the act of reading, and for good reason: there seems to be no way to study the dynamics of reading without interrupting or otherwise altering the act. But, as I argue in greater detail elsewhere (Kintgen, 1983), the tape recorder allows us to study something quite close to the reading process itself, rather than a later response to that process. To illustrate this, I will first introduce my general approach, then discuss a range of responses to a syntactic problem in a poem, and then deal with the experience of one reader reading a poem. On the basis of these discussions, I will finally make a few suggestions for future research along these lines.

I wanted to find out how expert readers actually comprehended a poem, how they converted a series of marks on the page into a unified mental conception. Presumably, there were discrete stages in this understanding, independent and relatively elementary cognitive processes which were applied sequentially to the text at hand. But what were they? Did all readers use exactly the same elementary processes, or was there some variation in individual inventories? Did readers have favorite organizations of processes; did they perhaps rely more heavily on some than on others? How much did the text affect the choice of cognitive processes: did some readers use the same processes, no matter what the poem? Did some poems require certain kinds of processing that others did not? Given a specific problem in a text, would all readers solve it the same way? And if not, what was the range of variation?

To find the answers to these and similar questions, I asked eight graduate students enrolled in a seminar I taught on the perception and comprehension of literature as well as eight faculty members to verbalize into a cassette recorder whatever they did while they tried to understand a poem. The poem and the instructions I gave them follow:

Winter Piece

Black town, beige woods, green frozen creek
All now, this moment, stilled,

Our steeple clock
Transfixed, the mineral twigs
Intact, this park's arterial loss
Suspended, do rebuke me,
Gone amiss
In minute thefts to break
My bond, who set my face, my sticks,
My springs, against a thief,
Time on my crux
To nail: my thirty-three
Deliquesce, so sly, I might now wink
My hand, bone, lymph, away:
Not all my ink
Keeps to my word or want,
Arrests the sun, resurrects the tree,
Or translates out of my water
So little wine:
All miracles not done.

Tick, town; rot, wood;
Run, you winter crook, run.
—Gibson, 1948

Please try to verbalize everything you do in coming to a complete understanding of this poem, as if, say, you were preparing to be on a panel discussing any and all aspects of it. Try not to censor anything—if you read the poem several times, if you start in on one train of thought and then switch to another, if stray thoughts occur to you, if you look some words up in a dictionary or use any other references—whatever, please try to do it verbally rather than silently so it will be included. This verbalizing will undoubtedly interfere to a certain extent with your normal practice, and may be a bit frustrating, but please try to include everything.

I chose the poem partially for its unfamiliarity—I was reasonably confident that everybody reading it would be doing so for the first time—but mainly for the opportunities it offered: though short, it is highly structured; the initial triplet of town, woods, and creek is echoed in various triplets throughout the poem (the clock, mineral twigs, and arterial loss; face, sticks, and springs; hand, bone, and lymph; the three miracles not done; and the coda at the end). It offers a number of syntactic and lexical problems, a few allusions to be identified, and a clear—if untraditional—form. There are two areas of concern in the poem—one relating to time, specifically the stopping of time, and the other to religious history—that have to be unified. Perhaps best of all, to some extent it turns literary expectations upside-down: instead of exploiting a kind of pathetic fallacy in which the frozen scene either reflects the speaker's own inner frigidity or reminds him of it, the poem reverses the situation, so that the frozen scene rebukes the narrator for his own lack of stasis; and the narrator, rather than seeing himself crucified by events, is out to crucify something else. To ensure that my readers would confront these rich interpretive possibilities, I tried to forestall any lapse into biographical or historical speculation by omitting the author's name.

The tapes the readers recorded were typed up into protocols (when double-spaced on an elite typewriter, protocols run between six and 28 pages); it is these that I have mainly worked with. It seems to me that there are two basic ways you can analyze the protocols: you can take a particular problem in the poem—finding the meaning of a word, identifying a reference, unraveling a difficult syntactic construction, and so on—and study the range of variation in approaches to that problem, or you can take a particular reader and study the development of his or her understanding of the poem by examining the entire protocol. I will consider later the possibility of unifying these approaches, but first I will illustrate each.

DIFFERENCES IN SYNTACTIC PERCEPTION

As an example of the first approach, we will observe how the sixteen readers attempted to solve a syntactic problem. Syntactic problems are particularly instructive to study for a number of reasons (see Kintgen, 1978b, for further discussion and examples). First, though different theories do not always agree, linguistic analysis provides what may be thought of as a reasonably objective method of describing the situation. This differs significantly from identifying an allusion, interpreting what a symbol symbolizes, or deciding whether a particular meaning of a lexical item is activated in the poem, since in all these cases there is little recourse except to intersubjective agreement. Second, the perception and comprehension of syntax are usually so automatic that most readers are almost unaware of the syntax of the poem and the demands it makes on them. By studying a syntactic problem we will see at least the conscious mechanisms people use when syntax demands it. Finally, studies have indicated that different subjects may understand some constructions differently (Langendoen et al., 1973; Kintgen, 1978a); it will be interesting to see whether there is much variation in the perception of this (apparently the most determinate) aspect of the poem.

Of the various syntactic difficulties in the poem, two are absolutely crucial: the referent of *gone amiss* in line 7, and the antecedent of *who* in line 9: readers who differ in their assignments of these references will have entirely different understandings of the poem. We will look at the first of these. By purely linguistic analysis, *gone amiss* could modify either of two constructions: the *me* it immediately follows, or—somewhat less plausibly—the compound subject of *do rebuke*. Eight readers thought that *gone amiss* modified *me*, and four of them had little or no difficulty with the construction; sometimes, as in the first example, they barely mentioned it:

> All these things rebuke me, *gone amiss in minute thefts to break my bond.*
> Gone amiss in minute thefts, meaning the thefts weren't successful, apparently.
> (H, 1-2)[1]

---

[1] The protocols have been lightly edited to avoid repetitions, false starts, and so forth. Ellipsis marks indicate that a little has been left out; asterisks, that at least a page has been skipped. The readers are

Okay: *do rebuke me, gone amiss. Gone amiss.* I was looking for the grammatical tie here. Me gone amiss as in done amiss? Me, I've gone amiss in minute tiny thefts . . . (A, 2)

suspended, do rebuke me, the person who's gone amiss in minute thefts. (C, 1)

Do rebuke me, gone amiss. Gone amiss—the me—that seems to refer to me. The me has gone amiss . . . (L, 3)

One reader puzzled over the construction the first time through, but then decided that *gone amiss* modifies *me*:

our transfixed clock, the intact mineral twigs, the suspended arterial loss of the park rebuke me. Me, gone amiss? Or the clock, twigs, and loss gone amiss? Don't know. * * * *Do rebuke me, gone amiss,* assuming it's, presumably he's gone amiss. * * * *Do rebuke me, gone amiss in minute thefts to break my bond.* He presumably, is gone amiss in minute thefts to break his bond. How? How? (J, 1, 2, 6)

Another reader noticed twice that the construction was potentially ambiguous, but concluded both times that it referred to *me*:

Gone amiss in minute thefts to break my bond. Gone amiss is syntactically ambiguous, anyhow, at least in the first notice. It seems to refer to *me*: that's the reason that the me, whoever it is, is being rebuked. * * * Could the *gone amiss* refer to anybody else, to anything else? Could it refer to the other things— the clock, the twigs, the arterial loss? *To break my bond.* Let's see how—the thing is ambiguous. I'm assuming it does refer to *me*. (B, 2, 10)

Another repeated this same process of deciding that *gone amiss* modified *me* and then returning to the passage and wondering again whether it could modify anything else six times.

The next example is not altogether clear, but it seems that at first the reader concludes that nature, specifically the noun phrases in lines 3 to 6, has gone amiss, since they are associated with the thefts. Later he changes his mind:

Now I continue with this grammar, try to get some sense out of it—*do rebuke me, gone amiss in minute thefts.* Now the minute thefts, it would seem to me, would be connected with the loss, the arterial loss, the loss, the mineral twigs perhaps, the fact that winter has crept up slowly and has taken life of some kind out of the surroundings, slowly, minutely. * * * As I look this over now, it seems to me there is a direct opposition here between the kind of suspension, as in the natural world, and the what might be called entropy, the running down of the speaker's own body . . . *To break my bond, do rebuke me, gone amiss*: that he has gone amiss, he who has set his face is the way I see it now. (M, 2, 6)

---

identified by initials. Reference in this section is by page; in describing M's protocol below, the numbers refer to lines in the protocol in the Appendix. I'd like to thank Janet Pocock for transcribing the tapes, and Indiana University for a Faculty Grant-in-Aid of Research.

The interesting thing about this excerpt is that although the reader announces his intention to try to figure out the syntax, he relies on the sense of the passage rather than on any syntactic considerations: at first, he connects *gone amiss* with nature because nature seems to be associated with the thefts; later, he connects the *gone amiss* with *me* because the speaker, in his inability to arrest his own running down or entropy, seems to be at fault. In both cases, the syntactic assignment depends on a prior semantic decision.

Of the other eight readers, one never confronted the problem—he was distracted by the reference of *who* in *who set*—and four decided that the phrase modified the aspects of the natural scene specified in the first few lines. Two made this interpretation as quickly and automatically as those who had related the phrase to *me*:

> And if we take the *gone amiss* to refer to the speaker, but more probably the subject of *gone amiss* is the same as the subject of do *rebuke me*. (P, 1)

> It's probably they do *rebuke me*. They are *gone amiss in minute thefts to break my bond* . . . All these natural—I mean all these suspensions and transfixions do rebuke me. They're gone amiss in minute thefts. (S, 2, 3)

Two other readers considered several possibilities before settling on an interpretation:

> *Gone amiss in minute thefts to break my bond.* Who has gone amiss? * * * I would stop time. I would, by means of my poetry, arrest the sun, make something immortal. Perform a miracle. And yet I am rebuked. Perhaps I have not gone amiss. Perhaps the syntax is just that the stopped clock, the frozen twigs, perhaps these things have themselves *gone amiss in minute thefts to break my bond.* * * * Nature has gone amiss for a moment but it comes out again. (F, 1, 5, 8)

> So those are all *suspended.* They *do rebuke me.* Now is it me who's *gone amiss*? And *gone amiss in minute thefts to break my bond*? Well, no. Well then maybe since it's something going to break my bond, then it's probably not me who's initiating the action. Maybe it's them again, those bits of scenery which are in minute thefts to break my bond, or they're doing something to break my bond. * * * All of those things do rebuke me, me who has gone amiss in minute thefts to break my bond. Well, no I think that they have gone amiss to break my bond. They have appeared this way to me, or somehow gotten distorted out of a natural, dynamic, and lively aspect, they've gotten frozen in, to show me that I've become frozen in, that I ought to break my bond. (W, 2–3, 7)

Again it should be noticed how much of the evidence readers use in making a difficult syntactic decision is actually semantic. The first reader prefers not to think that performing a poetic miracle could be characterized as going amiss and deserving a rebuke; both problems clear up if something else goes amiss and rebukes the poet while in that errant state. The second reader, taking *bond* as a "shackle" or "fetter," reconciles his feeling that breaking such bonds is a good thing with the poem by seeing the frozen aspects of nature as that which has gone amiss.

Semantic evidence clearly predominates over syntactic for the three readers who concluded that the subject of *gone amiss* was something other than the two possibilities we have considered so far:

> And now I'm in a notion of time, that it is time that has gone amiss, it is time that has, that is the thief, and time that has nailed him on the crux, the crux being this moment, this fixed moment, this stilled moment. (G, 2)

> *Gone amiss*. What's gone amiss? What's the subject of that? * * * Next, *gone amiss*: I'm still baffled about what has gone amiss. Is it the mere fact that the steeple clock is transfixed, the mineral twigs intact, and the park's arterial loss suspended? Is that something that's gone amiss? Is the fact that time has somehow halted, has time halted simply because it's winter? Is it the natural world, is it the life world that is halted? Is that's what's gone amiss? * * * *Gone amiss in minute thefts to break my bond*. Mínute and minúte thefts to break my bond. *Gone amiss*: what has gone amiss? The promised rebirth? The promised life here? (E, 1, 2, 10)

> But these twigs are suspended and they're rebuking the unknown author or whoever the me represents in this case. Something has gone amiss. Perhaps this is the green frozen earth. Everything is still, to include the clock. Wooden twigs have become mineral, they're suspended from what we know not. Obviously something has gone amiss. * * * *Gone amiss in minute thefts*: something has gone wrong in small ways. His bond, perhaps, with God. * * * Everything has stopped, everything is suspended, rebuking the poet, gone amiss. Things have gone awry. Why is *gone amiss* a line in itself? It must be to focus our attention on it for some reason, but why? *Gone amiss in minute thefts to break my bond, to set my face, my sticks, my springs against a thief, time on my crux to nail*. If we think of the me as the poet, what has gone amiss then? * * * *This park's arterial loss suspended*: all the leaves are gone from the arterial branches of the trees. They're dormant, like suspended animation: they're just there. And all of this is making fun of the poet—the helplessness, the powerlessness of the poet to do anything about this dormancy of life. Perhaps this is what has gone amiss or gone awry. (D, 2–3, 5, 7, 9)

In all three examples here the reader abstracts something out of the poem, reifies it, and makes it the syntactic head for *gone amiss*. For the first reader, it is "time," for the second, something like the natural order of the world, for the third, the poet's inability to counteract the stasis of the winter scene. Their goal is not to identify something which *gone amiss* could modify syntactically, but rather something which would be a plausible semantic agent.

From these excerpts we can perhaps hazard a few conclusions. The most obvious is that poetic syntax can force itself into the reader's consciousness. This point is worth making only because many discussions of response seem to ignore syntax altogether. When it does, readers try to apply their normal mechanisms of syntactic perception—in this example, the fact that modifying phrases must have heads to modify. But when these mechanisms do not automatically or immediately provide a solution—and these solutions are not necessaily "right," since some of those who settled on the subject of *do rebuke* as the antecedent for *gone amiss* did so as confidently as those who identified *me*—semantic considerations are likely to take over: the reader first decides, in a general way, what the passage (or the whole poem) means, and then tries to fit the syntax to that conception. As the last three readers illustrate, the fit does not have to be particularly good, since all were willing to accept as part of the syntax of the poem something that never actually occurred in the poem.

Linguistic analysis may thus provide a description of the syntax of the poem, but it does not describe how readers perceive that syntax. This raises several questions. If linguistic descriptions do not correspond to readers' perceptions, are there nevertheless some areas of overlap betwen them? What kinds of conscious or unconscious knowledge of syntax do readers activate when confronted with a syntactic problem? Do readers differ in their store of linguistic knowledge or in their ability to use it? Can one define basic perceptual or cognitive styles for individual readers based in part on the relative weight accorded semantic and syntactic factors in solving syntactic problems? More speculatively, can what seems problematic to a reader be related to his cognitive or perceptual style? These questions are framed in terms of syntax, because we have looked at a syntactic problem, but they clearly apply, *mutatis mutandis*, to all levels of linguistic description— phonological, morphological, lexical, and textual. Taken together, they imply a description, not of the text, but of the knowledge structures necessary to perceive and comprehend the text.

ELEMENTARY PERCEPTUAL PROCESSES

The second basic approach in studying the perception of poetry is to analyze the activity of one reader. Here we are interested in discovering both the basic processes the reader uses in coming to an understanding of the poem and the temporal development of his conception of the poem. To illustrate this, I have included as an appendix the protocol of M, a full professor who worked on "Winter Piece" for about half an hour, producing about 230 lines of typescript. The protocol is interesting because of the economy of its interpretive moves even though M insisted from the beginning that he disliked the poem, and because there is one of those sudden illuminations when a reader realizes that he has been on the wrong track and completely changes his way of looking at the poem. It would be a good idea to read through the protocol before proceeding; the shift occurs at line 164.

The first thing to do with an individual protocol is to divide it into units—words, phrases, or clauses—that seem to express single cognitive operations. This initial segmentation must be relatively impressionistic, simply because there is no isomorphic relation between thoughts and their expressions, and consequently no formal algorithm for analysis. It seems best to treat it merely as a first hypothesis, open to later modification if further analysis requires it. In purely practical terms, it is best to overdifferentiate at first, and later to combine succesive units assigned to the same elementary process. (The slashes in the protocol in the appendix indicate my segmentation.)

The real problem here is the development of an inventory of elementary processes to characterize the activity of the reader. Schemes such as those proposed by Alan Purves in *Elements of Writing About a Literary Work* (Purves and Rippere, 1968) and by Lee Odell and Charles Cooper in "Describing Responses to Works of Fiction" (1976) are useful, except that they are designed to describe the statements readers make when writing relatively formal esays about their reading; they deal with the expressed response rather than with the evocation of the work during reading. This differs from the present research situation in three major ways. First, there is the problem of rhetorical contamination: the reader's conception of how knowledge should be presented in a class paper, no matter how rudimentary, is indistinguishable in the final product from the knowledge itself, and so it is never clear whether a particular statement reflects knowledge of the work or conception of the rhetorical situation. Second, any written response—and especially an assigned paper—is produced at some temporal distance from the experience of reading, and so is at best a memorial reconstruction of the reading rather than a report of it, with all the blurring and loss of detail that entails. Third, limitations on the length of class essays (often to five hundred words) hardly encourage much specificity about the details of the reading process. At best, one gets summary re-creations of small proportions of that process, and much more frequently, later reactions to some summary of that act. These schemes, then, though they are impressive when applied to the expressed response, are less useful in describing the act of reading.

More useful for the present study (because it is more oriented toward identifying the specific processes which occur during mental activity) is the type of production system, or information-processing, approach used by Allen Newell and Herbert Simon in *Human Problem Solving* (1972). As one of their tasks, they asked subjects to solve cryptarithmetic problems, puzzles in which two words each of whose letters represent a digit are added together to form a third; the subject must "solve" the addition by figuring out what digit each letter represents (e.g., DONALD + GERALD = ROBERT or SEND + MORE = MONEY). The subjects verbalized what they were doing into a tape recorder; later, the tapes were transcribed and analyzed. The result of such analysis is, typically, a relatively small number of basic processes such as *assign* a value to a letter, *test* the assigned value, *process* a column, *find* a column containing a given letter, and so forth, which can be applied over and over until the problem is solved. These processes are stated as part of a production system, a completely explicit (i.e., programmable) listing of the processes and when to apply them.

Obviously, understanding a poem and solving a cryptarithmetic problem are vastly different undertakings. The domain of the latter is severely restricted, the processes likely to be useful are limited (note that even subtraction, multiplication, and division are useless), and there is a way to test the validity of the final answer. None of this is true of understanding poetry. A poem may refer to anything past, present, or future, real or imaginary, and most good poems exist in a mode that makes these terms seem inadequate. The processes likely to be useful in understanding a poem are not limited in any way, since different readers may utilize a wide variety of memories, associations, allusions, and so on in their attempts to comprehend the poem. Finally, there is no one "right" answer to a poem, no one "correct" interpretation, and consequently no way to test the validity of a reader's understanding. In short, understanding a poem is an open-ended process.

In spite of these differences, however, it is worthwhile trying to characterize what a reader does in reading a poem in terms of similar elementary processes simply because psychological economy suggests that there should not be many elementary processes; intellectual range can be achieved by allowing relatively few different processes to apply recursively to a relatively large set of memories and perceptions, just as a transformational grammar uses relatively few different transformations and phrase structure rules and a large inventory of lexical items to generate an indefinitely large set of sentences. The list of processes below is tentative; more are perhaps necessary, and some on my list can be further analyzed. But these 21 processes illustrate the kinds of operations I have found in my protocols, and I would hypothesize that they (or some extension of them) will describe the activities of any reader.

- Comment, Narrate
- Read, Select, Locate
- Word, Phonology, Syntax, Paraphrase, Form
- Deduce, Generalize, Connect: Poem, Connect: Nature, Connect: History, Connect: Literature
- Test, Justify, Qualify, Specify
- Interpret

First, there are two processes that are ancillary to the others, and they stem from the fact that the subjects I used were not specifically trained in verbalizing their thoughts. *Comment* refers to any personal comment the reader may make about the poem: what he is doing, where he is, and so forth: "and I'm a little put off already," "I guess at . . . my impression . . . and this is unfortunate, is that at first reading I don't particularly like the poem" (4, 8–10). *Narrate* refers to the reader's explanation or narration of what he is doing; he narrates about his thought processes rather than directly verbalizing them: "I'm going to read the poem now as I would to myself" (7–8).

In the first group of processes dealing with the poem itself are those which provide the reader with something to work on. The simplest of these is *Read*, in which the reader just reads either the whole poem or a portion of it. M reads the entire poem through before beginning work on it, and (like most other readers) reads a phrase or a line before commenting on it. More specific is *Select*, which specifies just what the reader is going to work with. Sometimes *Select* and *Read* coincide, but often a passage is read and then some part of it is selected for special comment: "*Our steeple clock transfixed, the mineral twigs intact, this park's arterial loss suspended, do rebuke me,* and I've got to stop here. The *do rebuke me*" (22–23) illustrates a *Read* followed by a *Narrate* and *Select*. A third operation in this group is *Locate*, which occurs when the reader either searches for something in the poem or specifies where something is to be found: "the *away* coming at the end of the next line" (120).

The third group of processes consists of the simplest operations, linguistically defined, that can be performed on the text. These proceses are severely underdifferentiated, partly because they rely on psycholinguistic proceses which are themselves only vaguely understood, and partly because M's protocol dos not contain enough references to them to allow much fuller analysis. In fact, the first is not contained in M's protocol at all: *Phonology* refers to any comment about the phonology of the poem, including such things as rhyme, alliteration, assonance. *Word* refers primarily to looking up or stating the meaning or etymology of the words in the poem but also to comments about diction, lexical choice, and so on. "My dictionary suggests that 'rebuke' means to criticize, reprove sharply, to reprimand, and then obsolete meaning, to check or repress" (47–49). *Word* also includes identification of a pun (i.e., that a word has two meanings that may operate simultaneously). *Syntax* is the process by which the reader attempts to unravel any aspect of the syntax of the poem: "What is the subject of that verb *do*? . . . it is the clock, the mineral twigs, and the park's arterial loss suspended" (24–25). *Syntax* can hardly be an elementary process, since presumably the perception of syntax requires hypothesis formation and testing on its own (Bever, 1974; Fodor, Bever, and Garrett, 1974); and as the first selection of this paper illustrated, there is a great deal of variation in the way different readers process syntax. Since this is a category that obviously needs more work, I have also included here comments on tone, which could well be a process by itself, except that I am not clear on the relationship between illocutionary force, which should probably be considered part of syntax, and tone.

Paraphrase refers to a very close restatement of what the poem says, either by a kind of linguistic transformation or by substitution of synonyms: "*Time on my crux to nail*. To nail time on my crux" (84–85) illustrates a *Read* followed by *Paraphrase*. Unfortunately, not all cases are this clear, and *Paraphrase* often shades off into what we will later call *Deduce*, which deals with the implications of what is said. For instance, "So these thefts are somehow working toward breaking a bond and nailing" (89) represents M's understanding of the construction, even though it is deducing something to say that the thefts work toward anything. In general, *Paraphrase* is used when the reader is trying to ascertain what the poem *says*; when he moves on to what it *means*, some other process is usually being used. The final member of this group is, like *Syntax*, underdifferentiated, mainly because M spends so little time on it. *Form* refers to any comments about the form of the poem: meter, line length, stanzaic pattern, the placement of words within lines, and so on: "And I wonder whether there is some extra weight given to that word *stilled*, the way it comes at the end of that second line" (15–16). Even here, *Form* is not pure; it is being used to *Justify* a *Connect* (for these, see below) between an aspect of form (*stilled* at the end of the line) and content.

The operations in the next group seem to deal with what we think of as interpretation itself, since they are concerned with identifying allusions, establishing connections, and finding implications. The first operation here is *Deduce*, which covers two slightly different processes. First, there is the identification of what a unit of the poem, a word, or a phrase implies: "*Keeps to*, as if his ink is in some way recalcitrant, won't bend to his own will, wants to go in another direction, won't be controlled, I suppose, won't express what he wishes" (144–46). This is a kind of extended paraphrase, and is distinguished from *Paraphrase* proper only so that *Paraphrase* can be linguistically defined. The other aspect of *Deduce* identifies implications of elements of the poem: "But a bond obviously does refer to the hardening substance like glue or plaster, and suggests again something about this speaker is held together in a kind of artificial manner" (129–31). Here a *Word* is followed by a *Deduce*, which occurs from the comma on. *Deduce* is often identified by the reader's phrasing, particularly by such phrases as *suggests, as if, there's a sense that*, and *in a way*.

The second process in this group is *Generalize*, which analyzes two or more different elements in the text, identifies what they have in common, and then reifies that commonality: "And all of this motionlessness, things having been stilled" (44–45). Here the component of stasis has been extracted from *transfixed, intact*, and *suspended*; it is this the reader sees as rebuking the speaker of the poem. The major difference between *Deduce* and *Generalize* is that the latter deals with two or more different poetic elements and seeks to establish what they have in common. In this way it is very similar to the major process in this group, *Connect*. Actually, there are four different kinds of *Connect*, which might have been given individual names, except that would obscure the fact that very similar mental operations are involved in all cases. Readers may *Connect* an element in the poem with some other poetic element: "and that word *arterial* stands out and suggests to me a connection with the frozen creek"(42–43), *my sticks* suggests "some kind of vague parallel to the mineral twigs and the hands of the steeple clock" (67–68). A poetic element may be *Connected* with an element of nature—and here the term *Refer* might be used, for this is essentially what a word or phrase in the poem refers to: "and *the mineral twigs* could of course refer to the frozen branches" (37–38), "referring to his limbs as sticks" (67). Third, the reader may *Connect* a poetic element with something stored in his memory, usually something from (intellectual) history: "and in some way is related to the crucifixion" (34). This might have been called *Allude*, since it is primarily concerned with identifying historical allusions. Finally, the *Connection* may be made to another literary work, an author, or to literary history in general: "which reminds me of Shakespeare" (155–156), "So if we cannot make our sun stand still, at least we can make it run: that kind of, I suppose, Marvellian notion here" (168–169). This category could have been included in the previous one, except that experienced readers tend to read a literary work against a background of literary history, and it seems a good idea to recognize this fact.

The next group introduces most obviously the possibility of recursion, for the operations here are performed on other operations instead of being performed on the text. *Test* assesses the validity of a previously identified connection, deduction, generalization, syntactic conclusion, and so on: "but that isn't—that isn't the meaning here, not the primary one" (34–35), "Now the *who*, I suppose again could go with the landscape, but that's forced" (63–64). In the latter example, we see a syntactic hypothesis *Tested* and found wanting. The second process in this group is *Justify*, which is similar to *Test* insofar as it deals with the validity of other operations, but differs from it in that it presents evidence of some kind instead of questioning whether there is any: *Justify* can refer either to a poetic element, in which case it adduces almost a kind of *Connection* to explain why something in the poem is happening ("Our steeple clock transfixed, in this sense held motionless, transfixed, I take it, by the winter" (35–36): *Read* followed by *Word* and the *Justify*, which explains what causes the motionlessness), or to a perceptual process, in which case it presents evidence for that process ("as if the speaker is incorporating or including some sort of community here with the reader—it's our clock, not the steeple clock" (17–19)—here a *Justify* for a *Deduce*. Finally, there are two minor processes in this group that serve to modify the scope of a previous operation, *Qualify* and *Specify*. The first reduces the scope of, or mitigates, a previous operation: "There's a formality in a poem whose title is 'Winter Place' that I don't particularly like, unless of course the poem in some way turns out to qualify that stilted kind of language in some fashion" (5–7). Here we have part of a continuing *Justify* for M's initial dislike of the poem *Qualified* at the end by the *unless* clause. In general, the phrases such as *it seems to me*, *I suppose*, and *I take it* with which the protocol is peppered are all examples of *Qualify*. *Specify* restates more specifically something which has just been said: "Also could apply to the clock, the hands of the clock, the workings of the clock" (40–41) shows a connection between the mineral twigs and the clock which is further specified in the hands and workings of the clock.

In a column by itself is *Interpret*, a category containing processes I cannot now account for otherwise. For instance, "Maybe there is somethng within him which tends to work in another fashion, doesn't want to be still, and there's a—he's being held in check by the stillness of the scene" (51–53) is an attempt to *Justify* the use of 'rebuke,' but the vagueness of the suggestion and the fact that it cannot be related to anything in the poem indicate that it is not really a justification. Or again: "And that perhaps there is a kind of envy, in spite of the bleakness of the situation, of the landscape—in this way, the speaker wanting to be at one with this winter piece [peace?] as a piece which is stark and unmoving" (199–202). Here, I have no way to account for the idea of envy or the desire of the speaker to "be at one" with the landscape.

In other instances, however, what seems to be a reader's interpretation of the poem is analyzable as a sequence of the processes I have identified. Consider the following:

> So that ultimately it's the speaker in a very unusual context, it seems to me: rather than being depressed by the stasis, cold, frigidity of his surroundings because of its suggestion of barrenness, sterility, he's depressed by the contrast, I suppose, between himself as one who runs down constantly, deliquescing slowly, and the kind of stasis, the kind of staying power, that he sees around him in the clock, in the streams, and so on, that he himself would like to nail time in this way. And the contrast between his own flowing down the stream of time and the way winter seems to freeze that movement is, I think, what bothers him here, in the poem. (202–211)

This statement of the general meaning of the poem seems to be built on a number of *Generalizations*—"the stasis, cold, frigidity of his surroundings," "the kind of stasis . . . that he sees around him in the clock, in the streams, and so on"—two *Paraphrases*—"deliquescing slowly," "to nail time"—and several *Deductions*—"its suggestion of barrenness, sterility," "himself as one who runs down constantly," "the kind of staying power," "the way that winter seems to freeze that movement." These are linked together by several *Connections:* the contrast between the static nature and the aging speaker, repeated twice; the connection between the speaker's situation and the Heraclitean stream of life (the speaker's situation here is itself the result of a number of generalizations, deductions, and connections not overtly represented); the contrast between being bothered by the sterility of the situation and being bothered by the difference between the narrator and the situation, and finally, a literary *Connection* in the "unusual context," which is unusual only if you expect something like the pathetic fallacy. In addition, there are a number of obvious qualifications: "It seems to me," "I suppose," "I think." What I cannot account for is how M decides that these various contrasts depress the speaker rather than exhilarate him. That is, right now the following phrases would have to be called *Interpret*: "Being depressed by," "he's depressed by," "what bothers him," and "that he himself would like."

Finally, we have to recognize modalities of the processes as well as the processes themselves: Readers do not always state. Sometimes they question, and sometimes they advance a point so tentatively that it must be considered a hypothesis. These last two processes could perhaps be combined, and contrasted with statements, but the difference between them can be seen in "What is the subject of the verb *do*?" (24) and "I wonder if the word could be an adjective" (108). In general, anything can be questioned or hypothesized about, except perhaps *Read*, and the extent to which a reader questions or hypothesizes rather than states seems to be connected to his interpretive style, as do the processes *Qualify* and *Specify*: M, as I have already said, works very economically, spending little time on hypotheses. Other readers, however, devote almost their entire time to deriving and testing hypotheses: "Could this refer to . . . ?" "Is there a connection between this and that?"

Tentatively, then, there are twenty elementary processes, three modalities, and the wastebasket *Interpret*. Some of the categories, especially *Syntax* and *Form*, are underdifferentiated; others, notably *Deduce* and *Justify*, must be more rigorously defined. Moreover, there may be processes that M does not use on "Winter Piece" that other readers do use, or that he would use elsewhere—*Phonology* is one of these, and there may be others. Even so, in its present form, this scheme of elementary processes accounts for over 95% of what M does, which leaves less than 5% in the *Interpret* category.[2] This suggests that it is reasonable to think that a relatively small number of elementary processes, say about two dozen, may be

---

[2] This is a very approximate figure. To arrive at it, I counted the number of phrases assigned to *interpret* and divided by the total number of phrases in the protocol. This ignores the number of words involved and the importance of the phrases for the understanding of the poem.

able to account for what an experienced reader does when he reads a poem, and that an even smaller number (those in the fourth column, plus perhaps *Justify*) may constitute the core of what we think of as literary interpretation.

In addition to identifying the elementary processes a reader uses, analysis should seek to characterize the temporal course of the entire process of understanding a poem. Ideally, this would take the form of a problem behavior graph, which represents the successive states of knowledge achieved by the subject, and relates each state to the succeeding one by one of the elementary processes (Newell and Simon, 1972). Here, however, to save time and space (problem behavior graphs are tremendously prodigal of both), I will informally characterize the course of M's perception. Like most readers, he begins with a brief introduction (1–8), sets the stage, and follows with a complete reading of the poem. M progresses methodically through the poem, freely interlarding his interpretive efforts with comments on the poem. Most of the first four pages, until a telephone interrupts him at 1.122, consists of going through the poem phrase by phrase, figuring out the meaning of the words, the syntactic constructions, and establishing internal and external connections; the usual progression is something like *Read, Select, Connect*, or *Read, Select, Word*, or *Read, Paraphrase*. M is relatively thorough: he uncovers all the meanings or connections for a word or a phrase before he leaves it, and this results in one progression through the poem with a return to selected portions at the end. (In this way, he differs from many readers who *Select* a word or phrase and then perform just one operation on it—establishing its meaning, settling the syntax of a construction, paraphrasing, or making a connection—before progressing to the next *Select*. This latter method leads to a number of passes through the poem; a dozen is not uncommon.) A turning point occurs in M's protocol at 1.164: working with a *Deduce*—that the sun offers potential warmth to thaw the frozen situation in the first few lines—he suddenly considers the implications of that deduction, that the speaker may, in fact, want to cultivate the frozen situation since it is one way of stopping time (I have considered this move an *Interpret*, but it might be a *Deduce*). From here to the end of his protocol, M moves away from the poem to a certain extent, working with *Generalizations* and *Deductions* rather than phrases from the poem, and establishing *Connections* between these generalizations and deductions rather than between poetic elements and something else.

FUTURE DIRECTIONS

Having illustrated the two basic approaches to the protocols that I have used, I would now like to consider some ways of developing and improving the study of literary perception. The first desideratum is to use readers who are trained in two senses: first, people trained in literary interpretation, and by this I mean, at the very least, good graduate students or outstanding undergraduates. The perceptual processes of any reader can be interesting, of course, but to discover what is involved in understanding poetry it makes the most sense to study first those who do it best. When the processes constitutive of the comprehension of poetry are better understood, we can turn to other readers and study what they do, and how that differs, either qualitatively or quantitatively, from what the experts do. The other sort of training involves learning to verbalize thought processes directly without first censoring them. "Introspection" is the name usually applied to this activity, but three different types of introspection should be distinguished. The first is "retrospective introspection," where the subject tries to recall or reconstruct what he or she has thought. The second and third are both "simultaneous introspection," in which the subject tries to verbalize his or her thoughts as he or she is thinking them (Eysenck, Arnold, and Meili, 1972). Here we may distinguish two subcategories: "objective," in which the subject observes his or her thoughts as something to be reported and perhaps commented on—what I have called *Narrate*—and "subjective," in which the subject verbalizes his or her thoughts directly without suggesting any split between the thinker and the reporter. The last—subjective simultaneous introspection—is what subjects should be trained in, for here there is the greatest possibility that the basic thought processes will appear undistorted.

Second, it would be desirable to expand the experimental paradigm so that subjects can return to the poem over a period of time and record their second and third thoughts. Many of my readers complained that they did not normally understand a poem in one sitting, that a period of fermentation was necessary during which problems magically disappeared. Clearly, any study that ignores the utility of returning to a poem is going to be severely limited, but extending the experimental situation in this way introduces its own problems, primarily because thoughts about a poem often occur when no tape recorder is handy. Reports of these thoughts at a later time—retrospective introspection—will be better than nothing, but they will have a different status than simultaneous introspection. However the practical problem is solved, it will be necessary to allow the reader time for a hundred visions and revisions in constructing an understanding of the poem.

Third, each subject should work with several different poems so we can distinguish what the reader habitually does from what a particular poem elicits. Further, ancillary information, such as author, date, and so on could be supplied to see how it affects the reader's perceptions. Obviously, both the poem and the information available about it will affect the readers' perception of it, but the relevant questions are *how* and *how much*. As an illustration, note that M hardly notices the form of "Winter Piece" at all; he comments only on the placement of *stilled* at the end of a line. Other readers devoted a good deal of time to the form, identifying a final couplet and a stanzaic form, comparing it to concrete poetry and some of Herbert's poems, and even, in one case, discovering it to be a crypto-sonnet, fourteen more or less pentameter lines linked by half-rhyme fractured into its present twenty-two line form. Now the relevant questions are whether M typically ignores the form of poems, whether there is a kind of threshold of form at which he begins to take notice (say, the sonnet form), and—most importantly—what he does with the form when he notices it. (Another question, of course, is whether he would have gotten around to commenting on the form of "Winter Piece" if he had taken more time.) These are questions that can only be answered by observing his interaction with several different poems.

As the ultimate outcome of this kind of research, I envision a series of characterizations of the operations of many readers reading several poems. The most detailed description would consist of a listing of the elementary operations in the order in which they were used in reading each poem. This can be efficiently represented by numbering the segments in the protocol and then providing a corresponding list of the operations. At a slightly higher level of abstraction would be a description of a reader's typical sequences of operations. Early in the reading experience these will probably begin with *Read* or *Select*, as the reader identifies a portion of the text to work with, but later the topic may be set by earlier deductions or generalizations about the poem. Various comparisons would lead to the next level of abstraction. By comparing one reader's experiences on several poems, it should be possible to characterize his or her general approach to poetry, and to discover which aspects of his or her reading are dependent on the poetic text and which are relatively independent of it. By comparing the activities of several readers on one poem it should be possible to assess the range of variation possible, and to distinguish each reader's idiosyncratic approach from what (if anything) seems to be demanded by the text. In making these comparisons, however, we must be prepared for the enormous influence of memory, so that even readers whose general approaches may be similar—say in emphasizing *Connect:Literature* or *Connect:History*—may arrive at quite different readings because they draw different literary or historical connections (for further discussion see Kintgen, 1983).

Assuming that the elementary operations can be defined precisely enough, it seems likely that it will be possible to characterize a reader's cognitive activities at any desired level of specificity. In order to do this, however, a better system of analyzing the basic perceptual processes is necessary—the fourth desideratum. As is clear from my sample analysis of M's protocol, I think the aim here should be to specify elementary cognitive or perceptual processes, ideally as few as possible, and allow them to combine or act recursively on each other. This will undoubtedly lead to some complexity in the description of readers' activities, but it will reflect the intuition that a relatively small number of basic cognitive operations are used in a large number of different situations.

My hypothetical descriptions may seem more than sufficiently complicated already, but even so I have ignored one important dimension of literary perception, that pertaining to how interaction with other readers affects understanding. The research paradigm I am proposing could be extended in a natural way to include this dimension by recording group discussions of the poems read. While this would isolate each reader's contribution to the discussion (which could, in turn be related to the processes used in comprehending the poem), it would not necessarily reveal the effect of the discussion on his understanding of the poem. This is another practical problem I have no solution for. One possible solution—to ask each reader to record after the discussion how it changed his or her understanding of the poem—introduces again the problem of retrospective introspection. Collecting simultaneous introspection reports would involve something like providing the participants with a tape recorder and having them record whatever trains of thoughts the discussion engendered. This does not seem particularly feasible, though it is amusing to contemplate a roomful of people all talking simultaneously to each other and into their private recorders. However, it might be that simplifying the situation by limiting it to a discussion between two or three people, for example, would produce interesting data.

Finally, I have two caveats. The first is that one should not expect to catch in a tape recorder everything that occurs while a reader reads a poem. The language which must be used to verbalize mental events is primarily linear, unidimensional, while at least some of the mental processes involved are likely to be parallel, occurring simultaneously. Similarly, a reader may be reading one part of the text but glancing at another—I often do this myself, and another reader also reported doing it—and the glance is impossible to include in any verbalization without completely altering the temporal sequence. If one stops to report the glance (and note here again the difficulty of reporting rather than verbalizing, inherent in this case because of the different perceptual modalities involved), the report takes longer than the glance, and so distorts the chronology of the process. Now this particular example could, in fact, be circumvented by monitoring foveal fixation, but that does not affect the main point, which is that some mental processes may, by their very nature—either because they are parallel processes or because they are "right brain" processes—be impossible to verbalize veridically.

The second caveat is that all experiments have "demand characteristics" and all subjects have assumptions and expectations about what they are doing (Orne, 1973). This is clearly too large an issue to discuss here, but the central point is that what subjects do will depend to a large extent on what they think you are doing. If you encourage readers to arrive at an understanding of a poem by themselves, they will probably do it. If you encourage them to stick close to the text by denying them the author's name and dates, they will spend gratifyingly little time on biographical and historical speculation. On the other hand, if you encourage group interaction, your readers will almost certainly illustrate how much their comprehension depends on discussion with others. And if you encourage them to relate the poem to their own lives in one way or another, you will get quite a bit of autobiography. So in drawing any conclusions from research of this kind, we must always add—in a kind of mental footnote—"these processes occur in *this* situation." That is, until we understand much better than we currently do how the situation affects what goes on in it, results cannot be generalized beyond the situation studied. And so, questions about whether the processes discovered occur in situations different from the one studied and whether they occur normally—when the reader is not taking part in some sort of study—cannot be answered yet. But it is good to have more questions than answers, or what's a heaven for?

APPENDIX A

I should mention that I'm lying on my back, / my back aches, / feeling a little crotchety / as I open up this piece of paper / and see a poem— / it's printed not very darkly on the sheet, / and I look at the title, /

Winter Piece, / am I'm a little put off already / because I find such titles
pretentious. / There's a formality in a poem whose title is Winter Piece /
that I don't particularly like, / unless of course the poem in some way turns
out to qualify that stilted kind of language in some fashion. / I'm going to
read the poem now as I would to myself. / [One complete reading.] / I guess
at—my impression—and this is unfortunate, / is that at first reading, I
don't particularly like the poem. / It seems to me quite stilted, / un-
conversational, forced, / in what seems to me grammatical incongruities. /
And I guess it is to these incongruities / that I would start trying to piece
together how this thing runs. / I go back now to the opening lines / and
find those two lines not very difficult to comprehend. / All now, this moment,
stilled. / And I wonder whether there is some extra weight given to that word
stilled, / the way it comes at the end of that second line. / Obviously it
does take an emphasis. / We turn then to our steeple clock / as if the speaker
is incorporating or including some kind of community here with the reader /
—it's our clock, not the steeple clock; / something familiar, / and I suppose
he's going to render it in unfamiliar or perhaps threatening terms / as I
remember having read it the first time. / And I'm going to reread it— /
our steeple clock transfixed, the mineral twigs intact, this park's arterial
loss suspended do rebuke me. / And I've got to stop here. / The do rebuke me. /
What is the subject of that verb *do*? / Well, we go back / and it is the clock,
the mineral twigs and the park's arterial loss suspended. / All seem in some
way to rebuke the speaker of this poem. / Now why this inverted order, / and
this difficulty with subject, / I'm not exactly clear, / unless the next line,
gone amiss / which I suppose could also apply to the scenery, / but certainly
must apply to the me, / me gone amiss, / and in that way perhaps accounts
for this rather tortured syntax as I see it. / Transfixed. Our steeple clock
transfixed. / That word seems to me, / and I guess I should look it up, /
although I don't think I will, / —to transfix means to pierce as with
a weapon / and links with the later line, I suppose, / my crux and nail / and
in some way is related to the crucifixion. / But that isn't—that isn't the
meaning here, not the primary one. / Our steeple clock transfixed, / in this
sense held motionless, / transfixed, I take it, here, by the winter, / frozen
in other words. / And the mineral twigs could of course refer to the frozen
branches, / in the village, whatever in the town, / which is described, I
see, as a park. / It could also—They— / the term mineral twigs intact: /
they're still whole . . . / also could apply to the clock, / the hands of
the clock, the workings of the clock. / This park's arterial loss suspended. /
And that word arterial sticks out / and suggests to me a connection with
the frozen creek, / the flowing of streams which are suspended now in the
winter, / in the cold. / And all of this motionlessness, / things having been
stilled, / as he says, or she, / somehow rebuke the speaker. / And I guess I
have a little trouble with the word rebuke / and I'm going to look that up /
to see in what way all of these things might rebuke me. / My dictionary suggests
that rebuke means to criticize or reprove sharply, to reprimand, / and then
obsolete meaning, to check or repress. / I suppose both of those things
may be working here . . . / I suppose that the man is being criticized
somehow by these things. / Maybe there is something within him / which . . .

tends to work in another fashion, / doesn't want to be still, / and there's
a—he's being held in check by the stillness of the scene. /
    Now I continue with this grammar, / try to get some sense out of it— /
55   do rebuke me, gone amiss in minute thefts. / Now the minute thefts / it
would seem to me would be connected with the loss, / the arterial loss, the
loss, / the mineral twigs perhaps, / the fact that winter has crept up
slowly / and has taken life of some kind out of the surroundings slowly,
minutely . . . / In minute thefts to break my bond. / Break a bond, / as if
60   now the speaker is no longer in harmony with his surroundings, / and I suppose
in that way the surroundings rebuke him / because he is out of harmony with
the environment. / To break my bond / and I interpret that, my bond with
my surroundings. / Who set my face. / Now the who I suppose again could go
with the landscape, / but that's forced. / Who I suppose would have to go
65   with me, / or two or three lines above. / Me, to break my bond, / me who set my
face, my sticks, / and here again—again I suppose suggesting in some way his
own paralysis, / referring to his limbs as sticks / and some kind of vague
parallel to the mineral twigs / and the hands of the steeple clock. / My
sticks, my springs, and here a pun perhaps: spring as the season within
70   him. / He feels or at least has an inclination toward the vitality of spring /
as opposed to the landscape where he finds himself, / but also springs, his
innermost workings / and that also connects with the steeple clock. / Again,
I find this very forced as poetry. / These connections seem to me very very
consciously offered, / and I don't particularly like this kind of poetry. /
75   My bond, who set my face, my sticks, my springs against a thief. / Well we've
already had some thefts, / those minute thefts which in some way are connected
with winter as I see it. / Against a thief. / Who is the thief? / Well, maybe
winter. / Time on my crux to nail. / There's an inversion here, I suppose; /
I'm not really clear again on the syntactical relationships. / Now I inter-
80   rupt my look at this poem to see if the tape has run out, / since I'm very
good at talking into expired tapes. / And I don't think it has run out, / but
that is something I keep thinking about as I talk into this microphone. /
Okay. /
    Where were we? / My sticks, my springs against a thief. / Time on my
85   crux to nail. / To nail time on my crux, / I suppose, is the way we're to
read it / if its going to make any sense at all. / In minute thefts to break
my bond. / Me who set my face, my sticks, my springs against a thief. / He's
opposed to the natural situation here, winter. / To nail time on my crux. /
So these thefts are somehow working toward breaking a bond / and nailing . . .
90   / this is difficult. I'd have to parse that out a little bit more I suppose. /
Going back at the risk of boring the listener to this—listener of this
tape. / Transfixed, the mineral twigs intact, this park's arterial loss
suspended, do rebuke me, gone amiss in minute thefts to break my bond, / to
nail time on my crux, I suppose. / Again, the element of time, / the clock
95   earlier, the springs, / there's some kind of continuity here among the words
and images chosen. / Somehow time, nail, time is standing still. / I suppose
the connection between time as—as a stream might be made / between the arterial
loss which is suspended, and time here, frozen. / Crux, time on my cross. /
Crux also means, I guess, a difficult point, / a critical turning point, the

100   crux of it all, / nailing time to my crux. / My 33, / and then of course this
word which I must now look up. / I've heard of deliquescence— / I think Thoreau
uses it a few times. / I believe it means to—to melt, / something like that. /
And so I'm going to look up that word. / And also try to find its pronunciation.
/ Deliquesce, to melt, my dictionary tells me, / to melt away or disappear
105   as if by melting. / To dissolve and so on. / Botany: to branch out into
numerous subdivisions. / Well, let's say to melt here. My 33. Well, what
can he be talking about, his age? / her age? / To nail, / my 33 deliquesce. /
I wonder if the word could be an adjective, / except that would be deliquescent.
/ It is a verb, / and I'm perplexed as to how the verb works. / Subject, my
110   33, deliquesce. / My 33 years melt so sly I might now wink my hand, bone,
lymph away. / Well, I suppose now we're—we're back opposing the stillness, /
frozen scene / where time seems to be nailed momentarily. / That's somehow
being opposed or compared to the years, / the aging process, / the speaker
somehow more aware because of the frozen landscape, / of his own approaching
115   frigidity, / I suppose, which he / —well, his own years, as they become
fluid, / certainly opposes the frozen stream, / the suspension again in the
landscape, / and the minute thefts that we have earlier / are paralleled with this
so sly deliquescence. / 33 deliquesce so sly I suppose is a kind of adverbial
phrase / that goes with deliquesce: / the way in which those 33 become fluid /
120   and I suppose slip away, / the away coming at the end of the next line: / I
might now wink my hand, bone, lymph away. / How the hell does one wink a
hand away? / You don't see it? / Oh, there's the telephone. /
        I've now been sort of looking over some other parts of this poem. / And
I see a kind of double meaning / which I hadn't seen before / on the word
125   bond, / to break my bond, / which I earlier interpreted as a kind of community, / communion with the natural world, / but bond here as a kind of glue
I suppose. As things harden, / form a bond in that sense, / and I guess if
I were going to do this thoroughly, / I'd look that word up to get more meanings
from it. / But a bond obviously does refer to the hardening substance like
130   glue or plaster, / and suggests again something about this speaker is held
together in a kind of artificial manner. / At the same time, the possibility
that he might melt / and disappear, I suppose, into the landscape. / How
could he melt, / why could he deliquesce with such cold as he describes, /
that even the steeple clock is transfixed? / I suppose there's also a con-
135   nection with this arterial business / —we have the lymph—lymph / my
physiology isn't very good. / I suppose I should look that up too. / But
that's related to this business of artery earlier. / Now also we've got a
different thing flowing here, / aside from lymph, perhaps blood, / suggested,
the life-blood of this park. / Arterial loss perhaps as I think of it / . . .
140   the speaker's referring to himself now, as—as—as a park, / as a part
of the landscape, / and now suggesting that his ink, / which I guess is
not dried up in this way / is flowing . . . /
        His ink doesn't keep to— / Not all my ink keeps to my word or want. / A
weird way of putting it. / Keeps to, as if his ink is in some way recalcitrant,
145   / won't bend to his own will, / wants to go in another direction, / won't
be controlled I suppose, / won't express what he wishes. / Not all my ink
keeps to my word / or want, arrests the sun, resurrects the tree. / And now

we're back in that religious context. I suppose, / of crux and transfix. /
Resurrects the tree / —curious things going on there. / Christ nailed to the
150   tree, Christ resurrected. / Here the tree itself is to be resurrected /
—unusual notion, / but connected with this frozen landscape that we have in
the first few lines. / Arrests the sun. / Now why would he want to arrest
the sun? / Again is there a pun on that arrest? / Bothersome, these words,
it seems to me. / Arrest—we've got thief earlier, / and perhaps there's a
155   connection between that and the sun as a thief, / which reminds me of Shakespeare— / which play is that? The sun's a thief, the moon— / or is it the
moon that's a thief? / Well, I think they're all thieves in Timon of Athens. /
And maybe I'd go look that up before fully finishing with this poem. / I'd
go to Shakespeare / and I suppose I'd also go to my Bible / to find out the—
160   the exact context of the water and wine business. / I don't have my Bible
here / so I'm not going to, / but that's a miracle of sorts. / Keeps to my
word or want, arrests the sun. / Now why would he want his ink, as I say,
to arrest the sun / if the sun offers potential for warmth / to unfreeze the
mineral twigs? / Or is that the situation that he wants? / Does he actually
165   cultivate this frozen situation? / Maybe that's it . . . / Obviously if you
can stop the sun you're also stopping time itself / and I guess there's a
sense that he wants to do that / so that his 33 doesn't continue to melt away,
/ wants to make time stop. / So if we cannot make our sun stand still, at
least we can make it run. / That kind of I suppose Marvellian notion here /
170   that he would like that kind of power as an artist, / to be able to hold the
sun still / in that sense of the larger cosmic time. / Resurrects the tree
or translates out of my water so little wine: All miracles not done. / I
don't know what's going on here. / I take it that wine here has a kind of
positive connotation / and that the poet wishes to translate out of his water,
175   / perhaps thinking of his own body as a bunch of water, / which, I guess we
are—mainly water / which is to go beyond that, / to see himself as of worth,
/ of greater worth than water. / Wine in here again, connection I suppose,
with Christ and the sacrament. / But again I find this really un—unrealized,
/ so little wine. / The miracles are not done / and it seems to me that that is
180   an appropriate statement for this poem; / that for me, at any rate, it performs
no miracles. /

   Tick, town; rot, wood; run, you winter crook, run. / Does very little
for me. / The thief business comes in again: / you winter crook, perhaps
referring back to the stream. / Is he—is he actually imploring winter as
185   a crook to run? / Or is he in a sense exclaiming and criticizing, / run,
you winter crook? / Is there a real bitterness here in the tone? / Run . . .
I just really don't know. /

   As I—as I look this over now / it seems to me there is a direct opposition
here / between the kind of suspension as—in the natural world / and the—what
190   might be called entropy, / the running-down of the speaker's own body. /
And perhaps I would interpret time on my crux to nail, / in a different way
I think from the way I did before. / Do rebuke me, gone amiss. / The rebuke
here, in a sense, yes, that I—that—that the speaker would like to be able
to suspend his own deliquescence / as the landscape seems to be in a state
195   of suspension. / To break my bond, do rebuke me, gone amiss. / That he has

gone amiss, / he who has set his face is the way I see it now, / and so on, against a thief, in order to nail time on my crux. / That is to be wished for I think. / The speaker would want to nail time here in this sense, / to stop time / as opposed to the melting away. / And that perhaps there is a kind of
200 envy / in spite of the bleakness of the situation, / of the landscape— / in this way, the speaker wanting to be at one with this winter piece, / as a piece, / which is stark and unmoving. / So that ultimately it's the speaker in a very unusual context, / it seems to me, / rather than being depressed by the stasis, cold, frigidity of his surrounding / because of its suggestion
205 of barrenness, sterility, / he's depressed by the contrast, / I suppose, / between himself as one who runs down constantly, deliquescing, slowly, / and the kind of stasis, / the kind of staying power / that he sees around him in the clock, in the streams and so on, / that he would himself like to nail time in this way. / And the contrast between his own . . . flowing down the
210 stream of time / and the way that winter seems to freeze that movement is, / I think, / what bothers him here in the poem. / It seems to me the major consideration. / That's why I suppose at the end he is bitter: / Tick town. / He wants the town to join him. / He's ticking, he's running, he's running down. / And the winter crook he wants to run as a kind of vindictiveness
215 here / as he I suppose anticipates the spring / and in some way perhaps the summer / when wood will, in fact, rot, / as it is not now doing, / having been transformed somehow to mineral in the mineral twigs up above. / So I guess in that way this poem makes a little more sense. / In this way the usual term, / you know, run, you crook— / he wants it to run, he wants winter
220 to run / as it is not doing now. / Now it's—it's frozen, it's still, / and he wants in this way winter, I suppose, to go away, / but also to turn into a kind of deliquescence, / to move on / and to reflect the passage of time / which he is a part of / and which he obviously I think now wishes he could escape / as the scene around him itself appears to him to have escaped. /
225 I do think I could get a bit further with this, / especially with that translates business . . . / and I guess I'm—I'm ready to stop. / I'm not satisfied with my own work on this poem / and I feel that if I could give it another hour I could do more. / But in all honesty, / I don't have that time, / and so, run, you winter crook, run.

REFERENCES

Bever, T. G. The interaction of perception and linguistic structues: A preliminary investigation of neo-functionalism. In T. A. Sebeok (Ed.), *Current trends in linguistics*, XII. The Hague: Mouton, 1974.

Cooper, C. R. Empirical studies of response to literature: Review and suggestions. *The Journal of Aesthetic Education*, 1976, *10*, 77–93.

Eysenck, H. J., Arnold, W., & Meili, R. Introspection. *Encyclopedia of psychology*. New York: Herder, 1972.

Fodor, J. A., Bever, T. G., & Garrett, M. F. *The psychology of language.* New York: McGraw-Hill, 1974.

Gibson, W. Winter Piece. *Winter crook.* New York: Oxford University Press, 1948.

Kintgen, E. R. Psycholinguistics and literature. *College English*, 1978, *39*, 755–69. (a)

Kintgen, E. R. Perceiving poetic syntax. *College English*, 1978, *40*, 17–27. (b)

Kintgen, E. R. The perception of poetry. *Style*, 1980, *14*, 22–40.

Kintgen, E. R. *The perception of poetry*. Bloomington, IN:. Indiana University Press, 1983.

Langendoen, D. T., Kalish-Landon, N., & Dore, J. Dative questions: A study in the relation of acceptability to grammaticality of an English sentence type. *Cognition*, 1973, *2*, 451–78.

Newell, A., & Simon, H. A. *Human problem solving*. Englewood Cliffs, NJ: Prentice-Hall, 1972.

Odell, L., & Cooper, C. R. Describing responses to works of fiction. *Research in the teaching of English*, 1976, *10*, 203–25.

Orne, M. T. Communication by the total experimental situation: Why it is important, how it is evaluated, and its significance in the ecological validity of findings. In P. Pliner, L. Kramer, & T. Alloway (Eds.), *Communication and affect*. New York: Academic Press, 1973.

Purves, A. C., & Beach, R. *Literature and the reader*. Urbana, IL: National Council of Teachers of English, 1972.

Purves, A. C., & Rippere, V. *Elements of writing about a literary work: A study of response to literature*. Champaign, IL: National Council of Teachers of English, 1968.

Chapter 9
Theoretical and Methodological Issues in the Empirical Study of Metaphor*

Andrew Ortony

Center for the Study of Reading
University of Illinois at Urbana-Champaign

Language is a strange and interesting tool. We use it all the time with great familiarity, yet the mechanisms underlying its operation are almost total strangers to us. Of course, we all know that language is a system of rules and conventions that makes possible the expression of thoughts, aspirations, promises, requests, questions, and so on. However, particularly when one comes to the study of metaphor, this does not tell us very much. One reason is that a metaphor, at least at first glance, seems to depend on the *violation* or rules and conventions for its success and intelligibility. But nonsense also depends on such violations for its failures and unintelligibility. If, therefore, one attempts to treat metaphors (and other tropes) as violations of conventions, one will have to be sufficiently specific about which conventions are violated and in what manner, to distinguish metaphors from nonsense. To do that would be tantamount to providing a definition of metaphor, something that I shall not attempt in this paper (but see, Ortony, 1980; Ortony, Reynolds and Arter, 1978, for discussions of this issue).

Whether or not metaphors are to be accounted for in terms of conventions for violating conventions, there are several reasons why the topic of metaphor is a particularly interesting and challenging one. Which of these reasons one finds most compelling depends a great deal on one's perspective. From the perspective of a *scholar of literature* an important reason might be that a better understanding of the mechanisms underlying tropes in general, and metaphors in particular, is likely to lead to a better understanding of the nature and functions of literature itself. This is especially true if one views tropes as an essential ingredient of literature; metaphors, after all, have traditionally been regarded as the archetypal trope. For the *teacher of literature* (particularly to preadolescent children) one might have some quite practical reasons for wanting to understand the nature of figurative language. Children certainly cannot understand all of the metaphors they encounter (indeed, many adults cannot either), and from this fact at least two interesting questions arise. First, what are the limits or constraints that exist on the comprehension of metaphors?

* This work was supported in part by the National Institute of Education under Contract No. US-NIE-C-400-76-0116, and by a Spencer Fellowship awarded by the National Academy of Education.

Are they, as some psychologists (e.g. Asch and Nerlove, 1960; Cometa and Eson, 1978) have suggested, cognitive constraints, or are they merely the constraints imposed by a limited experience of the world? Second, if metaphors fulfill a necessary communicative function by permitting the articulation of literally inexpressible ideas (Ortony, 1975), how is one to explain to someone who fails to understand a metaphor what that metaphor "means"? These questions are also of concern to the *developmental* and *cognitive psychologist* interested in the psychological processes underlying the comprehension of language in general. Furthermore, for psychologists, metaphors and other figures of speech seem to constitute an interesting "special case" with which a comprehensive theory of language development and language comprehension ought to be able to cope. Finally, from the perspective of those interested in the *teaching of reading comprehension*, it would be helpful to know whether (and if so under what conditions) children's reading materials make unreasonable demands on their cognitive capacities. If one could answer this question, it might be possible to determine whether and when metaphors in texts facilitate or hinder learning.

These and many other questions about metaphors and figurative language need to be answered. Many of them are closely related to the nature of language and communication in general, and to the nature of language acquisition. However, I shall only consider some of these issues, and my discussion will often serve to block off dead ends rather than to cut new paths through the forest. A comprehensive treatment of many of the philosophical, psychological, linguistic, and educational aspects of metaphors can be found in Ortony (1979a).

METAPHOR AND MEANING

If metaphors are to be explained in terms of convention-violating conventions (which certainly is not a foregone conclusion), then at least some of the conventions violated must be meaning conventions. This is because the meanings of expressions used metaphorically somehow depart from their usual meanings. The basic issue is brought into focus in one of those charming exchanges that takes place in Lewis Carroll's *Through The Looking Glass*. Humpty Dumpty is talking to Alice:

> "When *I* use a word," Humpty Dumpty said in rather a scornful tone, "it means just what I choose it to mean—neither more nor less." "The question is," said Alice, "whether you *can* make words mean so many different things." "The question is," said Humpty Dumpty, "which is to be master, that's all."

In metaphor one might think that Humpty Dumpty's case is made; for in metaphor, an author uses words to mean what they do not usually mean. But Alice has a point too. One cannot, either in metaphorical or in literal uses of language, allow a word to mean just whatever one chooses, unless one does not care about successful communication. To put the matter another way, one cannot *arbitrarily* assign an old word to a new meaning. The existing meanings associated with the word impose constraints on how a hearer or reader will construe it. So, whom are we to believe, Humpty Dumpty or Alice? The answer is that there is truth on both sides. The relationship between language users and language is not that of master to servant, but of partners. Each influences the other. On particular occasions, one of them may gain the upper hand. If I walk outside into a torrential downpour and remark "It's raining quite heavily," my communicative intention has been achieved with language constraining what I say. If I had chosen to express the same idea, taking advantage of Humpty Dumpty's license, by saying "My sister got married last year," I would have no right to expect anybody to take me to mean that it was raining. But suppose I had remarked "It's a beautiful day". Then, while the language still imposes constraints, I have stretched it and, in stretching it, I temporarily became the master. My sarcastic remark ought not to be taken literally, for it was not intended to be, yet its relationship to my intentions was not as arbitrary as Humpty Dumpty would have it. The same is true of metaphors.

Now all of this boils down to recognizing a distinction that has prevailed in the philosophy of language for quite some time, namely, the distinction between *meaning* and *use*. When people use a metaphor, meaning and use become about as remote from one another as is possible in the course of successful communication. When they use metaphors, people do not mean exactly what they say, and they do not say exactly what they mean. If someone says that politics is a rat race, he or she does not mean *exactly* that, for politicians are not *really* rats, and what they do is not *really* to race. Presumably, what is meant has something to do with competitiveness, and perhaps ruthlessness, but that is not exactly stated. By contrast, in so-called literal uses of language, people mean what they say, and they say what they mean.

If we accept this conclusion, the question of how people understand metaphors immediately arises. If what is said is not what is meant, how do we discover what *is* meant? Do people manipulate the meaning of a metaphorical statement to fit with the emerging picture of the world that the author is presenting? Do they manipulate an emerging picture of a world so as to permit the literal interpretation of the words? Or, do they sometimes do one and sometimes do the other (Levin, 1979)? Whatever the answer, how are such manipulations achieved? The way that one approaches such question depends, at least to some extent, on the position one takes with respect to what metaphors are.

There are three predominant views of metaphor. First, there is the *substitution* view, which maintains that metaphors are essentially linguistic ornaments for which their more prosaic literal equivalents can readily be substituted. According to this view, when John Dean told Richard Nixon that there was a cancer on the Presidency he merely meant that something was seriously wrong, and he could as easily have said just that. Second is the *comparison* view which maintains that metaphors are implicit comparisons. Here, the cancer metaphor is seen as being, at least potentially, a little richer, for it implies that there is a similarity between the state of the Presidency and a cancer-ridden patient, and the possibility that some aspects of the similarity are literally difficult or impossible to express is not ruled out. Finally, there is the *interaction* view which is based on the idea that the terms in a metaphor (the topic and the vehicle) somehow interact to produce some new, emergent, meaning. On this view, the juxtaposition of the notions of the Presidency and a cancer result in some new conception that is at once greater and less than the two together. The interaction view was first proposed by Richards (1936, pp. 89–138) and was subsequently championed by Black (1962, 1979).

These views are not totally incompatible with one another; in fact, many proponents of the substitution view have also been proponents of the comparison view, most notably, perhaps, Aristotle. From the perspective of how metaphors are understood, however, the real contrast seems to be between the comparison view and the interaction view. While the interaction view is rather difficult to shape into a coherent psychological process theory—not least because of its vagueness (but see Black, 1979)—there have been attempts to employ the comparison view for this purpose (e.g., Kintsch, 1974; Miller, 1979). Such accounts usually postulate a comprehension process wherein the metaphor is converted into an explicit comparison. It is translated, these authors suppose, from the metaphorical to the (presumed) literal—from something ornamental to something transparent and prosaic. This conception of the nature of metaphors, however, suffers from a number of serious defects (Ortony, Reynolds, and Arter, 1978; Ortony, 1979b). One problem is that the translation of a metaphor into an explicit comparison cannot always be realized. For example, how does one translate Macbeth's remarks about sleep into explicit comparisons?

> the innocent sleep,
> Sleep that knits up the ravell'd sleave of care,
> The death of each day's life, sore labour's bath,
> Balm of hurt minds, great nature's second course,
> Chief nourisher in life's feast

(Incidentally, in the next line Lady Macbeth asks, "What do you mean?")! The translation of these lines into literal language (comparisons or otherwise) would seem to be not only difficult, but pointless as well. The metaphors pick out and emphasize certain aspects of sleep in a manner that cannot be comparably achieved with literal language.

Still, it might be objected, there are many instances of metaphor in which it is possible to effect a translation from a metaphorical statement to a simile. Surely, in such cases we have transformed a statement from one that is literally false (the metaphor) to one that is literally true (the simile). I think that this line of reasoning will not work. Even if such a transformation were normally possible, the desired conclusion implicit in such a proposal would still not follow. It is precisely this conclusion—that similes are the literal counterparts of metaphors—that I think is wrong, because the explicit comparisons to which the metaphors are allegedly reducible are themselves metaphorical in nature. Just as metaphors assert that things have properties that they do not in fact have, so similes express similarities between things that are not really similar. It cannot be argued that the terms in a simile are (literally) similar *by definition* because to say that two things are similar, and to say it literally and nontrivially, is to say that there are attributes that are important or salient to both and that are shared by both. But in similes we do not find this match of salient features across the terms of the comparison; rather, what we find are that attributes that are important and salient to one of the terms are only partially applicable to, or less important, attributes of the other (see Ortony, 1979b, for a more detailed discussion of this). Thus, when Wordsworth writes, "I wandered lonely as a cloud", the solitude that is so essential to an individual's "lonely wandering", is certainly not an essential feature of clouds (particularly in Britain). It is, however, a feature that can sometimes be applied to clouds. Typically, clouds are not mavericks, they are too gregarious for that. Of course, all these things are matters of degree, but I think it is important to recognize that one cannot explain away the interesting features of metaphors by reducing them to comparisons, because even when such a reduction is possible, the resulting simile raises exactly the same question as does the metaphor from which it came.

The fruitlessness of attempting to reduce figurative language to literal language is perhaps only obvious to scholars of literature who may wonder why anyone should even entertain the idea. Linguists and psychologists, concerned about understanding the intricacies of language and its comprehension, get stuck when the rules appear to be broken. The attempt to reduce metaphorical to literal language seems appealing as a way out of the impasse. One conclusion that could be drawn from our observations so far is that, while classroom teachers can help children to understand simple metaphors by looking for similarities between topic and vehicle, this strategy is unlikely to be successful for complex literary metaphors. Such metaphors, when they are understood, are often understood in a personal, holistic, and unanalyzable fashion. To peer too closely, searching for a rational understanding, is like moving too close to an impressionist painting. In such paintings, a particular brush mark often gets its meaning not from within itself, but from the larger context of surrounding marks. An impressionist picture contains an economy of representation compared to, for example, a photograph. It conveys a *feel*, without providing the details. So too with many literary metaphors. It can be just this holistic economy of description that makes it possible to say anything at all. Our understanding of such metaphors has more the character of what Polanyi (1966) called *tacit knowledge*, than it does of explicit knowledge. That is at once their beauty and their cleverness.

My main purpose in this section has been to discredit the notion that the meaning of a metaphor can normally be explicated in literal language (the substitution view). In particular, I have argued that the reduction of metaphors to explicit comparisons (similes) cannot explain the metaphorical nature of metaphors because the resulting comparisons are themselves metaphorical. However, this does not mean that the empirical study of metaphors is impossible; it means only that we have to be very careful about how we do it.

MEANING AND COMPREHENSION

In order to lay the groundwork for my discussion on research relating to the comprehension of metaphors, I first want to establish a framework in terms of which comprehension in general can be viewed. When people read a text they normally expect it to be meaningful. If they encounter an obscure turn of phrase, or a complex, convoluted sentence, they still seek to understand it because they believe it is there to be understood. So, in some sense, the comprehension of a text presupposes and depends upon the meaning of the text. The account of the relationship between meaning and comprehension that I wish to propose is a very general framework in which the text, the reader, and some other factors interact to produce a resultant interpretation. It is intended to be just as applicable to parts of a text (e.g., metaphors) as it is to entire texts. The system of conventions of the language serves to delimit and constrain ranges of meanings of texts "in themselves." In other words, they serve to prevent authors who hope to be understood from arbitrarily assigning linguistic units to intended meanings. It is in this limited sense, and only in this sense, that I am willing to say that texts themselves have meaning. It is in exactly the same sense that the paragraphs, sentences, and words that may constitute them also have meaning. Thus, the meaning of a text can be more or less well defined according to the constraining influences of the language it embodies.

To understand a text, the reader has to *do* something. (It is unfortunately not enough for the printed marks just to float past one's eyes). Readers are individuals with a (necessarily) personal history. The knowledge accumulated during the course of a reader's life is potentially all available for the comprehension process in which the reader must engage if the text is to be understood. This knowledge has to be conceived of in a very broad manner. It encompasses not merely knowledge of facts, but beliefs, attitudes, prejudices, aspirations, hopes, and fears. It is a notion that includes the emotional as well as the intellectual, the probable and possible as well as the certain. Much of a person's knowledge is idiosyncratic, resulting from his own unique experiences. But much of it is also shared by others who speak the same language, share the same culture, have similar interests, and so on (Clark and Marshall, 1981). Thus, some knowledge is unshared and some is shared. An emphasis on the role of background knowledge is now commonplace in accounts of reading comprehension (see, for example, Spiro, Bruce, and Brewer, 1980). These accounts generally assume a theory of the organization of knowledge called schema theory (Rumelhart and Ortony, 1977) in which concepts are regarded as structured representations of what is known.

Such a broad conception of knowledge, together with the shared/unshared distinction is essential for several reasons. First, people communicating with one another must of necessity have some shared knowledge (for otherwise their communication could never get off the ground) and, in general, there must be some unshared knowledge (for otherwise there would be nothing new to say). Second, the shared knowledge can be of different kinds, thus permitting different genres of text to achieve different communicative goals. This is obvious if one considers texts with respect to different audiences. The art historian is not expected to share the requisite knowledge with the author of a technical article in a medical journal, but has as good a chance as most other people of understanding a detective story. Even here, however, notice that knowledge about the structure of such stories may give rise to a different (deeper?) understanding than would be normally achieved without that knowledge. Finally, different texts and text genres make differential demands on the shared/

unshared knowledge ratio. For example, it is presumably a purpose of a legal document to be unambiguous. Its author wants to minimize its dependence on unshared knowledge. So, too, with recipes and instructions. By contrast, many works of literature and much poetry invite "interpretation."

We have, then, these two principal components: texts with their meaning, and readers with their knowledge. The result of the interaction of the two is an interpretation. Texts have meaning in the sense that they impose constraints on probable, perhaps even on possible, interpretations. Readers draw upon their knowledge in order to generate an understanding, or interpretation of a text. There is one other important factor that has to be included. I shall refer to it as *ambiance*. By *ambiance*, I mean the total situation in which a text is read. It includes linguistic context in the usual sense, but it also includes many more general aspects of the situation, including such things as the reader's purpose for reading the text, and the reader's mood while reading it. Ambiance affects the interpretation that a reader makes of a text by selecting or suppressing knowledge that could be used in the comprehension process. Consider, as an example, the different interpretations that an imaginary reader might impose on a novel like *Crime and Punishment*. Suppose, in the first case, our reader was planning a murder just to see what would happen and how he would feel. In the second case, let us suppose that he has just committed such a crime, while in the third case, we will suppose that he had done so a year earlier and was beginning to feel that he would get away with it. It seems reasonable to suppose that, in each case, different aspects of the novel would take on more importance in the reader's interpretation. In the first case, perhaps the novel would be read as a "blueprint." In the second, the descriptions of anxiety and nervous excitement might be highlighted and, in the third, it might be interpreted as a vindication (or partially so). Of course, in these three hypothetical situations, the knowledge we suppose the reader to possess is different, but so too are those things which are prominent. These changes in prominence are the results of the filtering effects of ambiance. That the perspective a reader takes has dramatic effects on what he or she attends to and considers important in a text has been convincingly demonstrated in an experiment by Pichert and Anderson (1977).

The general conception of the relationship between a text and its meaning, and a reader and his or her interpretation is as applicable to parts of texts as to complete texts. So, returning to metaphors, one can view their comprehension as involving many of the same fundamental processes that are involved in the comprehension of any other piece of language. The comprehension of metaphors, and of the texts in which they occur, very often manifests itself in the reader's recognition that he or she has achieved some kind of insight into the author's meaning or intention. I have been arguing that metaphors (especially good ones) frequently resist translation into literal language. I have taken the position that metaphors are a principal means of expressing the literally inexpressible. One of the features of language in general is that one can use it to say "old" things or "new" things. Sometimes one remarks on things that are obvious, or that have been forgotten by one's addressee, and that one knows are not going to come as a revelation. But, on other occasions, one uses language to convey new information. In these cases, the speaker or writer knows, or believes, that the hearer or reader does not know what the speaker knows. In the realm of literal uses of language, this distinction goes more or less unnoticed. In the realm of figurative uses of language, the distinction can be very important, for there one has the opportunity to say something radically new that cannot be said literally.

It seems to me that one of the ingredients of creativity is the ability to break away from the traditional ways of seeing things into new ways of seeing things. It is probably the case that our language has developed in just such a way as to permit the expression of things within the framework of a particular perspective, or way of seeing the world, so that if we do come to see the world, or some aspect of it, in a totally new way, our language will be poorly equipped to express the novelty. Poetry is an example par excellence of text that permits readers to see things in new ways. In some cases, a deep understanding of it can result in the comprehender discovering something new, rather than recognizing something already known. Thus an author's insight can lead to the same, or a related, insight in the reader. The creative component of literature (as well as of the other arts) need not, therefore, be merely stylistic. It can often be cognitive too. All of this, however, is speculative. The investigation of the relationship between insight and the comprehension of (nontrivial) metaphors is an interesting, if difficult and largely unexplored research area. There are less difficult problems that one can address, and it is to these that I now turn.

INVESTIGATING METAPHORS EMPIRICALLY

So far I have suggested that meaning should be conceived of as conventionally imposed constraints on possible or probable interpretations of texts, or parts of them. The real work of comprehension arises as a result of the filtering effects of ambiance determining which aspects of a reader's knowledge will be brought to bear in generating an interpretation. Once we accept this framework, it becomes obvious that empirical investigations into the nature of metaphors, and into any special psychological processes that might underlie their comprehension, is better conducted when the metaphors being studied occur in appropriate contexts. Yet, attractive though it might be to confine one's discussions of and research into the nature and functions of metaphor to genuine novel metaphors found in works of literature, such a goal is impractical for a variety of reasons. One reason is that it is much easier to develop a theory in such a complex domain if one starts by focusing on simple clear cases. One can then go on to see if it can be extended to more complex cases. If one tries to start with complex cases, there tend to be too many unrecognized factors at play, and theory construction becomes much more difficult. In the case of metaphors, it can be very difficult to find "pure" cases, that is, cases that are not contaminated with other tropes such as oxymoron ("a living death"), synesthesia ("a dazzling sound"), metonymy ("The White House refused comment"), and synecdoche ("let's take a head count"). A simple example of this from the Macbeth quotation is the case of synesthesia in "hurt minds." It is, of course, true that there is a close relationship between metaphors and the various other tropes, but their different characteristics make it possible that the comprehension process required to understand them might be different, if only subtly so. A good modus operandi, therefore, is to ensure that initial research in the area considers simple and clear cases. Of course, a corollary of this is that it may sometimes be necessary to construct "artificial" materials so that the characteristics of the materials are known, rather than use naturalistic materials where it is much less likely that they will be.

An example of this kind of approach is provided by a number of studies recently conducted in our laboratory. Some of these studies (e.g., Reynolds and Ortony, 1980; Vosniadou, Ortony, Reynolds, and Wilson, in press) were designed to investigate whether young children would be able to understand metaphors, and if not why not. There is a history of psychological research which suggests that children cannot really master metaphorical language until they reach 10 or 11 years of age (e.g., Asch and Nerlove, 1960; Cometa and Eson, 1978; Winner, Rosenstiel, and Gardner, 1976). If this were true, one might need to review very seriously what children below these ages are expected to read. However, much of the research suffers from conceptual and methodological problems that render it suspect (see, Ortony, Reynolds, and Arter, 1978, for a review).

Theoretically, there are at least three reasons why young children cannot understand metaphors, if they cannot. First, there may be special cognitive processes required to relate the disparate domains that are involved. Second, a child might have the requisite processes, but he or she might lack the knowledge of the domains that is required to recognize the relationships between them. Third, a child might have both the processes and the knowledge required, but might lack the metalinguistic skill needed. This would mean that the child would not know that there was a convention that permitted one to say what one did not really mean.

In an experiment designed to examine some of these issues (Reynolds and Ortony, 1980), children were given a number of specially constructed short stories, each about 70 words long. The stories were accompanied by pictures. After the child had read through one of the stories with the experimenter, he or she was shown four sentences and asked to select the one that best "fitted" the story just read. The sentences were constructed with the following characteristics: either, (a) one of the four fitted the story if interpreted literally, and none of the other three made sense under any interpretation. If a child saw a set of sentences with these characteristics he was said to be in the "literal" condition; or, (b) the sentences were such that none of them fitted if given a literal interpretation, but one of them could be interpreted metaphorically—the "metaphor" condition. Or, (c) the sentences were all transformed from those in the metaphor condition into sentences in a "simile" condition, wherein the same sentences were modified to include the word "like" to mark an explicit comparison. Children in the experiment received four items in the literal condition, followed either by four in the metaphor condition, or four in the simile condition. So, each child saw eight stories in all. For each story, if the child were merely guessing, he or she would be right 25% of the time, since there were four alternatives from which to select a response. One of the stories was about an unfortunate racehorse called Jack Flash:

The Old Racehorse

> Jack Flash had been a great racehorse when he was young. But now he was too old to race. His owner thought Jack Flash wasn't good for anything any more. None of the other people who worked at the ranch where Jack lived paid any attention to him. No one wanted to ride an old broken-down horse. The owner decided that he did not want Jack around where people could see him.

Children in the literal condition had to select the most appropriate continuation sentence from:

1. Jack was sent to one of the pastures in the back of the farm.
2. The owner of the ranch played with Jack every day.
3. Jack was given the best stall in the ranch to stay in.
4. Jack hated eating oats for breakfast.

Children in the metaphorical condition saw:

1. The saddle was polished and shiny.
2. The worn out shoe was thrown into the trash.
3. The race was going to begin.
4. The raincoat was new.

Those in the simile condition had to choose from among:

1. It was like a saddle that was polished and shiny.
2. It was like a worn out shoe that was thrown into the trash.
3. It was like a race that was going to begin.
4. It was like a raincoat that was new.

In this example, a response would have been considered correct if it was 1. in the literal condition and 2. in the other two conditions.

The results showed that in the literal condition the children (at grade levels 2 through 5) were virtually perfect. In the simile condition they were performing at about the 50 percent level, and in the metaphor condition performance improved from about 20 percent (approximately at chance level) for second graders to about 50 percent for fifth graders. The fact that the children were able to perform almost perfectly in the literal condition tells us that they understood both the story and the task. The fact that they performed significantly better than chance on the similes shows that for the most part they had the cognitive processes required to relate the two domains and that, at least in some of the cases, they had enough appropriate knowledge of the world to enable them to do so. That leaves only the metalinguistic hypothesis open to explain their much poorer performance in the metaphor condition. It suggests that the reason that they could not select the sentence that fitted in the metaphor condition was that they could neither see a literal interpretation that made sense, nor—more importantly—could they construe what they saw as making any sense at all. It either did not occur to them, or they were unable to conceive of the possibility that language can be used to say what is not meant. In other words, with reference to the general framework of comprehension outlined in the last section, the problem appears to lie not with the "meaning" of the metaphors, but with the knowledge-filtering effects of ambiance. It is as though the children were operating with an insufficiently liberal mechanism for imposing an interpretation on a text.

In another series of studies (Vosnidou, Ortony, Reynolds, and Wilson, in press), we explored the abilities of (especially) four-year-old and six-year-old children using a rather different experimental paradigm. In it, children were asked to act out the events described in stories in a toy "world" comprised of models of familiar buildings (a school, a church, a MacDonald's restaurant, houses and so on). Even the four-year-olds were able to understand the metaphors in the context of the stories. Judging from the three experiments, it seems that different variables cumulatively contributed to the overall difficulty of comprehending the metaphors in the context of the stories in which they appeared. These variables were: (a) the extent to which the event described metaphorically was predictable on the basis of the context alone, (b) the complexity of the metaphor itself, and (c) the explicitness of the metaphor (i.e., whether it was presented as a metaphor or as a simile). The complexity of the metaphor was manipulated by varying the number of words that required a metaphorical interpretation in the concluding metaphorical sentence. In particular, in the less complex condition, the metaphors included two nouns that required a metaphorical interpretation (e.g., "Sally was a *bird* going to her *nest*") while in the more complex condition, the verb also required a metaphorical interpretation (e.g., "Sally was a *bird flying* to her *nest*"). Finally, as in the Reynolds and Ortony study, the explicitness of the metaphor was manipulated by using either the metaphor form (implicit) or the simile form (explicit).

The data showed that children produced significantly more appropriate enactments of the metaphors when these metaphors described predictable rather than (relatively) unpredictable events. However, they also showed that the predictable events were much more likely to be enacted given the preceding context *and* the metaphor than they were given the context alone. We know this because when the children were asked to show us how they thought the story would end, given only the initial context, they were much less likely to produce the "correct" enactment than when they were given the outcome in a metaphor. The data also showed that for both age groups, performance with more complex metaphors was poorer than with less complex metaphors, and that performance with metaphors was poorer than performance with similes. However, four-year-old children were performing at about the 75 percent correct level with the easiest combination of the variables. This compared to a 50 percent probability of the children providing the same correct enactment when given only the context and asked to produce the most likely ending.

The findings from such experiments lead to an interesting speculation about how one might be able to train children who apparently are unable to understand metaphors, to come to understand them. Suppose that one finds a child who can understand metaphors in their simile form, but not in their metaphor form. One might first have the child do the task successfully in one of the simile conditions in the experiments described above. Then one might present the child with a set of items in their metaphor form. Between the two sets of items one might say something like "These are really exactly the same, but they don't have the word 'like' in them." Now we might expect that insofar as they can do the similes, they will be able to do the corresponding metaphors.

Notice that in the experiments I have described we used metaphors that have corresponding similes. As I argued earlier, this does not commit us to the view either that all metaphors have corresponding similes, or to the view that similes are literal. It merely enables us to look at comprehension differences in cases where there are corresponding similes. Indeed, it is precisely because young children can understand similes (at least significantly better than chance would predict) that I wish to argue that they possess the essential skills required to understand metaphorical language, provided that they recognize that it is metaphorical.

It seems to me that this is an example of an approach to research that carries with it some interesting possibilities for the teaching of this aspect of language use, even with very young children. But notice this: it is not very easy to find naturally occurring cases of metaphors which can be easily transformed into corresponding similes. In fact, it is difficult enough to find metaphors in first and second grade texts that are amenable to any kind of experimental manipulation. So if one is interested in investigating the ability of young children to understand metaphors, and if one is interested in investigating their sensitivity to them, it is almost essential to use the kind of artificial materials that we did. One alternative that researchers have tried is to elicit from children reports about how they understood metaphors (Billow, 1975; Malgady, 1977; Cometa and Eson, 1978; Winner et al., 1976). However, research shows that the ability of young children to understand and articulate their own cognitive processes and products lags far behind the development of these processes and products themselves (see for example, Brainerd, 1973; Brown, 1978). Consequently, this approach can be very misleading.

Another piece of research (Ortony, Schallert, Reynolds, and Antos, 1978), conducted with adults highlights a second serious difficulty associated with investigating people's responses to metaphors. Since one cannot measure various kinds of responses in absolute terms, it becomes necessary to compare responses to metaphors with responses to something else. But, what else can one compare them to? If we have to be wary of the notion of a literal translation of a metaphor on the grounds that it may be cognitively, phenomenologically, and informationally different, the most obvious yardstick seems to be problematic. In the experiment I shall describe, we compared comprehension of a sentence used metaphorically to the comprehension of that same sentence in a context in which it was interpreted literally.

The main question that we addressed in this experiment was whether or not metaphors are necessarily more difficult to understand than literal sentences. To address this question, we constructed a number of vignettes in which a short passage (about 50 words in length) was defined as the context. Then, for each context, we constructed a perfectly ordinary literal sentence to follow. This sentence we called the target sentence. Each target was matched with two contexts, one that induced a metaphorical interpretation of it, and one that induced a literal interpretation of it. So, for example, one of the targets was: *The castle was crumbling at its very foundations*. Any particular subject would see it preceded by one of two contexts, a literal-inducing context (1), or a metaphorical-inducing context (2).

> (1) The old fortress on the Rhine needed major repairs because an underground stream was slowly eroding its base. Unfortunately, the government was reluctant to appropriate the money needed to maintain it. One needed only to visit the dungeons to see gigantic cracks in the walls and to become convinced that unless repairs were begun, the fortress would soon be lost.

> (2) The established theory was being seriously questioned because of emerging critical findings. Although it had been accepted for many years, the theory was now incapable of explaining some newly discovered phenomena. Its deficiencies were deemed so serious that there seemed to be no way to save it. Even the most basic assumptions of the theory were being challenged.

For every item, subjects were presented with the context and when they had read and understood it, they pressed a button. The target sentence was immediately displayed on the computer-controlled screen and subjects were instructed to again press the button as soon as they had understood the displayed sentence. The time required to understand the target sentence was measured. Results showed that there was no significant difference in the time that subjects took, regardless of whether the sentences required a literal or a metaphorical interpretation. Our explanation of this finding was that if the idea expressed by the target sentence is sufficiently compatible with the context then it really does not matter whether that idea is expressed literally or metaphorically. In other words, what determines the ease of comprehension is not so much the manner in which the ideas are expressed, but the degree to which they are thematically related to what has preceded them. This was, to some extent, confirmed by the data from another condition in the experiment. In some cases, subjects were presented not with the entire context, but only with the first phrase or sentence from it (e.g., *The old fortress on the Rhine needed major repairs*, or *The established theory was being seriously questioned*). In this "short context" condition, subjects took much longer to understand the target sentences, whether literal or metaphorical, than in the long context condition, but this was especially true for the targets requiring a metaphorical interpretation. The interaction between the degree to which the target is thematically related to the context and the kind of target (literal or metaphorical) suggested to us that metaphors do contribute some difficulty of their own, but that this difficulty is negligible if the text as a whole (context plus metaphor) is coherent and well organized.

Notice that in this experiment we were able to make a meaningful and valid comparison between a metaphor and a literal statement. Although I have argued that, in general, this cannot always be achieved, we selected metaphors for which this was not a problem. These metaphors I call "whole sentence" metaphors.

Characteristically, they are not internally anomalous or semantically deviant. By contrast, a "part sentence" metaphor is one in which individual words or expressions within a sentence are anomalous with respect to that sentence, regardless of the larger context in which it occurs. Part sentence metaphors are often impossible to paraphrase, except by using other metaphors (e.g., *the ship plowed the seas*).

If there is a generalization to make about methodology here, it is that one's conception of what a metaphor *is* inevitably influences the kind of research that one can do. In rejecting standard definitions of metaphor in favor of one that permits a normal sentence to sometimes require a metaphorical interpretation and sometimes a literal one, we can investigate all kinds of questions that would otherwise have been difficult or impossible to study rigorously. This approach has the added advantage of forcing us to examine metaphors in a reasonable (if not totally naturalistic) context, and this is essential if one holds a view of the comprehension process of the kind I have outlined above.

Even from the few studies that I have described, I think one can draw some interesting conclusions about the comprehension of metaphors. For example, although metaphors do seem to constitute an intrinsic source of comprehension difficulty, it appears that this difficulty is normally overshadowed by sources of difficulty which have no particular connection to metaphors at all. For example, our studies suggest that the thematic relatedness of the idea expressed to the preceding context makes a big difference to the ease with which a metaphor can be understood both by adults and by children. However, this is a general factor in language comprehension. There are no doubt countless examples of thematically related metaphors being easier to understand than (relatively) less related literal language. When we come to consider what unique source of difficulty to comprehension metaphors might provide, the only answer one can seriously contemplate suggests that even this may be a general language processing variable. Thus, my hunch is that the problem of understanding metaphors is, in most cases, a problem of determining the referents of the terms that are used metaphorically. In the case of the Ortony, Schallert et al. (1978) study, for example, subjects had to make sense of the statement *The castle was crumbling at its very foundations* in the context of a collapsing scientific theory. The sentence employs the definite article which ordinarily indicates that the referent has already been mentioned, yet there was no mention of a castle. What can the reader do? Presumably the reader does exactly the same as he or she would do if instead of *The castle* the sentence had started with the word *It*. The reader tries to determine the referent, and the context really does not provide very many candidates. When we read on and discover that the castle was *crumbling* we know that whatever the referent of *The castle* is, it must be something that is being threatened. In other words, the metaphor carries with it a set of implications which, in a general way, can be matched with a set of facts already stated, or inferences deducible from those facts. Notice, however, that the process of determining the referents of referring expressions is a perfectly normal aspect of literal language comprehension. In this particular case the main difference seems to lie in the fact that the referent cannot be what it would normally (literally) be. This could be momentarily misleading, but if the reader assumes that what is written is written in good faith, it is indeed only momentarily so. Once the reader has identified the castle with the theory, the rest of the sentence is smooth sailing.

My arguments so far have suggested that the comprehension of metaphorical uses of language probably does not require any special cognitive machinery over and above that required to understand literal uses of language. If this is correct, then one would expect young children to be able to understand metaphors to the extent that they already have the ability to understand literal language. Our developmental data are in line with this prediction. They show that if one does not introduce too many sources of difficulty even four-year-olds can understand metaphors in context. This finding may be at odds with the received wisdom about children's ability to understand metaphors, especially when that wisdom is based on a Piagetian approach to cognitive development. But if the facts show that the received wisdom is incorrect, it seems better to revise the received wisdom than to ignore the facts. The area of metaphor comprehension is by no means the only one in which recent research has demonstrated cognitive abilities in children at much younger ages than predicted by Piagetian theory (Gelman, 1978; Chi, 1978; Markman and Siebert, 1976).

CONCLUSION

To conclude, I want to summarize the main points, and then outline some future directions that I think research in the area might take. I have argued against the notion that metaphors are routinely translatable into literal language. I have argued that even their reduction to similes, in cases where it is possible, solves only methodological problems. It does not, however, explain the mystery of metaphor. For these reasons, among others, I have emphasized the advisability of using artificially constructed metaphors in artificially constructed contexts as materials for use in initial research efforts. The use of such materials permits one to exercise some control over the variables at work, as well as reduce the constraining influences of untranslatability. I should emphasize again that, whether something is a metaphor, a literal statement, or nonsense depends on the context in which it occurs, so metaphors should always be investigated within some reasonable linguistic context. What else should be done? What else could be done? Naturally, there are far more unanswered questions than answered ones; I shall only pose a few of them.

First, there are two issues raised by Levin (1979). One of these has to do with the question of construal that I mentioned earlier. Can one distinguish between metaphors that are comprehended by modifying meanings, from those that are comprehended by modifying the model of the world that the reader constructs on the basis of his or her understanding of the text? If this emerging model is manipulated by the reader so as to be consistent with the metaphor, is it really a metaphor at all? Perhaps it is merely a highly context-sensitive literal statement. The other issue raised by Levin has to do with what controls the way in which metaphorical meanings are construed. Here one might investigate the comprehension of ambiguous metaphors, that is, metaphors in which there are two candidate terms for metaphorical interpretation such that if one is given a metaphorical interpretation the other must be given a literal one, if the sentence is to remain coherent. For example, either *flowers* or *smiled*, but not both, must be interpreted metaphorically in *The flowers smiled at him in the park*. In cases where the context does not make it clear, is there any evidence that people show patterns of interpretive preference (e.g., treating the noun metaphorically rather than the verb). If such pattern do appear, what explanations can be given for them?

Second, is it true that part of the power of metaphors lies in their vividness and the ease with which images of them can be constructed, as I have suggested elsewhere (Ortony, 1975)? If so, they should be very memorable, provided that they are understood. I believe that these are features of fundamental importance, but there is still very little concrete evidence. In fact, the whole area of the relationship between metaphors and imagery is very murky. Presumably, if a reader were to spontaneously construct an image of the metaphorical vehicle, that image would be full of details that could not possibly facilitate the comprehension of the metaphor. So, if one were to read that skyscrapers are the giraffes of cities, it is not at all clear how one could take advantage of the fact that it is easy to construct a mental image of a giraffe. There currently exists no coherent theory of the role of imagery in the comprehension of metaphors.

Third, what role does metaphor play in the creative use of language by children? How can we distinguish metaphors from mistakes and misconceptions in the early stages of language development as when, for example, a child uses his word for moon to refer to cakes (Chamberlain and Chamberlain, 1904)? Do metaphors figure in the writing of children before, after, or at about the same time that they come to comprehend the metaphors that they encounter in the texts that they read?

Fourth, what *are* the constraints governing children's use of metaphors? I have outlined one way of addressing the issue; there are surely others. It would be very useful to discover the nature and frequency of metaphors as they occur in different kinds of texts for children of different ages. Judy Arter and I once scanned fifth and sixth grade social studies texts, looking for metaphors. We were amazed at the sophistication of some of those that we found. Is it in fact the case that excessively high expectations on children's comprehension are being unwittingly placed upon them by authors? How do children's stories compare with expository texts in this respect? And, how do these compare with poetry through the grades? Finally, it would be interesting to know how the results of such an investigation relate to the popularity and comprehensibility of the texts.

There are many other difficult issues to be studied; some are very theoretical, and some are very practical. An example of a theoretical question concerns the relationship between metaphors and similarity. During the last few years, we have been developing a theory of similarity that includes metaphoricity as a component (Ortony, 1979b). Whether such a theory can have sufficient explanatory power to elucidate the nature of metaphors that are not obviously based on similarity statements is still not clear. Another interesting issue relates to the three views of metaphor discussed earlier. It is quite possible that what these views actually reflect are not alternative theoretical treatments of one phenomenon but rather complementary accounts of three phenomena. In other words, it might be that some metaphors are substitution metaphors, others are comparison metaphors, and still others are interaction metaphors. If this should turn out to be so, it might provide the basis of a very helpful taxonomy of metaphors.

Finally, as an example of a more practical issue, one might enquire as to whether what we already know, or what we might discover, ought to suggest a reanalysis of certain classroom and instructional practices. Should it suggest a reanalysis of the teaching of reading and of literature—what to teach, when to teach it, and how to teach it? Certainly, when one reviews those sections of basal readers concerned with figurative language what one finds is very misleading. Of course one cannot wait to teach until the theoreticians can provide a solid theoretical basis for doing so, but we know enough already to be able to say with some confidence that much of what is taught about figurative language to children in the early grades is based on theoretical quicksand.

REFERENCES

Asch, S., & Nerlove, H. The development of double function terms in children: An exploration study. In B. Kaplan & S. Wapner (Eds.), *Perspectives in psychological theory*. New York: International Universities Press, 1960.

Billow, R. M. A cognitive developmental study of metaphor comprehension. *Developmental Psychology*, 1975, *11*, 415–423.

Black, M. Metaphor. In M. Black (Ed.), *Models and metaphors*. Ithaca, NY: Cornell University Press, 1962.

Black, M. More about metaphor. In A. Ortony (Ed.), *Metaphor and thought*. New York: Cambridge University Press, 1979.

Brainerd, C. J. Order of acquisition of transitivity, conservation, and class inclusion of length and weight. *Developmental Psychology*, 1973, *8*, 105–116.

Brown, A. L. Knowing when, where and how to remember: A problem of metacognition. In R. Glaser (Ed.), *Advances in instructional psychology* (Vol. 1). Hillsdale, NJ: Erlbaum, 1978.

Chamberlain, A. F., & Chamberlain, J. C. Studies of a child. *Pedagogical Seminary*, 1904, *11*, 264–291.

Chi, M. T. H. Knowledge structures and memory development. In R. S. Siegler (Ed.), *Children's thinking: What develops?* Hillsdale, NJ: Erlbaum, 1978.

Clark, H. H., & Marshall, C. R. Definite reference and mutual knowledge. In A. Joshi, B. Webber & I. Sag (Eds.), *Elements of discourse understanding*. New York: Cambridge University Press, 1981.

Cometa, M. S., & Eson, M. E. Logical operations and metaphor interpretation: A Piagetian model. *Child Development*, 1978, *49*, 415–423.

Gelman, R. Cognitive development. *Annual Review of Psychology*, 1978, *29*, 297–332.

Kintsch, W. *The representation of meaning in memory*. Hillsdale, NJ: Erlbaum, 1974. .

Levin, S. R. Standard approaches to metaphor and a proposal for literary metaphor. In A. Ortony (Ed.), *Metaphor and thought*. New York: Cambridge University Press, 1979.

Malgady, R. G. Children's interpretation and appreciation of similes. *Child Development*, 1977, *48*, 1734–1738.

Markman, E. M., & Siebert, J. Classes and collections: Internal organization and resulting holistic properties. *Cognitive Psychology*, 1976, *8*, 561–577.

Miller, G. A. Images and models, similes and metaphors. In A. Ortony (Ed.), *Metaphor and thought*. New York: Cambridge University Press, 1979.

Ortony, A. Why metaphors are necessary and not just nice. *Educational Theory*, 1975, *25*, 45–53.

Ortony, A. ed. *Metaphor and thought*. New York: Cambridge University Press, 1979. (a)

Ortony, A. Beyond literal similarity. *Psychological Review*, 1979, *86*, 161–180. (b)

Ortony, A. Some psycholinguistic aspects of metaphor. In R. P. Honeck & R. R. Hoffman (Eds.), *Cognition and figurative language*. Hillsdale, NJ: Erlbaum, 1980.

Ortony, A., Schallert, D. L., Reynolds, R. E., & Antos, S. J. Interpreting metaphors and idioms: some effects of context on comprehension. *Journal of Verbal Learning and Verbal Behavior*, 1978, *17*, 465–477.

Ortony, A., Reynolds, R. E., & Arter, J. A. Metaphor: Theoretical and empirical research. *Psychological Bulletin*, 1978, *85*, 919–943.

Pichert, J, & Anderson, R. C. Taking different perspectives on a story. *Journal of Educational Psychology*, 1977, *69*, 309–315.

Polanyi, M. *The tacit dimension*. Garden City, NY: Doubleday, 1966.

Reynolds, R. E., & Ortony, A. Some issues in the measurement of children's comprehension of metaphorical language. *Child Development*, 1980, *51*, 1110–1119.

Richards, I. A. *The philosophy of rhetoric*. London: Oxford University Press, 1936.

Rumelhart, D. E., & Ortony, A. The representation of knowledge in memory. In R. C. Anderson, R. J. Spiro, & W. E. Montague (Eds.), *Schooling and the acquisition of knowledge*. Hillsdale, NJ: Erlbaum, 1977.

Spiro, R. J., Bruce, B. C., & Brewer, W. F. (Eds.), *Theoretical issues in reading comprehension*. Hillsdale, NJ: Erlbaum, 1980.

Vosniadou, S., Ortony, A., Reynolds, R. E., & Wilson, P. T. Sources of difficulty in the child's understanding of metaphorical language. *Child Development*, in press.

Winner, E., Rosenstiel, A., & Gardner, H. The development of metaphoric understanding. *Developmental Psychology*, 1976, *12*, 289–297.

Chapter 10
Once Upon a Time:
The Development of Sensitivity
to Story Structure*

Shelley Rubin and Howard Gardner

Harvard Project Zero
Psychology Service
Boston Veterans Administration Medical Center
and
Department of Neurology, Boston University School of Medicine

INTRODUCTION

From the first years of childhood, stories offer an important forum of interaction between adults and children; they establish a powerful point of connection between the child's world and the larger culture. Most normal children hear, view, or read a variety of narrative forms from early childhood until the adult years: for both educational and scientific reasons, it is important to determine the extent to which—and the manner in which—they understand the stories which they encounter. It is, of course, possible that children's comprehension is equivalent to that of adult's, and is simply less well-articulated, but a great deal of research in developmental psychology suggests that children of different ages may understand stories in fundamentally different ways (Gardner, 1973; 1977; 1982a; Winner and Gardner, 1979). The forms of understanding (and misunderstanding) displayed by children will not only clarify the child's own relation to narrative but also help to explicate the basis upon which adult competence comes to be built (Piaget, 1970).

To begin with, it may be helpful to elucidate some of the skills a normal adult reader brings to the task of comprehending the plot, or anticipating the ending of a simple story. For example, consider the following story:

---

*This paper was prepared for presentation at the Conference on Researching Response to Literature and the Teaching of Literature, Buffalo, New York, October 27–29, 1977. The research reported in this paper was supported by the Markle Foundation, the Spencer Foundation, the Carnegie Corporation, and the National Science Foundation. We are grateful to the following individuals for their help: Jane Hanenberg, Peter St. Louis, Lowell McGee, Dennie Wolf, Jennifer Shotwell, Hope Kelly, Patricia McKernon, and the rest of the staff of Project Zero. We would also like to thank the following members of the Cambridge school system for their kind assistance: Leslie Oliver, Director of Reading; Richard Phelps, Director of Language Arts; Paul Mahoney, Headmaster, Fitzgerald School; Ruth Murray and Tom Scalese, Sub-Masters, Fitzgerald School; and William Edmunds, Headmaster, Kennedy School.

> Once upon a time, at a time when dragons still roamed the earth, there was a king. His wife had died and left him with a beautiful and clever daughter. The King was very happy because he lived in a land with such beautiful weather that many different song birds from far and near came there to enjoy the sun. He was also very proud of his daughter, for he thought she could do anything.
>
> The King had one weakness. He was very greedy. So, when he married again, he thought only of adding to his riches. The new Queen was very rich, but she was also ugly and mean. She was jealous of the Princess, and grew furious every time the King bragged about his daughter . . .

Although the story opening presented above is an unfamiliar one (written in the late 1970s), adult readers could probably infer the plot developments likely to ensue. They might well assume that the jealous stepmother is likely to pose a set of tasks to thwart the princess. The princess, after solving the first two of these seemingly impossible tasks, may need to call on outside aid (perhaps in the form of a prince) to accomplish the third and most difficult task. The queen will be punished for her weakness, and the other characters will be rewarded by living "happily ever after."

What must children understand to draw these inferences? Such an appropriate apprehension of the tale clearly depends on certain skills on the part of the reader. If children are to anticipate a plausible conclusion for the story, they must possess a set of assumptions derived from the opening paragraphs of the story; they must be able to recognize the story as a fairy tale, and have some appreciation of the elements appropriate to that genre. In this regard, they must be aware of the conventional settings of such tales, and the nature and identity of the stock characters. They must be able to generate narrative solutions to the problems posed in the story in a way that addresses both the dictates implicit in the plot and the psychological tone of the story.

These skills are only the most rudimentary prerequisites to working competently within the story. In addition, there are also deeper levels of symbolic significance to which readers may attend. Indeed, once one begins to consider the many complex assumptions and skills that we as adults bring to this tale, it becomes apparent that the task of story apprehension represents a considerable developmental achievement for the child.

Tracing just how children arrive at the achievement of story competence promises to be a fertile area of investigation. After a long period of neglect, psychologists in the mainstream of Anglo-American empiricism have begun to focus increasingly on stories. Gordon Bower, an American experimental psychologist, has gone so far as to proclaim stories "the royal road" to the understanding of the human mind (1976). Practitioners representing such disparate pursuits as artificial intelligence, computer science, the study of memory, and the examination of moral development have each found within stories a fruitful ground for probing issues central to them (Applebee, 1978; Brown and Smiley, 1977; Kohlberg, 1969). Of special note are those investigators who have applied a mode of grammatical analysis to stories in order to probe subject's apprehension and retention of narrative materials (See Mandler and Johnson, 1977; Rumelhart, 1975; Stein, 1979; and Black and Seifert, chapter 11). Research into the more purely literary and aesthetic aspects of narrative development promises to be yet another provocative vantage point from which to explore how stories are represented in the human mind (Gardner, 1978).

Even for those committed to pursuing the literary foundations of narrative competence, identification of the issues to pursue poses a formidable challenge. Not only may stories function for children in ways quite differently than they do for adults, but responses to stories may vary both *across children* (i.e., a particular story may provoke varying reactions from different children) and *across stories* (i.e., a response to one story may not predict the response to a second story). How then can one arrive at an understanding of the child's mind as it becomes engaged with stories? Such is the challenge which confronts those developmental researchers who take narrative as their domain for investigation.

The tools used to elicit information from children may vary considerably from the means used to assess adult reactions. When working with adults, one can request their interpretations of stories, solicit their difficulties in interpreting, or instruct them to compare one literary work with another. Such introspective descriptions, while never the sole source of information, form a logical point of departure in an empirical investigation. The responses of young children to stories may reflect an intense involvement, on the other hand, but they are less adept at publicly expressing these reactions in the form of a linguistic analysis. When faced with direct questions, children will often invent answers simply to evade the interrogations of the experimenter (Piaget, 1965).

Asking children to invent stories is another means of securing information on their story competence, but there are difficulties with this method as well (Pitcher and Prelinger, 1963; Sutton-Smith, 1981). Children's failures at such an activity may reflect an unwillingness rather than an inability to master stories; successes, on the other hand, may signal competence in narrative, but may also testify to a keen memory for a story already heard. Similarly, investigations which expose children to a story and simply ask them to repeat the story are difficult to interpret; they may measure memory rather than understanding of stories.

For these reasons, it is desirable to have a method which, while less direct, provides more reliable information on the child's apprehension of the essentials of narrative. Optimally, this entails a task which will encourage the child to exhibit his or her mastery of the genre under discussion, without either requiring the child to invent the story out of whole cloth or reducing the task simply to a measure of memory. One promising approach is to present the child with elements appropriate to a specific story genre (e.g., the opening framework of a fairy tale) and allow the child to complete the story on his or her own. Examination of the child's responses can reveal which facets of the genre have been assimilated, and which remain to be mastered (Scarlett and Wolf, 1979).

Following along these lines, we sought to devise a study of elementary school children which would provide information about the growth of narrative competence. Clearly, the full picture of the story competence of school-aged children surpasses the scope of any one study, but we hoped to take some first steps toward tracing its evolution in young children. To this end, we elected to construct a story which we could then ask children both to complete and to retell. By manipulating the story in various ways, we hoped to provoke children to confront key problems posed by the story, which would enable us to infer from their responses the level of their story apprehension. Broadly speaking, we hoped that our investigation would help us to understand children's emerging grasp of some central narrative issues: how children develop the capacity to maintain a particular story "frame"[1] and to elaborate within that frame; how they come to understand issues of character and tone; how, in completing a story, they can both solve problems embedded within the story and integrate their ending with the preceding narrative; and to what extent they can understand and utilize the motivational dimensions of a story.

A word is in order concerning our decision to focus on the results of a single study. All too often, in our view, surveys of research race across scores of studies, providing some sort of an overview of the general drift of findings but conveying little sense of why the study was conceived, how it was carried out, and what steps were involved in proceeding from results to conclusions. In a book designed in part to introduce readers to methods of research in the psychological sciences, we felt it would be preferable to spell out our own thinking and procedures in some depth and to make explicit those choices and consequences which are typically only implied. There is, of course, a cost in this decision: readers will have to consult the other studies cited in this chapter, and the other chapters in this book, if they want to gain a more veridical sense of the full terrain of psychological investigations of literary responses. Still, given the newness of this area of study, and the dearth of investigations which probe aspects *central to the story as a literary creation*, we hope that our strategy will be viewed as a reasonable and justifiable one.

THE STUDY

In any investigation, the particular story chosen will be very influential in determining children's responses (Meringoff, 1980). In our own case, we needed a story that, although unfamiliar, carried with it powerful expectations against which we could measure the children's performance. In many ways, the fairy tale genre was well-suited to our task. By composing a prototypical fairy tale, we presented a story that, while specifically unfamiliar, drew largely from the stock elements ("long ago," a royal family) and featured an established form (three tasks in order of progressive difficulty) characteristic of the genre. In addition, a fairy tale consists of more than a series of actions; it contains a complex but unified set of psychological features. Physical traits ascribed to an individual in a fairy tale have profound psychological resonances as well; beauty is equated with moral purity, for example. The threat that the queen poses in a fairy tale is not only physical (in the sense of

---

[1] By frame, we refer here to the narrative skeleton of a specific genre. In the case of a fairy tale, this incorporates such elements as stock characters (i.e., the wicked queen), motifs (three tasks), and conclusions (retributive justice).

bodily menace); it is also psychological, as the queen's dominance has more subtle repercussions on interactions between characters.

In order to look specifically at children's handling of the psychological dimension, we devised two versions of our fairy tale. Some children were presented with the complete story; others heard an extremely skeletal version in which all instances of "motivation" were deleted (see Appendix A for the text of stories). "Motivation" was broadly defined as phrases or character traits which made comprehensible the actions of the protagonists. Deleted from this latter version, for example, was not only the description of the princess's cleverness and beauty, but also any explanation of why the queen issues her harsh commands, or why the king does not step in to protect his daughter. Our deleted fairy tale was a sparse account of the story with no explanations of why any of the characters acted as they did.

The format of the study, then, was as follows: ten children in each of grades one, three, and six heard a recording of the full story with motivation included; an equal number of children in each of the three grades heard the same story with all motivation deleted. In all cases, the story ended abruptly when the princess, in the middle of the third task, was unable to find enough feathers for the skirt the queen has demanded. Children were asked to supply an ending for the story, and were then asked three short questions: whether they had liked the story, who their favorite character was, and what they would title the story.

We returned three days later, reminded children of the title they had provided, and asked them to repeat the story, from the beginning we had originally played for them through the ending they had furnished. We theorized that, in reconstructing the story three days later, children who had a firm hold of the scheme of a fairy tale would supplement the deleted version of the story with motivation where it was called for. In addition, our hypothesis was that the two versions of the story would provoke the most widely divergent responses in the third grade; first graders were likely to be overwhelmed by either story, while sixth graders would be able to compensate by supplementing the story with appropriate motivation. To determine whether the three-day period did, indeed, increase such supplementations, we also included a control group of ten children in each of grades one, three, and six, who were asked to retell the story on the first visit, shortly after having heard it. In all cases, experimenters were friendly and encouraging, but offered no prompts that divulged story information.

We were aware that children might well understand more about motivation than they could articulate in a story format. For this reason, after retelling the story, children were asked a series of twenty-four questions, most of which focused specifically on the issue of motivation. Since we did not want to bias our findings against younger children, who often find it difficult to answer questions about something as intangible as how a character *feels*, we included not only direct questions pertaining to motivation ("How does the queen feel about the princess?" and "Why does the queen ask the princess to do all those things?"), but also questions which tried to get at this indirectly ("What does the princess say when the queen tells her to do all those things?" and even "Would you like the king to be your friend?"). Finally, we included three questions not addressed by the story (such as asking the color of the princess's hair) to see how readily children would fabricate information (see Appendix B for complete list of questions). After each question, children were encouraged to give reasons for their answers.

Before turning to our results, it may be helpful to underscore the rationale of our approach. We sought to devise a task which the children would find intrinsically interesting, so that their responses would reflect a full engagement with the issues we had deemed central in story apprehension. We aimed to make the fairy tale we constructed as representative of the genre as possible, in order that our results could be generalized with some confidence to other instances in the domain of fairy tales. At the same time, we wanted to gain considerable information about the extent to which children had mastered the explicit and the implicit themes and messages of the story; and we wanted to offer children an opportunity to share what they knew without making excessive demands on their abilty to spin a story. For this reason, we administered an extensive interview at the conclusion of the session.

As with any experimental investigation, this design balances strengths and limitations (see Gardner, 1982a, Introduction, for a discussion of the variables which can be manipulated in a study of this sort). For example, we might have decided to retell the story a number of times, thereby simulating more closely young children's experiences with stories. However, this procedure would have increased the possibility that our results reflected sheer memory rather than narrative understanding. Alternatively, we might have asked the children our long series of questions directly after the initial retelling. This procedure would have secured much fuller information about the children's memory for details, but it ran the risk that a subsequent retelling might incorporate aspects of the child's own answers, rather than reflect only on the child's initial recall of the story itself. Finally, we felt the need to include two control groups: one heard the story with all motivation included; a second was asked to retell the story immediately after its initial presentation. Their inclusion was essential to contrast the precise effects of the experimental manipulation in which we had the greatest interest: the motivation-deleted condition.

FINDINGS

Motivation

As we have explained, "motivation" was broadly construed. From our original story, we deleted not only stock character traits (The king "was very greedy") which might account for a character's course of action, but also statements about a character's emotional reactions ("He was filled with fear") that described how the character felt about the train of events. Also deleted were statements pertaining to the characters' feelings about one another, both those that might affect how a character would act "The king was proud of his daughter"), as well as direct explanations of why a certain character behaved in a certain way ("He dared not refuse the queen"). In short, the deleted version that some children heard consisted of a series of events, with no explicit motivational logic to glue them together, and no accounting for personal relationships between the characters.

One way of gauging the children's integration of the motivational element was simply to count the motivational phrases they supplied in their endings and retellings. In the case of children who had heard the motivation-included story, we looked at how much motivation from the original story they incorporated, as well as how much "new" motivation they interjected; for children who had heard the motivation-deleted story, we looked at how much they supplemented their contribution with motivation.

Not surprisingly, we found that those children who had heard the motivation-included story provided more motivation in their endings and retellings than those who had heard the motivation-deleted version. In other words, children were more likely to recall motivational phrases from the original story, as well as to invent their own, when they had a motivationally complete story to which they could refer. Although first graders supplied very little motivation on the whole, those who had heard the motivation-included story included five times more motivation than those who had not. The motivation provided by first graders consisted primarily of repeated one-word character traits, as in this retelling:

> This man, the king married a lady who was kind of mean and he had a daughter.
> And the mean lady wanted the daughter to do everything for her.

In this way, first graders distill the motivation into a few potent words.

Similarly, third and sixth graders included twice as much motivation when they heard the motivation-included story. Third grade motivation consisted primarily of stock character traits embedded in sentences that often fail to make explicit the motivational connection:

> Once upon a time there was a king. He had a wife. She had a beautiful daughter, but she wasn't very jealous and she died. So she married another one. She was so jealous because she was very beautiful and he kept on bragging, "My daughter can do anything." So she got mad. . .

Sixth graders went beyond stock character traits to describe incidents between the characters that convey the quality of the interaction between them:

> The king and the wicked lady got married. The king wanted all the riches for his lovely daughter. The queen got mad at her and kept telling her to do things. . .

That children contribute more motivation when they have heard the motivationally complete story is not an unexpected finding. However, one interesting pattern did occur, in contrasting children who retold the story shortly after hearing it with those who did not retell the story until three days later. Our original hypothesis was that, in recollecting the story three days later, children who had heard the motivation-deleted story, and who had a well-internalized fairy tale frame, would supplement their retelling with the motivation that had been lacking. Younger children, having less defined expectations of the fairy tale genre and more difficulty with the task of narrating a story, would be less likely to do so.

Turning to our results, we found that first graders contributed more motivation when they retold the story immediately after hearing it than when they waited three days. In their case, they were better able to latch on to the motivational implications (at least in terms of character traits) of the story when they repeated it back with no delay. For third graders, the time interval made no difference; they included approximately an equal amount of motivation in both cases.

In sixth grade, however, the results were the most striking. *Sixth grade children actually included more motivation when they retold the story three days later.* That is, sixth graders who repeat the motivation-deleted story back immediately make few additions; they repeat the story more or less as they have heard it. Asked three days later to tell the story, they automatically compensate by providing motivation. Sixth graders have enough knowledge of the ingredients of a fairy tale to fill in the absent motivational connections.

In any case, relying on the specific motivational phrases employed by children is only one of several ways of gauging the effects of our motivational tampering. We looked also at the indirect effects—how children solve story problems, how well they integrate their ending with the rest of the story— and from this deployment of converging measures, we were able to draw further inferences about the ramifications of our approach.

Problem Solving

As we mentioned earlier, we left off our fairy tale at a point where the princess cannot find the requisite number of feathers to make the skirt the queen has commanded. Children were asked to remember everything that had happened up until then, and to tell us how the story might end. In examining the endings generated by the children, we have considered the story as posing two levels of problems: one explicit, one implicit. The first problem is what we will call the "skirt task": namely, the princess's difficulty in carrying out the last of the three tasks that have been presented her. The problem is basically a concrete one; it is the problem insisted upon as the story breaks off, and addressing it means simply picking up at that point. The immediate options for handling this problem are restricted; either the princess succeeds at the task, or she does not. The consequences of either of these outcomes leads us to our second level of problem.

The other, less concrete, problem posed by the story, we will refer to as the "queen threat." By this, we mean that the story also leaves unresolved the troublesome issue of the queen's place in the household. The story paints her as having bullied theking and tyrannized the princess, and it poses a dilemma about how the tension between these three characters is to be resolved. The solution to this threat, then, will not be a mechanical one of finding a certain number of feathers, but a psychological one which must incorporate interactions between the characters. Furthermore, while the skirt task problem is made explicit as the story breaks off, this threat is less direct, and must be inferred from the interactional tensions present.

The other, less concrete, problem posed by the story, we will refer to as the "queen threat." By this, we mean that the story also leaves unresolved the troublesome issue of the queen's place in the household. The story paints her as having bullied the king and tyrannized the princess, and it poses a dilemma about how the tension between these three characters is to be resolved. The solution to this threat, then, will not be a mechanical one of finding a certain number of feathers, but a psychological one which must incorporate interactions between the characters. Furthermore, while the skirt task problem is made explicit as the story breaks off, this threat is less direct, and must be inferred from the interactional tensions present.

Skirt Task

The tendency to respond at all to this problem increases with age. Whether or not motivation was present in the story they heard, half of the first grade children ignored the skirt task in their story endings. A typical first grader concluded the story in the following way: "At the end she says, 'Tell you daughter that I want the house clean.' " This child generates another task in the pattern the story sets out, but fails to deal with the princess's immediate predicament. First graders, when they address the problem at all, do little towards integrating it in a continuing narrative; many commenting simply, "She did it, I think." (Gardner, 1982b)

In both the third and sixth grades, however, children are more likely to touch upon the skirt problem in their endings if they have heard the motivation-included story. In both grades, children who have heard the motivation-deleted version are more likely to pass over the skirt problem. One third grader ended her story by declaring, "I think that the king should get a divorce with the mean one . . . and that he should marry a nicer queen." A sixth grader suggested:

> She got sent away to prison and there was lions in the cave and they was chasing her and then she got out of there and then she was in a prison and she died of starvation. And then, that, that would say, "Tell your daughter to do one more thing," um, went to her funeral and she got buried.

The disjointed story produced by the lack of psychological motivation seems to lead these children to continue the action in a similarly unconnected fashion.

Indeed, several third and sixth graders, rather than narrating one ending, instead proposed a list of possible endings, as in this sixth grade response:

> Maybe she went to a big mountain and there's a nest full of all kinds of birds and she plucked 'em. Maybe she unstuffed a pillow? Painted leaves? Maybe she found a whole mess of feathers and sewed 'em up to it. Or maybe she had a dress with feathers and cut off the skirt. It was one feather short. She stuck it on.

These suggestions are at once ingenious and non-narrative; children who furnish such endings treat the task as one of extended problem-solving, rather than as the creation of an integrated ending that calls on all levels of the story. Independently, each of the suggestions are clever solutions within the frame, but in listing rather than narrating, their authors have opted not to enter the narrative frame (Scarlett and Wolf, 1979).

Queen Threat

Not surprisingly, first graders generally ignore the threat of the queen, while sixth graders usually fashion some sort of resolution. In resolving this task, the differential effects of the two versions of the story surface primarily in the third grade. Strikingly, third grade children were *twice* as likely to resolve the threat of the queen when they had heard the motivation-deleted story than when they had heard the story with motivation included. In other words, *hearing the entire story actually lessened the likelihood that third graders would address the psychological dilemma of the threat posed by the queen.* It may be that the full weight of motivational detail—having the situation presented in all its motivational complexity—enhances the queen's power, making it more difficult to tie up the ends of this complex motivational problem.

We were also interested in the ways in which children who touched upon the queen threat went about resolving this problem. To this end, we devised six categories which seemed to encompass the range of possible outcomes:

1. Queen is vanquished by princess.
2. Queen is killed by some outside force (dragon, natural disaster).
3. Queen repents or gives up.
4. Queen leaves kingdom, or gets old and dies.
5. Queen triumphs (banishes or kills princess).
6. Queen is repudiated by king.

Despite the fact that the story centers on the problems of the princess and ends with her dilemma, only four children in all (and those, sixth graders) recounted an ending in which the princess overcomes the queen. Clearly, she was not seen as a powerful enough figure to successfully confront the more potent queen.

Of the third and sixth graders who do attack this problem, three of the above options are most commonly employed: the queen repents, the queen triumphs, or the king repudiates the queen. A solution in which the queen repents or ceases her demands is most frequently called upon by sixth graders, regardless of the version of the story that they heard:

> The daughter got the feathers and she made the skirt. And then the queen saw
> that the king was right that his daughter could do that, so the queen let the
> daughter stay with the king and never bothered them again.

In other words, it is chiefly sixth graders who conclude the story by allowing the queen to revise her conduct. Third graders, who apparently see the queen as extremely powerful, do not usually formulate such a solution.

Endings in which the queen actually triumphs occur most often in third and sixth grade children who heard the motivation-included story. This is, it appears that children who hear the motivationally rich story, in which the details make the queen more potent in relation to the other characters, cannot resolve the situation other than to have the overbearing queen emerge as victor. On third grader explained,

> She just couldn't do it, so the king lost his fortune and the queen was happy
> ever after and the king was sad because his daughter was sent away some far
> place where he's never find her and the queen was glad she was gone.

In such cases, the fairy tale tradition of a "happy ever after" for the "good" character
gives way to a triumphant finish for the "bad."

Among those children who most frequently address the problem of the queen
threat—third graders who heard the motivation-deleted story and sixth graders who
heard the motivation-included version—a solution in which the king repudiates the
queen is most often invoked, as in this sixth grader who expressed the king's
exasperation:

> He got very mad. "Why am I doing this?" And the king said to the queen, "I
> call divorce, I call divorce. And you must take your belongings and get out of
> here." So the queen left, and the king and his daughter live happily ever after.

Once again, it is significant that third graders are able to use the king to dismiss
the queen when they have heard the motivation-deleted story, in which details and
repercussions of the queen's dominance are absent. In contrast, sixth graders,
presumably more conversant with the "ways" of fairy tales, are consistently helped
by the addition of motivation. The reminders of how "things usually work" apparently
suffice to stimulate a classic ending to this contrived tale.

Retributive Justice

In the solutions in which the queen is, in some way, overcome, we looked for
endings in which the evil queen faces punishment for her misdeeds: in other words,
retributive justice. This tradition of the evil character getting her comeuppance is
common the the fairy tale. In *Hansel and Gretel*, the witch is burned in her own
oven; in Grimm's ending to *Cinderella*, pigeons pluck out an eye from each of the
stepsisters to punish them for their wickedness.

In looking at the use of retributive justice among school-aged children, we found
that sixth graders are almost three times more likely than third graders to make the
queen suffer for her evil ways. This is true for sixth graders, regardless of whether
or not the story they heard included motivation. On the other hand, third graders
who heard the motivation-deleted story invoke retributive justice three times more
often than those who heard the motivation-included version, as in this third grader's
ending:

> She should go to a dresser or a zoo or something, and if they have any animals
> that have plumes, she should plume them. She should put all the feathers together
> to make a dress. And then, if the mother—I mean, stepmother—made her do
> anything else, I'd tell her father and her father would feed her to the dragons.

Again, third graders seem better able to vanquish the queen when they are deprived
of motivational information that increases her potency. Sixth graders, on the other
hand, are able to conceive of overpowering the queen regardless of which version
of the story they heard.

Action vs. Interaction

In addition to examining the tactics children called upon to solve the story problems, we looked as well at the quality of their endings. On the one hand, we grouped together children who ended their stories through a series of actions ("She didn't find the feathers and she was sent away forever"); on the other hand, we included children who incorporated interactions between characters into their endings ("She made a skirt and the queen was very happy"). This is clearly related to the interactional motivation we considered earlier, but we are looking here specifically at two options for ending the story. Incorporating interactional themes would, it seemed to us, exhibit a greater sensitivity to the psychological strains which underpin the plot.

Not surprisingly, we found that younger children utilize a sequence of actions to end their stories, while other children call upon resolutions that take into account the effect of those actions on the other characters. Interestingly, though, third graders vary as to what method they favor, depending on which version of the story they heard. Third graders who heard the motivation-deleted story respond more like first graders, providing endings which describe a series of actions. Third graders who heard the motivation-included story resemble sixth graders, utilizing themes of interaction. In this case, the presence of motivation which gives life and body to characters seems to encourage third graders to pay attention to the interactional issues of the story.

Degree of Integration

Another important question to be raised concerning story endings is the degree to which children integrated their endings with the beginning of the story. This ability obviously increases with age; sixth graders are far more skillful than first graders in this regard. First graders are more successful at integrating their ending when they have heard the motivation-deleted story; this appears to be another example where first graders are overwhelmed by the motivation-included story, and perform better after hearing the deleted version. For both third and sixth graders, however, endings are more likely to be integrated by children who heard the motivation-included story; apparently in this case, children are able to draw upon the fuller story. Again, one finds a similar split in the third grade: half of the third graders who heard the story without motivation perform more like first graders, while the other half, whose story included motivation, are more akin to sixth graders.

Children's Knowledge of The Fairy Tale Frame

Perhaps the clearest way to sum up the children's overall grasp of the fairy tale frame is to offer a portrait of each grade.

First Grade. In general, our study tells us more about what first graders cannot do than what they can do; their achievements tend to be obscured in contrast with the performance of the older grades. To begin with, first graders simply talk less in a testing/story context than the older children, and one often finds oneself in the position of making assessments about what they meant to say. Nevertheless, without reading into the answers they did provide, we can make certain statements about their story knowledge.

Because, as we have already suggested, physical traits in a fairy tale embody psychological qualities as well, the fairy tale is a useful vehicle for considering how children view characters in a story. The first graders, in their answers, appear to see the fairy tale characters as personifying opposing psychological extremes:

> The mad princess said to the good princess, "Wait until the birds shed off their feathers and she'll be punished and the bad princess will forgive the good princess."

Quite often, first graders distill the story into a potent listing of these oppositions. One first grader, who had heard the motivation-included story, ended the story by ceremoniously repeating the qualities of the characters:

> The king and the queen and the wicked witch. The angry witch and the king and queen. The angry witch and the good princess.

Referring to the queen as a witch is typical of first graders, who have only the most gross psychological understanding of the characters. Another first grader who had heard the motivation-included story retold the story by explaining:

> The lady was mean to the princess and the princess was mean to the lady. The princess and lady was mean to each other, and the princess talked mean to the lady and the lady talked mean to the princess.

In general, first graders are able to identify the story as a fairy tale, but seem not to differentiate among fairy tales. Asked to title the story, first graders frequently respond with the names of other fairy tales similar to them. Asked to choose their favorite character, regardless of which version of the story they heard, first graders select each of the characters about equally, favoring the princess only slightly; the princess was selected because of physical characteristics ("because she has a pretty dress") rather than because of her psychological role in the story. That is, although they recognize the story as a fairy tale and ascribe certain traits to the characters, first graders are equally impressed by each of the characters. Those who favor the queen do so, "because of her voice," (expressive in the recording), "because she was mad," or because "queens are beautiful." Asked if they would like the queen to come visit them, many first graders answer in the affirmative, "because she is royal" or "because I've never seen a queen."

While the first graders can see the queen as "bad" or "mean" in the context of the story, they do not seem to see her as consistently and overpoweringly evil. Instead of seeing her character as fixed by the content of the story, they draw upon a more general notion of royalty as exotic, powerful, and beautiful.

As for the content of first grade endings and retellings, their stories are shorter and more sparse than those of the older grades. They recollect primarily the final task, alluding either to the queen's command, or commenting on the princess's difficulty in fulfilling her request. Half of the first graders repeat the refrain, "She will be punished."

On the whole, first graders perform better when they hear the motivation-deleted story; their endings are better integrated and they call upon more of the story in their retellings. It appears that they are overwhelmed by the wealth of detail (and, hence, the greater length) in the motivation-included story. Children who heard the story with motivation include more direct phrases of motivation, though, in both cases, they supply very little. Finally, first graders remember more of the story when they tell it immediately after hearing it, rather than waiting the three days.

Third Grade. While first graders chiefly employ fairy tale titles, third graders acknowledge the fairy tale frame by incorporating themes, characters, or events from other fairy tales into their stories. Several children, revealing their awareness of this tale's affinity to one of the classic fairy tales, concluded the story by invoking *Cinderella*. One child explained that, "She's gonna pull off her shoes . . . and she didn't have any clothes but rags"; another child recounted, "so the princess got new, all new clothes, and went to the ball." Several children imported whole episodes from other fairy tales into their stories:

> She couldn't find the feather and when her mother heard about it, she sent her huntsmen into the woods. The girl was lost in the woods and someone found her and took her home and she fell asleep in a big bed . . . Then she woke up and saw someone and the man said, "I am a prince." He rode her to the castle.

Of all the children, third graders seem to get most actively involved in the task and contribute the most exhaustive endings. Unlike the first graders, two-thirds of the third graders included a setting statement which introduced the characters, while one half alluded to each of the three tasks in their retelling. Half of the third graders repeated the refrain, "she will be punished."

It was notable that children in the third grade name the princess three times more often than the others as their favorite character. They choose her because, "she could do many things," "she was beautiful," "she tried hard," and "she didn't yell." In other words, apart from admiring her physical characteristics, many of the reasons for preferring the princess center on her opposition to the queen. In addition, third graders who heard the motivation-deleted story name the queen in their titles five times as often as the other characters; those who heard the motivation-included story mention the princess twice as often. By examining the other effects of the two stories on third graders, we hope to suggest a reason for this.

Of all the children, third graders display the most variation in their response to the two stories. Children who heard the motivation-included story make use of the additional information to provide more integrated and sophisticated endings. They include more phrases of motivation, especially those which reflect on interaction between the characters. The endings supplied by these children usually describe a triumphant queen who overpowers the king. On the other hand, third graders who heard the story with motivation deleted, are more likely to overcome the threat of the queen, include more retributive justice, and portray a more active, powerful king. In short, motivation is, in some ways, a help to them and in some ways a hindrance.

In an attempt to categorize the effects of the two stories on third graders, we can make the following generalizations. On one hand, the details of the motivation-included story allow third graders to excel at the technical level of telling a story; their endings are more integrated and they include more phrases expressing motivation. On the other hand, since the third graders appear to be somewhat overwhelmed by the queen's power, depriving them of the motivational information may, paradoxically, make it easier for them to confront the psychological tensions of the story. In this latter case, they are able, not only to dispel the threat of the queen, but also to fill out the role of the king in this conflict. In this latter case, then, children are more likely to name the queen in their titles, as they face up to the problem of what to do with her. Finally, we should note that for third graders, the three-day time interval makes little difference; they include the same amount of motivation and recall as much when they retell the story immediately as when they retell it three days later.

Sixth Grade. Sixth graders, while calling upon a good deal more fairy tale motifs and themes than do third or first graders, tell stories that are a blend of fairy tale elements and ingredients derived from modern adventure tales:

> The queen hired a lot of woodsmen to chop down the tree and the daughter started running and hid in the woods . . . and had a wolf with her and she made it attack the queen . . . The wolf bit her and she had an hour or else she'd die . . . Then the only shot for her arm was in another kingdom, miles away. The daughter got on a wild horse and finally got the cure. She got on the back of a cheetah and it ran about sixty miles. She made it back and saved the queen's life and they were friends.

We have already quoted the sixth grader who portrayed the king asking for a divorce. Another child described the princess getting the feathers from a zoo, then, in more suitably fairy tale fashion, had the queen fed to a dragon. While such anachronistic touches are blatant violations of the fairy tale frame, this may be a deliberate ploy for sixth graders, who feel themselves "above" the fairy tale frame. For example, when first and third graders were asked if they liked the story, they usually responded in the affirmative. Sixth graders, in contrast, frequently commented that the story was too childish for them. This may lead them to mix the fairy tale genre with a more modern literary frame.

In all cases, hearing the motivation-included story spurs sixth graders to perform better. When they have heard the complete story, their endings are more integrated, they include more motivational phrases, and they are more likely to solve the problems posed by the story. They are also more likely to use the king to defeat the queen when they have heard the full story. In addition, regardless of which version of the story they heard, sixth graders overwhelmingly name the princess as their favorite character, apparently perceiving her as the heroine of the story.

Summary

To gain some insight into the story competence of school-aged children, we presented children in first, third, and sixth grade with one of two versions of a fairy tale: half the children heard a complete story; the remaining half heard one in which all "motivation" was deleted. Children were asked to provide an ending for the story. Experimenters then returned three days later, and asked the children to retell the entire story. A control group of children who retold the story immediately was also included.

As hypothesized, we discovered that sixth graders who had heard the motivation-deleted story actually supplied more motivation when they repeated the story three days later than when they retold it immediately after hearing it. This appeared to confirm our speculation that sixth graders, possessing strong expectations of what a typical fairy tale is apt to include, would be likely to supplement a later retelling with motivation. The time interval made little difference to the third graders, who performed about equally in either case, while first graders were more successful when they retold the story immediately.

We looked at children's ability to solve problems posed by the story. First graders often passed over both of the tasks in their endings. Third and sixth graders were more likely to solve the skirt task when they heard the motivation-included story. Some children in third and sixth grade, rather than narrate an ending, instead proposed a list of possible endings. Third graders tended to have the queen vanquished when they heard the motivation-deleted story; including motivation appeared to make the queen more powerful, and third graders who heard that version furnished endings in which the queen emerged as victor. Sixth graders who heard the motivation-included story were especially likely to attack the problem of the queen. In addition, sixth graders employed retributive justice three times more often than third graders.

Different grades displayed chracteristic ways of acknowledging the fairy tale frame. First graders used titles from other fairy tales to name the story. Although first graders divided the characters up into "good" and "bad," they tended, in answering questions, to make statements about the characters that were outside, or even opposed to, the context of the story. First graders had no clear preference for a favorite character. Third graders imported fairy tale themes or episodes into their retellings, borrowing from familiar fairy tales. Third graders named the princess most often as their favorite character, apparently recognizing her as the heroine of the story. Sixth graders told stories that blended fairy tale elements with more modern literary frames and selected the princess overwhelmingly as their favorite character.

Of all the grades, third graders were the most vulnerable to the effects of varying the story. First graders were often overwhelmed by the fully textured story with motivation. They performed better after hearing the motivation-deleted story, telling more integrated endings and supplying more detail in their retellings. Sixth graders, in contrast, always performed better when they heard the motivation-included story; their endings were more integrated, they included more motivational phrases, they were more likely to solve the problems posed by the story, and they more frequently used the king to overthrow the queen. Third graders, as we have suggested, were the most variable. Those who heard the motivation-included story told more integrated endings, included more motivational phrases, and supplied more information on interactions between the characters. Those who heard the motivation-deleted version were more successful at overthrowing the queen, ascribed a more active role to the king, and included more retributive justice.

CONCLUDING NOTE

As a means of charting the development of narrative competence in children, we devised a single study: 90 children from one working-class community were examined as they attempted to complete and recall a fairy tale written by us. The limitations imposed by each of these facets of our approach should be evident. Our findings might well have altered had we constructed our study differently, examined children from other backgrounds or of different ages, utilized an alternate fairy tale, explored another genre, or employed a familiar story rather than manufacturing our own. It is possible that the children would have appeared more sensitive to the fairy tale genre, if, for example, we had tested them using familiar or often repeated tales; on the other hand, it is possible that the children would have appeared less sensitive to the genre, if we had asked them to create stories from scratch or to discuss the characteristics of the genre in a more explicit fashion. Clearly our results must be replicated and expanded before their ultimate value can be assessed.

Given the inherently fragile nature of experimental results, then, what is the hope that any line of research can illuminate what we have so broadly termed narrative competence? To begin with, it seems crucial that the steps we take in acquainting children with literature be informed by our best conception of children's narrative abilities. Thus, while the importance of fairy tales in children's lives has been justly asserted (Bettelheim, 1976), it is only carefully designed and controlled research which can provide reliable information on which aspects of these tales are in fact understood (or misunderstood) by children at various levels of sophistication (Gardner, 1977).

Similarly, while our study does not pretend to explain all aspects of narrative achievement, we hope that it may provide a valuable paradigm for how such research might profitably proceed. In essence, the experimental method has as its chief virtue the fact that it can confirm or disconfirm claims about the phenomenon under discussion. Moreover, to the extent that the present design seems revealing, it can be adapted to study additional aspects of children's narrative competence, ranging from their mastery of other genres, to their understanding of other narrative features (i.e., plot or character development), to their appreciation of the more formal aspects of a story (i.e., the relations among episodes, the structure of an ending). (See Honeck and Hoffman, 1980; Madeja, 1978; Perkins and Leondar, 1978; McGhee and Chapman, 1980; Winner and Gardner, 1979; O'Hare, 1981, for some suggestions about other psychological approaches to the understanding of linguistic art forms.)

As with all experimental investigations, ultimate goals may become submerged in the details of the technical execution of the study. How many subjects to run? What is the proper control group? Which means of coding the responses is most accurate? How can one gain adequate reliability among the judges? Clearly, no study can rise above the care entailed in the design, execution, analysis, and write-up of the investigation. Yet, on the other hand, one must beware the empiricists' fallacy in which the experiment one happens to have devised becomes confused with the phenomenon which originally inspired it. Ultimately, researchers must balance a perspective on the limitations of a particular design with a recognition of its potential for illuminating the central issues that have prompted the study (Winner, 1982). Just as no one story encompasses all narrative possibilities, so no one study can uncover all the skills involved in the attainment of narrative competence. As one study leads to and informs the next we can begin to assemble a portrait of the way in which children's experiences with literature change over time.

In this spirit, we hope that the present study can serve as a model for how research into the development of narrative skills might proceed. Compared to the richness and complexity of a fairy tale, our observations are necessarily limited. Yet we hope that even those involved with readers of a much greater sophistication and age will recognize, in the efforts at understanding and problem-solving of young children, some echoes of the processes in which all individuals are engaged as they come to understand, to interpret, and to cherish literature of importance to them.

APPENDIX A

Motivation-Included Story

Once upon a time, at a time when dragons still roamed the earth, there was a King. His wife had died and left him with a beautiful and clever daughter. The King was very happy because he lived in a land with such beautiful weather that many different song birds from far and near came there to enjoy the sun. He was also very proud of his daughter, for he thought she could do anything.

The King had one weakness. He was very greedy. So, when he married again, he thought only of adding to his riches. The new Queen was very rich, but she was also ugly and mean. She was jealous of the Princess and grew furious every time the King bragged about his daughter.

The new Queen wanted to get rid of the Princess, so she said to the King, "If your daughter can do anything, tell her the chattering of the birds keeps me awake all night. If she cannot quiet them this very night, she shall be punished."

The King loved his daughter, but he was afraid of angering the Queen and losing a fortune. So he gave the command.

The Princess knew she could not silence the birds. However, she placed near the Queen's window a jar of honey that drew many hummingbirds. Their hum put the Queen gently to sleep.

The Queen slept very well and the next morning the King remarked, "I told you. My daughter can do anything."

Once again, the Queen became furious. "Tell your daughter I want my house filled with a hundred and one swan eggs tomorrow morning. If even a single one is broken, she shall be punished." This was no easy task, for the swans all lived on the other side of a wide river.

Soon the Princess set out with a large basket. She wrapped each egg in a leaf and then floated the basket beside her as she returned across the river.

Upon the Princess's return, the King repeated, "I told you. My daughter can do anything."

The Queen looked at the King. "We'll see if she can do anything," the angry Queen snapped. "Tell your daughter to weave me a skirt for the ball tomorrow night. It must have 1,001 feathers in it, one from each kind of bird in the kingdom. If it is short one feather, she must be sent away forever!"

Though the King was filled with fear, he dared not refuse the Queen, for he did not want to lose her fortune.

The Princess picked up many feathers, but there were still hundreds she could not find. Finally, she burst into tears. "How can I get feathers which have not yet fallen from the birds?" she cried.

Motivation-Deleted Story

Once upon a time, at a time when dragons still roamed the earth, there was a King. His wife had died and left him with a daughter. The King lived in a land with such beautiful weather that many different song birds from far and near came there to enjoy to sun.

The King married again. The new Queen said to the King, "Tell your daughter that the chattering of the birds keeps me awake all night. If she cannot quiet them this very night, she shall be punished."

The King gave the command.

The Princess knew she could not silence the birds. However, she placed near the Queen's window a jar of honey that drew many hummingbirds. Their hum put the Queen gently to sleep.

The next morning, the Queen said, "Tell your daughter I want my house filled with a hundred and one swan eggs tomorrow morning. If even a single one is broken, she shall be punished." This was no easy task, for the swans all lived on the other side of a wide river.

Soon the Princess set out with a large basket. She wrapped each egg in a leaf and then floated the basket beside her as she returned across the river.

Upon the Princess's return, the Queen looked at the King. "Tell your daughter to weave me a skirt for the ball tomorrow night. It must have 1,001 feathers in it, one from each kind of bird in the kingdom. If it is short one feather, she must be sent away forever!"

The Princess picked up many feathers, but there were still hundreds she could not find. "How can I get feathers which have not yet fallen from the birds?" she cried.

APPENDIX B

List of Questions

1. Would you like that Queen to come visit you?
2. How come?
3. How does the Queen feel about the Princess?
4. Why?
5. How does the Princess feel about the Queen?
6. How come?
7. What kind of food do the King and Queen eat?
8. Would you like the King to be your friend?
9. Why?
10. What do you think the King says at the end of the story?
11. How does the King feel at the end of the story?
12. How come?
13. Why does the King marry the Queen?
14. How old is the Princess?
15. How does the King feel about the Queen?
16. Why?
17. Why does the Queen make the Princess do all those different things?
18. What do you think the Princess says when the Queen tells her what to do?
19. Why does the Princess do what she is told?
20. What is the color of the Princess's hair?
21. What do you think the King says when the Queen tells him what she wants the Princess to do?
22. Why does the King do what the Queen tells him to do?
23. What do you think the Queen says when the Princess *does* all those things that the Queen asks her to do?
24. How does the Queen feel when the Princess *does* all those things that the Queen asks her to do?

REFERENCES

Applebee, A. *The child's concept of a story*. Chicago: University of Chicago Press, 1978.

Bettelheim, B. *The uses of enchantment*. New York: Knopf, 1976.

Bower, G. H. Comprehending and recalling stories. American Psychological Association, Division 3. Presidential Address, Washington, D.C., September, 1976.

Brown, A., & Smiley, S. S. Rating the importance of structural units of prose passages: A problem of metacognitive development. *Child Development*, 1977, *48*, 1–8.

Gardner, H. *Arts and human development*. New York: Wiley, 1973.

Gardner, H. Review of B. Bettelheim, The uses of enchantment: The meaning and importance of fairy tales. *Semiotica*, 1977, *21*, 363–380.

Gardner, H. From Melvin to Melville: On the relevance to aesthetics of recent research on story comprehension. In S. Madeja (Ed.), *The arts, cognition, and basic skills*. St. Louis: CEMREL, 1978.

Gardner, H. *Developmental psychology*. Boston: Little, Brown and Co., 1982. (a)

Gardner, H. The making of a story-teller. *Psychology Today*, March, 1982, *61*, 48–53. (b)

Honeck, H., & Hoffman, H. (Eds.) *Cognition and figurative language.* Hillsdale, NJ: Erlbaum, 1980.

Kohlberg, L. Stage and sequence: The cognitive-developmental approach to socialization. In D. A. Goslin (Ed.), *Handbook of socialization theory and research.* New York: Rand McNally, 1969.

Madeja, S. (Ed.). *The arts, cognition and basic skills.* St. Louis: CEMREL, 1978.

Mandler, J., & Johnson, N. S. The remembrance of things parsed: Story structure and recall. *Cognitive Psychology,* 1977, *9*, 111–151.

McGhee, P., & Chapman, A. (Ed.). *Children's humour.* London: Wiley, 1980.

Meringoff, L. K. Influence of the medium on children's story apprehension. *Journal of Education Psychology,* 1980, *72*, 240–249.

O'Hare, D. (Ed.). *Psychology and the arts.* Sussex: Harvester Press, 1981.

Perkins, D., & Leondar, B. (Eds.). *The arts and cognition.* Baltimore: Johns Hopkins University Press, 1977.

Piaget, J. *The child's conception of the world.* Totowa, NJ: Littlefield, Adams, 1965.

Piaget, J. Piaget's theory. In P. H. Mussen (Ed.), *Carmichael's manual of child psychology* (Vol I). New York: Wiley, 1970.

Pitcher, E., & Prelinger, E. (Eds.). *Children tell stories.* New York: International Universities Press, 1963.

Rumelhart, D. E. Notes on a schema for stories. In D. G. Bobrow & A. M. Collins (Eds.), *Representation and understanding: Studies in cognitive science.* New York: Academic Press, 1975.

Scarlett, G., & Wolf, D. When it's only make-believe. In E. Winner and H. Gardner (Eds.), *Fact, fiction, and fantasy in childhood. New Directions in Child Development,* 1979, *6*, 29–40.

Stein, N. The concept of a story: A developmental psycholinguistic analysis. Paper presented at the American Educational Research Association, San Francisco, April, 1979.

Sutton-Smith, B. *The folk-stories of children.* Philadelphia: University of Pennsylvania Press, 1981.

Winner, E. *Invented worlds: A psychology of the arts.* Cambridge: Harvard University Press, 1982.

Winner, E., & Gardner, H. (Eds.). Fact, fiction, and fantasy in childhood. *New Directions for Child Development,* 1979, No. *6* (Whole).

Chapter 11
The Psychological Study of Story Understanding*

John B. Black and Colleen M. Seifert

Department of Psychology
Yale University

Stories are a microcosm of life. When people read stories, they use the same psychological processes to comprehend the events in the story that they use to comprehend life. Even brief stories are condensations of life's complexities into a simpler, manipulable form. By studying how people respond to stories, psychologists can address the issues of how people understand and remember. For example, when we read a story about a character going into a restaurant, we have expectations about some of the actions that will probably occur (e.g., the character will sit down, order food from a menu, eat it, and pay for it) just as we would expect if we actually went into a restaurant. Likewise, if we learn that the character has gone there to meet his girlfriend, and that he has brought an engagement ring with him, we have expectations about what will happen in the episode (e.g., he will propose to his girlfriend) as well as predictions about how the character feels, how his girlfriend will feel, and so on. We know the character is trying to attain a goal (becoming engaged) and, as readers, we will analyze his actions, goals, and feelings just as we would interpret any person's actual efforts to attain that goal. Thus, at all levels, reading and responding to the story is similar to understanding the real events in the world.

When we attempt to understand someone's actions, either in a story or in life, we depend on our knowledge of the world to predict and to explain what is happening. In the example, explaining why the character brought a ring and expecting him to propose both depend on knowing how people usually act in the social interaction of getting engaged. Without this information, we could not connect the ideas together, ignore irrelevant events, expect what may be coming, explain what has happened, analyze the character's intentions, empathize with his feelings; in short, we could not *make sense* of the situation. Understanding a story can be viewed as finding the right knowledge of the world to give the events coherence and explanation. Thus the knowledge of the world we use to comprehend the story will determine how we respond to it.

The goal of the psychological study of story understanding is to determine the way in which the reader's response to a story depends on the knowledge used to

*The writing of this paper was supported by a grant from the System Development Foundation.

understand. The crucial tasks are to investigate the kinds of knowledge people use when reading a story, the form in which this knowledge is stored in memory, and how the application of this knowledge affects the reader's memory for and responses to the story. In addressing these questions, we will take the interdisciplinary approach of cognitive science by drawing on related results from cognitive psychology experiments and from artificial intelligence attempts to write computer programs that understand.

WHAT IS A STORY?

Part of our knowledge of the world is our concept of what a story is; that is, when something is a story, what is in a story, its structure, and the order of its parts. A prominent set of theories of story understanding have been proposed in the form of "story grammars." These theories attempt to set out a theoretical account of story structure that causes one text to be a coherent story, while another arrangement is not. There are two basic parts to the theories: first, a set of categories that are included in stories, and second, a set of rules that specify the relations between the categories. These "rewrite" rules, widely used in linguistics to specify grammar rules, gave the story grammars their name. Rumelhart (1975) was the first to propose a story theory of this type, followed by Thorndyke (1977), Mandler and Johnson (1977), and Stein and Glenn (1979). The theories use goal and subgoal analyses to separate the story into episodes. Because the stories are based on achieving goals, they can be viewed as "problem solving" stories. Most of the stories used in this type of research are goal-based—that is, a character is trying to achieve some result. To illustrate this approach, here is a simple example from Thorndyke.

Figure 11-1 gives the rewrite rules that define a story schema in Thorndyke's system. The rules are to be specific enough to determine what is a "legal" story

Figure 11-1. Sample of rewrite rules from Thorndyke's story grammar (1977)

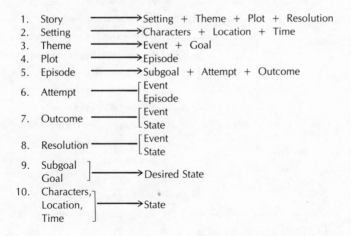

and what is not. The first rule states that a story is composed of a setting, a theme, a plot, and a resolution. These are each defined by other rules. In particular, the second rule says a setting is composed of character, location, and time descriptions. The setting thus describes the state of the world (see rule 10) needed for the rest of the story to occur. The next rule defines the theme as a goal with perhaps one or more events that establish it (parentheses indicate options and an asterisk means there can be more than one). The goal is the state of the world (rule 9) that the character is trying to attain.

The plot then relates the character's attempts to achieve this goal. Specifically, the plot is a series of one or more episodes (rule 4) where an episode is a subgoal, one or more attempts to attain the subgoal, and the outcome of the attempts (rule 5). An attempt can then be either a simple series of events or an entire subgoal-attempt-outcome episode (rule 6). Finally the outcomes of the episodes and the resolution of the whole story relate events or states which tell the reader whether or not the character attained the subgoals and the overall goal.

Figure 11-2 shows how these rules can be used to create a hierarchical structure linking story statements and showing their roles in the story. The story diagrammed in the figure is rather trivial, but it provides a simple example of an application of a story grammar theory to a text. The story can be read by scanning down the right side of the figure. John, a Stanford University undergraduate (setting) needs a course book (theme-goal). His first strategy is to look in the library (first plot episode subgoal), but the book is not there (first plot subgoal outcome). He tries a second strategy of looking in the bookstore (second plot episode subgoal) where he succeeds

Figure 11-2.   Diagram of a sample story using a story grammar hierarchy

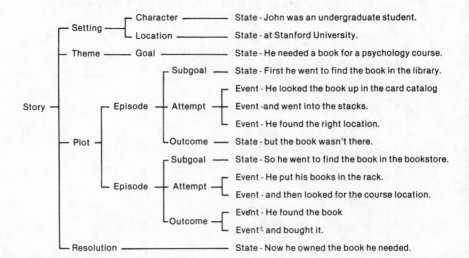

in finding and buying the book (second plot episode outcome). Thus the story ends with John owning the needed book (story resolution).

Some of the empirical predictions of story grammars have been validated. The simplest comparison was memory for texts based on a story grammar and the same texts with the statements reorganized. Thorndyke (1977) found that the story grammar texts were more comprehensible than the same texts with different statement orders. A second issue is the role of the hierarchy in memory for the stories. A common experimental procedure has been to give a group of people one or more stories to read, and then after a delay (e.g., 30 minutes) have them recall the stories. This allows comparison of how often the different story statements are recalled.

If we assume that what is stored in memory about a story is a structure like Figure 11-2 and that memory retrieval starts at the top level of this hierarchy (the far left side labeled "Story" in Figure 11-2) then we would predict that the farther a statement is from the top of the hierarchy the harder it would be to remember. Thus, in Figure 11-2, the resolution statement "Now he owned the book he needed" would be recalled most often (by most of the people) because it is only three steps from the top (Story-Resolution-State). The setting and theme statements, "John was an undergraduate at Stanford University. He needed a book for a psychology course," would be next in frequency of recall, because they are four steps from the top (Story-Setting-Character-State). Finally, the plot statements would be the least frequently recalled, since they are five steps from the top (Story-Plot-Episode-Subgoal-State).

In a more realistic story there would be more levels in the hierarchy. For example, a lower level can be embedded in the sample story by complicating one of the attempt-events. Instead of saying "John went into the library stacks" the story would read

> John went to the entrance of the stacks and the librarian asked for his ID. He remembered that his ID was back in his dorm room. Therefore he went to his room, picked up his ID and returned to the library. When he showed his ID to the librarian, she let him into the stacks.

Now instead of the attempt being the simple event of going into the stacks, it becomes the entire episode (see rewrite rule 6 of Figure 11-1) with its own subgoal (showing the ID), attempt (return to room to fetch it) and outcome (finally showing his ID to the librarian). If we added these elements to the hierarchy, they would be at least six steps from the top and therefore harder to remember than any of the statements in Figure 11-2.

Thus the story structure in memory acts like a wilting tree with the part labeled "Story" on the left being the trunk and the story statements on the right being the leaves. As the tree wilts (the story is forgotten), the leaves farthest from the tree wither first. In Thorndyke's experiments, he indeed did find evidence that information higher in the hierarchy was better recalled. In fact, numerous investigators (e.g., Thorndyke, 1977; Rumelhart, 1977; Black and Bower, 1980; Graesser, 1981) have now found that when they asked people to recall stories, the lower in the hierarchy a story statement was, the less likely it was to be recalled. Rumelhart (1977) also found that when people summarized stories, statements high in the hierarchy were more likely to appear in the summaries than those low in the hierarchy. To pursue the analogy: when the tree is pruned, the longer branches are cut off first. In addition, temporal order of information was shown to be better recalled when it was organized in a way consistent with the story grammar (Mandler, 1978; Thorndyke, 1977).

In addition to establishing a hierarchy among story statements, the story structure in Figure 11-2 also groups them into clusters. The major clustering is by subgoal: that is, all the first subgoal events cluster together with the subgoal and their outcome in the first episode, and all the second subgoal events cluster together with it and their outcome in the second episode. Mandler (1978) validated this subgoal clustering empirically by showing that people tend to recall the events related to a subgoal together even when the events were separated in the story text. Black and Bower (1979) have also shown evidence for grouping by subgoal. Specifically, the recall of an event in an episode was unaffected by the number of events in other episodes (i.e., related to other subgoals), but was affected by the number of events in the same episode. The more events in the same episode, the worse memory was for the individual events.

These results indicate that the story structure defined by the story grammar was successful in making some predictions about what would be remembered, especially in its use of hierarchies to define the importance of information. The notion of hierarchies of information, with relative degrees of importance, plays a crucial role in other text theories which use different schemes to develop the hierarchy. For example, Meyer (in press) proposes grouping the information based on rhetorical relations among the concepts. Clustering in memory is also important to other classification schemes. While these ideas have been empirically validated, and the general class of story grammars have met with some success, more recent evidence indicates they are an incomplete characterization of story understanding.

While story grammars provide the overall structure of a story, they are unable to make important distinctions about the parts of stories. For example, the grammars are unable to distinguish between failed and successful outcomes of episodes. Evidence from both problem solving and story understanding suggests this distinction determines what people remember. If we have people solve a problem, and later test their memory for what they did, they remember the best path to the solution of the problem (Egan and Greeno, 1974; Reed and Johnson, 1977). If people are using some of the same mental processes when they are solving a problem as when they are reading about a character solving a problem, then the solution paths in the stories, like those in the problems, should be remembered better. For example, in the story shown in Figure 11-2, the strategy described in the first episode (looking in the library) failed, while the strategy in the second episode (looking in the bookstore) succeeded. The second episode should be remembered better than the first, because the second actually leads to a solution. Black and Bower (1980) demonstrated that when people read and later recall stories of this kind, they remembered successful episodes better than episodes that failed.

Another problem with the story structure (Figure 11-2) is that the main role of setting information in stories is to set the stage for the plot events to occur. Thus, knowing that John is an undergraduate at Stanford explains why he needs a book for a course. Also, since Stanford is a large university, it probably has a large library, and large libraries usually store their book collections in "stacks," which explains why John "went into the stacks." In this story, all the setting information is necessary to the story, and used as background by the plot. However, the story setting could have given more information about John that would not have been connected to the plot. For example, it could have informed us that John was tall and blond. Would this additional setting information make any difference, considering it is not used in the episodes? In an experiment Black conducted (Black & Bower, 1980), people read and later recalled stories which contained setting statements used by plot events, and some not used. The results showed that people remembered the used setting information well, but tended to forget the unused setting information. Thus the primary role of setting information in problem solving (goal-based) stories is to provide the background information that establishes the conditions needed for the plot events to occur. The story grammars are unable to distinguish among the statements in the setting that were later used in the story, and those that were not. They treat all the setting information equally, while people's memories do not.

The problem of how to construct the story grammar structure for a story points out this problem of needing other types of knowledge to explain story understanding. These story grammar structures are not built automatically during reading. The key to building it is knowing the overall story goal and understanding how the story statements relate to that goal. Thorndyke (1977) showed that the more obscure the goal structure of a story is, the more trouble people have understanding and remembering the story. In particular, when he placed the theme-goal statement at the end of his stories, people rated the stories as less comprehensible and had a harder time remembering them than when the goal statement was at the beginning. When he removed the goal statement entirely, there was a further decline in comprehensibility and memorability. Another method of obscuring the goal structure of a story is to have the reader and the story be from different cultures. Bartlett (1932) and Kintsch and Greene (1978) also found that people write inferior summaries of stories from a different culture. They simply do not know what in the stories is important and what is unimportant. Thus when people lack the knowledge to infer the goal structure of a story, they demonstrate a poor understanding of the story.

These results are very important, as they demonstrate the structural information contained in story grammars is not enough to explain people's story understanding behavior. While these models tell us what parts are usually contained in stories, and demonstrate a hierarchical ordering among these parts, they clearly leave the reader lacking in even enough information to recognize the parts. Other experiments have shown that people need more knowledge to infer the story goal, connect setting information with events in the story, and determine when unsuccessful goals should be forgotten. Perhaps the story structure is not the most important information a reader needs. In fact, Stein (1982) found that the functions of story telling embody the wide varieties of motives underlying human social behavior. Specifically, she found that the concept of a story is a "fuzzy set"; that is, there is no unique set of features that characterize stories, but that the more story features present in a text, the more likely people will judge it as a story.

These results suggest that is it knowledge of the world, and not structure, that is important in understanding. The extent to which story grammars can successfully predict what people will remember may depend upon how closely the structure coincides with other world knowledge in the story. People do have information about what the typical parts of stories are, and they have developed a concept of what counts as a story and what does not. But it appears that the knowledge crucial for understanding is not structural parts of stories, but knowledge about events in the world. It is knowledge about the content of the story that allows a reader to make the right connections, predict and explain events, empathize and understand— in other words, to respond to the story. We will discuss this world knowledge in the next section.

WHAT DO YOU NEED TO KNOW TO UNDERSTAND?

We have proposed that the understanding of stories and episodes in the world is based upon the application of many different kinds of content knowledge (Black, Wilkes-Gibbs, and Gibbs, 1981). This knowledge is not a disorganized collection of isolated facts. Instead, related facts are organized into knowledge clusters called "schemas" (Bartlett, 1932; Rumelhart and Ortony, 1977). For example, your knowledge about what chairs look like, what personality types are from the Midwest, and what happens when you go to the store is organized by a schema. When a situation calls a schema into use, the schema adds to your understanding of the particular instance by bringing in more general information about the instance. The advantage of this organization is that once the appropriate cluster is accessed, all the related information in the schema is now available to aid in understanding. In this way, schemas organize related information in memory, and are the key to using the information in the understanding process.

Schemas can organize any type of information, from pictorial to affective. Obviously, different types of schemas will be needed to handle the wide variety of situations we encounter in life. Since the schemas are built from our experiences, the kinds of schemas we learn will reflect the diversity around us. In order to examine the knowledge we bring to bear in understanding, we need to categorize the schematic knowledge about a smaller set of knowledge. Addressing the class of goal-based (problem-solving) stories we have been discussing, can we conclude anything about the types of schemas required to understand? How do we know, in the example story, that going to the library and the bookstore are reasonable things to do given that you are looking for a book? How do we know that looking in the card catalog and going to the stacks are reasonable actions if you are looking for a book in a library? How much of this type of information is specific to libraries and books, and how much is useful in other, related situations? Schank and Abelson

(1977) have attempted to categorize the rather mundane information that people—and computer programs—would need to make these kinds of judgments. Of the schemas they propose to organize this information, plans and scripts are useful in the stories we have been examining.

A plan is a set of actions that are appropriate to perform in order to attempt to create a certain desired goal state. For example, if the goal is to use an object for some purpose, the plan could be to go to that location, gain control over the object, and then use it. In the example story, John needed a book to use for a course, so he thought of a place it might be (e.g., the library), went to that place, and tried to gain possession of it. Thus we "understand" this specific attempt to get a book for use in the course by recognizing it as an instance of a general "use plan." This plan describes the general actions to do in order to get to use an object. In addition, the schema allows access to other information about use, such as possible problems, other times the plan worked, and alternative possibilities. Most important, the schema explains what has happened, and predicts what will come next.

A script is a group of actions that typically occur in a particular situation. Thus while plan schemas are clusters of actions related to goals, scripts are plans that commonly occur in a particular setting. For example, one script in the example story was "getting a book in the university library." The actions in this script are ordered and more fixed than plan actions: going to the card catalog, finding the book number, go to stacks, show ID card, go into stacks, and so on. John's actions are understood as a subset of this script. If something in the script is mentioned, the rest of the actions are inferred to have happened, without having to describe each action. Scripts are very stereotyped plans, and together they are used in understanding how people try to achieve their goals.

Schank and Abelson use an interesting methodology to determine what schemas are needed in story understanding. They generate and analyze short narratives that range from easy to understand to the bizarre. By analyzing what makes the stories different, they determine what knowledge is needed to understand the comprehensible episodes. For example, this story is trivial to understand:

John went to a restaurant. He asked the waitress for roast beef.

Later, he paid the check and went.

On the other hand, the following analogous story is nonsensical:

John went to the football stadium. He asked the midget for air.

Later, he paid the box and left.

The difference in the stories is that the first fits a restaurant script, while the second fits no script. When we go to a restaurant, we expect to ask a waitress for food and pay for a bill later. However, we have no expectations of finding a midget selling air at a football game. Scripts exist to help us connect and understand the first paragraph, but not the second.

Consider another example:

> John knew that his wife's operation would be very expensive.
>
> There was always Uncle Harry. He reached for the phone book.

Here there is no script; that is, there is no stereotyped sequence of actions to do. Instead there is the goal (getting money) and a plan or set of more loosely connected actions to attain the goal. Again, the modified version is nonsensical:

> John knew that his wife's operation would be very expensive.
>
> There was always the mirror.
>
> He reached for the cat.

There is no obvious plan for getting money using mirrors or cats, but phoning a rich uncle is a reasonable method for obtaining emergency funds. Thus the set of actions in the episode must fit a plan schema in order for the episode to be understandable.

These schemas, plans and scripts, appear to account for one kind of information that is present in the stories. What empirical evidence is there that people use script or plan schemas in understanding stories? A series of experiments by Bower, Black, and Turner (1979) examined how people used scripts in understanding narratives. One implication of script theory is that people should largely agree on the typical actions for a common situation, since our experiences are similar even for different people. Indeed, when groups of subjects wrote down what would happen in five common situations (going to a restaurant, seeing a doctor, attending class, getting ready in the morning, and grocery shopping), there was a high degree of overlap in the actions people grouped in each situation.

Another implication of scripts is that stories can invoke an entire script in the mind of the reader by mentioning only a few of the actions in the scripts. Two memory experiments support this by showing that people could not remember what specific actions had been stated, and even claimed some had been stated that actually had not been. The design involved reading script-based stories where only some of the total possible actions were mentioned. Later, these subjects were asked to either write down all the actions they could remember, or rate a test list of actions according to how certain they were that the action had been explicitly present in the story. The results show that people remembered that the story tapped a certain script (seeing a doctor), but tended to lose track of exactly which actions they had read. Their answers show that they omitted some actions that were in the story and added some for the script that weren't in the story. Clearly, people are using scripts to aid their understanding of the story episodes.

In another experiment, scripts were shown to have a direct effect on the reading process. In this experiment, people read script-based stories one at a time, pressing a button on a computer terminal as they finished reading each action. The time between button presses is the reading time for each action. Because the script actions occur in a particular order, the amount of intermediate actions between two actions could be varied. For example, a restaurant script based story begins like this:

John sat down at the restaurant table. (action 1)

John looked at the menu. (action 2)

John finally decided what to order. (action 3)

The waiter came over to the table. (action 4)

John gave the waiter his order. (action 5)

Two sentences can be presented so that there is a large gap between them (action 1 followed by action 5, with 3 intermediate actions missing), or so that there is little or no gap (action 4 and action 5, with no intermediate actions). If we compare the time to read action 5—"John gave the waiter his order"—we find it is read faster when there is no gap in the action sequence. People do appear to use the scripts while they are reading to fill in information.

This section has presented evidence that people use plan and script schemas when understanding a story. One type of evidence, offered by Schank and Abelson (1977), argued that plan and script schemas are needed to distinguish the understandable stories from the nonsensical ones. A second type of evidence, from Bower, Black, and Turner (1979), showed empirical effects of the use of scripts to help understand stories. The evidence for the use of plan schemas in story understanding has grown rapidly in the last few years. For the remainder of this section, we will examine two experiments in this area with two goals in mind: first, to illustrate the types of experiments that are addressing the use of schemas in understanding; second, to demonstrate in detail the methodology common to these experiments. The methodology used in Bower, Black, and Turner (1979), specifically the reading time, recognition test, and free recall test, has been a basic and fruitful approach to testing what happens during story understanding. In addition to the experimental methodology, the computer modeling summarized in Schank and Abelson (1977) has added greatly to our knowledge of what must be known in order to understand.

There is ample evidence for the use of scripts in understanding. But what about other types of schemas? Are plans also used in reading to fill in information? An experiment by Seifert, Robertson, and Black (1982) examined the use of plan information, as well as goal, action, and state information, in reading narratives. The assumption was that if schematic information is needed during reading, and it is not supplied in the text, it will take some processing time during understanding to activate or "infer" the correct information. For example, if a text tells you explicitly what plan the character is using, you should be able to understand the events sooner than if you have to determine (infer) which plan the character is using from the situation. Accessing the appropriate schematic information takes extra time during understanding. In this study, reading time for the statements in the text is used as a reflection of when additional processing is required. If a statement which requires inferring information takes longer to read than the same statement when the information was already given to the reader, then the time difference is attributed to the additional processing needed to infer the information. Here is an example from the experiment:

> Mary planned to go out to lunch shortly with her friend Kate.
>
> Each was supposed to pay for her own lunch.
>
> Mary needed to get some money.
>
> Mary's pocketbook was empty.
>
> (She decided to ask Kate for a loan.)
>
> She told Kate that she had no cash.

The statement in parentheses is the plan Mary will use in the story. For some people, this plan is presented in the story, and the reading time for the last line is recorded. For other people, the line in parentheses is left out of the story. These readers need to infer or figure out the plan from the last statement, "She told Kate that she had no cash." When the plan had to be added by the reader, the reading time for the last statement should be longer than when the plan was given to the subjects just before the last line. The results showed that people took longer to read and understand the statements when they had to infer the plan, compared to when the plan was stated for them in the story. This shows that people are accessing the planning schemas when they need them in understanding, and that this process takes more time during reading.

Goals, states, and actions were also tested in this way. The assumption was that if a goal or plan schema was needed during reading, it would take some processing time to activate it. If action information was needed, this would also require extra time to fit the action into the schema. The results supported these predictions, as people took longer to understand the statements if they needed to infer goals, plans, or actions. The state information alone was different. States were included because it was expected that state information was not needed in understanding these stories, and so if it wasn't present, people would not need to add it. For example, the statement "Kate had cashed a check that day" allows the inference that "Kate had some money." This inference is logically true. However, it is not as useful as the schematic inferences, and so was not predicted to be added by people as they read. The reading time data showed that people were not taking extra time to add the state information as they read, while they did take extra time when they needed to add the goals, plans, and actions to the stories.

The reading time results showed that people were taking longer to understand at the points that we expected they needed the information. How do we know they inferred the same goals, plans, and actions instead of something else? How can we be certain they were adding the expected information to their memory of the story? The method used in the experiment to test what information the people had actually added to what was in the story was a recognition test. The test consisted of story statements, information that could have been added or inferred during reading, plus some wrong information. After the reading portion, the readers would go through the test, rating their certainty that particular statements had actually been in the stories. In general, subjects are good at recognizing statements that were stated in the story texts, and rejecting those that had not appeared. Sometimes, though, subjects could not distinguish whether a statement had been stated or whether they had added or inferred that information. In our plan example, a subject might "remember" seeing the plan statement "She decided to ask Kate for a loan," even though it had not been in the story, but the subject had added it during the understanding process. This phenomena is called "false alarming." If people "false alarm" to the goals, plans, and actions, this would indicate they must have added the information as they were understanding the stories. Indeed, the false alarm rates were high for these types of information, while the false alarm rate was very low for states. This supports the reading time data: when people took more time to read, it seems they actually added the information to their understanding and memory for the stories. When there was no reading time difference, as for the states, there was also no evidence that people had added that state information to their knowledge of the stories.

This experiment provided strong evidence for the use of schematic knowledge (i.e., plans) during the understanding process. It also demonstrated how reading time results can be supported by methods such as recognition testing. A third method used to tap people's understanding of stories has been the free recall test. Typically, people are given texts to read, and after some time are asked to reproduce, as accurately as possible, whatever they can remember of the texts. An example of this method is an experiment by Abbott and Black (1982). In the experiment, the question of how information is organized in memory was addressed by comparing two types of organization. One was "argument repetition" (Kintsch, 1974), where statements that are about the same thing would be related together (i.e., the arguments would be repeated in different propositions in the story). This would predict statements like "John has blond hair," "John's wife grew up in Texas," and "The boss called John" would be stored together, since they all share the argument "John." An alternative proposal is the one we have been advocating: that people use schematic knowledge about the world to impose order on what they read (Schank and Abelson, 1977; Bower, Black, and Turner, 1979; Graesser, 1981). Thus schemas would allow a reader to understand the relations between the statements "The sun was hot. The children were sweating. The pool was inviting." These statements share no arguments, but nevertheless, people can easily see the relations between them.

The stories in the experiment were designed to have statements related by either argument repetition or by schematic world knowledge. Subjects were given six stories to read; after an intervening period, they were asked to write down all the information they remembered about each story. The subjects' answers were scored according to how many of the three related statements from each story they had remembered. The conditional probability of recall was then calculated for each of the two relations. That is, given that subjects recalled one of the three statements in a story, how likely were they to recall another of the statements? For the argument repetition stories, the conditional probability of recall was .38, while the schema-based stories had a much higher average of .82. It appears the schematic organization helped the subjects remember related statements together. The free recall data reflected the knowledge organization of the readers, and indicated the schematic approach produced better recall.

WHAT MAKES A STORY INTERESTING?

A striking characteristic of the stories used in psychology experiments is that they are terrible stories. Certainly no one would claim that they are literature. Why are these stories so dull? The purpose of the experiments was to test the validity of the theories about standard knowledge schemas. Therefore, the stories were written to embody the schemas in pure form. For example, a character would go to a restaurant, and nothing would happen that was not expected or explained by the restaurant schema. If a story matches a common schema completely, then it tells the reader little that is new or unusual, and therefore it is uninteresting. An essential attribute of literature, on the other hand, is to be innovative.

Does this difference make the psychological study of story understanding irrelevant to the study of how people respond to literature? No, because before we can tell what is innovative, we need to know what is standard, particularly since being innovative does not mean being completely arbitrary. A random collection of ideas would have no meaning rather than a novel meaning. The key is to be novel in a way that stretches our existing schemas, but not in a way that defies them completely. A simple script-based episode will illustrate this point. First, here is a standard, uninteresting script episode:

> John went to a restaurant.
>
> The waiter came over to his table.
>
> John ordered roast beef.
>
> He ate the dinner.
>
> He paid the check and left.

But if this episode is changed so it departs from this standard sequence of events, the episode becomes more interesting:

> John went to a restaurant.
>
> The waiter did not come to his table, so
>
> John started making loud, obscene remarks
>
> about the women patrons in the restaurant.
>
> Then the waiter quickly came over to the table.
>
> John ordered the roast beef.
>
> He ate the dinner.

He paid the check and left.

Here, instead of the waiter coming over to the table automatically, as in the standard script, John has to create a disturbance to attract his attention. This episode is not great literature, but it is considerably more interesting than the previous one. The same increase in interest can be produced by departing from the standard script at any point; for example,

John went to a restaurant.

The waiter came over to his table.

John ordered roast beef.

He ate the dinner.

He went to the bathroom and started a fire.

In the ensuing confusion,

he left without paying.

This episode departs from the script by having a nonstandard exit from the restaurant, and again, it is more interesting than the first story. In the interesting stories, some of the events are nonstandard. The script stills plays an important role, however: it helps you to determine what is going wrong, and therefore what is interesting.

Episodes like these were used in a memory experiment (Bower, Black, and Turner, 1979). Specifically, people read script-based stories that contained some deviations from what the scripts predicted. These deviations were much less vivid than the examples given above. For example, in a restaurant episode, the customer would either talk to a friend before he sat down, yell at the waiter to attract his attention, or the waiter would bring a hot dog instead of the hamburger he ordered. However, even with these mundane deviations, the people recalled the deviations much better than the script actions. People focused on the deviations as the interesting and important part of the episodes while the standard actions fade into the background.

But if the deviations are too extreme, the episodes again become uninteresting. For example, the following is a restaurant episode that deviates too much from the script:

The waiter came over to the table.

John went into a restaurant.

He left.

He ate the dinner.

He ordered the roast beef.

He paid the check.

Here the actions are the same as in the standard script episode above, but they have been randomly reordered until the episode is incoherent. Meyers and Boldrick (1975) reported an experiment in which they had people read and later recall a story with 50 percent, 20 percent, or none of its statements randomly rearranged. The measurement of interest here is the number of ideas present in the recalls that were not in the original story texts. These new ideas represent inferences that people made while attempting to make sense of the story, like the "false alarms" on the recognition test. The results showed few new ideas when none of the statements were rearranged and when 50% were rearranged, but when only 20% of the statements were rearranged, there were a lot of new ideas in the recalls. The readers showed little creativity when the story was normal or when its deviation was too extreme, but there was a magic region between these two extremes where the interesting phenomenon was taking place.

A proposed explanation for this effect may lie in how people are using schemas to help them remember. If the story exactly fits a schema, then the reader has only to remember the schema to remember the episodes. There is nothing distinctive to mark the story as a separate incident. When asked to recall the episode, there are no special cues to help, and the story is simply reconstructed from the schema. At the other extreme, stories that are very different from the closest schema, such as the scrambled statement stories, have so little to match with the schema that the schema is useless in organizing the recall. The advantage of clustering is lost because the schema cannot be used, and people have to resort to remembering as many individual items as they can. Finally, the case where a schema clearly matches the story, with some deviations, is the best for producing a good memory of the story. First, there is the relationship to the schema, which organizes most of the story and points out where the deviations are. These deviations are then noted, and "hung off" the schematic structure. Remembering these stories is not just remembering the schema: there are important differences. Since these differences are remembered as exceptions to the schema, remembering any of them will aid in recalling the whole episode. For example, in the fire story above, the memory representation of the story could be the restaurant schema plus the deviations of setting the fire and getting away without paying. Since fire is so unusual, it may be remembered later when readers are trying to remember all the stories they read. Once they remember "fire," that distinctive cue plus the restaurant schema will help pull together the other deviations, such as getting away without paying.

The role of interesting deviations in memory has been analyzed by Schank (1980, 1982) using the phenomena of reminding. Reminding occurs when a particular situation causes you to remember another experience that is similar in some way. The relationship between the new input and the old memory retrieved can be at any level of abstraction or similarity. For example, seeing a bearded man in a red suit may remind you of Santa Claus, going into Burger King for the first time could remind you of McDonald's, and seeing "West Side Story" may remind you of "Romeo and Juliet." Schank proposes that in understanding the new situation, you are led to structures in memory that categorize the input; then, if a particularly interesting or unusual characteristic is present in the input, you may find an episode from the past stored in the same way. In the example above when the waiter did not come to take John's order in the restaurant, John used the plan of making loud, obscene comments to get the waiter to come over, and it worked. The next time John is in a store, and the salesperson will not come over to assist him, he may be reminded of the incident in the restaurant. In both cases, he wanted service from a person who is in the role of assisting him for pay, and the person is ignoring him. From the old restaurant experience, John may remember what he did, and try to use the same plan of making loud comments about the other patrons.

In this way, matching a new situation to a previous experience provides understanding and possibly a way of solving a problem. Accessing the old episode in the process of understanding is advantageous for other reasons as well. The reminding may add to your understanding by pointing out similarities in the two experiences that you hadn't noticed. The old episode may have additional information comparable to the new situation, such as what you did in the old situation that might be possible in the new, problems to watch for, and expectations about what will happen. For example, recognizing that Burger King is like McDonald's will tell you a lot about how to order, how the food will be served, and so on. Finally, the reminding may point out that you have processed the new episode incorrectly. If the old and new episodes aren't really comparable, then the way you are understanding the new situation is in error.

One level of relationship between episodes is particularly interesting for literature. This is the thematic level; for example, the similarities between "West Side Story" and "Romeo and Juliet" (Schank, 1982). These thematic structures are based upon relationships between the goals in the episodes, and interesting deviations in the situation. Schank calls this similarity in abstract patterns of elements a TOP (thematic organization point). In these two stories, the two characters are pursuing the same goal while outsiders oppose their goal. When an episode involves a complex goal pattern, similar episodes that had been understood using that goal pattern may be brought to mind. Then, the old experience can be further used to aid in processing the current episode. This can be very useful in making predictions about what is likely to happen, and it may prevent one from making the same mistakes in a similar situation.

So far we have been discussing reminding as an individual experiences new situations. However, reminding can be useful in reading to bring to mind related information that adds to the ideas. In literature, readers can be aided in understanding by reminding them of their own similar experiences or ones they have read about. A reader truly "understands" a story when he has accessed his closest related experiences. Recognizing an episode as something experienced before gives the reader a head start in expectations about what will occur, and encourages active participation in analyzing the course of events. Reminding in reading may add appreciation to the ideas being stated, as well as new ideas to enrich the text. From this point of view, good literature is that which maximizes remindings from the life of the reader. Recent experiments by Reiser, Black, and Abelson (1982) have examined how remindings can be facilitated. They have found that subjects are reminded of an experience more quickly when schema cues are presented before deviation cues. From our earlier example, giving "restaurant" and then "person fails to take order" as cues more effectively remind the person of an experience than the same cues presented in the reverse order. Other experiments have focused on remindings while reading thematic-based texts (Seifert, Abelson, McKoon, and Ratcliff, 1982). Further progress in discovering how remindings are evoked in readers will provide ideas about how texts can be written to help readers tie in their own experiences, and thus add to their understanding.

Higher level remindings (thematic) seems the most fruitful for comparisons with themes in literature. Some theories of thematic level structures have been proposed, such as macrostructures (van Dijk, 1980) and plot units (Lehnert, 1981). Plot units focus on components of goal interaction, such as "retaliation" and "competition." Plot units have been investigated in a series of experiments that demonstrate how an abstract relation between two episodes can be used in perceiving stories as similar (Reiser and Black, 1982). Schank's TOPs address a more abstract pattern of these components. Dyer (1982) has developed a class of thematic structures like Schank's called TAUs (Thematic Affect Units). A TAU describes a common plan that has an interesting deviation in its outcome. TAUs focus on mistakes people make in certain planning situations, and how people recognize (or fail to recognize) that the same mistake is about to be made. The TAU structure often includes information about how to prevent or recover from the mistake in the future. The patterns are often captured in the form of cultural adages, such as "counting your chickens before they're hatched." In this situation, a character is trying to achieve a goal, and decides that it is likely she will succeed. Based upon this belief, the character goes out and pursues other goals. When the original goal actually fails, the actions based upon its success naturally also fail. The character's overconfidence causes him or her to perform actions based upon success before the success can be certain. Since TAUs represent the abstract relations in an episode, they are the point, or "moral," of a story.

Here is a story based upon the TAU "counting chickens":

> Ernie was really encouraged about his interview for a security guard at the new factory in town. The interview was long, and Ernie thought he had done well. He assumed his employment as a guard was imminent. He went to the shopping mall and hunted around for a dark blue security guard uniform, and finally bought several. The next day he received a phone call from the factory personnel director saying he was not selected for a security guard position. Ernie was dismayed he has wasted money on uniforms.

In the story, Ernie counts on getting the job before he really has it. He then buys uniforms, and when he finds out his original goal did not succeed, he loses the uniform money too.

An experiment designed to test people's sensitivity to these TAU patterns involved showing subjects three example stories based on the same TAU pattern, and asking them to write a story that is similar (Seifert and Black, 1982). The three sample stories were 'about' very different things, such as jobs or auto mechanics, but shared the same abstract pattern of making a planning error. For example, here is a second story based on the "counting chickens" TAU:

> Judy was overjoyed about the fact that she was pregnant. She looked forward to having a baby boy, and wanted one so badly she felt absolutely certain it would be male. As a result, she bought all kinds of toy cars, trucks, miniature army soldiers, and even painted the nursery blue. Finally, the big moment came, and she was rushed to the hospital. Everything went smoothly in the delivery room, and at last she knew. Judy's lively, bouncing baby was actually a girl.

Judy also counts her chickens in assuming she will have a boy; she acts based on that belief, only to find she was wrong. If subjects are able to reproduce the same abstract pattern in a context that they choose, it would indicate the pattern is cohesive and subjects are sensitive to it.

The subjects were asked to write three stories based on three different sets of sample stories, of a total of nine possible TAU patterns. The subject-generated stories were scored for which TAU pattern, if any, was in the story. For the "counting chickens" TAU, 78 percent of the stories clearly matched the TAU pattern in the examples. Over all the TAUs, 82 percent of the stories matched the TAU. The subjects used familiar contexts, such as school, jobs, and dating to express the TAU pattern. In general, then, the subjects were able to recognize and reproduce the TAU in a story.

In a second experiment, the relationship between stories based upon TAUs was examined. Three TAUs were chosen: "counting chickens," "the blind leading the blind," and "pot calling the kettle black." In the first, the character errs by counting on success before it is certain; in the second, the character chooses someone to help him who obviously has done it wrong himself; and in the third, the character tries to injure another with accusations, only to be proved guilty of the same. Eight of the stories for each TAU were chosen randomly from the stories written by subjects in the first experiment. These 24 stories were presented in random order to a new set of subjects. These subjects were to group the stories together using any criterion they wished. They were told to form as few or as many groups as they wished.

The results were analyzed using Johnson's hierarchical clustering algorithm (1967). The stories were reliably sorted into three groups which corresponded to the three TAUs the stories were based on. Only one story was placed in the wrong group: this story was written based upon "counting chicks," but involved elements of "blind leading blind," and was sorted with this other group. These results show that subjects are, again, sensitive to the abstract, thematic structures. Further, they can use these relationships to perform tasks based on similarities between stories.

While these results are encouraging, there is still no evidence for the use of the thematic pattern "during" the understanding of similar stories. So far, all the evidence for reminding consists of analysis of individual reminding experiences. However, the goal of examining reminding empirically has resulted in exploring methodologies such as free recall testing. Another methodology that may be useful is priming, where response time is used to determine how related two items are in memory. Demonstrating whether and when a previous episode is called to mind is a challenging experimental goal. Investigation continues into the use of reminding in both personal experiences and texts.

Thematic structures like TAUs provide a connection to how the characters feel in a story. From the pattern of the theme, the reader can predict how the character will respond. For example, in the "counting chickens" story, the character is first hopeful, then devastated as all his plans fall through. The role of themes in producing affect is another area of application to literature. The reader's empathy with the character will depend on his understanding of the character's response. Affect seems closely connected to knowledge structures and specifically to the deviations from the expected course of events.

Another approach to story understanding has focused on arousing and reducing affect in the reader. Brewer and Lichtenstein (1981) have examined how the arrangements of events in a story provokes different affective responses in the reader. They divide knowledge about a narrative into two levels: first, the event structure, which is the underlying temporal event sequence (i.e., a script); and second, the discourse structure, which is the linguistic presentation of those events. Using the same event structure, the information can be presented in different discourse structures to arouse suspense, surprise, or curiosity in the reader. For an experiment, they wrote stories and manipulated the discourse structure while leaving the event structure the same. The stories were compared to "base stories" which had "no significant event." For the stories that would produce emotive effects, it appeared there had to be a significant (interesting) event present.

While the subjects read the stories, they were interrupted to rate the surprise or suspense at certain points in the story. At the end of the story, they rated how much they liked it. For the most part, the subjects' ratings corresponded to the manipulations of discourse structure: they thought a story was surprising when the events were arranged so as to introduce information in a particular sequence. The base stories, on the other hand, were rated low on the surprise and suspense scales. These results supported Brewer and Lichtenstein's view of rearranging the content structure in order to provoke a response in the reader. These three particular patterns—surprise, suspense, and curiosity—were directly related to the discourse structure of the story.

While this experiment adds important information about the emotive effects of story, the role of the discourse structure is not separate from the role of content knowledge we have been discussing. World knowledge is still a determinant of whether a story is at all interesting. The manipulation of the discourse structure depends on a significant (interesting) event to be present in the story. How is this determined? Clearly the content of the story is crucial to any further manipulations. In addition, the memory processes and knowledge structures also affect the discourse structures. Patterns of discourse are episodes too, and may remind a reader of similar patterns, allow him to predict what is coming, and so on. For example, the discourse pattern of presenting an important fact to the reader, but not to the character, allows suspense while the reader waits to see whether the character will notice it in time. This pattern would at first be memorable, and would be recalled when a similar device is used in another story. After many episodes, it would be readily recognized, and another problem develops for the writer: how to create a deviation from this pattern that will make it interesting? Patterns of discourse may be analogous to themes, where patterns that become familiar require some unexpected changes to make the pattern novel and unusual. In summary, the structure of the events in a story is an additional factor that affects response in the reader. While the discourse structure is also dependent on content structures in memory, and the pattern of discourse in the story can be used as a theme in analysis, it is an important addition to the study of how people understand stories.

CONCLUSION

What do we have to contribute to response to literature and the teaching of literature?

What has research in the psychology of story understanding contributed to our knowledge of response to literature? The basic tenet is that response to a text is determined by the knowledge the reader brings to it. Understanding and remembering a story depends upon knowledge of the world. Cognitive science research has shown that this knowledge is organized around schemas in memory, such as plans and scripts. Deviations from these schemas make episodes interesting and memorable.

During reading, specific episodes are called to mind to add to understanding of the text. This process, called reminding, involves finding similar episodes in memory that are related to the story. When a reader is reminded of an episode, it increases understanding of the situation and allows the reader to predict what may happen. Good literature maximizes the ability to evoke remindings in the reader. A particular kind of reminding—thematic reminding—seems particularly related to the kinds of themes used in literature.

The cognitive science approach to story understanding also provides ways to research response to literature. The methodology of story understanding research addresses the questions of what people know and how they use that knowledge in understanding. The artificial intelligence technique of computer simulation forces the researcher to define the tacit knowledge that is involved. To examine the representation in memory, measures such as free recall and recognition testing are useful. For processes involved during comprehension, concurrent measures such as reading time and priming prove useful. Additional approaches are being developed to examine how remindings are evoked in readers.

Through the examination of what knowledge is needed, and how this knowledge is used, the psychological study of story understanding has addressed the determinants of people's responses to literature. Further research in this area will address the more complex relations between higher level knowledge and good literature.

REFERENCES

Abbott, V., & Black, J. B. A comparison of the memory strength of alternative text relations. Paper presented at the meeting of the American Educational Research Association, New York, 1982.

Bartlett, F. C. *Remembering.* Cambridge: Cambridge University Press, 1932.

Black, J. B. Memory for state and action information in narratives. Twenty-first annual meeting of the Psychonomic Society. St. Louis, Missouri, 1980.

Black, J. B., & Bower, G. H. Episodes as chunks in narrative memory. *Journal of Verbal Learning and Verbal Behavior,* 1979, *18,* 309–318.

Black, J. B., & Bower, G. H. Story understanding as problem solving. *Poetics,* 1980, *9,* 223–250.

Black, J. B., Wilkes-Gibbs, D., & Gibbs, R. W. What writers need to know that they don't know they need to know. In M. Nystrand (Ed.), *What writers know: Studies in the psychology of writing.* New York: Academic Press, 1981.

Bower, G. H., Black, J. B., & Turner, T. J. Scripts in memory for text. *Cognitive Psychology,* 1979, *11,* 177–220.

Brewer, W. F., & Lichtenstein, E. H. Event schemas, story schemas, and story grammars, In J. Long, & A. Baddeley (Eds.), *Attention and performance IX.* New York: Academic Press, 1981.

Dyer, M. G. In depth understanding: A computer model of integrated processing for narrative comprehension. Technical Report 219, Department of Computer Science, Yale University, 1982.

Egan, D. E., & Greeno, J. G. Theory of rule induction: Knowledge acquired in concept learning, serial pattern learning, and problem solving. In L. Gregg (Ed.), *Knowledge and cognition.* Potomac, MD: Lawrence Erlbaum Associates, 1974.

Graesser, A. C. *Prose comprehension beyond the word.* New York: Springer-Verlag, 1981.

Johnson, S. C. Hierarchical clustering schemes. *Psychometrika,* 1967, *32,* 241–254.

Kintsch, W. *The representation of meaning in memory.* Hillsdale, NJ: Lawrence Erlbaum Associates, 1974.

Kintsch, W., & Greene, E. The role of culture-specific schemata in the comprehension and recall of stories. *Discourse Processes,* 1978, *1,* 1–13.

Lehnert, W. G. Plot units and narrative summarization. *Cognitive Science,* 1981, *5,* 293–331.

Mandler, J. M. A code in the node: The use of a story schema in retrieval. *Discourse Processes,* 1978, *1,* 14–35.

Mandler, J. M., & Johnson, N. S. Remembrance of things parsed: Story structure and recall. *Cognitive Psychology,* 1977, *9,* 111–191.

Meyer, B. J. Prose analysis: Procedures, purposes, and problems. In B. Britton & J. Black (Eds.), *Analyzing and understanding expository text.* Hillsdale, NJ: Lawrence Erlbaum Associates, in press.

Meyers, L. S., & Boldrick, D. Memory for meaningful connected discourse. *Journal of Experimental Psychology: Human Learning and Memory,* 1975, *27,* 2, 146–152.

Reed, S. K., & Johnson, J. A. Memory for problem solutions. In G. H. Bower (Ed.), *The psychology of learning and motivation (Vol. 11).* New York: Academic Press, 1977.

Reiser, B. J., & Black, J. B. Thematic knowledge structures in the understanding and generation of narratives. Cognitive Science Technical Report #16, Yale University, 1982.

Reiser, B. J., Black, J. B., & Abelson, R. P. Retrieving memories of personal experiences. Proceedings of the Fourth Conference of the Cognitive Science Society, Ann Arbor, MI, 1982.

Rumelhart, D. E. Notes on a schema for stories. In D. G. Bobrow & A. Collins (Eds.), *Representation and understanding: Studies in cognitive science.* New York: Academic Press, 1975.

Rumelhart, D. E. Understanding and summarizing brief stories. In D. La Berge & J. Samuels (Eds.), *Basic processes in reading and comprehension.* Hillsdale, NJ: Lawrence Erlbaum Associates, 1977.

Rumelhart, D. E. & Ortony, A. The representation of knowledge in memory. In R. C. Anderson, R. J. Spiro, & W. E. Montague (Eds.), *Schooling and the acquisition of knowledge.* Hillsdale, NJ: Lawrence Erlbaum Associates, 1977.

Schank, R. C. Language and memory. *Cognitive Science,* 1980, *4,* 243–284.

Schank, R. C. *Dynamic memory: A theory of reminding and learning in computers and people.* New York: Cambridge University Press, 1982.

Schank, R. C., & Abelson, R. P. *Scripts, plans, goals, and understanding*. Hillsdale, NJ: Lawrence Erlbaum Associates, 1977.

Seifert, C. M., & Black, J. B. Thematic relations between episodes. *Proceedings of the Fifth Conference of the Cognitive Science Society*, Rochester, NY, 1983.

Seifert, C. M., Abelson, R. P., McKoon, G., & Ratcliff, R. Memory connections between thematically similar episodes. Cognitive Science Technical Report #27, Cognitive Science Program, Yale University, 1984.

Seifert, C. M., Robertson, S. G., & Black, J. B. On-line processing of pragmatic inferences. Cognitive Science Technical Report #15, Yale University, 1982.

Stein, N. L., & Glenn, C. G. An analysis of story comprehension in elementary school children. In R. Freedle (Ed.), *Discourse processing: Multidisciplinary perspectives*. Norwood, NJ: Ablex Publishing, 1979.

Stein, N. L. The definition of a story. *Pragmatics*, 1982, *6*, 75–83.

Thorndyke, P. W. Cognitive structures in comprehension and memory of narrative discourse. *Cognitive Psychology*, 1977, *9*, 77–110.

van Dijk, T. A. *Macrostructures: An interdisciplinary study of global structures in discourse, interaction, and cognition*. Hillsdale, NJ: Lawrence Erlbaum Associates, 1980.

Chapter 12
Verbal Scales in Research on Response to Literature

Gunnar Hansson

Department of Communication Studies
University of Linköping

INTRODUCTION

Anyone with an experience of reading or teaching literature, or writing interpretative essays about it is familiar with the fact that the words we need to describe the meaning of the works are often missing or hard to find. The meaning of a work may be vividly present in our response, but the words to describe the meaning are not available, or they are felt to be insufficient or partly misleading. The expressed response is not an adequate representation of the clearly felt or grasped response.

This is a problem in all communication about literature, whether in teaching, in writing, or in private discussions. It is also a problem in all kinds of research dealing with the meanings and qualities of literary works, regardless of whether this research openly refers to responses or not. Particularly, however, it is a problem in research on response to literature.

One sector of such research is deliberately working with the expressed responses: how different groups of readers articulate their interpretations and evaluations, how various ways to express responses and justify evaluations are acquired in the literary and cultural milieu or learned in the educational system, and so on. In these and similar cases the readers' difficulties in finding the "right" or "sufficient" words to represent their responses is not a serious problem, since the aim of the research is to study the ways various groups of readers describe and articulate their responses. Their ability to find "right" or "sufficient" words is an integrated part of such research.

Another sector of research on response to literature is, however, less interested in the expressed response than in the response itself. Such research is working with questions such as the following: what meanings and qualities were actually present in the response, though not expressed in a descriptive statement; where and when a specific meaning nuance was brought into the response; what other meaning nuances it was connected with in forming larger meaning units and the like. This is where missing or insufficient descriptive words becomes a crucial methodological problem. Research devoted to elucidating the full response to literature cannot be content with verbalized descriptions of meanings attributed to literary works, with analytical statements about structures and organizations that have been consciously discerned among these meanings, or with evaluative statements based on a reasoned inspection of these meanings and their apparent structuring. It has to go beyond such descriptions and statements and try to get closer to the response itself.

One way to eliminate the effects of variations in the ability to verbalize responses, interpretations, and evaluations is to make use of verbal scales. Such scales have been developed and have often been used for research by psycholinguists (Aaronson and Rieber, 1979; Rommetveit, 1968). The best known and most often used instrument is the so-called "semantic differential," which has been constructed and empirically tried out by Charles Osgood and his collaborators. The theoretical and technical aspects of their work have been fully discussed in C. E. Osgood, G. J. Suci and P. H. Tannenbaum in *The Measurement of Meaning* (1957). The instrument has since been used in hundreds of investigations and in many different branches of research. A sample of such applications is presented and discussed in J. G. Snider and C. E. Osgood, *Semantic Differential Technique* (1969). The latter book also contains a bibliography.

THE SCALES AND WHAT THEY MEASURE

Different types of scales have been tried out and used in various investigations. The type that has been used most often is a 7-point, bipolar scale, where the two poles are defined by opposing adjectives ("cold—warm," "strong—weak," etc.). Such scales may look like this: "cold 1 2 3 4 5 6 7 warm." Scales with more than seven points—15 or even more—have also been used, however. One reason for using scales with a greater number of points is that only three grades of, for example, "coldness" may be felt to put undue restrictions on persons responding to works of literature or to other objects with aesthetic qualities. It has also been argued (Gulliksen, 1958) that more than three grades of meaning at each end of the scale are preferable from statistical points of view.

Some investigators have preferred unipolar scales in studies of response to literature. In these scales there is a zero-point outside the scale as such, and the scale is defined by only one adjective (e.g., "0 − 1 2 3 4 5 6 7 happy"). In these cases the responder is instructed to use the zero-point when he or she finds the scale to be not relevant to what is being judged, or when he or she is uncertain whether it is relevant or not. One advantage to such unipolar scales is that they do not force the responder to decide that a work of literature, or a particular part of it, is *either* "cold" or "warm," *either* "simple" or "complex," and so on. Instead, they make it possible for him to say that the work, or a particular part of it, is *both* "cold" and "warm," *both* "simple" and "complex," if that is what he or she finds to be the case, and if both the opposed adjectives are included among the scales. People familiar with literature and other works of art often argue that such seemingly conflicting qualities may be simultaneously present in aesthetic responses. If this is so, bipolar scales will force the responder to choose one of the qualities and neglect the other, unless he denies his own response and puts his mark at the neutral midpoint. As a matter of fact, there are investigations in the aesthetic field where some responders have refused to make such forced choices on bipolar scales, or where they deliberately have checked on both ends of some of the scales.

How responders are supposed to use the scales may be seen from the following instruction, which was given in one of the investigations which will be discussed later on in this chapter.

When we read a poem, we normally grasp the sense of the words rather directly. Besides this, however, we often feel more or less clearly that the single words, the parts of the poem, or the whole poem are connected with certain words, or that they are on a distance from other words. We often say that we get "associations" in certain directions, or that we attach certain qualities to the poem and its parts. This applies not only to poems, but also to paintings and musical compositions, for instance.

Your task in this investigation is to compare a number of parts of a poem, and finally also the whole poem, with a series of opposing words, e.g., "strong–weak," "pleasant–unpleasant." Each pair of words represents the poles of a 7-point scale, e.g.,

strong 1 2 3 4 5 6 7 weak

If you feel that a particular part of the poem is *very closely* related to the pole "strong," you should put a circle round the figure 1. If, on the other hand, you feel that the part in question is *very closely related* to the pole "weak," you should put a circle round 7. If you think that the part is *not at all* related to the pair of words, or if you find it *difficult to decide*, you should put a circle round 4. The grades in between should be used for varying degrees of closeness, like this:

2 = *rather closely related* to the pole "strong"
3 = somewhat nearer the pole "strong" than the pole "weak"
5 = somewhat nearer the pole "weak" than the pole "strong"
6 = *rather closely related* to the pole "weak"

In principle you should do the same with all pairs of words. Each part of the poem should be compared with all pairs of words (one page in the booklet for each part). Do not worry or puzzle over individual items but do your markings at fairly high speed, since it is your first impressions we are interested in. Do not try to "check" your markings by looking back and forth through the items. Make only one circle on each scale. The aim of the investigation is not to register your complete response but only certain aspects of it.

The poem you will be working with is XYZ by ABC. To begin with, you should use 5–10 minutes (or more, if you want to) to read the poem and let your response develop and be stabilized.

When verbal scales like the ones discussed here are applied to single words or concepts, and still more to parts of literary works or even to complete works, it is evident that they do not measure the kind of meaning we find registered in dictionaries. On the contrary, what is measured is the more or less vague body of connotative meanings: associations, evaluative qualities, emotive nuances, and so on, that are grouped around such kernels of denotative meaning which we can look up in dictionaries. Figuratively speaking, the scales can be regarded as measuring rods placed in all kinds of directions through such bodies of meaning, and each responder is then asked to check how much meaning—if any—he can find in his personal response along the various directions provided by the different scales. Thus, what is measured are eminently subjective meanings—the subsequent analysis of a great number of scaled responses will show whether any of the meanings are intersubjective for larger or smaller groups of responders.

A set of scales can also be regarded as an instrument by which a group of people can make a systematic analysis of particular dimensions of the subjective meanings that constitute their individual responses. The particular dimensions, the "system" of the instrument, are given to the responders with the set of scales. This means limitations of two kinds: one is that the total meaning that was elicited in the response cannot be registered in one set of scales; the other is that the persons who construct the instrument are responsible for which questions can be answered in the final analysis of the scaled responses and which cannot.

Standardized versions of the scale instrument, such as those tried out by Charles Osgood and his colleagues, contain a fairly small number of scales that have been chosen because they register general dimensions of meaning ("cold–warm," "strong–weak" are examples of such standardized scales). In the field of literature, as well as generally in the field of aesthetics, there is no need for the researcher to limit himself to these standardized sets of scales. Most of the potential meanings of a subtle poem—or of a painting or a piece of music—must be registered by other scales that have been constructed for a particular investigation and according to specific hypotheses concerning potential meanings of this work ("simple–complex," "quiet–unquiet," "tragic–happy," "purity," "disappointment," "confidence" are a few dimensions that have been used).

STUDIES USING VERBAL SCALES

So far, there are not too many studies in which verbal scales have been used to investigate problems directly concerned with the understanding of literature. There are enough such studies, however, to allow an outlining of some research fields and some problem areas where they have already delivered promising results and opened up new perspectives. In the following sections, a few of these studies will be presented, and their implications for further research will be discussed.

Effects of Teaching
A Swedish study (Lindholm, 1963) tried to measure the effects of teaching the understanding and appreciation of poetical metaphors. Participants were young people with little formal education and limited training in the reading of literature. The objects of the study were a number of metaphors which were taken from actual texts of modern poetry. Some of the participants had a period of teaching and training (24 lessons in all), including opportunities to use "poetic" language actively and creatively (somewhat along the lines presented by Kenneth Koch in his well-known books *Wishes, lies, and dreams. Teaching children to write poetry* (1970),

and *Rose, where did you get that red? Teaching great poetry to children* (1973). A control group was not given any training.

Lindholm then constructed a series of scales intended to measure, among other things, the "quantity" of the meaning and the richness of nuances of meaning in the responses. In a pilot study, he used the usual bipolar scales, but for the main investigation he preferred unipolar scales, each defined by one adjective. Three measurements were made: just before the training period, just after this period, and two months later.

Although the differences between the experimental group and the control group did not quite reach statistical significance, Lindholm found that the students who had had teaching and training could discern more nuances of meaning and had a higher appreciation of the metaphors than the students who had had no training. There were other positive results as well: the students in the experimental group appreciated the training they had had, they had a more open attitude to poetry, and they started using more expressive words to describe their responses.

Problems of Interpretation

Another Swedish study (Hansson, 1964, 1973) took as its starting point some theoretical considerations about a class of interpretative statements. Certain statements made by critics and scholars about the meaning of a work of literature clearly refer to what the author of the work intended it to mean, or to what he said it meant when he had written it. Others refer to the printed text—metrics, composition, and so on. Still others refer to what people in the past have found in the work when reading it. Such statements were not dealt with in the study.

There are many other statements, however, which upon closer analysis will be found to refer—more or less clearly—to the response of somebody who *now* reads the work. Such statements may be like the following: "Act two is the most tragic"; "The compassion is most moving in the last two lines"; "The suggested tension in the first lines is held in suspense and then reaches its climax in the last three lines."

When a person interested in the study of response to literature is confronted with statements like these—and we meet them everywhere—it is quite natural for him to start asking questions. *Who* feels like that when reading the text? *Who* is responding like that? Do students in the elementary school or in college respond like that? Do literary critics and scholars unanimously respond like that? It is not difficult to see a research strategy in such questions: the original, incomplete, and elliptical statements about the meaning and structure of the work can be restated as a series of hypothetical statements about the responses of specific groups of readers; these statements can then be used for the construction of a series of verbal scales intended to measure the meanings or other response qualities which the hypothetical statements are referring to; these scales can be presented to specified groups of readers who, by marking their judgements on the scales, provide data which will show whether these particular readers responded to the work in a way which confirms the hypotheses or not.

This was the design of the study presented in *Dikt i profil*. Altogether, 25 bipolar 7-point scales were used. They were chosen on the basis of an analysis of an extensive discussion among scholars and critics about the meaning and proper interpretation of a subtle and not easily interpreted nineteenth-century poem (called *Endymion*) belonging to the Romantic period of Swedish literature. In this discussion of the meaning of the poem it was maintained, for example, that the first two stanzas suggest a contrast between the happy life of a dream world and the bitter life of reality, and that this contrast is sharply accentuated in the last two stanzas. This was one of the statements that was used as a hypothesis in designing the investigation, and because of it scales like "tragic–happy," "bitter–sweet," "simple–complex," "expressive–expressionless" were included in the final set of scales.

The poem was divided into 12 parts, each consisting of two lines which, apart from their contextual relations, were complete meaning-carrying units. Three groups of readers took part: experts (scholars and teachers of literature), university students studying literature, and skilled workers with only seven years of compulsory school in their childhood. After a period of private reading and thinking about the poem, all persons participating had to judge each one of the 12 parts as they read them in turn, and finally also the whole poem, using the set of 25 scales.

The results of this investigation demonstrated a striking similarity in most of the "profiles" for the three groups of readers, as can be seen in Figure 12-1 showing means and distributions on two of the scales ("tragic–happy" and "resting–mobile").

The same similarity between the three profiles appeared on almost all of the 25 scales. Since the poem is difficult to interpret and the meaning qualities judged by the readers are subtle and not easily accessible, there is no doubt that marked differences would have been found if the readers had been asked to write down their interpretations. This justifies the conclusion that the *passive* ability of the less-educated readers to notice and judge linguistic, literary, and experiential qualities were much more developed than their *active* ability to verbalize their interpretations and experiences in written statements.

Another conclusion that could be drawn was that the readers were given in the scales an instrument by which they could make fine distinctions in their responses and in their use of language when reading the poem. More important perhaps, with this instrument as an aid the less-educated readers could make more or less the same judgments as the readers with more extensive education. The scales made it possible for them to identify and "describe" meaning qualities for which they had not had enough opportunities to acquire a descriptive language.

There was one exception to this conclusion, however. On the scales that register formal qualities (like "simple–complex," "fast–slow," "vibrant–static") the readers with less formal education could not make as diversified judgments as the readers with more extensive education. Part of this effect—though not very strong in this case—can be seen in Figure 12-1, "resting–mobile," where the profile for Workers is somewhat more of a straight line along the neutral midpoints, while the other two groups of readers have found more varied qualities of that kind in the different parts of the poem. The differences in this respect can easily be explained. The

Figure 12-1.   Means and distributions for three groups of readers on two scales: 1. Tragic—Happy, 2. Resting—Mobile

1. Tragic–Happy

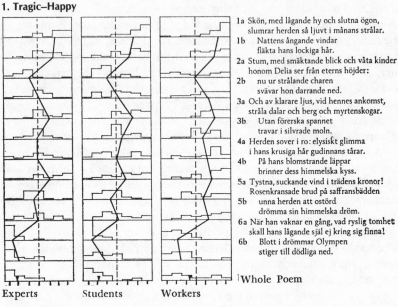

1a Skön, med lågande hy och slutna ögon,
    slumrar herden så ljuvt i månans strålar.
1b   Nattens ångande vindar
     fläkta hans lockiga hår.
2a Stum, med smäktande blick och våta kinder
    honom Delia ser från eterns höjder:
2b   nu ur strålande charen
     svävar hon darrande ned.
3a Och av klarare ljus, vid hennes ankomst,
    stråla dalar och berg och myrtenskogar.
3b   Utan förerska spannet
     travar i silvrade moln.
4a Herden sover i ro: elysiskt glimma
    i hans krusiga hår gudinnans tårar.
4b   På hans blomstrande läppar
     brinner dess himmelska kyss.
5a Tystna, suckande vind i trädens kronor!
    Rosenkransade brud på saffransbädden
5b   unna herden att ostörd
     drömma sin himmelska dröm.
6a När han vaknar en gång, vad ryslig tomhet
    skall hans lågande själ ej kring sig finna!
6b   Blott i drömmar Olympen
     stiger till dödliga ned.

Experts   Students   Workers   Whole Poem

2. Resting–Mobile

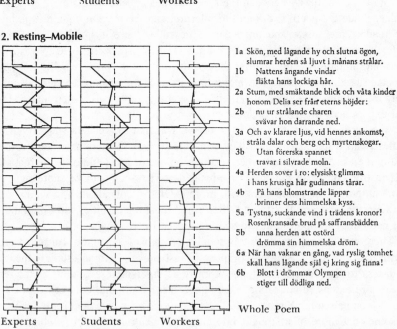

1a Skön, med lågande hy och slutna ögon,
    slumrar herden så ljuvt i månans strålar.
1b   Nattens ångande vindar
     fläkta hans lockiga hår.
2a Stum, med smäktande blick och våta kinder
    honom Delia ser från eterns höjder:
2b   nu ur strålande charen
     svävar hon darrande ned.
3a Och av klarare ljus, vid hennes ankomst,
    stråla dalar och berg och myrtenskogar.
3b   Utan förerska spannet
     travar i silvrade moln.
4a Herden sover i ro: elysiskt glimma
    i hans krusiga hår gudinnans tårar.
4b   På hans blomstrande läppar
     .brinner dess himmelska kyss.
5a Tystna, suckande vind i trädens kronor!
    Rosenkransade brud på saffransbädden
5b   unna herden att ostörd
     drömma sin himmelska dröm.
6a När han vaknar en gång, vad ryslig tomhet
    skall hans lågande själ ej kring sig finna!
6b   Blott i drömmar Olympen
     stiger till dödliga ned.

Experts   Students   Workers   Whole Poem

judgment of such formal qualities presupposes not only ability to give meanings to words and sentences, but also practice in literary analysis and knowledge of critical terminology. These things form a kind of expert knowledge, which the less-educated readers could not have acquired.

Evidently, results of this kind can be used to demonstrate whether the qualities which scholars and critics have attributed to a particular text are present in the responses of specific groups or readers or not. If the analyses of the scaled responses were carried further on, for instance, by using established statistical methods, it could also be demonstrated whether there were in the responses of groups of readers such structural relations as critics and scholars had found and described in their interpretations. The conclusions drawn from such analyses would have a direct bearing on many crucial problems in literary theory and in the theory and practice of literary interpretation.

Literature in the Classrooms

The scales used in *Dikt i profil* were derived from a large number of statements made by scholars and critics in the interpretations of a poem. There are other ways, however, to collect similar data which can be used to design a research plan and to construct a series of scales. One of these ways is to gather information from teachers about their experience in teaching literature. Such information can be collected systematically for various levels of the education system, for different kinds or periods of literature, for specific problems or larger problem areas, or for particular works of literature.

This procedure was followed in a 1974 Swedish study (Hansson, 1974, chap. 10). The objects of this study were four poems which are very often studied in the Swedish schools. As a first stage of the investigation a questionnaire was sent out to a sample of teachers in different parts of the country. The teachers were asked to describe in detail their teaching practice when studying these four poems in class: what kind of problems (concerning history of literature, author's life, genre, style, etc.) they tried to deal with in the study of the texts, how they generally introduced the texts and carried through an analysis of them, what they expected from the students and their responses, and what in their experience was easy or difficult for the students to master in the study and analysis of the four texts. The reports from the teachers were then used for the formulation of hypotheses and problems, and thus for the choice of dimensions in which to construct the scales.

If many teachers said that in their teaching they regularly tried to bring out qualities of loneliness and despair in one of the texts, and qualities of purity and longing in another, scales were chosen to register such nuances. If, on the other hand, many teachers said that they would like to discuss qualities of, for instance, confidence and tenderness in a work, but that they had found it difficult to do so in the lower grades, scales covering such qualities were included so as to show whether young boys and girls could discern them when using the scales (which they, as a matter of fact, quite often could).

Altogether, 14 unipolar 7-point scales (with a box for "not relevant" outside the scale) were used for each text in this study. Four of the scales were common to all four texts; they were chosen so as to register qualities which, according to statements made by the teachers, were relevant and important to the study of all four texts. Six of the scales were chosen so as to be relevant to one of the texts; thus there were four different sets of these six scales. The remaining four scales were intended to register qualities which the teachers had *not* mentioned in their reports: a kind of "open" hypotheses as to the meaning of the poems.

Besides applying the set of 14 scales, the readers had to write "protocols" in which they formulated their opinion on one or two problems of interpretation or characterization. These problems had also been chosen because the teachers often mentioned them in their reports. Finally, the readers were asked to evaluate the poem and to give as many reasons as they could for their evaluations. Three groups of readers representing three stages in the education system took part in the study: grade 9 in the compulsory school (age 16), grade 2 in the gymnasium (age 18), and university students studying literature (age 20–25). All three groups were given exactly the same assignments.

A number of useful results came out of this study. One was that the striking similarity between markings of groups of readers with large differences in age, knowledge, and experience of reading literature was confirmed here. This can be illustrated by Figure 12-2, in which means and distributions of the markings on two typical scales ("fear" and "calm") for the six consecutive parts of one of the four poems are shown.

In this study, the scaled responses could be compared with the written responses in the protocols. There were conspicuous differences in these written responses between the three groups of readers: in the amount of what they had written, in their ability to use descriptive and expressive language to communicate what they had found in the poems, and—most important perhaps—in the content of their interpretations. Most of the interpretations of the poem represented by the scaled responses in Figure 12-2 could be classified in three categories. The interpretations of the three groups of readers are shown in Table 12-1, where A is the "expected" interpretation of this poem, and B and C are two variant interpretations proposed by the readers.

As can be seen in Table 12-1, the students in the compulsory school arrived at three different interpretations (apart from a group of miscellaneous interpretations), and they divided themselves fairly evenly among these three. Two of the interpretations were then gradually abandoned by the students in the gymnasium and at the university. Thus, there was a marked difference between the three groups of readers in the verbalized interpretations, but a striking similarity in the scaled responses.

In their reports, many teachers were outspokenly pessimistic about the possibility of studying these four poems with the 16-year-old students. Undoubtedly, this pessimism was founded on long and profound experience of the difficulties in getting the students to verbalize their interpretations in a discussion or an analysis of the poem. However, the scaled responses clearly demonstrated that these young students

Figure 12-2.   Means and distributions for three groups of readers on two scales: 1. Fear 2. Calm

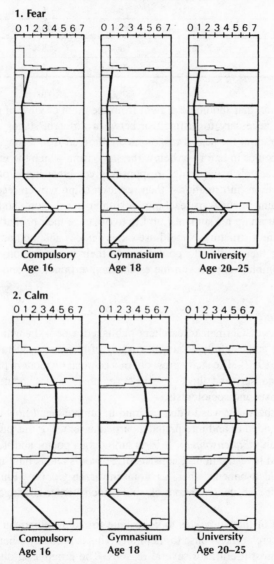

1. Fear

| Compulsory Age 16 | Gymnasium Age 18 | University Age 20–25 |

2. Calm

| Compulsory Age 16 | Gymnasium Age 18 | University Age 20–25 |

had the basic linguistic ability to give such meanings to the words of the poems and to make such distinctions between meaning qualities that the teachers had declared that they would like to deal with in their teaching. What the students lacked, to a certain extent, was the ability to organize these meanings and qualities into a coherent whole which they could put into words and communicate as an interpretation or an analysis of the poems.

Table 12-1.   Interpretations of a Poem by Three Groups of Students

	Interpretation			
	A	B	C	Mis.
Compulsory	32%	22%	22%	24%
Gymnasium	70%	16%	5%	9%
University	70%	9%	1%	20%

One conclusion that should be drawn, from the point of view of research, seems to be that it is necessary to distinguish between different stages or levels in the response to literature: the scaled responses are derived from a stage of the reading process which comes in before or below the stage from which the written responses are derived. Research using scaled responses gives other kinds of information— and sometimes more information—than research using written responses only.

From the point of view of teaching, a similar conclusion should be drawn: a teacher who is training his students' ability to organize their primary responses into larger and coherent structures should use other devices and methods than a teacher who is training their ability to communicate their interpretations and to present more or less complete analyses in the established terminology and analytical categories.

A Poem in Detail

In 1972 a group of German researchers published a book in which an unusually well-thought-out and carefully-documented study of response to literature is presented (Mauser, et al., 1972). The study grew out of a seminar on modern poetry conducted by Wolfgang Mauser, and the extensive research activities included cooperation with psychologists and sociologists.

One aim of the study was to demonstrate in minute detail how different groups of readers responded to and interpreted a particular text. For this purpose the group chose Paul Celan's *Fadensonnen*. It is an ambiguous poem, and it is short enough to allow detailed investigation: it consists of 21 words and is built up by only three metaphors ("Fadensonnen / über der grauschwarzen Ödnis. / Ein baum- / hoher Gedanke / greift sich den Lichtton: es sind / noch Lieder zu singen jenseits / der Menschen."）.

Another aim of the study was to contribute to the development of theories and methods in research on response to literature. This is probably where the study will turn out to be most useful, for several reasons. The group used different points of departure and tried different research methods, and they made a number of pretests with successive revisions of aims, methods, and research instruments. Each step of the planning and analysis is carefully described, even when they demanded revisions or ended in a failure. Furthermore, each step of the investigation is theoretically explained and analyzed to make clear the background and aims. To be sure, work of this kind is particularly important in a new research area.

No less than 664 persons were engaged as responders. Most of them were pupils from seven different grades of the school, and university students representing nine different subject areas.

In the main investigation, the responders were first asked to answer a large number of questions about themselves, their attitudes to modern poetry, their literary frames of reference ("Erwartungshorizont"), and Celan's *Fadensonnen*. Then they wrote down their free associations from the three metaphors and three key words of the poem ("Ödnis," "Lieder," "jenseits"). After that they judged the meaning of each of the three metaphors on a series of 7-point bipolar scales. Finally, they read the poem once more and answered a great number of questions about the poem and its author.

The testing instrument included 18 scales representing Osgood's semantic differential, the same scales for all three metaphors. These scales were intended to cover not only the three factors (evaluation, potency, and activity) that Osgood and his colleagues regularly have found to be the strongest, but also two other factors (unreality and exceptionality). As a matter of fact, 9 of the 18 scales represented these two factors. Besides the 18 scales there were a few others, which varied with each metaphor and was chosen to register specific qualities in each of them. They were chosen on the basis of the free associations that were collected in the pretests.

The analysis of the very large body of data was painstakingly carried out along three different lines: *semantic*—asking, among other things, if a structuring of the textbound associations could be found; *literary*—asking, for instance, what role the reader's "Erwartungshorizont" was playing in his interpretation; and *didactic*—where one of the questions was whether the reader, by step-by-step analysis, could be led to a deeper understanding of the text.

The tangible results of these analyses do not quite match the efforts put into the planning, the pretests, and the handling of the data; the first ones to realize this were the members of the research group themselves. The meaning dimensions that were brought out in the analyses were almost identical for all the three metaphors. The differences that were found applied to nuances of meaning only. The researchers suggested as an explanation that the total impression of the poem was so intense that it permeated all meaning dimensions of the three metaphors. Another, and perhaps more plausible explanation,—or at least part of the explanation—might be sought in the choice of scales which, in this case, did not grow out of particular problems or hypotheses. The scales most often used in Osgood's semantic differential are deliberately chosen so as to represent general meaning dimensions. It is very likely that there are such general dimensions in the language of poetry too—and perhaps that is what the German researchers found. But it is not very likely that a set of "general" scales that have been found to be useful in work with the semantic differential will bring out specific meaning qualities in a particular poem, or in three metaphors in one and the same poem.

Thus, one conclusion that might be drawn here is that studies of particular works of literature—and probably also most other studies dealing with literary or aesthetic problems—will be more fruitful if they already are oriented toward specific problems and hypotheses in their conception. Nevertheless, *Text und Rezeption* is a most useful study, because of its many contributions to the theory and methods of research, and because of its minute presentations of what was done, why it was done, and what came out of it.

Scaled Responses Related to the Text of a Play

In the Swedish studies presented above, details—as well as larger units of the scaled responses—could be related to specific words or parts of the poems. Also, structural relations in the scaled responses could be related to corresponding parts of the texts. This line of research was one of the guiding principles when James DeVries designed the studies which he presented in his unpublished thesis, *A statistical analysis of undergraduate readers' responses to selected characters in Shakespeare's "The Tempest"* (1973).

DeVries focused his research on three main problems: the technology of constructing a test which measures response to literature; an objective or statistical description of readers' responses; and the relation of these responses to the text. He did not perceive the literary text as just a stimulus to elicit the response, but regarded reading as including both the reader and the text. Therefore, he wanted to focus his study on the text by showing how the readers' responses relate to the text. Moreover, he primarily wanted to study the evaluative aspect of literary response, since affective evaluation is a large and important part of such response.

To elicit affective responses and to lessen the chances of readers' misunderstanding the questions, the researcher has to choose some important aspect of the work to be studied. DeVries found such an aspect in the characters of a play—Shakespeare's *The Tempest*. Thus, DeVries' research was focused primarily on the readers' evaluation of characters, and also on some general evaluations of the play, to see what effect the readers' perception of the characters has upon their evaluation of the play. Besides his interest in the general response to the play, DeVries was particularly interested in the readers' changing responses to the protagonist Prospero and the antagonists Caliban, Sebastian, and Antonio.

DeVries used bipolar scales defined by opposing adjectives, but instead of 7 points (he calls them steps or boxes) he had as many as 15 points on each scale. In this he follows suggestions by Harold Gulliksen (1958) who, in a discussion of Osgood's work, gave statistical reasons for the use of scales with more than seven points. DeVries himself adds several good reasons for the use of scales with many steps in research on response to literature.

The text of *The Tempest* was divided into ten parts; the reasons for the divisions are carefully stated in the thesis. After reading each one of the divisions, the responders had to fill in a questionnaire containing seven scales describing responses to the play, and ten scales describing responses to one or more of the four characters of the play. The seven play response scales were the same for all ten parts, and the ten character response scales were the same for each character. Besides these scales there was also a self-concept measure consisting of 28 scales, a short essay question, and some questions asking for information about the reader and his background. Altogether, 100 students taking undergraduate Shakespeare courses at the University of Illinois voluntarily read the play and filled out the questionnaires.

The sets of scales that were used in the main investigation were carefully chosen and empirically tried out in pilot studies; this important stage of the research is described in detail in the thesis. Thus, the character response scales were chosen according to three criteria: they should be comprised of adjectives which people might ordinarily use in describing other people; they should elicit the reader's impression of the character's inner and social self; and they should be relevant to the characters surveyed. To ensure the relevancy of the scales DeVries analyzed well-known critical articles about *The Tempest* to determine what adjectives had been ascribed to the characters of the play. Some adjectives were taken directly from the critics' texts, others were converted from other words or statements used by the critics. A number of scales were then chosen to be representative of the critics' comments about the characters. The adjectives that defined the final sets of scales were used in everyday language and were related to different psychological and social dimensions of personality.

In his analysis of the data, DeVries found some influence of the readers' self-concept on their response to characters. This influence was relatively small, however, and it was noticeable only in response to the character the readers were presumably identifying with, that is, Prospero. For the other characters, there was an almost total lack of difference between readers with high and low self-concept, a finding which DeVries interpreted to mean that the text of *The Tempest* influenced their responses much more than did their own predispositions.

A large part of the thesis (chap. 4) is devoted to the aspect which DeVries set up as his main object of study: the analysis of the readers' responses in relation to the text. His results cannot be summarized here, but they provide ample evidence of the fruitfulness of the research method and of the design of the investigation. Under headings like "Prospero's Reminiscence," "Prospero and Caliban Exchange Insults," "Caliban's Rebellion Thwarted," findings in the scaled responses are related—often in minute details—to descriptions or characterizations of the text of the play. Surely such a procedure involves some unresolved problems—for example, how to establish "the text" without an undue introduction of some critic's or the researchers' own interpretation of the same text. In a conscious and carefully planned treatment of the data such problems can be handled, however.

The scaled responses could also be used to draw tentative conclusions about the structure of the play and its relation to reader response. One conclusion of this kind is the following: the available data suggest a structure which includes a reader's perception of characters that increases in complexity as the play proceeds and involves a shift from preoccupation with plot in the beginning to a focus upon character interaction further on.

Another finding was that the scales that were most clearly evaluative discriminated better among the characters than the other scale groups did. This led DeVries to the conclusion that most scales in reader research should continue to be evaluative, because they offer the greatest variation in reader response.

CONCLUSIONS AND IMPLICATIONS

Although only a few studies using verbal scales have been made so far, there is already enough evidence to justify the conclusion that such scales will continue to be a useful instrument in future research on reader response. The scales give us information about such stages of the reading process and such levels of the response that cannot be reached by other research methods. The scales overcome many of the difficulties in getting information about responses and interpretations among readers who, for various reasons, have not had the opportunity to acquire the terminology and descriptive language which more trained readers ordinarily use to communicate their experiences and evaluations of literature. They also provide data which lend themselves to analysis with a variety of objective methods. At the same time, these data can easily be related to many other kinds of data, quantitative as well as qualitative, which are gathered by the use of other research methods.

Most of the work that has been done in the studies reviewed in this chapter has been exploratory—we have just started finding out what possibilities verbal scales may offer in research on literature. This means two things: that there are many more possibilities to discover, and that much work remains to be done before the method as such has been consolidated and adapted to the special problems and demands raised in research on literature. These are things—promising and exacting at the same time—which are facing every researcher who explores a new research area or uses new research methods.

Thus, there are methodological problems which will require serious efforts by researchers in many different fields of interest. But there are several other areas which invite researchers interested in the use of verbal scales. A few of these areas will be briefly outlined on the remaining pages. Such choices always reflect personal priorities—others may find areas more important, and they are right in doing so!

The Response to Literature

Considering the time and efforts that are spent in teaching how to interpret and appreciate literature, we know shockingly little of what constitutes response to literature. There are almost no limits to the amount of research that is needed before we know even the gross outlines of what goes on in the reading processes where the latent meanings, qualities, and structures of works of literature are realized in the minds of readers. The number of books containing theories, ideas, suggestions, or prejudices about these transactions is almost innumerable. Such books are of great value to empirical research—wise and clever people have written most of them—but what we badly need is a great quantity of empirical research that has been specially designed to investigate basic problems in the response area.

Some of this research will have to be exploratory, like the early but still very important studies by I. A. Richards (1929) and Louise Rosenblatt (1938, reprinted 1968). Such studies provide a gross body of data that can be used for formulating hypotheses, defining research problems, and designing more limited studies. Other investigations will have to be of a survey type, yielding reliable but rather "shallow" data from large and representative groups of readers. Such studies are needed in all new branches of research. Still other studies can start out from already existing theories of literary response, making use of them in designing research strategies that may provide empirical evidence for or against the particular theory.

Evaluation
Many of the crucial problems in different branches of human life sooner or later turn out to be closely related to evaluations. The same applies to the reading and understanding of literature: evaluations of one kind or another enter from all directions. Yet we do not know more about the principles and processes of evaluation than we do about the general response to literature.

In all their "differential" research on language, Charles Osgood and his colleagues have found the evaluative factor to be by far the strongest. James DeVries presented empirical evidence as well as other reasons to justify his conclusion that the evaluative aspect is basic in the appreciation of literature. Verbal scales can easily be adapted to the exploration of the dimensions of literary evaluation. There are solid reasons to expect that such research on evaluative problems will produce vital and useful knowledge in almost any area where it is applied.

Such areas of evaluative problems abound in our society: in the publishing houses, where a few persons decide which literary manuscripts to print and not to print; in the libraries, where other persons decide what books to buy and not to buy; in the universities, where students and researchers choose topics for essays, dissertations, and books; in schools and universities, where literature is taught and a small number of texts are canonized; in journals and daily papers, where critics print more or less authoritative statements about the quality of published works and so on.

In research on problems of literary evaluation, as well as in research in many other branches of response to literature, verbal scales may best be used in combination with other research instruments. One such instrument could be the "elements of evaluation" presented by Alan Purves in his *Elements of writing about a literary work* (1968). These elements are intended to contain all the evaluative criteria that are currently used in the field of literature. The instrument has been applied in empirical research (Hansson, 1975; Purves, 1973, 1981; Spenke, 1982), and it has already proved its usefulness.

A way of combining evaluative criteria and scales has been demonstrated by the Dutch researcher Rien Segers (1978). His investigation was carried out in the United States: his readers were undergraduates, graduate students, and teachers at Indiana University and Yale University. Segers derived his set of evaluative criteria from statements and preferences of a group of graduate students. He then used these criteria to define a number of 7-point scales, which his three groups of readers applied in their evaluations of four short stories.

The Meaning of Literary Works
James DeVries wanted to demonstrate in his thesis how the readers' responses relate to the text of a work. In other studies there have been tentative efforts to "construct" the meaning of a work on the basis of the responses only, without making use of

"the text" (which in the final analysis will always include some specialist's inter-pretation of the printed text). These two lines of research need not be very far from each other in their theoretical points of departure, in their methods to collect and analyze data, or in the kind of results they arrive at. Both will in the end present knowledge about the meaning of literary works as they were understood by particular groups of readers.

If it is important to have critics and scholars presenting their personal readings and appreciations of the best and most influential works in the cultural heritage, then it is just as important to have researchers finding out—as objectively as possible—how groups of people from all parts of a society read and appreciate the same works. We need such studies on works which have been unusually influential in the past, which are key works in an epoch, which are important in the study of literature at school, which are more often read than most other works, and which are now appreciated more than other works. The interpretations and evaluations of such works among groups of readers representing the whole society are a most vital part of the life of literature, and we need reception studies in order to understand the conditions of this life.

We also need reception studies repeated at intervals. We need to know what changes important works undergo from generation to generation of readers. This will also serve future historians of literature. Most likely future histories of literature will be written from a wider perspective than that of a few critics and scholars. A complete history of literature will have to include the understandings and appreciations of the literary works by successive generations of readers. Provocative demands of such histories of literature have been raised (Jauss, 1970, 1975), but the research that is necessary before these new histories can be written is almost completely lacking.

Style and Structure

Analyses of style and structure are important in the writing about literature and in the teaching of literature. Many of the categories used in such analyses are not too well-defined, but it is evident that much of what is stated about style and structure refers to response qualities. *Whose* response those qualities have been located in is seldom made clear in the statements, but it has to be in somebody's response. Any study or handbook dealing with stylistic or structural aspects of literature will have a great many examples of such arguments and descriptive statements referring to qualities that cannot be located in the texts but are to be found in some individual person's response to the texts. The abundance of such arguments and descriptions are enough evidence of the need for response research. At the same time, however, most of these arguments and descriptions can be used constructively for defining research areas and formulating more specific research problems.

Verbal scales seem to be unusually well-suited for research on all kinds of problems related to the presence of stylistic and structural qualities in the responses of groups of people, and consequently on problems of the relation of such qualities to elements in the texts. The style and structure of works that are often called expressionistic or that were written in the expressionistic tradition is just one example of such studies. The style and structure of works which belong to a particular genre or of works by an individual author are other examples. Clearly, results from studies using verbal scales and response qualities can also be related to results from studies using other methods, for example, objective descriptions of the language of the printed texts.

Literary Theory

In the theory of literature there are many problems that could be fruitfully attacked through research on response to literature. "A book is a machine to think with," said I. A. Richards in one of his books. The results of well-planned and well-executed empirical studies are also excellent machines to think with. What is, for instance, the status of the critics' statements about the meaning and qualities of works of literature? Are they valid outside a limited circle of experts? What claims do they make or can they make on the whole? Empirical research on reader response will be in a position to provide at least partial answers to such questions.

I. A. Richards maintained that "balanced interests" was the aesthetic and psychological effect of reading good literature. Can such a balance between interests, which in everyday life often are in opposition or conflict with each other, be observed in the responses of groups of readers—or are they just a piece of interesting literary theory? T. S. Eliot claimed that a good work of literature establishes an "objective correlative" between an author and his readers. Do we find evidence for such a thing as an "objective correlative" in successful literary communication, or is it just another piece of literary theory?

René Wellek and Austin Warren stated that a literary work exists as a "structure of norms," an "object *sui generis*," unlike all other objects we know of. "Significant form" is a key term in the theories of Susanne Langer, as is "symbolic action" in the theories of Kenneth Burke. Knowledge in the field of literature would be advanced considerably if we started designing empirical studies that could provide evidence for or against these and many other theories of literature, which to a large extent turn out to be theories of response to literature. Any book on aesthetics or theory of literature contains ideas, statements, suggestions, or claims that can be used in planning studies on response to literature in which verbal scales are part of the research design. Even if few of these problems can be definitively resolved through such research, many of them can be elucidated, better defined, and restated on new and more solid grounds—which amounts to making progress in this much-debated branch of knowledge.

Literary Criticism

Some of the studies reviewed in this chapter have demonstrated the usefulness of critical or scholarly interpretations of literature in generating problems and hypotheses for empirical research. Since, upon closer analysis, a very large part of what is stated in literary criticism will turn out to be referring—explicitly or implicitly—to response categories, it is evident that there is almost no limit to what a researcher can find and use in works of criticism. There may be limited problems, like statements about the meaning and significance of an individual poem compared to the meanings and significances found by groups of people when reading the same poem. Or there may be more general problems, like the study of categories of twentieth century Anglo Saxon criticism in relation to the response categories of a representative sample of adults with a high school education.

There are many other kinds of problems close at hand, however. Many literary critics have an innocent and unreflecting attitude to what they are doing; they write as if they were writing *about* something, not *for* somebody. The writings of a critic or a group of critics could be studied and then compared with the conscious expectations and the (probably less conscious) response categories of one or more groups of people who are or are not reading those critics. In criticism there has, for some time, been a strong interest in formal aspects of literature. The effects of this interest could be studied in the writings of some critics and then related to what specific groups of readers actually pay attention to in their reading.

Any book that contains interpretative criticism will offer more suggestions, debatable or unfounded statements, and unresolved problems than can be handled in a lifetime of research on reader response.

Teaching Literature

The teaching of literature on various levels of the education system is another area with unlimited problems which lend themselves to empirical research using verbal scales as one of several research strategies. One aim of such research might be to provide a basis of empirical knowledge, for use by teachers, for curriculum makers, editors of anthologies, and others who choose particular works of literature to be studied at a certain age level or in a specific context. When are students ready to study a particular work, in the sense that they have at their disposal the linguistic and experiential qualities which are a prerequisite for development of a personal response, or in the sense that this personal response can be verbalized and communicated in an analysis or an interpretation of the work? Which works may preferably be read for personal appreciation but without any extensive analyses at a specific age level, and which are suitable for more systematic exercises in the use of descriptive, analytical, and evaluative terminology?

Other kinds of research in the teaching area might concentrate on problems which have been delimited more or less narrowly in the research design. What stylistic properties might be discussed in a particular grade, since research has demonstrated that at that age most students can discern the response qualities that make up the properties? What structural properties might be discussed on similar grounds? What value qualities can be discerned by the students, and what kinds of value arguments may, as a consequence, be brought into the analysis? How do response qualities which constitute stylistic, structural, and value properties develop through the grades, or under the influence of different ways of teaching literature?

These are just a few examples. Curricula regulating the study of literature on all levels of the education system contain—explicitly or implicitly—goals, aims, and strategies which will point out many other tasks for empirical research. Systematic or even informal interviews with students and teachers will uncover more areas. In their aims and ambitions and in their experience of successes and failures in the teaching of literature, any group of teachers or students will have more problems and insights than can be handled in several lifetimes of research on reader response.

Most of the research proposals which I have outlined very briefly on the last few pages are broad ones which will require the use of several research techniques and methods. The use of verbal scales is just one of these several techniques and should not be regarded as an exclusive method. There may be cases where scales could be used as the only research instrument, but on the whole they will—like most other techniques—yield their best results when they are used in combination with other methods.

One of the advantages with verbal scales is that they bypass the difficulties many people have in verbalizing their responses and describing qualities in these responses. Thus, in the dimensions which the researcher has delimited for his investigation, he or she will get more information—and very likely also more reliable information— than if he asks his readers to verbalize their reactions. At the same time, however, the information the researcher gets will be limited to the dimensions in which he has defined his scales. That is one reason to combine them with other techniques.

A set of scales will also help readers—experienced as well as inexperienced— to see deeper into their responses and to discriminate between qualities which they had not consciously thought of before. This also applies to very young children: since their passive linguistic capacity develops much earlier than their active ability to use words, they can apply a series of scales even if they are incapable of using their own words to describe their responses. Thus, verbal scales will enable the researcher to get closer to the actual response, and also to work with very young or otherwise inexperienced readers.

Students and researchers who want to probe further into the possibilities and limitations of verbal scales as a research technique may find the studies by Wolfgang Mauser, Rien Segers, and James DeVries particularly rewarding. For the general theory underlying the scales and for specific problems of measurement, the original work of Charles Osgood and his colleagues in *The Measurement of Meaning* is still an indispensable source.

REFERENCES

Aaronson, D., & Rieber, R. W. (Eds.). *Psycholinguistic research: Implications and applications*. Hillsdale, NJ: Lawrence Erlbaum, 1979.

DeVries, J. *A statistical analysis of undergraduate readers' responses to selected characters in Shakespeare's* The Tempest. Unpublished doctoral dissertation, University of Illinois at Urbana-Champaign, 1973.

Gulliksen, H. How to make meaning more meaningful. *Contemporary Psychology*, 1958, *3*, 115–118.

Hansson, G. *Dikt i profil* (Poetry in profile). Göteborg: Akademiförlaget/Gumperts, 1964.

Hansson, G. Some types of research on response to literature. *Research in the Teaching of English*, 1973, 7, 260–284.

Hansson, G. *Litteraturläsning i gymnasiet* (Reading literature in the gymnasium). Stockholm: Utbildningsförlaget, 1974.

Hansson, G. *Läsning och litteratur (Reading and literature)*. Stockholm: Almqvist & Wicksell, 1975.

Jauss, H. R. *Literaturgeschichte als Provokation (Literary history as provocation)*. Frankfurt: Suhrkamp, 1970.

Jauss, H. R. *Der Leser als Instanz einer neuen Geschichte der Literatur* (The reader as instance of a new history of literature). *Poetica*, 1975, 7, 325–344.

Koch, K. *Wishes, lies, and dreams: Teaching children to write poetry*. New York: Random House, 1970.

Koch, K. *Rose, where did you get that red? Teaching great poetry to children*. New York: Random House, 1973.

Lindholm, S. *Att uppleva metaforer (Responding to metaphors)*. Stockholm: Pedagogiska institutionen, Stockholm University, 1963.

Mauser, W., Bauer, W., Braunschweig-Ullmann, R., Brodmann, H., Bühr, M., and Keisers, B. *Text und Rezeption* (Text and reception). Frankfurt: Athenäum, 1972.

Osgood, C. E., Suci, G. J., & Tannenbaum, P. H. *The measurement of meaning*. Urbana, IL: University of Illinois Press, 1957.

Purves, A. C. *The elements of writing about a literary work*. Champaign, IL: National Council of Teachers of English, 1968.

Purves, A. C. *Literature education in ten countries*. Stockholm: Almqvist & Wicksell, 1973.

Purves, A. C. *Reading and literature*. Urbana, IL: National Council of Teachers of English, 1981.

Richards, I. A. *Practical criticism*. London: Routledge & Kegan Paul, 1929.

Rommetveit, R. *Words, meanings, and messages: Theories and experiments in psycholinguistics*. New York: Academic Press, 1968.

Rosenblatt, L. M. *Literature as exploration*. New York: Noble and Noble, 1968. (Originally published, 1938.)

Segers, R. T. *The evaluation of literary texts*. Lisse: Peter de Ridder Press, 1978.

Snider, J. G. & Osgood, C. E. *Semantic differential technique*. Chicago: Aldine Publishing Company, 1969.

Spenke, C. *Läsa—lära—förstå (Reading—learning—understanding)*. Lund: Liber, 1982.

Chapter 13
Q-Methodology and English Literature

William Stephenson

School of Journalism
University of Missouri-Columbia

Yet there is something for which Newton—or better to say not Newton alone, but modern science in general—can still be made responsible: it is the splitting of a world in two . . . the world of science—the real world—became estranged and utterly divorced from the world of life, which science has been unable to explain—not even to explain it away by calling it "subjective." (Koyré, 1965)

INTRODUCTION

Though we are to be scientific, it is with an understanding that is the great novelists, dramatists, poets, biographers, historians—the Tolstoys, Shakespeares, Emily Brontës, Boswells, Burckhardts—who provide true knowledge of the "world of life," not academic psychologists. Our approach is to seek what is *truth* in such great literature, and to indicate how to find it.

There are many who will proclaim that these great minds have grasped truths that scientific investigation could never attain, that they give answers to life's *purpose*, which is altogether outside the purview of science. The very notion of studying them scientifically is unthinkable: so, for example, spoke Simone Weil (Rees, 1965).

This, however, applied to science in the manner of Newton: the modern revolution in science, of quantum theory and relativity, has altered investigative matters profoundly, and it is to this advance that the present essay is directed. The quotation which opens this chapter calls attention to the split of knowledge into two—the sciences and the arts—and it asserts that a profound problem remains unsolved. It concerns "subjectivity."

The present essay addresses itself to this question: Can there be a science about "subjectivity"? and answers yes.

THE MAJOR PROBLEM

R. G. Moulton, a well known professor at the University of Chicago, said in 1915 that literary study is a country without a map, and that the "unity of literature" was the major problem for future literary scholars.

233

The problem remains, but we can solve it.

We consider, first, an essay called *Art and Science* by professor of literature Elder Olson (1976). Olson posits that knowledge in science is far superior to knowledge in the arts for a number of reasons. Theory and practice go hand in hand in science. Discussion is clear and uniform. There is agreement about method; when there are disagreements they are recognized as such and the methods are dubbed hypothetical or speculative. Different scientists, working independently, arrive at the same conclusions: what is a fact and what is not is well understood. A scientist's findings live on after his death.

The reverse of this, Olson says, holds for the arts. Theory and practice are disjointed. Terminology is unclear, and no doctrine is beyond dispute. Nobody, Olson concludes, even seems to know what poetry is.

Why, then, the difference, and why is so little known for sure in the arts? The reason, Olson argues, is that science has a *method* and has remained with it, whereas the arts have nothing of the kind.

What, then, is the method? Olson said it is a "sense of evidence":

> There is a clutter of absurd interpretations of Hamlet, which most scholars recognize as absurd but are unable to refute; indeed, in most areas of literary study it is impossible to establish a small point about a poem or novel without first clearing away all the rubbish that has accumulated about it. A sense of evidence is of course required. (Olson, 1976, p. 305)

In science, the "sense of evidence" comes from scientific method, which has certainly undergone a revolution during the past fifty years. The emphasis used to be on prediction, that is, in which hypotheses had to be formulated before testing; this hypothetico-deductive methodology was adequate until investigations discovered subatomic particles and the infinitude of the universe, at which point an inductive methodology became necessary. The scientist now faces the uncertainty principle and the inseparability of object and measuring instrument. Experiments in the ordinary sense are impossible—one has to make observations to find quarks and quasars, and explanation (as theory) follows suit rather than determines what is predictable. Scientists now try to *understand* phenomena, using models in which understanding rather than a priori hypothesis-forming and prediction is at issue.

But if every scholar uses his or her own model, sufficient for a particular problem, the situation described by Olson is not much improved. He argued that this does not matter, because the various theories and their models need not be contradictory: the scholars are merely using different dialectics—different rules of logic and ways of thinking about their problems, as may be the case in the chapters of this book. Olson therefore wonders whether there can ever be *one* dialectic, one system of discourse. He says:

> Surely there can be discovered a set of statements conveying the whole truth, and one single method which is the right method. (Olson, 1976, p. 299)

But he concludes that there can be no such single dialectic: Art is a plurality of systems, and requires a plurality of theories for its understanding.

Q-methodology denies Olson his conclusion. There is, in fact, one "set of statements," one body of methodology and theory, which encompasses all "subjectivity" in the arts, to which we now attend.

IMMEDIATE EXPERIENCE

Our concern is with language (or its surrogates in art) in a subjective form, as when a person says "I feel (something)" or "I am enjoying (something)" or "I have a hunch that (something)." *Feelings are at issue about something, and there is always self-reference.*

We should look first at what happens when the language is *objective*, as when a person examines an antique urn from ancient Greece, such as the one Keats made immortal in his *Ode on a Grecian Urn*: Some remarks, for example, may be: "It is brown-colored, like all Greek urns"; "The crack marks show that it must have been patched up from broken pieces"; "The decor of human figures runs right around the urn"; "They are youthful men and women"; . . . and so on. All such statements are objective, not subjective. They are spoken by a person, but are observations about testable things or events in the world outside. But if the same person says, instead, "I don't like the brown color"; "The cracks destroy the beauty of the urn"; "The human figures look stilted to me"; "The bull is being sacrificed, I'm glad I'm not there to see it"—all such remarks are subjective. The person is expressing his or her feelings about something, from "inside."

What you can observe objectively about such an urn is apt to be finite: there is only so much you can see and describe. An archaeologist may be able to give the approximate date of its making, or the meaning of the decor; a chemist may add some knowledge about the chromium content, or refractibility. All such knowledge is objective. But what we can say subjectively is infinite, limited only by our imagination—its beauty, its calm delight, its charm, its quiet dignity, its haunting memories, the ecstacy it unfolds, its youthfulness, its mellowing by wine encuffed, its lovers forever anticipating kisses, its dancing joy, its voluptuousness, and so on ad infinitum.

Everyone will agree that objective matters are for scientific concern. But how is it possible to be scientific about an urn viewed by people with infinite subjectivity? Especially an imaginary urn, such as Keats wrote of in *Ode on a Grecian Urn*:

> Thou still unravished bride of quietness,
> Thou foster child of Silence and slow Time,
> Sylvan historian, who canst thus express
> A flowery tale more sweetly than our rime—
> What leaf-fringed legend haunts about thy shape
> Of deities or mortals, or of both,
>   In Tempe or the dales of Arcady?
> What men or gods are these? What maiden loath?
> What mad pursuit? What struggle to escape?
> What pipes and timbrels? What wild ecstacy?

And it ends with an enigma:

> Beauty is truth, truth beauty—that is all
> Ye know on earth, and all ye need to know.

The urn was a figment of Keats' imagination, and every thought and feeling in the *Ode* is intrinsically *self-referent*, projections of Keats' own feeling. If Keats had spoken prosaically, and not poetically, he would have mused somewhat as follows, speaking to himself:

> I feel the silence, quietness, timelessness of the urn and what it depicts; it is sylvan history for me; somehow it makes me feel that the songs I hear are sweet, but those I imagine are sweeter; and I wonder about the lovely shapes, are they meant to be gods or human beings? And that maiden, is she merely being coy? I suspect otherwise, she is enjoying the chase . . . I suppose it could have happened at Tempe (the beautiful valley I've read about in Thessaly, Greece), or in Arcadia, the pastoral home of shepherds in Greece.

Such—and a thousand other—musings, recollections, and feelings must have been in Keats' mind as he wrote the *Ode*. Something similar happens when we read the *Ode*: we read it over and over and expeience such moods, questionings, and delights. Surely Keats hoped that poetry-lovers would enjoy reading his *Ode*, and would experience some of his own feelings, rather than regard it as a crossword puzzle or as an enigma—that beauty is truth, and truth beauty, in everlasting perplexity.

Our body of theory begins with the assumption that the primary step in understanding literature from the subjective standpoint, is to study it as immediate experience.

The scientist then takes over.

He or she notes that immediate experience is described in self-referent language, and is about *feelings* for something distinguishable; also, that the number of such statements a person can make (or understand) about anything is enormous.

Take, for example, "rain." You can see it outside, and one can say "It is raining." But ten thousand statements can not exhaust what "rain" may mean subjectively to people or to one person—has it a father, asked Job, and did he beget the drops of rain? Is it not a sign of resurrection, asks the Koran? Do I really need to put something by for a rainy day? It comes dancing down? And how beautiful is the rain, quoth Longfellow. It is warm as tears. Or, as Coates Kinney said, in *Rain on the Roof*,

> And a thousand recollections
>   Weave their bright hues into woof
> As I listen to the patter
>   Of the soft rain on the roof.

The feelings we can have about "rain," or "It is raining," find expression in a thousand thoughts, all of which follow a simple form:

> *"I . . . feel . . . (something)"*

A long-forgotten branch of psychology—called systematic or subjective psychology—begins with such self-referent statements as the simplest form of "psychical life"

(Ward, 1933). They are its elements, as atoms are in physics, molecules in chemistry, genes in biology. They are the bricks of "psychical life," and it is with these that the present author tried to revive subjective psychology with Q-technique and its methodology (Stephenson, 1953).

We begin, then, by examining *immediate experience* in terms of self-referent statements.

CONCOURSE THEORY

A collection of subjective statements about an experience is called a *concourse* (Stephenson, 1978). Thus, about "It is raining," the following would be typical statements of its concourse:

- I watch thunderstorms from inside a nice, safe place—it's exciting.
- If it rains a lot you smell the earth (Statement *a*)
- I like to put on old clothes and take a walk—it's sort of romantic to walk in the rain.
- Makes me feel sad, if I'm alone or depressed for some reason.
- I go to bed and sleep when it rains—it's boring.
- I like the taste of kisses in the rain—I really like that taste.

The self-reference is evident: thus, it may be a fact that a person watches thunderstorms from a safe place; it becomes self-referent when he or she adds "It is exciting." Statement *a* seems to be a fact, but the feeling could be that it is *me* smelling the earth with delight. The feelings cover a wide range of experience— safety, excitement, romance, depression, boredom, sensuality. No statement is purely factual, as in "Water is a compound of oxygen and hydrogen in liquid state convertible by heat into steam and by cold into ice."

There are concourses for everything people experience. A child of three or four seems to be *au fait* with every picture you can show him or her in story books, and can talk to every one of the pictures, not merely to say "*that* is a teddy bear" (which is *not* self-referent), but to say "that's *my* teddy" (which *is* self-referent). By the time a child reads and writes, concourses abound for him or for her. The child can give a meaning about "raining" to hundreds of the statements of its concourse.

This is a remarkable achievement. *By adolescence, all statements of almost all concourses are comprehensible to most young people.* The reason for this is that concourses are not about facts, which have to be learned, but about feelings which are lived every day. Formal learning and teaching at school tend to concentrate on facts (in algebra, spelling, physics, grammar, literary works, etc.); feelings have to fend for themselves, and they are subject to fortuitous experiences (singing, reading to oneself, viewing television, socializing, dating, etc.). We experience feelings and emotions ostensibly, not as knowledge, but in countless immediate experiences, lived through almost randomly.

Nor need the concourses be in language form, as sentences. They may be single words, such as all the words implying subjectivity in *Roget's Thesaurus*, that is, all words relating to "voluntary powers" (will, desire, pleasure, necessity, devotion, humor, earnestness, indisposition, resolution, patience: . . . there must be 10,000 in the *Thesaurus*). The concern would be with "my will," "my desire," "my pleasure," "my necessity," "my devotion," "my humor," and so on. Or concourses may be photographs, for example, of "vases," like the ones we can purchase in museums in large cities of the world: in such cases, the immediate experience would be aesthetic—but again each person's own, *mine*. Or, there can be a concourse of colored prints (or postcards) of religious paintings in churches, museums and cathedrals in Europe: the concern would be with "religious affections," that is, with the feelings people have when looking at the pictures—feelings of mystery, truth, the angelic, the cloistered, the heavenly, of revelation and myth, and a thousand more, *always a person feeling something*. Concourses provide the stimuli upon which a person can project states of feeling.

The semantic differential method (see chap. 12) deals with subjectivity, but in an analytic, not a synthetic context. In Q-methodology a concourse is the universe of statements possible about a particular situation, concept, a notion, out of which *new* ideas are formed, by feeling imposed upon the universe. We shall see that *creativity* is locked into concourse.

For theoretical purposes a concourse is assumed to be a "statistical population," whose items are random, like marbles in a bag. The statements are therefore subject to "sampling theory"—a sample can be drawn randomly from a concourse, and this is the origin of the Q-sample in Q-methodology. Q-samples may be of any size, but they are 30 to 50, approximately; the size is a matter of design and convenience. Sometimes we may be satisfied with 50 statements without collecting the hundreds more we know exist: but that involves a statistical trick, called "balanced block designing" (Stephenson, 1953).

THEORY OF MEANING

Another part of our body of theory concerns what is to be meant by *meaning*. Professor Elder Olson refers to this dictum from Aristotle:

> Things are infinite, words are finite.

Words, it seems, fix the meaning of things. The sounds we utter are given meaning, and once this happens, they become words. Olson adds:

> The giving of meaning is always determinate—that is, the word means *this* and does not mean *that*. (1976, p. 299)

For us this is only half a truth. It is true that modern science gives precise definitions to its words; but it would be more true to say that in literature and the arts Aristotle's dictum should be reversed:

> Words are infinite, things are finite.

Olson got it wrong for literature, because the meaning given to words is the crux of the creative mind; and it is from this standpoint that we develop the first *law of subjectivity*—called the Law of Mind originally by Charles Sanders Peirce (1839–1914), the great American philosopher.

An example will show how this law operates: suppose I give a random set of statements to a person, from the concourse on "It is raining," with a request that he or she read them, and tell something of what "It is raining" means to him or to her, that is, what he or she feels about "rain." The person is put into a situation of immediate experience, and will no doubt mull over the various ideas of the statements, thinking about one or another in a mishmash of cogitation, recollection, and all else of immediate experience. The statements are all self-referent, and they all involve feeling, but the ideas expressed are all different—about thunder, romance, smell of earth, sadness, boredom, and so on. Peirce's law says, in effect, that reasoning about the statements won't help much, but that feelings will. In experiencing the ideas, their feelings will "flow together in a continuum of feeling," *from which a new idea will come to mind*. Peirce applied the law, initially, to explain how different ideas gain a certain generality, but it covers the situation for the statements on "It is raining,' and for a person "generalizing" about the disparate statements, to form a new idea (Peirce's theory of mind is described in J. Buchler's *The Philosophy of Peirce*, pp. 339–353.

Thus, even from the few statements about "It is raining" to which I have made reference, one might imagine a young person musing about them in some such manner as this: "Thunder and romance don't go down well with me, and the smell of earth, sadness, and boredom are destructive to romance." But another may feel, instead: "Romance is like a burst of thunder and a smell of earth; but its end is sadness, boredom, it never lasts." The building blocks are used very differently in the two cases. And each has in it the possibility of a new idea: for is there not a touch of poetry in the following statement?

> Romance is thunder,
> A smell of earth.
> Its end is sadness, boredom.

Charles Peirce said he did not know what governs such "unifications," such putting together of ideas and feelings—not as matters of grammar, of course—but as ideation, as immediate experience. Obviously it is a complex matter.

Q-TECHNIQUE

How, then, are we to stimulate such feelings, and arrive at new formations?

It is done by way of Q-technique and factor-theory. Q-technique had its origins in a branch of experimental psychology (psychophysics) in the middle of the last century; its concern was with the body-mind problem—is mind one thing and body another, or are the two one and the same? The technique deals with feeling as a fundamental principle of subjectivity, and it does so in relation to the theories of concourse and meaning briefly outlined above.

The technique puts an individual in a situation calling for expression of feeling, not use of intellect, judgment, or reasoning. It does so by confronting him or her with a set of "statements" from a concourse about an object of inquiry. Thus, to know what "It is raining" means to a person, one begins with a collection of statements made empirically, as when people talk about the weather, or in dictionaries of quotations about "raining." From this concourse a Q-sample is taken to represent the concourse (Stephenson, 1953). As an example, I chose 30 statements, each typed on a 3 × 4-inch card. After being shuffled (as in card-playing) to randomize them, the cards are given to a subject to browse through, after which he or she performs a Q-sort with all 30 statements, to express his or her *feeling* about "It is raining."

A Q-sort consists of spreading the statements on a scale, from pleasure to unpleasure, such as the following:

Q-Sort Distribution

Score	Pleasure			Neutral			Unpleasure		
	+4	+3	+2	+1	0	−1	−2	−3	−4
($n = 30$)									
Frequency	2	3	3	4	6	4	3	3	2

The dispersion is a quasi-normal frequency distribution. This is a theoretical requirement; the spread of the scale depends on the size of the Q-sample. Feeling is always split into opposites, from pleasure to unpleasure; this was regarded by Charles Spearman as the cardinal principle of psychology. Freud based psychoanalysis on the same fundamental principle, *pleasure-pain*, (along with *reality* principle). The statements themselves have no normative values. The feelings are always relative to a given situation. In terms of Peirce's "continuum of feeling", (to which reference has been made earlier), subject to chance (and remembering that we are considering a concrete situation, such as one person performing a Q-sort), as many statements of a Q-sample will be felt by the person as *pleasant*, as there will be those felt to be *unpleasant*; most statements will be more-or-less *neutral* in the situation, with little or no feeling attached. The feelings, because of the "law of error," will tend to be normally distributed, in the familiar bell-shaped statistical distribution, as above.

Thus, of the 30 statements, one or two will evoke pleasure ("I like kissing in the rain.") and one or two displeasure ("It should rain every day."). Most feelings would be neutral. Nothing is standardized in the technique, except that the mean for feeling should approximate zero, to correspond to the point of *no* feeling on the scale.

The use of "forced" distributions is often queried: it is usual to ask whether it does not distort data, and whether it might not be better, and more true to matters, to allow the Q-sorter to use *un*forced distributions, to please himself (or herself) in the way he or she distributes the statements along the scale? This, however, assumes nominalism and a normative basis for the meanings of subjective statements, which contradicts the premises upon which Q-methodology is based. The "forced" distribution is a *theoretical* requirement.

THE IMPORTANCE OF Q-TECHNIQUE

The technique just described is of importance not because it finds wide use in psychology, social science, and science generally, but because it solves an age-old problem; measurement of mental acts directly, with a universality never achieved before.

Even though the statements are sorted physically, on a table, the acts of quantification are in the mind of the Q-sorter. Anyone, with a ruler, may measure length; but only the Q-sorter can measure his or her own subjectivity. The inseparability of object of measurement and measuring instrument is therefore complete, a basic axiom in relativity. Moreover, the measurement is in "pure numbers": whatever may be the unit used implicitly by the Q-sorter, the raw numbers assigned on the linear scale are transformed to a corresponding distribution of standard statistical scores whose mean is zero (0) and standard deviation (σ) 1.00—by the simple device of dividing deviations from the mean by the standard deviation of the distribution. This provides a distribution of pure numbers, free from the raw unit, whatever it was. There is now, therefore, a standard unit for all subjective measurement: we call it the *quantsal* unit. The limitation remains, that the Q-sorter alone can make these quantsal measurements, which is what everyone accepts about subjectivity—that it is locked in the person's mind. Here, in Q-methodology, we reduce what is "locked up" to one simple method of measurement—we can deal with everything else objectively in terms of this unit. Every other requirement of scientific method, such as reliability, testability, validity, falsifiability, is taken care of as thoroughly in Q-methodology as in any branch of science. What holds up acceptance of quantsal as a universal unit is what I have elsewhere called "The Shame of Science" (Stephenson, 1978), a dogmatic assertion that objectivity can be reached only "outside," not "inside" the mind; an assertion oblivious to the axiom of the inseparability of object and observer in relativity theory.

Q-METHODOLOGY

Q-methodology is not merely a statistical method, but a set of interlocking theories, including those of *concourse*, of *meaning*, and also *factor-theory* and *theory of communication* (Stephenson, 1953, 1980a). It uses factor-analysis, but not as Charles Spearman originally conceived of it, or as it is used widely today in psychometry for studies of intelligence, abilities, and personality, where the concern is with individual differences, that is, measurements of the intelligence, ability, (or whatever) of each individual in a population. In Q-methodology, on the contrary, the concern is with the *form* taken by samples of statements of a concourse during Q-sorting. It is not a matter of measuring or predicting the score gained by individual statements for the *feeling* they induce: *the concern is with the form taken by all the statements of a Q-sample, that is, with probability distributions, as if determined by quantum state vectors, as in nuclear physics* (Stephenson, 1982).

The concern is with feeling as a *state*, and the total amount of feeling expressed by a person will be *zero*, since there will be as much positive feeling as negative.

Factor-theory probes into this: it is, of course, too complicated to describe here, but is comparable to other widely used theories, such as Shannon's theory of information (1949) and Gabor's theory of communication (1951) upon which computer science depends. Our use of factor-theory, for analysis of total states of feeling, is as basic for subjective science as Shannon's and Gabor's are for information science.

KEATS' ODE ON A GRECIAN URN

Consider, for example, the problem of interpreting Keats' *Ode on a Grecian Urn*. When students in an English literature class read the poem, what do they feel about it? What is their understanding of it? Ordinarily, they could write an essay describing what it means to them, or the professor may ask for answers to some questions designed to probe into their interpretations.

With the theories of concourse, meaning, Q-technique, and factor-theory already in hand, we can go about the problem systematically. First, a concourse of self-referent statements made by literary critics in the past about the poem is collected: there is a considerable volume of interpretative literature on the *Ode*—by Edgar Allan Poe, T. S. Eliot, and many more—providing such statements as the following:

- It suggests (to me) a life of sensations rather than of thought.
- It is reminding us (me) that one's imagination is free to play its own tune— "heard melodies are sweet, but those unheard are sweeter."
- I feel that we die, like the heifer brought for sacrifice, with as little understanding of the reason for it.
- The setting (in my view) is sexual, but idealized and exquisite in feeling.
- (In my view) the message of the urn is that poetry can be a source of the highest form of wisdom and truth.
- To say that beauty is truth, and truth beauty, is (in my view) essentially meaningless.

And so on, one statement after another, all different, all self-referent, and countless in number. It is a straightforward matter to search through the literature and to collect such statements: there is art in the process, to be alert for interesting, pregnant viewpoints, expressed with brevity. Then one takes a Q-sample. If one is "playing the game" strictly, this would be a random sample, chosen by lot: but since Q-sorting has a theoretical basis, it is wiser to be sure that the Q-sample statements are all as different as possible, as widely expressive of different feelings as possible, and (from a preliminary try-out) well-balanced about zero in Q-sorting.

The Q-sample I used in a study of Keats' *Ode* (Stephenson, 1972) had 35 statements like those above. A class of 28 graduates in English Literature was given a copy of the *Ode* to read, after which each student performed a Q-sort to represent what he or she experienced during the reading, with the following frequency distribution:

	Positive	Neutral	Negative
Raw Score	+5 +4 +3 +2	+1 0 −1	−2 −3 −4 −5
(n = 35)			
Frequency	2 2 3 3	5 5 5	3 3 2 2

There are therefore 28 Q-sorts. The factor-analysis is performed on a digital computer: there is little need for the student to know how the calculations are done—he or she probably uses a transistor calculator every day and doesn't know how it provides answers to the buttons he or she presses. The same should apply to factor-analysis and, indeed, if it were not so complex, a transistor calculator could have been designed for it, for anyone's use.

Factor-analysis serves to distinguish what sets of coherent probability distributions are present in the Q-sorts. In my study, the computer indicated that there were four sets, A, B, C, D, for 11, 4, 5, and 2 students respectively. Six Q-sorts were idiosyncratic, that is, not attached to any factor.

A factor is a "theoretical" Q-sort, like any performed by a person. Eleven students had provided similar Q-sorts (providing factor A), pointing to a quantumized probability distribution, and therefore to an inherency of the concourse. Similarly for each factor, each for different students. The six Q-sorts which fall on none of the factors may be regarded as random.

In principle we expect a limited number of factors, which take the cream, so to speak, off the data. And according to our *theory of meaning* each factor involves the possibility of a *new* meaning. It is the investigator's main objective to grasp from the factors what the new meanings are; success in this depends upon how well the investigator can interpret data, not on how well the computer had made calculations.

The data are in tables of quantsal scores, showing the scores gained by the statements of the Q-sample on each factor, as in Table 13-1 for Factor A.

Table 13-1. Statements for Factor A

	Score on Factors			
Statement	A	B	C	D
35. The poem has no palpable design on us . . . it is unobtrusive, entering one's soul. It startles one's feeling.	5	3	1	−1
8. The "Ode" is wistful, freezing for eternity an instant of time—the bold lover who will never kiss: the lovers will remain so for eternity, he urgent, she fair.	4	2	−2	3
12. The trees and leaves are blissfully immortal . . . yet all are shown with deep human feelings . . . we feel them deeply . . . with "burning foreheard, and a parching tongue."	4	1	2	0

There are 32 additional statements in the table, of course, each with scores for the four factors, A, B, C, D.

As we see, the statements gain different scores on different factors—but their measurement as such is not the object of the analysis. What is at issue, theoretically, is a *feeling* underlying all 35 statements of the Q-sample, a different feeling for each factor. The three statements above have been selected to illustrate how interpretation is pursued. The statements discriminate A from the other factors. The hunch is, at once, that the meaning is going to be within a framework of *romance*, of sexual paradise, bliss, pure and innocent, idealized. Of all 35 statements, none could be more evocative of this than statements 35, 8, and 12 in Table 13-1—and we see that these are given highest scores by A compared with any for B, C, or D. With this suggestion in mind the investigator looks elsewhere in the complete table, to see if other statements (and their quantsal scores) fit into the pattern, that these 11 students appear to have experienced the poem as idealized romance.

So it was in the study: all 35 statements fitted into this interpretation for A relative to the other factors. One then wonders why, and it could be that the students were so steeped in knowledge of the Romantic Period in English Literature, in which Keats of course was a luminary, that they could not read the poem except as romantic bliss. All 11 Q-sorters had majored in English Literature, and one might suspect something of this had entered into their Q-sorts. But the Q-sort itself, as well as other evidence, suggested that the students really did *feel* the *Ode* as romantic: it "startled" their feelings; it was "wistful," "blissfully immortal," and so on. In follow-up discussions with the students, the conclusion was inescapable—*this is how they feel about the poem.*

Consider next, factor D, for a few characterizing statements as in Table 13-2.

Table 13-2. Statements for Factor D

		Score on Factors		
Statement	A	B	C	D
16. Truth is the satisfaction of reason; beauty is the satisfaction of pure pleasure; passion is the satisfaction of the emotions (of the heart).	3	2	−5	5
27. To say that beauty is truth and truth beauty is essentially meaningless.	−5	−5	−5	4
4. The imaginative insight of Keats is a basic and fundamental perception of essentials— . . . it is truth reached by beauty, not by reason.	1	2	3	−5
17. The urn is utterly beautiful . . . it will remain eternally so, reminder to us of these deepest feelings—of love, mortality, despair and immortality—but what is immortal is what we leave *behind*, the silence, because we are no longer present.	−1	−2	4	−4

The two students of this factor (Table 13-2) project total rationality, that truth can be reached only by reason. There is no sense of romance; the beauty of the poem is quite lost; there is no feeling of tragedy and despair (statement 17 is given almost the highest *negative* score). One might assume that the students were denying any value whatever to the poem, or had set out deliberately to distort the exercise.

These two examples will serve to illustrate what is involved in interpretation, and for the moment completes the formal exposition of Q-technique and its methodology. There is much more to learn about it, of course. But the method is quite straightforward: For any problem in the subjective domain, factor-analysis brings data to the investigator's attention, for his or her interpretation. The steps are always the same: put together the concourse; compose the Q-sample; perform the Q-sorts; have them factor-analyzed; and interpret the factors. All of this is eminently systematic, perfectly general in application, and basically scientific in a fundamental sense, granted a place for science in subjectivity. The end is always an interpretation, but it is easy to test whether different investigators arrive at the same interpretation, just as it is easy to determine how far different individuals give the same "interpretation" to our experimental piece of poetry:

> Romance is thunder,
> A smell of earth.
> Its end is sadness, boredom.

KEATS' ODES

The enigma of the final lines of Keats' *Ode on a Grecian Urn* has presented literary interpretation with a gnawing problem:

> Beauty is truth, truth beauty—that is all
> Ye know on earth, and all ye need to know.

I thought that if we think of Beauty as great art, and of Truth as reality, there is nothing enigmatical about these two lines. Keats was saying that really great art is not a denial of reality, but its poetic translation. Great art, in short, can only be great if it in some way reaches into reality.

Behind this, however, there was the gnawing problem of the split of knowledge in two, to which reference was made in the quotation heading the present chapter. Ages before Keats, there had been the same split. There had always been *Nature's Book* written by scientists, and the *Books of Scripture and Conscience* written by philosophers and theologians, as described in Benjamin Nelson's address to the Copernicus Symposium in 1972, and published in *The Nature of Scientific Discovery* (Gingerich, 1975, pp. 355–371).

Nature's Book was served by the fictionalistic theory of hypothesis ("saving the phenomena" in antiquity, which became the hypothetico-deductive method from the time of Newton). The other Books involved the *probabilistic casuistry of conscience, opinion and belief* (the scholarly domain of theologians and speculative philosophers down the ages and of literary philosophers today).

The founders of modern science, Copernicus and Galileo, maintained that the secrets of nature were to be found in mathematics—"numbers never lie"—whereas works on opinion and conscience are written in words "which are easy and tempting to misconstrue." To this day the same split is maintained: that science, with its numbers and invariances is the royal road to understanding nature. Unhappily, it left the *Book of Conscience* behind. For Keats, Beauty in art and Truth in science were equally real: We can now agree with him, not merely because mathematics and "numbers (which) never lie", but because there is a methodology to support it, as outlined in *Quantum Theory and Q-Methodology: Fictionalistic and Probabilistic Theories Conjoined* (Stephenson, 1983).

Keats knew what he was saying. His early poems are adolescent fantasies about "bowers of bliss," "lush sensualities," an all-absorbing pleasure in a sexual paradise, idealized, romantic, characterized by innocence and freedom from shame, guilt, and lust. It was this youthful fantasy, it seems, that the 11 students of factor A above were experiencing as they read Keats' *Ode on a Grecian Urn*.

However, it is not what Keats had put into this *Ode*. He had become aware of the fantasy of his early poems, which he had composed (admittedly) with such felicity and grace. He now felt something of the realities of life—sordid then, and all about him in the disease, ignorance, and poverty of London at the turn of the eighteenth century. He becomes depressed, and equated poetic creation with hard work, learning, wisdom, and intellectual maturity—all labor, he wrote, of "knowledge enormous." For a time he was unsure of himself, was depressed, and his writing suffered correspondingly.

But in a matter of a very few years Keats,—who died, remember, when he was only 26—came to grips with himself, to face up to the "agonies and strife of human hearts," and it was then that he wrote his *Odes*—the greatest poems, many would say, in the English language. There were four: *Ode to Psyche*, *Ode to a Nightingale*, *Ode on a Grecian Urn*, and *Ode on Melancholy*, all written around 1819. I set about examining the relationship of these different interpretations with the poetic development undergone by Keats. Factor A, we have seen, corresponds to Keats' adolescent fantasy. Factors B and C, however, reached toward serious regard of the *Ode on a Grecian Urn*. The four students of factor B responded to the *Ode* in terms of *taste*, that is, of poetic aesthetics, as the following key statements in Table 13-3 indicate.

Table 13-3. Statements for Factor B

Statement	Score on Factors			
	A	B	C	D
28. The poem is an expression of exquisite feeling and emotion—there is no need to look into it for deep philosophical meanings.	−4	5	−4	−4
21. The sole arbiter of poetry is *taste*—not intellect, not conscience; nor is duty, or truth essentially at issue—just taste.	−3	4	−5	2
20. Joy and sorrow in life are inextricably intermingled; but we feel that "beauty is truth, truth beauty," i.e., the highest value is a certain enjoyment, whether exquisitely "solidly pastoral" or other.	1	4	4	3

Notice the "exquisite feeling," without philosophical meanings; the *taste*, not the philosophies of intellect or conscience or duty or truth—just *taste*. The gist of the factor B is clear, that *aesthetic enjoyment* was the high point of the poem for these four students.

Factor C (Table 13-4) was for four students and myself. I had performed a Q-sort to represent my interpretation, as to what I felt, and my feelings were shared to some extent, apparently, by four students. I would like to think they were the most mature of the students! In any case, they apparently got more to the heart of the *Ode* (if I was correct), as the critical statements in Table 13-4 indicate.

Table 13-4. Statements for Factor C

		Score on Factors		
Statement	A	B	C	D
31. It represents a glorious clear-eyed apprehension of the spiritual eternity which art affords.	0	3	5	0
7. What is "true" is the conclusion that "immortality is silence" . . . This is the solution of Keats' enigmatical assertion that beauty is truth, truth beauty; both are immortal.	0	1	4	2
17. The urn is seen as utterly beautiful, in form and what it depicts . . . but what is immortal is what we leave *behind*, the silence, because we are no longer present.	−1	2	4	−4

The two statements, 7 and 17 (in Table 13-4), were my own contribution to the concourse. I did not want to say outright that by "immortality is silence" Keats was referring to *death*, as an end in silence:

> Thou still unravished bride of quietness,
> Thou foster child of Silence and slow Time . . .

But four students had felt something of this, and of the sadness and tragedy of the *Ode*.

I concluded that there is a relationship between Keats' own mature development as a poet, and the maturity of understanding of his readers. You are not likely to feel what Keats felt, unless indeed it is within you to do so.

One may imagine my pleasure when, two years after completing the study, a book appeared with the title, *Keats and His Poetry: A Study in Development*, by Professor M. Dickstein (1971), which described far better than I could possibly have done, the theme of Keats' development, attributing it to growth in the awareness of himself, as *self*. Dickstein indicates that writing the *Odes* was a confrontation of Keats with himself. Keats reverts to the early adolescent fantasies in *Ode to Psyche*, but now more thoughtfully he has set himself to

> build a fane
> In some untrodden region of my mind . . .

That is, a temple (fane) into which to put his newly-forming thoughts. The *Ode to a Nightingale* follows: he now "aches" and thinks of "easeful Death." The nightingale dies, but its song echoes on as art. But still Keats had not solved for himself the reality of death. Was it just a vision, he asks; am I awake or asleep? In the *Ode on a Grecian Urn* the truth is faced: the lovers on the urn can never kiss, yet their love will never fade—the art is transfixed. But the real lovers are dead. And in *Ode on Melancholy*, the truth is accepted: death, "veiled melancholy," ends all:

> Veil'd Melancholy has her sovran shrine,
> Though seen by none save him whose strenuous tongue
> Can burst Joy's grape . . .
> His soul shall taste the sadness of her might,
> And be among her cloudy trophies hung.

Only with maturity ("strenuous tongue") can we see life ("Joy's grape") for what it is, death being its sad ending ("a cloudy trophy hung").

The Q-technique study with students was an echo of this developmental thesis. The factors of Q-technique were evidence of a certain objectivity in Art, a certain *truth-value* in Keats' *Ode on a Grecian Urn*. Factors A (Table 13-1), B (Table 13-3), and D (Table 13-2) were "immature" responses, in different degrees; factor C (Table 13-4) was "mature" and "correct."

The student may recognize the enormity of such a conclusion. "Art is *I*," it has been said, "science is *we*": Art is what the individual cares to make of it—everyone is his or her own judge of it—unlike science, where there are correct answers about which everyone can agree. Q-theory is denying that "Art is *I*."

We reach, then, the real problem about literature and the arts: can there be an objective basis for it, as in science?

SELF-REFERENCE

The question is about "subjectivity," not about any acceptable findings in structuralism (which is a matter of Koyré's "world of science—the real world"), but about "the world of life." And the answer is affirmative.

Already, in the direction of an affirmative answer, a great deal of progress has been made in the system described above as Q-methodology. Every piece of art, every poem, every literary concept has its concourse, and can be subject to Q-technique and its methodology—all in the subjective domain, with specific reference to *self*, as Dickstein found, and as the above study of Keats' *Ode* indicates.

So it is for Keats' *Ode*: we can feel the despair, even if we do not face up to the reality ourselves. Most of the graduate students in the graduate English literature course were apparently incapable of feeling what Keats meant us to feel: but a few, unspoiled or able, could touch the tragic. The "world of life" is not an open book: its truths take careful finding.

This should not surprise us. America could sing no songs to honor either their own defeated, still less the victors, in the war with Vietnam. In Britain, during and after World War I (1914–1918), the popular poet was Rupert Brook, who wrote patriotic poems about British youth sacrificing itself for King and Country. Only later the poetry of Wilfred Owens was recognized as greater and profound: he was killed in France, a soldier, a few days before the war ended, and sang of war as Homer had done centuries before, doing honor to victors and victims alike:

I am the enemy you killed, my friend.
I knew you in this dark, for so you frowned
Yesterday through me as you jabbed and killed,
I parried; but my hands were loath and cold,
Let us sleep now . . .

It is this kind of truth-value that we can investigate, as in the above example with Keats' *Ode on a Grecian Urn*. Not by hypothesis-testing, but by determining operant *form*. We can reach, this way, what the philosopher Koyré described as the "world of life," by a methodology as fundamental for so-called mind as quantum theory is for matter.

We asked at the outset, what is truth in literature? It lies in self-reference (Stephenson, 1980b), and it is found by the methodology (Q) of which the above study is an example. It is established with a sense of evidence, as in all Q-methodological studies. When Olson asked, is there "one single method which is the right method," the answer is clearly yes. But when we ask what, really, is fundamentally at issue, it is a reply to Alexander Koyré's alarm at the splitting of knowledge into two— into the world of reality and the world of life. The two can now be conjoined. Fundamentally, theories of relativity, and of quantum mechanics, are as applicable to so-called mind as to matter—all are relative in Q, and factor-theory is analogous to quantum-theory. It is fundamentally relative, because "statements" take on feelings which are dependent upon concrete situations—nothing is normative or absolute; and objects and observers are indeed inseparable in Q-technique.

The closeness with modern scientific theory is best demonstrated, perhaps, by the reminder that for the past 2,500 years, since Democritus, the concept of the particle structure of matter has dominated scientific thought (the physicist thinks of electrons, hadrons, quarks, etc.), but now scientists are asked to think also of "fundamental symmetries," as Heisenberg invited them to do at the Copernicus Symposium in 1972 (Gingerich, 1975). "Fundamental symmetries" are matters of *inherent form*, from Plato's philosophy. There are also the self-structures of Q-methodology.

REFERENCES

Dickstein, M. *Keats and his poetry: A study in development*. Chicago: University of Chicago Press, 1971.
Buchler, J. *The philosophy of Peirce: Selected writings*, edited by Justus Buchler. New York: Harcourt, Brace & Co. 1950.
Gabor, D. *Lectures on communication theory*. Cambridge: MA: MIT Press, 1951.
Gingerich, O. (Ed.). *The nature of scientific discovery*. Washington, DC: Smithsonian Institution Press, 1975.
Heisenberg, W. Tradition in science. In O. Gingerich (Ed.), *The nature of scientific discovery*. Washington, DC: Smithsonian Institution Press, 1975.
Koyré, A. *Newtonian studies*. London: Chapman and Hall, 1965.
Nelson, B. The quest for certitude and the books of scripture, nature, and conscience. In O. Gingerich, (Ed.), *The nature of scientific discovery*, Washington, DC: Smithsonian Institution Press, 1975.
Olson, E. *On value judgments in the arts and other essays*. Chicago: University of Chicago Press, 1976.

Rees, R. *Simone Weil: Seventy letters*. London: Oxford University Press, 1965.

Shannon, C. & Weaver, W. *The mathematical theory of communication*. Urbana, IL: University of Illinois Press, 1949.

Spearman, C. E. General intelligence objectively determined and measured. *American Journal of Psychology*, 1904, *14*, 201–93.

Stephenson, W. *The study of behavior: Q-technique and its methodology*. Chicago: University of Chicago Press, 1953.

Stephenson, W. Applications of communication theory: II—Interpretation of Keats' 'Ode on a Grecian Urn'. *The Psychological Record*, 1972, *22*, 177–192.

Stephenson, W. The shame of science. *Ethics in science and medicine*, 1978, *5*, 25–38.

Stephenson, W. Consciring: Theory of subjective communicability. *Communication yearbook 4*. Edited by D. Nimmo. New Brunswick: Transaction Books, 1980(a).

Stephenson, W. Michael Polanyi, science and belief. *Ethics in science and medicine*, 1980, *7*, 111–133. (b)

Stephenson, W. Q-methodology, interbehavioral psychology, and quantum theory. *The Psychological Record*, 1982, *32*, 235–248.

Stephenson, W. Quantum theory and Q-methodology: Fictionalistic and probabilistic theories conjoined. *The Psychological Record*, 1983, *33*, 213–230.

Ward, J. *Psychological principles*. Cambridge: Cambridge University Press, 1933.

Part III:
The Study of Classroom
Literature Instruction

Chapter 14
The Identity of Pedagogy and Research in the Study of Response to Literature

David Bleich

Department of English
Indiana University

THE PROBLEM OF EPISTEMOLOGY

The study of response to literature has tried, generally, to use the epistemological standards and research procedures of the quantitative sciences. In this well-known method, a research site is established, the object of research is stripped of nonessential features, the researcher stipulates and seeks to maintain his or her independence of the object and its independence of the researcher, and he or she then draws conclusions that he or she believes others will have no trouble accepting. If accepted, the conclusions are considered objective knowledge and are discarded only when there is a more persuasive argument for another conclusion. Because both the old and new knowledge are considered objective, the new is considered true and the old false. True knowledge is understood as the representation of something intrinsic to the object of study; the process of knowing is the act of representing the object and its working in the correct way. The object of study, it is preassumed, is unaffected by the attempt to understand it.

In other work (Bleich, 1978) I have discussed how, in major areas of human knowledge, this objective epistemology has been questioned, and in some instances, suspended or discarded. Many who have studied response have indicated similar misgivings about the traditional research methodology and reasonings. Nevertheless, most researchers have continued to expect results from the approaches that have brought success in the past. The task of developing knowledge of response to literature, however, presents an especially clear occasion for showing how and why to change these expectations, and how to reconceive the problem of research in this area along more productive lines. This change in perspective involves identifying response research with literary pedagogy.

The interest in response has evolved historically from the growth of the pedagogical profession. It is one of the results of the gradual onset of universal literacy. When few could read, pedagogy aimed to develop reading skills and then reading habits. When the majority could read, literature became available for cultivating literacy, a capability which requires both response and intellection. In the study of literature, literacy entails interpretation, the aim of which is to establish the meanings and values of literature. As a rule, interpreters know just how tentative interpretive knowledge is. But if the knowledge yielded by interpretation must be presented on a large scale, it becomes easily ritualized, and it appears to have far greater certainty than it actually does have. The pedagogical failure to make such falsely certain knowledge "take" led to the interest in response both as a more reliable way to teach and as a more reliable source of knowledge about reading experiences.

Perhaps the earliest important statement assuming the intimate proximity of pedagogy and knowledge development is Louise Rosenblatt's *Literature as Exploration* (1938, 1968). Working from the tradition of Dewey and liberal humanism, Rosenblatt showed how, in the classroom, subjective, intersubjective, and social forces create valid individual perspectives on commonly known works of literature. Her work, however, was soon lost in the onrush of formalist exegetical criticism which emphasized the objectivity of literary knowledge. The gathering prestige of such criticism, along with ever-increasing university enrollments, seemed to dictate to teachers that they shall now instill in students well-disciplined formal techniques of literary interpretation. Because of the conceptual simplicity of this task, alongside its dignity among academic critics and the need to teach large numbers of people at once, it became the standard pedagogical practice. Knowledge and method were developed by an elite group of learning people, while teachers were agents of this group and middlemen in a clear hierarchy of academic authority.

By the late 1950s, teachers began to rediscover what Rosenblatt had advocated twenty years earlier, and they saw how their former practices were both personally demeaning and fundamentally inapplicable to the subject matter they taught. As Purves and Beach report in *Literature and the Reader* (1972), response became the object of study for a slowly growing group of graduate students planning to become teachers. The early research of James Squire (1964) and James Wilson (1966) began to show how attention to the fact of response raises problems of profound interest and subtlety in all aspects of literary ideation. Not even the common perception of texts could be taken for granted anymore, much less the interpretation or evaluation. These studies, and others which followed them, showed the senses in which pedagogy was an activity in which new literary knowledge was synthesized by each reader, and not one in which established knowledge was funneled into young and vacant minds.

Today, while it may be widely accepted that both readers and communities can develop their own knowledge, it is hardly accepted at all that this kind of knowledge-making can be understood by research. The notion of research has yet to shed its image as "the activity that only quantitative scientists do." In regard to the classroom, it is believed that because a teacher's observation of students is regulated, in large part, by the student's observation of him or her, the classroom cannot be a research site. To do research in pedagogy or response, one either removes the students into "neutral" territory where they are told that research is going to happen, or one distributes in the classroom nonnegotiable written questionnaires. Each of these methods, however, requires an implicit apology by the researcher. In placing students in the "laboratory" the apology takes the form of a compensatory wage for agreeing to be passive while being observed by others. (In daily life, one rarely agrees to be passive for the purpose of being observed; it is done in the doctor's office; other instances where we agree to be observed all involve a performance by us in which we are demonstrating an achievement of ours.) In the analysis of questionnaires, the apology is an acknowledgment of the inconclusive nature of the statistical results and of the fact that wider populations ought to be studied. The apologies enter the research atmosphere because the researcher is being conscientious; his or her own work is much less conclusive than scientific work, but there are, to the researcher, no alternatives if one aims to do research.

The limitation on research alternatives is the natural result of an underlying objectivist epistemology; the researcher *expects* that knowledge can come only from certain conventionally prescribed "neutral" sites and through mathematically organized procedures. Unless there is a "control" group, one cannot know anything about the "experimental" group; and each "group" must show "statistically significant" results. This epistemology achieved success when the object of investigation was either known or assumed to belong to a class of like objects and when there was no perceivable influence of the observer on the observed. Neither of these conditions obtains in the study of response, to wit: an individual's response is known in advance to be almost certainly *different* from responses even from similar readers of the same work; and, whoever is doing research on a person's response is almost certainly exercising an influence over the very response he or she is trying to study. As I discuss in *Subjective Criticism*, these two circumstances dictate the need for a subjective epistemology, and become the axiological bases for this epistemology.

Given this epistemology, the classroom is a natural research site; on the one hand, it provides a group of unique responses whose possible similarities with one another are discoverable only in retrospect; on the other hand, no one member of the classroom can observe others without him- or herself being observed. This does not mean that a classroom is necessarily a research site; it does mean that a gathering of those who call themselves students and teachers is as much a potential research site as the scene of pedagogy, therapy, torture, or orgies. Each of these purposes produces "knowledge," though each kind of knowledge will not be considered authoritative according to traditional concepts of scientific objectivity. The subjectivity of these knowledges, however, should be obvious. Our interest is to show how subjective knowledge acquires authority.

Pursuant to the two axioms cited above, any member of a classroom may, in principle, authorize knowledge. To do this, he or she must have a systematic means of articulating the uniqueness of his or her response, and of making this uniqueness available for observation and negotiation. Once the classmembers have gone through this common announcement, each has varying degrees of knowledge of oneself alone and of oneself as a class-participant. Whether and how such knowledge is published—that is, made available to other pedagogical communities—depends on what conscious purpose one or more members of the class has. But regardless of how widely circulated a particular claim may become, the nuclear authorization for that claim has taken place in a classroom. Pedagogy and research may be understood as identical when the classroom has a systematic means of authorizing knowledge of response.

THE RESPONSE STATEMENT AND ITS USE

The basis for presenting and authorizing unique responses is the *response statement* (whose nature and function I have discussed in detail in several other contexts). In the discussion to follow, I will present my own response statement to Franz Kafka's short story, "A Country Doctor," and I will try to show how it may be used to authorize four sorts of interpretative knowledge. I will thereby be acting as both a student and a teacher, an experiencing subject and an object of investigation. If others in my community present a similar statement, we will in one sense be teaching one another, but in many other senses we will be doing research in response. For example, depending on who else is in this community, we could "research" "this community's interpretation of this story by this author"; or, "these three readers' rejection of this story"; or, "this group's distaste for literature," and so on. If the issues are defined in terms such as these, it is easier to see the equivalence of research purposes and pedagogical purposes. Of course, in the present discussion, I will not have the benefit of being able to pursue purposes arrived at in community. Nevertheless, the discussion of my own response statement and the possibilities of its conversion into proposals of knowledge, will give an instance of the kinds of reasoning common to pedagogy and research when a subjective epistemology is presupposed. It should be clear, moreover, that when research is pursued in this way, one cannot seek rules of response that will be universally applicable. Nor can one circumscribe the possible responses to single works or single authors. In fact, no knowledge will be forthcoming that will *predict* anything. Rather, the knowledge sought will be of the kind relevant to the constituents of the classroom, and perhaps to the group in aggregate; it is knowledge that will create new mental orientations toward acts of reading in individuals and in groups. And, it will develop the foundations of *subjective interest and motivation* from which subsequent initiatives for knowledge derive.

The use of this procedure implies that the activity of reporting knowledge should take on a different meaning and role in professional life. First, it suggests that the frequency of reporting should diminish. One need not report every single case to public or otherwise impersonal forums; the pertinence of the knowledge developed in a group applies to the next steps the group hopes to take. Even if results are achieved over a whole course, such results pertain more to life in the local community at large—the school or the university—rather than to everyone teaching language and literature. We would be in more or less the same situation we are in now, where pedagogical journals regularly publish the interesting, but generally not useful, "here's what happened in my class" reports. Second, it would shift the kind of reporting toward an emphasis on group psychology and classroom functioning, issues of authority, gender, and motivation, for example, as manifested in work originally directed toward the study of language. We would be less constrained by traditional reporting categories such as "teaching" or "writing," and more concerned with the intersubjective options that arise in any inquiry into the mutual use of language. And third, the nature of the journals themselves would be different: There would be few individual reports and more collaborative studies, showing, within each essay, the multiple perspectives at work in any given project. Journals could address smaller constituencies, where the reported work could more actively be used as texts for further work; they would be less the collection of individual opinions, and more the presentation of how different communities actually function.

My use of the "response statement," therefore, ought not to be taken as an instruction; there are other ways to disclose these issues aside from my own way. However, I want to show that these issues should find *some* way into the existing vocabularies of research and pedagogy.

Here is my response statement to the Kafka story.

1. This story teaches me how to laugh at the most excruciating and painful frustrations. I can't tell any more whether I learned how to mouth proverb-like statements in the face of ridiculous adversity from Kafka, or if I did this before, and then found the same habit in the story. Of a piece with these statements—like "a false alarm answered in the night can never be made good—not ever"—are the earlier observations in the story, like "I was in great perplexity," which sounds to me like the narrator is going to decide whether or not to feed the pigeons on a sunny day.

2. I am greatly attracted by the seemingly violent and arbitrary motions at the beginning—the snowstorm and the helplessness of the doctor. The bad weather and cold reminds me of evenings when I used to return home with my father from visiting his parents in winter—it was cold and I comforted myself with the thought of my cozy bed at home. But also, I remember thinking that my father was not as well able to stand the cold as I was, and this thought was one of a series of such thoughts of his physical frailty, which I never mentioned to him or to my mother or took any action about. My father smoked on the subway going home; I subsequently noticed that signs prohibited such smoking and casually remarked to my mother that "people" smoke on the subway but do not "spit" (which prohibition was on the same sign); she promptly corrected me by telling me that the reverse was true, whence I observed again and found that behold, she was right, which put my father's behavior in a somewhat different light. When both my father and I were older, we had arguments about his smoking, which usually ended with his informing me that my arguing with him about it caused a "pain in the chest" that was far worse than the cigarettes I would not run down and buy for him. Again, I did not allow myself to feel the import of what he was saying, however.

3. I get a big kick out of the peremptory appearance of the horses with steaming flanks and the vulgar unrepressed groom that appears with them. The servant girl, also feeding pigeons in the park, says, "You never know what you're going to find in your own house," referring to this groom who is about to ravish her. What a jolly scene this is! All that heat in the middle of the

snowstorm with some sick person in the distance. Finally the doctor is at the patient's house and the groom is "splitting and bursting" into the girl. Good. What can we do about this, anyway? I wish I could feel as passive and helpless in the face of my responsibilities as the doctor does. I wish I could just write stories to complain about the situation. Yet, when the doctor says, "My horse was dead, and not a single person in the village would lend me another. I had to get my team out of a pigsty; if they hadn't chanced to be horses, I should have to travel with swine." This is just how I feel about the strokes of good luck that have come into my life.

4. My mother is fond of repeating that an old school chum of hers became Kafka's last lover. I imagine the poor tubercular hero trying desperately to make it with this girl and failing because of the arbitrary virulent disease. I also feel it painful that he did not live to write more such entertaining stories. And maybe live happily ever after with my mother's friend. And maybe my parents should have thus lived instead of struggling and blustering through life.

5. The boy's wound is just marvellous. Nice and red, ravished, with tiny—actually, big—white worms crawling around on it. Someone else's pain is giving me pleasure again—but not for long. But as the doctor's humiliation increases—gets undressed and into bed and hears insults from the boy—his verbal control of the scene becomes more and more arrogantly nonchalant: "Believe me, it is not too easy for me either," he says, when the boy says he'd like best to scratch the doctor's eyes out. My repeated pleasure in this story is the fun of always having the last word in a variety of situations. This is a skill I had to learn from my mother, for whom the last word was also the best word.

6. When you are naked and exposed to the frost of the ages, it is good to be able to have the last word. When I was about six years old, my mother urged me, when I went outside to play, to take my shirt off and get some sun. I was shy and reluctant, but finally she prevailed. Needless to say, the worst happened. There was Mary Ann outside, an imposing twelve-year-old girl with a big mouth who asked me why I did not take my pants off too. I did not have the last word on that occasion, or any other word, which made me feel as if the pants were already off. However, on future occasions I decided to keep my shirt on until I had enough last words for any emergency.

EVALUATION

I will understand this response statement as the representation of my reading experience in the form most viable for intersubjective negotiations—that is for both pedagogical and investigative purposes. The four questions I will ask of my reading experience should each be understood as deriving from each purpose. I will give two kinds of answers to the questions: first a more traditional answer that would be forthcoming had no response statement been given, and then another answer which takes into account the material in the response statement. I will then try to show how the second kind of answer makes it possible for both research and pedagogy to emerge from the same procedures of reading, thus broadening the interest, applicability, and significance of the literary knowledge represented in these answers.

Traditional Formulation

How good a story is this? This is an excellent story, full of literary virtuosity and emotional power, engrossing and moving the reader at every turn. For such a short piece, it has an unusual capacity to make a lasting impact on its audience. The narrator seems to be an extraordinary person, at once involved in a terrible and painful struggle and yet detached and thoughtful, strangely able to ignore the extreme physical adversity, yet able to comment on transcendental truths about his circumstances. He is able to see, in this crisis of medical responsibility, sexual forces at work, as he observes similarities between the sexual victimization of his servant, Rose, the illness of his patient with a rose-red wound, and his own naked helplessness in the snowstorm. Although every aspect of his being is challenged, even his ordinary sense of daily rationality, he remains observant and perceptive, as if knowing he will survive the onslaught of bestiality, sadism, and supernatural caprice. Each detail of his circumstance is related with calm and patience, each even with exactness and insight. He seems to be even eager to convert the repeated irrationalities into articulate thought and make a story out of what must be a nightmare to most people. What else makes great literature but its capacity for evoking in its audience real passions and comprehending assent to the authenticity of these passions for most people?

Formulation in View of Response

The grounds for my claim of the story's excellence, in this brief judgment of literary value, are that the feelings it evokes in "most people" are "real," and that these people know they have such feelings when they read the story. The judgment emphasizes that the character of the narrator is singularly able to evoke feelings of sexual victimization, bestiality, sadism, and supernatural caprice, and to describe them. I therefore conclude that *the story* is excellent.

The response statement says that my reading experience of the story is good. It does not say what I imagine others to be feeling when they read it, nor that these others know that they are having such feelings. My favorable affective response has to do with the verbal power and confidence the readings seem to have stimulated in me. I like the "proverb-like statements" (paragraph 1) the narrator is given to making; I like the invocation of clichés in unusual situations, such as the servant's remark (paragraph 3); and I like the narrator's heroic attempt to articulate the "last word" as a lawful principle of false alarms (paragraph 6). Several of my thoughts describe situations in which others have the last word—both my parents and Mary Ann in specific conversational contexts. When I read the narrator's words and identify with him, I am reminded how I learned the value of having the last word. This learning history, shown in the response statement, shows the affective lenses which made the story perceptible to me. The narrator does not describe his own behavior as having the last word. I describe my own responsive behavior in this way, and I objectify this behavior by saying it is descriptive of the story. Now, as I view both the response and the judgment of value, I see that the more objective I try to be, the less candid and less persuasive I get. In viewing my response, however, my coreaders can understand a clear and specific meaning of my usage of the term "excellent story."

In paragraphs 5 and 6, the response associates nakedness with humiliation, and I imply that my mother's initiative with me may be responsible for this association. In order to avoid future humiliations, I prepare myself with "last words." My judgment of the story's high value does not report the narrator as overcoming humiliation; rather he is heroic in fighting physical adversity and irrationality. When I indicate in the judgment that it appears to me as if the narrator knows he will survive his struggle, this alludes to the element and even the tones in the response statement that I claim I have already survived early humiliations which were brought to mind in my reading. Although humiliation may be absent from my judgment and from my present sense of daily life, it is not absent from my memory or my response to the reading, and it is thereby able to illuminate my judgment to others.

The response statement shows that I enjoy considerably various forms of violence I find in the reading; for example, the snowstorm, the groom's ravishing of Rose, and the aggressiveness of the patient. Paragraph 2 suggests that I associate the helplessness of the doctor with my memory of my father's frailty in a less extreme instance of cold weather. Although I know that the narrator does not report that he takes pleasure in anyone else's misfortune, I feel sadism in his casual perspective on others' pain. My associations suggest a retrospective guilt about my own detachment—"I did not allow myself to feel the import of what he (my father) was saying" (paragraph 2). Thus, my response statement shows a guilt attached to my lauding the doctor's imperturbable detachment; in the judgment, I am vague about whether he is a victim or a villain, and view him unambiguously as a hero regardless. Just as last words overcome humiliation, calm words overcome negligent detachment in my own system of linguistic self-regulation.

The rhetorical question concluding my judgment is a sentimentality that sounds nice but is so general as to be inapplicable. However, value judgments are customarily given in terms of unarguable standards of greatness. If a critic is conscientious in trying to present objective knowledge, such statements are the best he or she can do, because few will deny that great literature is *at least* that which "pleased many and pleased long." As long as subjective reasons are considered ineligible to support claims of knowledge, the claims remain anchored in sentimentalities. The response statement permits subjectivity to guide judgments without losing any of the discipline of rational discourse. My response shows just which "real passions" I am discussing, and just what I mean by "comprehending assent" in this reading experience. Every teacher in one way or another urges his students to "be specific," but teachers are usually uncertain regarding just what specificity is needed. The specificity I am urging is the subjective "etymology" of certain conventional generalizations about reading experiences. Thus, each reader "teaches" every other reader a certain new meaning for a conventional form of judgment; the judgment is no longer sentimental or general but real and well-authorized. From the research perspective, the group of so-authorized judgments becomes a reliable empirical basis for thinking about "this group's perception and evaluation of this particular story." Obviously, this knowledge will not allow others to predict their own responses; but once other responses and judgments are given, the knowledge of how other real readers thought about their readings is a reliable means of widening one's own vocabulary of potential interpretation. It is less remote from a given high school classroom that another class, say one thousand miles distant, had these detailed, subjectively authorized evaluations of the story, than that these 865 high school students from around the country all thought that the story was "strange." More is known about response and reading processes from small numbers of detailed reactions than from large numbers of one-word judgments. In this way, the process of teaching the development of detailed subjective response is simultaneously research into the nature of response processes.

The specific general issues of this first question I asked of my reading experience is that of literary (or aesthetic) *taste*. Most teachers do consciously aim to cultivate "taste" in their students, but it is usually done by exhibiting "classics" as those works which people of "good taste" will enjoy. Most students feel that such exhibitions do not constitute teaching in any dynamic sense. Only if a student can see his or her own existing habits of taste in operation—say in judging Shakespeare "boring"—can he or she ever gain enough control of his or her taste to make it more versatile, or even to abandon his interest in literature altogether for something he or she has a known taste for. Using response statements allows one's taste to become visible prominent, and intersubjectively relevant. A student will have begun his own "research" career by systematically inquiring into his own taste, that of his peers, and those of his teachers. These fundamentals of research are also the fundamentals of pedagogy. For a longer discussion of this issue, see Chapter Seven of *Subjective Criticism* (Bleich).

INTERPRETATION

Traditional Formulation
What principle of literary coherence best explains this story? The tale is built around the opposition of human rationality and the violent caprice of human experience. Rationality is presented in the form of the tale, which is the narrator's articulation of his experience; the content is given by the experience itself. In this way, form and content oppose each other and create within the process of reading a drama that enacts the doctor's struggle with his situation.

The determining feature of the doctor's experience is his frustration. Aiming to get to a patient some distance away in a snowstorm, the doctor has no means of transportation, and is unable to get these means, but horses finally do magically appear to take him, with supernatural speed, to his destination. However, the groom who tended these horses seems about to ravish his servant, Rose, as the doctor is taken away by the horses. The doctor doubts if the boy is sick, but after being persuaded to look more closely by the sister's waving of a bloody towel, the doctor observes a "rose red" wound on the boy's side, in which white worms are crawling about. As he is about to attend the boy, the latter's family and the village elders and a choir of children appear, while the elders and family undress the doctor and put him in bed with the boy, "on the side of the wound." The doctor is frustrated by his inability to heal the boy. His attempt to leave the sickroom is successful, but he remains naked, he barely gets his clothes onto the rig, and the horses move "like old men" through the "snowy wastes." Again the doctor is frustrated in his aim to move quickly out of the cold back home to rescue Rose.

The determining feature of the doctor's *presentation* of his experience is the reflective language he uses and reports having used in the incident. Trying to make sense out of the appearance of the horses, he says, "In cases like this the gods are helpful, send the missing horse, add to it a second because of the urgency, and to crown everything bestow even a groom." In explaining why he let the boy lie even though he thought him well, he says, "I was badly paid yet generous and helpful to the poor," or "To write prescriptions is easy, but to come to an understanding with people is hard." At the end of the tale, as he is slowly going home he says, "Naked, exposed to the frost of this most unhappy of ages, with an earthly vehicle, unearthly horses, old man that I am, wander astray." In addition to the doctor, both victims, Rose and the boy, are given to such reflective locutions: Rose remarks to the doctor on finding the groom, "You never know what you are going to find in your own house." The boy observes on his disappointment with the doctor's failure to help him, "I always have to put up with things. A fine wound is all I brought into the world; that was my sole endowment." In the face of incomprehensible adverse experience, the victims present rather formal, emotionally muted articulations of their circumstances. It is as if their only hope for survival is to issue strongly phrased language. This language is the core of the rationality that is brought in as mankind's main weapon against arbitrary experiences. As an aesthetic object, regardless of the fate of its fictional characters, the story persuades the reader of this special strength each person has to ameliorate his troubles.

Formulation in View of Response

My interpretative judgment of this tale is that its linguistic form overpowers its irrational content, and this action is the principle of its literary coherence. Presumably, I am claiming this is objectively true of the story. However, as most critics will allow, it is not possible to reach a final conclusion as to which aspect of a specific text is "form" and which "content," even though the distinction sometimes seems useful in discussions. For example, is it a piece of languge or a piece of behavior when the doctor says of himself, "Naked, exposed to the frost of this most unhappy of ages . . . "? Most people will probably agree that the statement can be viewed as both "form" and "content," in which case the distinction does not apply in any objective way. In the light of the response statement, however, the distinction applies very clearly as a description of different aspects of my response. What I had called, using traditional assumptions of criticism, a principle of *literary* coherence, more accurately describes the coherence of *my reading experience* of the story.

I, in my response statement, see the story's language as being careful, casual, and detached. There are several instances in the story which can easily be understood to contradict this perception. For example, the doctor tells the groom that he won't go on the journey unless the groom comes along. Or, just before the story's concluding sentence (quoted in the response), the doctor says, of himself, presumably, "Betrayed! Betrayed!" Even though I feel these thoughts as being "detached," it is easy for me to imagine another reader thinking them just the opposite of detached. However, my overall sense of the reading suggests how I am *motivated* to read them as I do. My response detailed a similarly motivated reading of the subway events in the light of the prohibitions against smoking and spitting: I did not let myself see that my father's offense was more than casual, and even later on, I did not let myself see that my father's pain was more than casual.

I often find the language of the tale amusing, but many readers with whom I have discussed this language don't find it amusing at all: they find it eerie and terrible. The laughter, while not necessarily unique to me, is, however, grounded in a unique configuration of feelings and associations each aspect of which occurs in a degree and combination in me not found in others. I actually laugh my way through this story and this is why I judge that the "form" overpowers the content. All the words in the story are, to me, last words, and I interpret this perception as a principle of literary coherence when I am speaking in the traditional critical language.

Paragraph 3 of the response suggests that my strong perception of the linguistic form justifies passive wishes that help inform my reading pleasure. Reading the story is a way of issuing complaints about things I ought to be responsible for. One such complaint is in the response, at the end of paragraph 4 which concerns my parents' difficulties in life, particularly my father, who did not usually complain of the struggle, but whose life I could have made less painful in small ways. My deemphasis of the pain in the story in favor of the witty verbiage comes from a greater identification with mother than I felt comfortable with, but which helps reduce the remembered claims of the guilty feelings.

I describe the content of the story as the series of frustrations that befall the doctor, who, in various ways, feels he cannot be as responsible in bringing the right help to those who need it, when they need it, as he wishes. However, my own response statement names "frustrations" in the opening sentence as the problem for which laughter is the solution. If the several linguistic features of the tale I already discussed are occasions for my amusement, then my perception of these features, and not some stable elements of the tale called "content," creates the category "content" with ingredients that should make sense of my response. For example, I may just as soon claim that when the narrator says his horse died in the night, it is only a metaphor for his never having had a horse. It is not possible to claim that one part of the narrator's tale is "facts" and the other "commentary," except if I am discussing my subjective resymbolization of the tale. The categories of form and content are created by interpretive purposes, which, in turn, are motivated by response and its psychological demands. If the categories are accepted as defined in my judgment, there will be an attempt to "verify" their truth relative to the tale, resulting in idle dispute over their objective presence. If the categories are understood as psychological, relative to the reader to begin with, they are more smoothly reprocessable by other readers.

The availability of particular reading experiences to others is a demand both of pedagogy and of research. The response statement makes it possible for a group of readers to know with far more certainty than before just how a single person assimilated his reading experience. Both the pedagogical and research interest are in what the reader has accomplished rather than in whether the accomplishment is right or wrong in an absolute sense. If I claim that my principle of literary coherence is true of the text of the tale, another reader may either believe me outright, in which case I am a priest and the text scriptural in character, or the reader will go through his own process of testing my assertion. If he or she disagrees with me, we will then dispute about which parts of the tale are form and which content, and we shall not be able to resolve the dispute. If the other reader, instead, tested his or her "objective" judgment in the same way I tested my own—that is, in the context of my response statement—both his or her and my judgments may be accorded truth-value on the basis of different subjective interests. To identify such interests in the classroom is both pedagogy and research; to relate interpretive judgments to such interests is likewise pedagogy and research.

Consider my final judgment of the story: "The story persuades the reader of this special strength each person has to ameliorate his troubles." If this judgment were taught in the traditional sense, students would write it down. Perhaps it would be discussed in class, but because the teacher is assumed to have objective knowledge of stories and how they work, students will consider this a discrete piece of knowledge capable of fulfilling examination requirements. The subjective tests for its viability, even if privately performed, will not get any functional exposure. When the judgment is given with the response statement, it is no longer examination knowledge but must be taken as a view of how another reader formed a judgment. What is taught is how to develop knowledge of this story on this occasion. The judgment may still be considered true, but in a different subjective sense than my judgment was true for me. Furthermore, the systematic tests of such judgments with response statements bring forth a collection of documented acts of mentation which form an empirical basis for research. Whether the response processes found on that occasion apply to other readers of other stories is the research issue; but, such research obviously can take place in the same pedagogical context—when the same class reads another story. The research into response and the teaching of literature is thus the same activity. Moreover, the research is no longer an activity of the elite, but the regular activity of daily schoolwork.

THE AUTHOR'S INTENTION

Traditional Formulation

What does the story show about the author's literary intentions, his personality, and his style of thought? Although the story does not prove anything, it does suggest a great deal about the author, particularly if we identify him with his narrator and hero. It is probably safe to assume that the hero's frequent self-justifications are attributable to the author, who, in his own life just feels beset by cascading irrationalities, analogous to those in the tale, which call into question his conscientiousness and self-esteem. Many of Kafka's other works, especially the novels *The Trial* and *The Castle*, have heroes who are likewise beset by social powers they don't understand, who are forever trying to reach a modest but rational goal, whose circumstances steadily deteriorate, yet who keep responding with an equally steady and rational attitude. Some biographical thought has explained the pattern in terms of the author's fear of his father as the "irrational" force in his life, and hence Kafka's continuing efforts to reach this force. However, other thought suggests that it is the impersonal force of modern civilization which Kafka is trying to outflank by writing about it. Or, it might be the case that, regardless of personal and social factors, Kafka is only expressing the permanent futility of being alive, and he is saying how he just continues his normal efforts in spite of the futility. As a major author, in any case, Kafka seems highly motivated to bring out in his work his deepest feelings and thoughts to a civilization that should be and ultimately is responsive to his work.

Formulation in View of Response
Once one has studied the biography of any author, it becomes clear that drawing strong conclusions about his life on the basis of just reading the literature is not reliable. Why guess before becoming familiar with the available facts? Yet, as my response statement shows, I imagine the author automatically, and this bit of fantasy, which bears an authentic element of my reading experience, becomes, in the judgment, a set of platitudes which must be true in some, probably trivial, sense. The formulations in the last part of the judgment are based on the assumption, only delicately made in the first part, that the hero is identified with the author. However, in my fluent imagining of the author in the response, there is no hesitation that he is the same figure as the hero. Some previous acquaintance with Kafka and his work contributed to my perception of the doctor in this biographical light; but the matter of concern is the fact that on this reading, I first understand the author-hero as a teacher (paragraph 1), and then as an analogue of my father (paragraph 4). These perceptions are essential features of my involvement in the reading experience. Insofar as Kafka is my teacher, I shift my learning of the "last word" from my mother to him, the author. When I see him as a father, he is a victim who overcomes with his own detachment, my detachment toward him; at the same time, my own detachment identifies with Kafka, through his hero. Whatever facts I subsequently discover in Kafka's biography are then negotiated with these basic psychological perceptions.

The elements of the biographical judgment I presented are clearer in the light of this perception. For example, my father is a better instance of struggling to reach a modest goal than is Kafka, whose goals were not modest and whose feelings were not stably rational. Similarly, my father, afflicted with heart disease for the last fifteen years of his life, never complained of the injustice of it; rather, I had this sense, but I remained calm and rational anyway—that is, less concerned than I ought to have been. My image of Kafka is myself with my father's illness. I, rather than my father had the greater sense of the "futility" of life. I combine my father's strength to endure with my own rationality and imagine this to be the historical figure, Kafka.

My judgment overlooks the faint note of derision of Kafka in paragraph 4, where I imagine him failing with his lover because of his illness. This may also be a perception of my father that I overlook when I aim for an "objective" judgment of Kafka. I subtly translate what I know must be weakness and failure in the author into his literary and emotional power. My biographical interest, which is authentic, is also authentically motivated by my persevering search for self-understanding. But without including my response statement in my preparations for biographical research I will have no reliable principle with which to organize the historical knowledge I might present.

Leon Edel wrote almost twenty years ago that "there seems to be considerable evidence that he (the biographer) is seeking to know the life of another in order to better understand himself." Because of Edel's work, biographical analysis has become a credible and authoritative means of developing literary knowledge. Every reader, at one point or another, imagines the author, in addition to the characters, as speaking to him or her. This subjective imagining is the basis of both pedagogy and research in biography. Once it is admitted that each reader's conception of the author is his or her own construction, teachers can no longer use the locution, "Shakespeare is telling us that . . . " or similar formulations which imply that teachers (or critics) know the intention of the author toward the reader. Rather, all those reading a work on a given occasion have images of the author, with associated invented intentionalities. When the psychological nature of these inventions is understood in the light of response statements, each reader has taught the others a potential new sense of the author. For the collective purpose of biographical research, these images become hypotheses to be tested by the available biographical facts. If Edel's view obtains, research cannot really begin until the biographer has defined the terms of his search for self-understanding. Such terms facilitate the reader's (researcher's) attempt to objectify the figure portrayed by the surviving personal documents. The terms use subjectivity to guide the process of objectifying the author for others. This process underlies both pedagogy and research in literary biography.

GENERIC CLASSIFICATION

Traditional Formulation

To what extent is the story illuminated when it is understood as an instance of a literary type? More than most fiction, this story could be made more accessible to many readers if it can be shown that it belongs to a familiar class of literature. Because it is unlike a fairy tale, a tall tale, a comic vignette, a fable, or an ordinary short story such as Poe's or Hemingway's, knowing how to associate it with other similar literature could be enlightening. Probably the closest fit of known literary types would be the parable or allegory. Other of Kafka's tales were announced as parables. The extreme form of the events in the tale suggest that they all may be systematically translated into a more rational allegorical picture. Viewed as a parable or allegory, the story's many proverb-like statements make more sense, particularly those coming at the end. If the final statement in the tale is understood as thematically conclusive, the tale is a parable about false alarms, for example. Or, if the hero's ultimate fate is taken as the conclusive element, then it is a parable about man's nakedness and its role as a punishment. In any event, both the material of the tale, and the narrator's habit of articulating experiences and responses in large-scale moral terms suggest that the tale is most directly understood as a kind of biblical document that has a clear moral posture to express.

But this may not be a fruitful path of study, after all. Because of the unusual character of the tale, familiar literary types may not be applicable as explanatory models. The literary type in which this story shares is uniquely modern, and other contemporary authors such as Beckett, Ionesco, Robbe-Grillet, or Borges have produced enough work along these lines to create the "absurd" or "irrational" genre. This explanatory type is not simply literary, as contemporary existentialism has consistently dealt with the issue of how single individuals, even the "single" human race shall deal with its feeling of isolation within an arbitrary universe. The story is explained as an expression of this uniquely modern *zeitgeist*, which has occasioned in many lives the kind of frustration and response shown in the doctor's narrative.

Formulation in View of Response
In a subjective sense, all of the foregoing typological judgments are false. While others may derive truth-value from them, they do not answer a demand made by my reading experience. I formulated the judgments, rather, in imitation of what I think are certain conventions of typological interpretation that are usually invoked in some phase of literary pedagogy. Given the reading experience I report in my response statement, I have no use for these judgments, as I might, for example, for the three sorts of judgment previous to this. That is, I shall not explain this tale to myself as a parable, an allegory, a biblical document, or an "absurdist" story.

The language of the tale seems to be an instance of my own language, though I also know that it is someone else's. Kafka's work had been familiar in my family for many years, and there is no aspect of his work which seems to pose some challenge to literary conventions that I am used to. In the reading experiences, I have no sense of subjective disharmony, no sense of mystery, no instinct to question, "What is happening here, anyway?" that I know many other readers have had. My sense of the language and meaning of the tale is, rather, "of course, I get this, this is familiar indeed." The terms of the familiarity are given in the response statement, and the abstractions given in my judgments are not the right ones to make my feelings communicable to others. As a matter of taste, habit, and experience, I do not explain my mentation very often in terms of allegory or existentialism, and to articulate a literary type as a way of explaining a reading experience seems rather odd; it would be as if I gained enlightenment when someone told me I were speaking in prose. It may be the case, but it is not what I want to know.

A typological explanation applies when one feels that the reading experience fails to correspond to anything in one's own experience; the type then becomes the link between this particular work and a whole class of others, many of which are familiar. To call this tale an allegory might perform this function for some readers. In my own case, I consider myself *within* the pale of reference for this story—that is, I am part of the community of address for that language; or, that I am speaking the "same" language in the metaphorical as well as literal sense. To type the story would be to type my own community—not an impossible task, but also not something one does when one feels that the reading experience needs no solution. To type a story there must exist the prior assumption that this type is different from the linguistic and literary idioms of one's own community; typing a story implicitly types one's own language system in the same act.

As a psychological act, typing is the appeal to known values of broad acceptance, and the attempt to make the story representative of those values. It is to discover an area of knowledge where the difference between the reading experience and the reader's sense of him- or herself is minimized or eliminated altogether. However, if no such difference is felt in the reading experience, typing is unnecessary. If I read Shakespeare, for example, it is of conceivable help to explain the reading by saying the words are "Elizabethan," knowing this term refers to certain dramatic conventions and language usages. But I need no such label as "modern" or "contemporary American" to describe *Death of a Salesman*, because the language and idiom seem immediately my own. It is a much more difficult problem to assign a type to one's own community than it is to assign one to a community distant in space or time.

Many of those with whom I have discussed this tale, and others by Kafka, have demanded, as a result of their intuitive sense of the reading, some kind of wider identification of the tale that would reduce their sense of its strangeness. The judgments I presented earlier could answer to this demand. However, it would probably be more germane to identify the difference in perception of the reading in terms of differing community values between myself and the other readers. The feelings of guilt, the style of aggression and hostility that I present in my response statement have communal origins, specifically in certain speech and thought habits of Jews from Eastern Europe where my parents and Kafka were both born. It is not surprising that readers of Anglo-Saxon (or perhaps Oriental) origin will find the language and experience alien. With the response statements of all readers at hand, it is easier to choose a germane explanatory type on the basis of the reader's community background than to try to seek from the list of known literary types the right formula.

The well-known literary types—such as Greek tragedy, for example—all have come down from reasoning identical to this just above. The meaning of these types comes from their reference to certain features of the originating community—classical Greek civilization in this case—though the term seems to apply only to the literature. Research into the generation of literary types is an investigation into how communities think of themselves and into how different communities characterize one another. Any classroom, especially in this country where there often are many people of different national and ethnic origin, is especially suitable for this sort of research. The response statement creates a basis for such inquiry in that it is an artifact of a certain community as well as the statement of an individual; this artifact automatically defines its own differences from the perceived community of the story. At the same time, the exposure of such differences is a common pedagogical task. Without the response statement, it is difficult to become aware of each reader's sense of his or her own community without relying on stereotypes and one-sentence characterizations. My own response statement presents a degree of subtlety and complexity that I think characterizes my own community that I could not present in any other form. It is a potential research *and* pedagogical project to define the relation between what I perceive as my own community and what I perceive as Kafka's. When such an inquiry is carried out by a group of readers, the use of possible explanatory literary types is grounded in both individual and community experience and is not the arbitrary selection of a plausible formula from a received list.

COMMENTARY

The recurring problem in research in response has been to create a systematic way of making it available for disciplined study. The approach of most of those interested in the topic has been to create "models" of response abstractly from different sorts of "data" they thought sensible to collect. It seems clear, though, that the willingness to think in terms of "models" and "data" bespeaks the reluctance to abandon the epistemological paradigm which uses those concepts fluently but for research interests altogether different from the present one. The "strange" experience of response has been repeatedly forced into the familiar paradigm of objectivity, even by the most ambitious of researchers.

As Kuhn discussed, to change a paradigm is to change the governing comprehensive attitude toward knowledge. As he further argued, pedagogical institutions are responsible for creating an illusory picture of "scientific truth" when claims of knowledge are given by textbooks without regard for their community or context of origin. In a sense, pedagogical action created the objectivity that scientists were not so sure of. Changes in paradigm come from scientific communities, and not pedagogical ones, and the two kinds of community were separate.

In the study of language and literature, the relationship of pedagogy and research is intrinsically different, the attempts to emulate quantitative scientists notwithstanding. The classroom is a standard forum for the discussion of reading and interpretive experiences, and it was teachers, rather than critics and scholars, who perceived this circumstance first. This perception is the basis of the literary profession's participation in the subjective paradigm. Unlike a chemistry class, where a student may actually receive knowledge of the periodic table as permanent, a student cannot receive an interpretation of "A Country Doctor" without creating his or her own and negotiating the two views. I cannot even "believe" my own interpretations without consulting my response statement. The role of subjectivity is active and fundamental in producing response and in negotiating it into knowledge. Pedagogy is research carried out with a subjective epistemology.

I consider an evaluative test of research in response to be a judgment of how easily it can be used in pedagogical situations. Taking large samples of response over thousands of classrooms is, by this test, unproductive: a questionnaire is not negotiable. Any discussion *about* the questionnaire in each classroom that uses it cannot be included when its results are presented in public. It is an equally doubtful process to collect variables such as age and sex and correlate them with answers to questions of binary judgment (yes or no). If you *define* response in this way, the results pertain to the definition; but I don't think the great majority of researchers and teachers understand response as being questionnaire-defined. These techniques, and ones like it which assume that regularities of response are statistically describable, depend on the traditional procedure of an external objective observer entering a "field" of research, neglecting his or her own action because of its apparent insignificance relative to the large sample, and then presenting "facts" about response thus obtained. In this procedure, the researcher invents the object to be studied, but reports it as knowledge. Such invention is negotiable if also the research motives are brought out. However, it is usually assumed that these motives are irrelevant. Finally, counting votes in class will not usually pass for teaching.

Using responses statements encourages pedagogy and research to be carried out under identical classroom circumstances. Response statements are not graded and teachers write them on the same basis as students. The contribution of each person in the classroom is the same on this basis. Those interested in response who seek to do "research" need not invent any new context, but use instead the one they are already in on a regular basis—the classroom. Most students enter classrooms— from childhood on—under the assumption that they will "receive" knowledge. Using response statements teaches that learning about language and literature is a process of self-regulation and not a matter of acquiring knowledge. To become aware of this process of self-regulation is to *teach oneself* to develop knowledge.

A survey of opinion becomes interesting among a group which has already been functioning together and has established an interactional pattern with one another. For example, if, as I have seen in one of my classes, six women and only one man "perceive" that Hemingway's "Hills Like White Elephants" is referring to a prospective abortion, this suggests a statistically significant gender difference in the perception of the story. If this statistic were received in isolation, we would be tempted to conclude, perhaps, that women are "better readers" than men. In the classroom, however, it becomes clear that women are more alert to *certain things* for psychological reasons. It is also clear that *these* women read differently from *these* men, where, in the class, each member knows why that person saw the abortion, and why that person did not. Some women give the same reasons for not seeing it as some men, however, which further suggests that values, and not competence, are the determining factor in the statistic. Instead of spending time perfecting the statistical technique, the effort is made to disclose the range of preexisting values in each person, and the various paths of reasoning. Therefore, the statistic is used to broach the question of gender-based values, which leads not to further surveys, but to further longitudinal inquiry into the development of values on individuals and group scales. The survey activity is understood only in connection with the local group, and not as a revelation of something objective about the story or something permanently true about reading. At one's own initiative and on behalf of oneself and one's community, to use the response statements regularly shows just how research is not something only a special group of people can do, but an activity organized by purposes available in principle to anyone with sufficient interest and discipline. Response statements function as a systematic way of identifying interests and exposing the forms of intellectual discipline unique to each reader. No matter how old or experienced an individual is, it is always important to develop new interests and new forms of discipline.

To propose knowledge is to take an initiative with one's own language and the language held in common with others. Especially with regard to language and literature, knowledge can not be conceived as something heretofore kept secret by God or Nature, but rather as the formulation of a new perspective that can enhance community interests. New knowledge often has this "revelation" effect because people are culturally trained to view knowledge in this way and to view teachers and researchers as members of a privileged group with special access to "truth." It occurs only to a few young people that intellectual leaders have no greater access to the ability to formulate knowledge than they—the younger people—have. Using response statements as teaching and research helps to demonstrate this equality of access, and encourages younger people to take more seriously their own natural initiatives with language as well as their perceptions of other people's language. The whole concept of intellectual authority is then shifted from that of a force to which one must accede, to one that can be independently developed by each person and by each community. Without a sense of one's own authority to propose knowledge, there is no motivation to make such proposals. And then neither pedagogy nor research will take place.

Disciplined study of anything is grounded in epistemology rather than theory. It is true that one usually begins looking for a new "theory" of such-and-such; the transformational project is a new "theory" of language, but its epistemology is the same as that of Newtonian physics. When a theory is carried to its furthest implications, epistemological questions arise: for example, did I want to know what this theory of language proposes? Or even though I now know that "rules" can be seen in grammar, does this really count as "knowledge"? In classical physics, the test of the knowledge was not in the intrinsic superiority of the theory, but in its technological consequences, which had a kind of phylogenetic survival value; in other words, it developed that people *needed* the knowledge proposed by Newton. By the same reasoning, it is not clear that people need to have transformational rules, and the future will tell if such a need arises. On the other hand, it is clearer that people need the kind of knowledge of language use which is not addressed in the transformational theory. However, there is no "theory" of language use because the epistemology in effect, as Chomsky explains, keeps language use in the realm of "mystery." In this sense, transformational knowledge emerges from an epistemology rather than a theory. As long as we look for new theories, we do not question whether our epistemology is inhibiting our search.

As I discussed in *Subjective Criticism*, the study of many subjects—including language—has at this time called attention to the defining role of epistemology, and has suggested that a new form of epistemology is more useful for contemporary interests. To think of teaching and research as the same activity, and to use response statements toward this end, is the result of what I think is a very large shift in our epistemology, from one which centers on knowing objects outside ourselves to one which aims to know the human means of objectifying things and the purposes for objectification. This epistemology converts the classroom from an exchange point for information to a research site at which new knowledge is developed and proposed. If classrooms can take on this new authority in producing knowledge of language and literature, it will acquire new importance for other forms of knowledge and for a whole new array of human interests.

REFERENCES

Bleich, D. *Subjective Criticism*. Baltimore: Johns Hopkins University Press, 1978.

Purves, A. C. & Beach, R. *Literature and the Reader: Research in Response to Literature, Reading Interests, and the Teaching of Literature*. Urbana, IL: National Council of Teachers of English, 1972.

Rosenblatt, L. *Literature as Exploration*. Urbana, IL.: National Council of Teachers of English, 1938, 1968.

Squire, J. R. *The Responses of Adolescents While Reading Four Short Stories*. Urbana, IL: National Council of Teachers of English, 1964.

Wilson, J. R. *Responses of College Freshmen to Three Novels*. Urbana, IL: National Council of Teachers of English, 1966.

Chapter 15
Studying the Effects of Literary Instruction in Classrooms: Collaborative Research in Schools

Agnes J. Webb

Empire State College
State University of New York

When I faced the prospect of choosing a dissertation research project in literature education, I was certain, at first, that I was once again a novice. Degrees in English literature and in education, as well as teaching experience, seemed to me to be a most inappropriate background for the unfamiliar and quantitative universe of educational research. The transition from instructor to an observer of the effects of instruction would not be made easily.

Since much of my maturing into a researching teacher occurred during the design and execution of the project itself, I thought it best to review here the year-long project which is the basis of my dissertation, *Introducing the Transactive Paradigm for Literary Response into the High School Literature Program: A Study of the Effects on Curriculum, Teachers and Students* (Webb, 1980).

What follows here is not a report of the results of the study, but a retelling of some of the events in a year's collaboration with four classroom teachers to study response to literature and to introduce changes in literature instruction. I am retelling these events to state the gradual emergence of one mode of collaborative research and, further, to urge others to engage in holist research studies.

In this chapter, I will refer to procedures and results briefly; more complete reports are in my dissertation and the concise report in ERIC (Webb, 1980). Here I will explain efforts to reconcile and balance the expectations and constraints of academic research, public education, and the study of literature. Those engaged in educational research will recognize the sequence of studying theory, piloting a small project, proposing a research project, executing the project, analyzing the results, and reporting the outcomes. Those engaged in public school education will be familiar with the ways in which new instruction is considered, judged, and accepted or rejected. All of us committed to the study of literature will have to remember that, although there is little mention of literature or response to literature here, the project year was spent reading, discussing, and teaching literature.

To encourage others to conduct research on response to literature in schools, I hope to describe the inquiry process that occurred during the project, the school's influences on the study, and some of the questions that arose during the year.

As the title of my dissertation reveals, I located the site of my study in a high school with the focus on education in the forms with which I was most familiar: curriculum, teachers, and students. I began with a theory of response to literature, developed some instructional strategies in my own Grade 10 classroom, and planned a research project to explore the activity of transforming theory into classroom instruction. At that point in the project, I was still functioning more as a teacher passing on a sound and effective idea than as a researcher systematically observing the outcomes of instruction. My proposal, though, had the familiar form of a statement of the problem, hypotheses to be tested, a plan for instruction, instruments to measure differences between an experimental group and a monitoring group, and an outline of measurement procedures. The proposal turned out to be little more than a self-contained plan of intention to be carried out during a school year. The composing of the proposal gave me no hint of the matters I was to question and think about during the year: the role of research in schools, the nature of information gathered in the midst of complex social activity, and the implications of my work for future research.

THE TRANSACTIVE THEORY

First, I will explain the theory of literary response which is the basis of the study. Transactive response to literature asserts that the reading of works is not merely the communication of a message to a passive receiver; the transaction is an internal activity in which the reader recreates the text and confers meaning on the work. As early as 1938, Louise Rosenblatt clearly directed the attention of educators to this theoretical perspective of reading and responding. Simon Lesser (1957) called this activity "analogizing" in his explanation of the response process from a Freudian psychoanalytic viewpoint. From a similar viewpoint, Norman Holland's case studies (1973, 1975) reactivated Rosenblatt's term "transactional" and documented readers' responses from the framework of current ego psychology. Holland says that the reader shapes the text to allow fantasy and transforms the text into meaning through ego strategies which are consistent with the reader's identity theme or personality organization. These ego strategies are the reader's habitual pattern of shaping and transforming other life experiences. These strategies protect the pleasure of fantasy and result in a selective perception of the text and unique responses from each reader. David Bleich's work (1975) on subjective criticism in classrooms and his outline for curricula also contributed to the plan for my study.

RESEARCH IN SCHOOLS

My proposal asked a general question: "Is the theory of transactive response to literature acceptable or useful in public school classrooms?" I found Holland's model of response to be well-documented and persuasive, but also dramatically different from the model which informs traditional teaching of literature in high schools. In order to find out whether this reader-centered view of response could be incorporated into a high school curriculum that was already successful, I had to convince the teachers and administrators of a school to allow me to initiate a program of transactive response to literature.

My general question about the acceptability or usefulness of the theory of transactive response to literature was restated in three hypotheses. The hypotheses predicted that the test performances of students in the experimental classes would be equal to or better than the performances of students in the monitoring classes. The test instruments would measure attitude toward literature, reading comprehension and interpretation, and cognitive development. These three quantitative outcomes of instruction reflect, in a general way, school objectives.

The very generality of the hypotheses was, I think, influential in gaining access to an Amherst, New York, senior high school. I wished to compare the growth of students in the experimental transactive classes with the growth of students in the school's present English literature program. I was clearly not interested in pointing out weaknesses in the existing instruction; to the contrary, I wanted comparison with a polished, established curriculum. The testing was only one way of determining the effects of the experimental curriculum. Other outcomes would certainly occur, ones which I could not predict. The planned case studies of teachers and students would record more subtle and gradual changes which might take place in the experimental classrooms. In other words, certain predetermined outcomes would be measured, but a far greater amount of time and thought would be spent on developing the new curriculum, evaluating the immediate effects on students, and recording the ways in which the new instruction differed from the established instruction.

As I talked with the principal and the Grade 10 English team leader at Amherst Senior High School, I realized that research in schools must fit smoothly into the general structure of the school program to avoid disruption of educational procedures which could be destructive to both the school and the research project. Further, research conducted in schools can be planned in such a manner that the particular style and issues in that school are acknowledged. This acknowledgement need not limit the theoretical basis of the study (ego psychology in my study) nor need it restrict the questions asked. But, to engage the serious efforts of those who will collaborate in the study, the theory and questions must be presented and explained in the context of instruction and the explanations must make immediate sense (Guba and Lincoln, 1981). Any requests for changes in the school's usual patterns of class meeting times and meeting places or requests for changes in course content must be essential to a study rather than a clever or complex design. Elaborate student groupings, rearrangements of schedules, expensive purchases, bizarre testing, or grandiose claims will only create objections to research.

The hypotheses of a research proposal may have to be reworded or elaborated to reflect the specific educational objectives of a particular school. Further, the testing instruments must clearly test the hypotheses. In my study, the test instruments for attitude and reading competence were taken from the International Education Association's study of literature education (Purves, 1973). These were familiar forms of academic testing, directly concerned with literature, which had been fully field-tested for use in an international study of literature education before I introduced them into this school. I requested that these two instruments be added to test the literture program; I did not request that these tests replace any existing testing. The instruments were accepted, not only because they clearly tested the hypotheses, but because they were not unduly time-consuming to administer nor were the teachers expected to score the tests.

The instrument to test the third hypotheses —equal or better growth in cognitive development—was more difficult to explain in terms of the school's present objectives in literature education. The Piagetian developmental theory which was the basis of the story-telling instrument I was to use (Feffer, 1959, 1960) was not familiar to all the teachers. However, the creative story-telling form of the test interested the teachers and they accepted it for use in the classroom. Even though the theoretical background of the test instrument was unfamiliar and the scoring criteria complex, the hypothesis of predicting equal or better cognitive development in the experimental classes was accepted because the medium of testing was a reasonable activity in literature classrooms.

I think, too, that studies which include current specific issues in education can complement a school program and encourage schools to permit research (Guba and Lincoln, 1981). A review of state-sponsored projects and grants will indicate possible special interest areas. Or, an administrator can alert the researcher to current priorities such as remedial education, programs for the talented, or new topics such as career planning. A researcher need not concentrate on a special interest but can accommodate it in reports to the school. For example, the population in my study included a state-funded remedial reading group. When I reported any findings to the school, I included a special section on the students who had been identified as having reading problems.

When a school admits a research project, the study is benefited by access to the records which are the history of the students' education. These records usually include a variety of testing results which would be too expensive or too difficult to obtain otherwise but which provide essential or interesting data to incorporate into the study. I was able to use reading testing scores, I.Q. scores, and Differential Aptitude Test scores in the multivariate analysis of the data I gathered.

Conducting research in the midst of an educational institution involves careful attention to the way one becomes a complement to the school's present activity while introducing change. Those most immediately affected by the changes are the teachers who take on additional work in collaborating in a study. They, too, must see some possible benefits to themselves from this added work. The four teachers who worked with me were able to fulfill a district requirement for professional development. Their participation in the study was accorded the same status as activity in a professional organization, graduate courses, or community involvement. Tuition waivers, in-service education credit, or contribution toward certification requirements would also be appropriate rewards to offer to collaborating teachers.

Once my study was accepted, I attended the preschool planning sessions of the Grade 10 English team and became familiar with the general functioning of the school, the grading policies, the assignment of students, the records available, and the elective course curriculum offered to the Grade 10 students. These early meetings helped me to define my role in the execution of the study. Even though I was a beginning researcher, I was not a novice in assessing schools and literature programs. I arranged to be in the school daily, to attend all meetings, and to assist the teachers in planning the instruction for the experimental classes. They, in turn, reported their classroom activities in the experimental groups and compared those activities with the instruction in their monitoring classes. I initiated a weekly report to summarize what each person had done and the follow-up instruction they anticipated. This summary became an important vehicle for explaining transactive response and for sharing the problems and solutions each teacher experienced.

COLLABORATIVE RESEARCH

My role was that of a participant observer. The clearest statement of participant-observer research is Paul Diesing's (1971) explanation of his role in discovering the methods of scientists. I have substituted "teachers" and "teaching" for "scientist" and "scientific."

> The participant observer approaches [teaching] method from the inside; he attempts to take the point of view of the [teachers] who are using a particular method. He does this by becoming, as far as possible, a member of the [teaching] community, sharing its activities and discussions, familiarizing himself with the literature, problems, and personalities that are discussed, helping with the daily work in whatever way he can. (p. 291)

Unlike the detached and objective laboratory researcher, the participant observer is engaged in the phenomena studied. Although I did not teach classes, I met with students to demonstrate the instruction and to compile case studies. In contrast with the researcher who must limit interpretation to the final data, I was engaged in interpreting, evaluating, and judging at all stages of the project. As the project continued, my observations and commentary were challenged and clarified by four other observers (the teachers themselves) as we shaped the direction of the new instruction.

During the first weeks of the school year, I became aware that my supervision of the instruction and, indeed, my continued presence in the school would depend in a large measure on the flexibility of the nondirective instruction that I recommended to explore personal and individual response to literature (Webb, 1982). I could demonstrate the extended dialogues, provide rationales for subjective response, and comment on student responses; but the frequency of the experimental instruction and its integration into the curriculum would be under the teachers' control. The study I had proposed was an intervention study, but one in which the teachers were more than a controlled, or uncontrollable, variable. The integration of change cannot, as Deising (1962) has noted, be forced on people. Change is integrated insofar as it is voluntary and, eventually, spontaneous.

The instruction for my study was not fully plotted out in advance of the school year, which is even more unusual in instructional research. I had developed a specific instructional strategy, nondirective dialogue, suggested two additional variations on this strategy, and waited to observe the further instruction which would emerge from this starting point. Such a "think-as-you-go" procedure would certainly be unacceptable in what Diesing (1962) calls technical research. In technical research, a guiding principle is the efficient achievement of predetermined goals. However, in the social sciences when research occurs in the midst of ongoing activity, the discovery process is facilitated by decision-making shared with those people responsible for the activity. The decisions are guided by the theoretical perspective and hypotheses of the study in addition to other considerations of that institution which are prior to and concurrent with the study. Research in schools planned as a collaboration between the researcher and the teachers closely reflects the actual functioning of teachers in schools as they take responsibility for curricula, daily instruction, and periodic evaluation of students' performance. In her studies of social patterns and learning, Hilda Taba (1955) states that research by two groups of experts is "designed for the purpose of improving some aspect of human endeavor which is therefore carried on within the context of that endeavor by persons who are at the same time responsible for the changes" (p. vi).

Not only does a collaborative study dictate the role of the researcher, a participant observer, and the inclusion of the teachers as decision makers, but it also affects the data gathering, its use and interpretation. My study's testing was preplanned, carefully executed, and rigorously analyzed outside the school. Nevertheless, the raw data contributed to the development and direction of the study. At the same time, it contributed to the school in matters outside the concern of the study. For example, the Attitude Questionnaire pretest indicated that the study population's mean score was lower than the mean reported for fourteen-year-olds in the United States. This was an uncomfortable statistic in a suburban school with students who, generally, were able readers. To verify this data, we administered the questionnaire to the rest of the Grade 10 students not included in the study. The extended testing confirmed the findings in the study population. Even though the school's own testing indicated that, with the exception of the remedial reading group, the students were performing above grade level in reading, it was clear to us that they found little relationship between literature and their own lives and that they were only moderately interested in reading. These pretest scores and extended testing convinced the four collaborating teachers that the proposed changes in instruction were appropriate for this school. Later in the year, the attitude testing results were used to discriminate among students chosen for a Grade 11 talented student identification—a use of testing data unrelated to the study but important for the English department.

ADAPTING THE STUDY

The four collaborating teachers like literature teachers elsewhere (Purves 1973), wanted the reading of literature to contribute to their students' self-knowledge and, at the same time, to their intellectual abilities of analysis and criticism. Their concerns about the personal value of literature were very closely bound to their commitment to developing competence in reading and to developing cognitive abilities of their students. The results of the attitude measure highlighted the need for attention to the autobiographical and personal stages of response; however, the post-test reading measure was a necessary complement to the attitude measure. Without the reading measure, I think there would have been doubts about the suitability of the study for that school. The third means of gathering data, the measure of cognitive maturity based on Piagetian developmental psychology, did not appear to have an effect on shaping the direction of instruction until mid-year when I discovered a major obstacle to transactive response in schools.

In January, we reviewed the first semester and the teachers elected to continue the study for the full school year. As I assessed the changes made in instruction, I noted that the greatest activity in transactive response took place in the first six weeks of a ten-week elective. In the last month of instruction, the differences between the experimental classes and the monitoring classes became less pronounced. Conversations with the teachers confirmed my observation of their timing of transactive response. The decline in transactive response occurred as grading time approached. The four collaborating teachers shared the school's concern for academic quality and test performance. In general, the quarterly grading of students was a rank ordering of students based on the quality of their writing about literature, and the letter grades were reports to the parents of the students' progress in gaining writing competence. During the last four weeks of each quarter, instruction time was spent in preparation for and practice in writing about the literature. Although I had purposely restricted my investigation to oral response and had avoided all commentary on grading, both matters became important to the study because they were important in the school. The decline in transactive response at the end of each elective (coinciding with a grading period) was a signal of a limitation of the study as proposed. The instruction in transactive classrooms had to be extended to include written response as well as oral response, as I will explain later. I chose again to remain uninvolved with grading, a responsibility of the teacher not to be confused with the evaluation procedures of the research.

Contrast of the experimental and monitoring classes led me to discover a tempo or movement of instruction in the monitoring classes which was not evident in the published curriculum nor in conversations with teachers. Subjective response to works had not been completely absent in the literature teaching at Amherst, but it was held in low esteem. In the past, the teachers had encouraged some personal anecdote and digressing discussions as they introduced a new unit. This activity was preparation for reading, a motivation or engagement stage of instruction—it was not learning itself, but getting ready to learn. The teachers were creative and skillful in these tasks and lessons. As a unit progressed, there was a change in the amount and kind of student participation. Individual responses became limited to brief question-and-answer exchanges to check comprehension and to lead to the theme statement or thesis of the elective. Any small group talk was controlled by prepared question guides. As the time for grading approached, the most valued and important activity became the written response—the literature essay. Usually, these essays followed the format of the New York State Regents literature question: a given theme statement or topic sentence to be developed and supported by perceptions recalled from a specific number of novels, short stories, and/or poems. Evidence to support the thesis might include personal experiences as well as text citation and analysis only if the experiences were objectively reported and were clearly instrumental in advancing the argument. During the last month of instruction in each grading period the personal response to literature was subordinated to the development of a single form of written response.

The rhetorical conventions of persuasive writing undeniably display intellectual ability and cognitive skills; however, the anonymous persona and the problems of organizing persuasive discourse constituted, in my mind, a difficult and unlikely vehicle for communicating the transaction between a reader and a literary text. These essays were written solely for evaluation and presented little opportunity to interpret the literature or to create meanings out of texts.

I presented these observations about the tempo of instruction at Amherst to both the collaborating teachers and other members of the English Department. They concurred that it was an adequate description of the usual instruction in the school.

In the monitoring classrooms, the teacher composed a limited number of closely related thematic questions to be answered in essay form. The same selection of questions no longer seemed appropriate in the experimental classes where students had become accustomed to creating a wide range of meanings for the texts read. The teachers and I resolved this problem through a return to the plan for the study, in particular, to the cognitive maturity measure, a story-telling task which required shifts in points of view.

We reasoned in this way: If the ability to write narratives from more than a single point of view is a logical cognitive activity as conceived by Piaget (1950) and demonstrated by Feffer (1959, 1960), then narrative writing tasks would be as appropriate as persuasive tasks for evaluation. Using the work of Moffett (1968) we composed a series of essay tasks which provided rhetorical context: a stated speaker, an audience, and an event from the literature—directions for a narrative point of view. These tasks evolved into varied literary forms: dialogues, interior monologues, dramatic monologues, diaries, letters, biographies. These fictional forms for response easily accommodated associational and affective responses as well as interpretation, some analysis, and evaluation.

In this way, the instruction was expanded to incorporate writing, the valued and evaluated form of response. The writing in the transactive classes differed from the writing in the monitoring classes in ways consistent with the theory, the hypotheses, and the testing of the research. In addition, the curriculum in the experimental classes was as comprehensive and unified as the polished curriculum of the monitoring classes.

The exploratory nature of my proposal and the flexibility it allowed in instruction led me to a clear insight into the limitations of a tempo in instruction common to schools other than Amherst. I realized, too, the extent of the change I was requesting. Transactive response to literature shifts the focus of instruction from a transfer of the teacher's experience of literature and a single rhetorical form for response to individual transactions with the text communicated in many forms drawn from literature itself. Teachers so often assert that they accept a wide range of interpretations of literature as long as good supporting reasons are present. I am now convinced that response to literature is restricted greatly by the question-answer instruction and by the constraints of the persuasive essay. Individual transactions with literature are digressions in comprehension quizzes and in thesis-seeking, but transactions are given essential articulation in extended dialogue with readers and in free association and narrative writing tasks.

RESEARCH IN COLLABORATION WITH CLASSROOM TEACHERS

So far I had composed a proposal for a study, gained access to a school, acquired four collaborators, and established experimental instruction; I could now state an important difference between the experimental instruction and the usual instruction in the school. All of this was taking place in a busy and complex social unit, but what kind of research was it? It certainly was not laboratory research; it seemed closer to anthropology, the study of a self-maintaining unit in society in which tentative and theory-based hypotheses are expected to be clarified and modified during the progress of the study. The research I had launched was the documented introduction of rational change and the systematic observation and evaluation of the effects of that change.

At mid-year, the most important reading I did was Paul Diesing's *Patterns of Discovery in the Social Sciences* (1971) and *Reason in Society: Five Types of Decisions and Their Social Conditions* (1962). His discussions of formalist and holist research were most helpful in understanding further the integration of descriptive and quantitative research I was attempting. Recently, several important books have extended the models of research beyond data gathering and data analysis (Cronbach, 1980, 1982; Guba and Lincoln, 1981; Patton, 1980). In these recent models, informal data gathering, spontaneous comparisons of perceptions and judgments, interviews, case studies, and interim reporting are included to provide depth of context and thick description as part of the outcome of the study. In studies in the social sciences, it is expected that the assumptions of the hypotheses will become known as the study progresses; it is also expected that the hypotheses will be restated, revised, and refined frequently. Although the hypotheses for testing by statistical analysis may still be a constraint in most dissertation research, the hypotheses can be challenged in discussions among the collaborators as more finely discriminating questions are asked.

In my study, the hypotheses became the subject of much discussion and conjecture. Despite our early agreement that self-knowledge was a primary reason for the study of literature, we began questioning the relationship between liking and enjoying literature and learning about literature. Was it possible to attend to students' attitudes toward literature and still attend to the expectations of other groups who influence educational practices: the Board of Education, administrators, other teachers, community members, parents, and prospective college admission boards? I began to appreciate the reasons why curriculum choices so often become safe compromises which can be easily defended and explained to others who are quite removed from the classrooms.

We questioned how much influence testing exerted on the ways the literature was presented and responded to. We wondered whether emphasis on individual transactions would impair the students' ability to perform on more conventional academic testing. Would the transactive responding cause regression to egocentric thinking, especially in adolescents just entering formal operational thinking? The teachers were very concerned about the psychoanalytic language of the transactive theory, and we discussed the differences between the theory which informs the teaching of literature and the actual instruction that takes place. In other words, the hypotheses were examined and challenged and supported in a variety of ways, incuding analysis of testing data, to gain internal validity (Cronbach, 1982, p. 113).

According to my definition of research in schools, I was satisfied that the introduced change was documented through weekly summaries and that the observation was frequent, varied, and systematic. The changes in instruction were appropriate for the school population under study. However, I still questioned the process of research.

Again, I turned to Paul Diesing's (1962) work on rationality and the study of change in society. The spontaneous decision-making characteristic of much of the instruction and planning of my study was not mere luck but the serious consideration of a theory of response to literature and its implications for the study of literature. These decisions are "substantially rational."

> A decision or action is substantially rational when it takes account of the possibilities and limitations of a given situation and reorganizes it so as to produce, or increase, or preserve some good. This definition includes two points: the decision must be an effective response to the situation in that it produces some possible good, and the effectiveness must be based on intelligent insight rather than on luck. (p. 3)

The openness of the instruction plan, then, not only reflected a common functioning of schools in integrating a new idea but also constituted a rational approach to discovery. It is a rational process which creates order bit by bit out of the disorderly matrix of necessity (Diesing, 1962).

Conducting collaborative research in schools rather than merely using schools as a convenient source of data can provide a reality check on theory. If well done, it can provide theorists with an essential complement already available to other fields such as psychoanalysis and medicine, a clinical interpretation of theory. Further, informed and attentive consideration of the limitations and capabilities of schools can suggest research that is needed by schools and classroom teachers. At the same time, researchers can provide conduits to the schools which make theory and research findings available to those most directly responsible for instruction.

FURTHER RESEARCH

Through this retelling of events in a collaborative research project, I want to encourage others to investigate the holist discovery procedures of social scientists and to bring their considerable knowledge of literature to the field of educational research. Particularly, I wish to see others study readers and their responses to literature in the social units in which public response most commonly occurs, in literature classrooms (Jacobsen, 1980, 1982). I am not arguing against laboratory studies, nor am I challenging the value of formalist procedures. Detached and objective investigation of response to literature can yield results that tell us a great deal about the phenomena of reading literature; that is, measurement and analysis of data is valuable when our measurement instruments are valid and our interpretations appropriate. However, while we continue to develop the technological means of research—all the testing, reporting, and evidence that we gather and take away to analyze—we ought simultaneously to expand the number of acceptable models of literature education research. I recommend participant-observer studies conducted in schools with the collaboration of teachers as an effective means of asking important questions. Further, I think that the answers which we will report to educators will be convincing enough to affect classroom practices.

Holist studies do not lose the certitude that detached laboratory study and analysis lends to research. In fact, the surrounding matrix of observation and reports by actively involved experts makes the boundaries of certitude clearer. The quantifiable data is given a larger context to indicate the ways the data can be interpreted and may even explain some of the apparent contradictions of the data. Reports of participant observers can create a community of descriptive observations adding rich context for the quantitative data. I recommend Scribner and Cole's study of literacy (1981) for descriptions of the flexible use of quantifying tests set in the context of observation.

Schools can provide researchers with collaborators—classroom teachers themselves—who are experienced observers of readers of particular ages. The primary researcher can provide whatever additional training is necessary to make them fully qualified observers. Classroom teachers can observe the same readers regularly for nearly two hundred school days. They are in the best position to observe, record, and make statements about the sheer quantity or density of events demanded by holist studies.

Holist studies of readers in schools can be not only more accurate about the nature of the event studied but can, even more importantly, add to the precision of our theories of literature and response to literature. Carefully thought out and well-executed holist studies can begin with complex theory, if refining our questions about the theory is an explicitly stated purpose of the study. Perhaps, in this way, researchers will ask bold questions, design imaginative ways of answering those questions, and be courageous in recommending future probes into theory.

The following suggestions for needed research are not extensions of my study but rather some of the areas which became important or interesting as we listened to student readers.

1. Avid readers can tell us a great deal about the response process. The observations of classroom teachers of those readers who read often and with great interest could make case studies more comprehensive. I think a school would welcome such a study if it included a section which looked at the role that in-school reading plays in readers' choices and preferences. Grant (1981) and Petrosky (1975) both included some school-sponsored reading in their case studies of young readers.

2. Existing response theory can be elaborated or challenged by scrutiny in schools. Rosenblatt (1978) disagrees with Bleich (1978) and Holland (1973) on the importance of the text in the response process. Rosenblatt (1978) states that the reader will always be conscious that the words of the author are guiding him. I am uncertain if this is a statement of a spontaneous response element or one which is a convention of talking about literature in classrooms. Studies of candid young readers which also examine the expectations of the teacher could clarify this theoretical ambiguity. If readers do refer to the text for support of their responses, when and how do they use text citations? Is specific instruction necessary to direct the attention of student readers to the language of the text? Does such instruction enhance or hinder other aspects or response?

3. Linguistic theory, particularly stylistics, can also be extended or limited by classroom research. Stylistics (Kintgen, 1977; Fish, 1970), the study of readers creating meaning from literary texts, is generating many assertions about the response process. As I read about the responses of ideal, informed literary readers and recognize their sophisticated semantic and syntactic competence (Fish, 1970) I have many questions about the educational and social experiences which must contribute to such an ideal. Not only do the terms "informed" and "competent" require redefinition at different stages of development, but the concept "literary reader" requires clarification. Classroom teachers are certainly the best observers of large numbers of readers at critical points of intellectual development (Jones, 1982).

4. Fantasy and fantasizing as part of the response process has been studied in individual readers (Bleich, 1978; Holland, 1973, 1975; Petrosky, 1975). Even though public classrooms are poorly suited for bringing unconscious fantasies to consciousness, this most personal dimension of response to literature is too important to be ignored in schools. Readers do fantasize, even in classrooms, and the fantasies can be inferred from written and oral responses. I found fantasy most easily discerned in the brief stories and anecdotes interspersed among other statements in small group conversation. The narrative forms of letters, and so on, also contain fantasy elements— embellishments on the text.

I think that a study of the personal experiences loosely associated to the literature and recounted in conversations with other readers would contribute to our knowledge of the public response process. The procedures of the Leeds' Children as Readers study (Barnes et al., 1971) provides a model for gathering responses likely to contain fantasies. In a similar setting, fantasy content could be studied in ways which would neither psychoanalyze individual students nor intervene in the recounting of associations to the text. Erikson's (1954) chart of the analysis of the manifest content of dream fantasies provide guidelines which have much in common with the analysis of literature. I think that his categories of verbal, sensory, spatial, temporal, and so on, would be valuable ways of looking at readers' associations to texts.

5. Since classrooms are the places where the individuality of response is most often challenged by group response, an investigation of the reciprocal effects of individual readers and groups could clarify the educational value of discussing literature with others. Story retelling is a common occurrence in classrooms. At times it is valued as a check on comprehension and at other times it is discouraged to make students comment about the text rather than recount it. I think this activity of reexperiencing the text or significant portions of the text, with all the inevitable deletions, omissions, and additions, is a rich source for examining responses to literature. Classroom teachers are not only able to gather retellings but are in a position to observe the ways groups of readers arrive at concensus about portions of texts in order to continue discussion beyond the retelling stage.

CONCLUDING REMARKS

The universe of research is now more familiar to me. Even though it is true that collaborative research in schools does operate in the disorderly matrix of necessity, I recommend that others risk all the things that might go wrong when educational research studies are located in the midst of the actual teaching of literature and language. Further, literature specialists have the talent and education to discover and preserve an essential dimension of truth in the sometimes sterile world of quantitative research. Much of our background has concentrated on the creative aspects of reason—the ability to view and make sense of phenomena in ways that differ from those who view the world with the limitations of a single, technical form of rationality. Research informed by literature studies and an understanding of schools can contribute substantially to our knowledge of the ways readers read and the ways schools help or hinder readers.

REFERENCES

Barnes, D., Churley, P., & Thompson, C. Group talk and literary response. *English Education* (Britain). 1971, *5*, 63–76.
Bleich, D. *Readings and feelings*. Urbana, IL: National Council of Teachers of English, 1975.
Bleich, D. *Subjective Criticism*. Baltimore: Johns Hopkins University Press, 1978.
Cronbach, L. J. *Toward reform of program evaluation*. San Francisco: Jossey-Bass, 1980.
Cronbach, L. J. *Designing evaluations of educational and social programs*. San Francisco: Jossey-Bass, 1982.
Diesing, P. *Reason in society: Five types of decisions and their social conditions*. Urbana, IL: University of Illinois Press, 1962.
Diesing, P. *Patterns of discovery in the social sciences*. Chicago: Aldine-Atherton, 1971.
Erikson, E. The dream specimen in psychoanalysis. *Journal of American Psychoanalytic Association*, 1954, *2*, 5–56.
Feffer, M. The cognitive implications of role-taking behavior. *Journal of Personality*, 1959, *27*, 152–168.

Feffer, M., & Gourevitch, V. Cognitive aspects of role-taking in children. *Journal of Personality*, 1960, *28*, 383–396.

Fish, S. Literature in the reader: Affective stylistics. *New Literary History*. 1970, *1*, 123–161.

Grant, A. N. *Young readers reading: A study of personal response.* Unpublished doctoral dissertation, University of Melbourne, Australia, 1981.

Guba, E. G., & Lincoln, Y. S. *Effective evaluation.* San Francisco: Jossey-Bass, 1981.

Holland, N. N. *Poems in persons.* New York: Norton, 1973.

Holland, N. N. *Five readers reading.* New Haven: Yale University Press, 1975.

Jacobsen, M. H. *The delphi method of teaching literature: A case study and discussion.* Unpublished doctoral dissertation, State University of New York at Buffalo, 1980.

Jacobsen, M. H. Looking for literary space: The willing suspension of disbelief revisited. *Research in the Teaching of English*, 1982, *16*, 21–38.

Jones, N. L. *Design, discovery, and development in a freshman writing course: A case study.* Unpublished doctoral dissertation, University of Iowa, 1982.

Kintgen, E. Reader response and stylistics. *Style 11*, 1977, *1*, 1–18.

Lesser, S. O. *Fiction and the unconscious.* New York: Vintage, 1957.

Moffett, J. *Teaching the universe of discourse.* Boston: Houghton Mifflin, 1968.

Patton, M. Q. *Qualitative evaluation methods.* Beverly Hills: Sage, 1980.

Petrosky, A. *Individual and group responses of fourteen and fifteen year olds to short stories, novels, poems and thematic apperception tests.* Unpublished doctoral dissertation, State University of New York at Buffalo, 1975.

Piaget, J. *The psychology of intelligence.* New York: Harcourt Brace, 1950.

Purves, A. (Ed.) *Literature education in ten countries.* New York: Wiley & Sons, 1973.

Rosenblatt, L. *Literature as exploration.* New York: Nobel & Nobel, 1968. (Originally published 1938).

Rosenblatt, L. *The reader, the text, the poem: The transactional theory of the literary work.* Carbondale: Southern Illinois University Press 1978.

Scribner, S., & Cole, M. *Psychology of literacy.* Cambridge: Harvard University Press, 1981.

Taba, H. *With perspective on human relations.* Washington: American Council on Education, 1955.

Webb, A. J. *Introducing the transactive paradigm for literary response into the high school literature program.* Doctoral dissertation, State University of New York at Buffalo, 1980. Eric Document Reproduction Service No. ED 203 322.

Webb, A. J. Transactions with literary texts: Conversations in classrooms. *English Journal*, 1982, *71*, 56–60.

Chapter 16
Studying Response to Literature
Through School Surveys

James R. Squire

Ginn and Company
Lexington, MA

THE IMPORT OF SCHOOL STUDIES

So much has been learned in recent years about the effectiveness of teaching from studies of selected schools that the neglect of classroom and school surveys in analyzing the teaching of literature is a major professional oversight. During the past decade more than 300 separate field studies of schools achieving high performance results with students in basic skills have revealed an important series of variables which are characteristic of effective schooling. (See especially the summaries by Association for Supervision and Curriculum Development [ASCD], 1980; Brophy, 1980.) The constellation of studies suggests that schooling and teaching is most effective when:

1. The principal functions as an instructional leader (Duckworth, 1981; Duffy, 1981).
2. Direct instruction is provided by the classroom teachers and children devote adequate classtime to academic tasks (Durkin, 1978; Denham, 1980; Duffy et al., 1981).
3. A structured curriculum provides for attention to priority skills (Venezky, 1979; Rutter et al., 1979).
4. An emphasis is placed on academic achievement (Venezky, 1979; Stallings, 1978).

Virtually all of the impressive cluster of school studies base identification of schools that perform on tested achievement in basic skills. The new body of research resulted largely from widespread professional attempts to discredit the findings of studies in the late sixties which suggested that schooling has no impact on pupil achievement in reading, writing, and arithmetic (Coleman, 1966; Jencks, 1972). To suggest that schooling can make a difference, a large number of researchers in both the United States and in England identified selected schools that were achieving recorded results and attempted through school visitation and classroom observation to define the characteristics of outstanding schools. (Excellent summaries of this work are provided by ASCD, 1980; Brophy, 1980; and Denham and Lieberman, 1980.) Whether the findings apply to the effective teaching of literature is less certain although numerous parallels exist between findings in these studies and those in one national high school English survey a decade ago (Squire and Applebee, 1968). There, too, time on task, a structured curriculum, stress on academic achievement, and the role of the principal were critical in schools noted for outstanding pupil performance.

But what is significant about the recent studies is the influence that they are presently having on the profession. Priorities in educational programming, in staff development for administrators and teachers, and in classroom teaching are being shaped by these results. Researchers who frequently despair that their investigations have little impact on the schools have demonstrated that when their work is directly related to practice and reflects a knowledge of school and classroom conditions, teachers and administrators seem overly eager to consider what such studies reveal about the differences between what is and what should be. Students of literary response can extend the power and practicality of their present work by initiating studies of schooling and investigations into how we are teaching literature and what our students are learning.

THE VARIETIES OF SCHOOL STUDIES

Status studies on the teaching of English have played an impressive role for many years in informing curriculum makers of current conditions and urgent needs. In many ways the Hosic report on the *Reorganization of the English Curriculum in the Secondary School* in 1917 was based on a general, if prescientific survey of schools. Dora V. Smith's national (1933) and New York State (1941) surveys, based on actual classroom observations, provided such telling observations as the statement that "more students are engaged in conjugating English verbs in six tenses than are engaged in all English activities alone." LaBrant and Heller (1939, pp. 127–164) applied school study approaches to the analysis of independent reading programs of students over a complete six-year-period. Robert Pooley studied schools and classrooms in Wisconsin to formulate recommendations for teaching (1948). Norvell surveyed student reactions to literature selections used in schools (1950, 1958). Jewett's national analysis of selected courses of study (1958) was also quoted in its time. During the early sixties in a specialized application of survey approaches, Corbin and Crosby headed a national task force reporting on characteristic English programs for disadvantaged youth (1963). All dealt with literary education as one dimension of English instruction.

Perhaps the most widely reviewed study of education in English during the sixties was the Squire and Applebee National Study of High School English Programs (1968) and their subsequent comparative report on literary and language schooling in England (Squire and Applebee, 1969).

During the early seventies, Purves compared international practices in teaching literature, although less from school studies than from tests, protocols, and selected course guidelines (1973). England subsequently saw reports of secondary school surveys from the national inspectors (Department of Education and Science, 1980) and a national review of the linguistic development of eleven-year-olds which revealed the beginnings of sensitivity to style (Gorman et al., 1981). In America, Durkin and others investigated the teaching of reading comprehension, including comprehension of literature (1978).

Recently Duffy has synthesized the implications of classroom studies for teaching reading and, hence, the comprehension of literature (1981), and Arthur Applebee has studied writing in the secondary school, which only tangentially deals with the teaching of literature but does employ school survey and classroom observation procedures applicable to any aspect of the discipline (1981). The Institute on Research on Teaching at Michigan State University has been particularly active in designing studies which describe current classroom practice, but thus far seems not to have concerned itself with the teaching of literature.

What the body of separate studies reveals is enormous variety of researchable questions that have been addressed by school and classroom studies. Among some of the more pertinent for those concerned with response to literature and the teaching of literature would seem to be the following:

1. What is the current state of the teaching of literature?
2. How is the teaching of literature changing from year to year? (Annual school surveys from Institutional Tracking Service from 1977 to 1980 explored such changes.)
3. How much classroom time is devoted to the teaching of literature? To reading literature? To writing about literature? To contemporary literature? To use of literary anthologies? And so forth.
4. What approaches to the teaching of literature are utilized in today's schools?
5. What is the content of the curriculum in literature and how is it changing?
6. What differences exist in the teaching of literature at various grade levels? In various kinds of schools? In geographical regions?
7. What is the preparation of teachers in literature?
8. How are students reacting to their literary education? Do their preferences for reading and approaches to reading reflect the kind of literary education they have experienced?

These and similar questions are best approached through school survey methods designed to yield substantive and replicable data on the current state of literature instruction in the schools.

DESIGN OF SCHOOL STUDIES

Supportable procedures for studies of schooling and teaching have been carefully summarized by Campbell and Stanley (1963), Flanders (1970), Rosenshine and Furst (1973), and Thorndike and Hogan (1977). Over the years, such studies have moved from an emphasis on the personality of teachers, educational characteristics as related to attitude and achievement, and contrastive studies of method, to systematic observation of classroom teaching, including patterns of classroom interaction.

More recent studies, often referred to as process-product research, have tried to relate clusters of teacher behaviors to learning outcomes and avoid overly-narrow and specific findings which sometimes are criticized for lack of sufficient reliability and validity. Medley provides a useful review of these recent efforts (1979). Some of the more recent descriptive or qualitative studies, as reviewed by Duffy (1981), seem less improvement-oriented than descriptive and influenced by anthropological traditions. A complex, multidimensioned series of snapshots of schools and classrooms is used to provide a kaleidoscopic portrait of schooling at a moment in time.

Selection of schools and teachers is basic in such surveys, as is training of the team of observers. In addition, special consideration—particularly as these may apply to literary education—pertain to classroom observation, teacher interviews, meetings with students, interviews with administrators, studies of tests and course guides, and analyses of instructional materials. Each will be discussed here in turn.

Selection of Schools and Teachers

Inevitably in any study that seeks to analyze school and classroom conditions in depth, the basis of selection of schools will influence subsequent generalizations to be drawn from the data. Warwick and Lininger (1975) provide useful recommendations on sampling populations.

Samplings have reflected geographical region or state as in Smith New York studies (1941) or the Pooley Wisconsin Analysis (1948); school size and geographical dispersion (ITS, 1980 or Gorman et al., 1981); ethnic composition; nonpublic or religious orientation; or, at times, geographical proximity to the investigator (Durkin, 1978). Where the basis of sampling is not widespread, generalizations applicable to all educational practice are hazardous. However an intensive analysis of a small number of variables in a limited sampling of schools can, in part, offset the bias of sampling error and yield insights too often obscured in broader surveys. Durkin, for example, limited her school subjects to institutions in the Midwest, but she analyzed more than 17,977 minutes of classroom observation. Industrial market research has clearly demonstrated the validity of data secured from small population samples where the sample reflects the total population. (See, for example, Kinnear and Taylor, 1979.)

When a researcher focuses on a single dimension of response to literature—say, the experiences of teachers of American literature with community censorship based on data gained through telephone interviews—he or she is advised to build a sampling population sufficiently large to minimize sampling error. But research that relies on school visitation, classroom interviews, and analysis of interviews in depth rarely permits more than a few score institutions as subjects. Experience suggests that carefully selected samples of thirty or even fewer schools can yield impressive findings if the basis of selection provides a sufficiently significant focus. Thus, a study of the language education of the disadvantage was restricted to programs for such children in major urban centers (Corbin and Crosby, 1965). Thus, too, many recent studies of effective schooling are based on findings in institutions which have consistently succeeded in achieving high pupil performance on standardized tests.

In the National Study of High School English Programs (Squire and Applebee, 1968), the researchers sought to identify throughout the United States institutions "known to have outstanding programs in English." They relied heavily on the opinions of directors of composition at universities, members of state departments of education, and on a national list of schools which consistently produced national Achievement Award winners in writing. The percent of graduates attending institutions of higher education might well have been an additional criteria. More than 80 percent did enter higher education, although the high percentage was a finding and not a criterion for selection. The investigators, however, found themselves unable to develop any replicative method of identifying high schools with outstanding programs for educating the non-college-bound in English. The characteristics of English teaching that they reported in this study thus clearly relate only to the excellence of programs for academic students.

At a time where much concern was being expressed about innovations in American education—team teaching, flexible scheduling, the humanities—the researchers found little evidence of such innovations in schools in their basic sampling. Thus, a second, related study sent teams into a selected group of high schools known for their innovations in English and the conditions in these schools were compared with those obtained in the initial study. In both studies the nature of the sampling was germane to the study objective and essential to its interpretation.

Similarly, the selection of teachers to be observed within a school can influence the nature of the findings. Seldom are all classrooms open to outside visitors; even less frequently can interviews be fully scheduled during school hours. Principals are frequently reluctant to require teachers to meet with researchers, and insecure (and even ambitious) teachers will sometimes either close classrooms or schedule atypical lessons to impress outside visitors. It is wiser to permit teachers to decline observation and interviews but, before they do so, provide a written description of the purposes of the study and, if possible, meet with the English faculty as a group to explain the approaches and the provisions for anonymity. Teachers who meet classroom observers and are reassured are more likely to participate.

Preparing Observation Teams
School surveys which involve the participation of teams of observers and interviews require diligent attention to advance preparation. Not only must schools and school administrators be alerted in advance, but members of visiting teams must be trained to understand the purposes of the study, the procedures to be employed within the schools, the responsibilities of each visitor, the uses of each instrument, the kinds of observer behavior that is acceptable and unacceptable, and the follow-up procedures.

Participants on visiting teams who lack familiarity with school customs, such as might be the case with some professors of literature, need to be oriented to the school culture. Others will need to practice interviews or have an opportunity to discuss the meaning of terms used in the interview and observation schedules. What is the exact distinction between lecture, discussion, and question-and-answer approaches being observed in class activity? How can one distinguish responses which signify emotional involvement from those which merely reflect detached understanding of a selection? A special training session which reviews the total study and its underlying assumptions is an imperative. In past surveys at least a full day has been required. Further, in large studies, a school tryout of procedures is highly commendable, particularly if time permits revision in approaches and in observer training. Again, the complexity of the study and the number of participants involved will determine the base requirements. The smaller the number of investigators, the greater the likelihood of securing reliable data. But interacting teams involving a substantial number of observers can add richness to interpretation. Including observers who have not taught in schools can add a freshness of view and a questioning of school practices which those steeped in institutional practice tend to accept uncritically.

Classroom Observation

Studies of teaching behavior can yield insights into the kind and amount of instruction in literature, the role of the teacher (director of learning? lecturer? tutor?), the approaches to the study of literature, the instructional materials actually used, the observed degree of student engagement, the percentage of class time devoted to the subjects, and similar considerations. Much depends on the purpose of a study. By providing checklists or similar response guides to make possible easy summarization of impressions, researchers can collect extensive data for later analysis. For example, in the Squire-Appleebee studies of high school English, observers used special observation cards (see Figure 16-1) to indicate the time devoted to various dimensions of English out of total English time (Squire and Applebee, 1968). Subsequently, the investigators could report that 60 percent of all high school English time is devoted to literature and its teaching. In Durkin's study, however, observers focused only on periods of reading instruction in the middle grades and thus categorized the number of minutes spent on instruction in reading, on testing, on various kinds of independent activities as a percentage of instructional time in reading (1978). Durkin was subsequently able to advance generalizations about the overwhelming emphasis on practice and assessment in teaching reading comprehension. The hypotheses underling each study determine the areas of emphasis, but no observer should be required to record data on more than a limited number of dimensions of what can be observed. The more precise, the more valid.

Further, following a series of classroom observations, investigators have found it productive to ask observers to provide an impressionistic account of what they have seen in the classrooms of a school. Such subjective accounts, when collected immediately following school visits, are useful not only in interpreting quantitative data but in capturing school-to-school variations in tone and atmosphere.

What can be gleaned from classroom observation and interviews about response to literature? Firm data on pupil involvement in literary experience must come from such observations, as well as reports on the uses of class time, on the relative emphasis on literature as contasted with language study or composition, and on the relative emphasis in the classroom on different genre or different approaches (close reading, wide reading, oral reading).

Figure 16-1.   Classroom observation card (used in Squire and Applebee, 1979)

Front of Observation Card

Name of high School: _____   Date: _____
Class and Grade: _____   Instructor: _____   Observer: _____
Grouping: A __ C __ T __ Other (specify) _____
Number of Students: ____   Time Observed: ____

Assignments: _____
_____

Physical features of classroom: _____
_____

Books, paperbacks carried by students: _____
_____

Describe the activity briefly (include teacher's apparent purpose, unique features, etc.): _____
_____

Back of Observation Card

Describe the continuity of lesson (its relationship to previous and succeeding lessons):

Pupil involvement (circle one):

                    completely involved   uninvolved

         1   2   3   4   5   6   7

Content (order of emphasis, *1, 2, 3*, only):

Literature ____   Reading ____   Mass media ____
Composition ____   Speech: formal ____   No content stressed ____
Language ____   informal ____   Other ____

Method (order of emphasis, *1, 2, 3*, only):

Lecture ____   Recitation ____   Student presentation ____
Demonstration ____   Discussion ____   Teacher operating equipment
Groups ____   Socratic ____   (specify) ____
Silent work ____   Other ____

At a time when direct instruction by the teacher is being heralded as a critical variable in basic skills instruction, one can only postulate about its importance in literary education. A solid study could reveal not only the amount of direct instruction, but also its kind and possibly its relationship to tested knowledge about literature or attitudes to literature of many kinds. For example, Purves (1973) suggested that prolonged emphasis on varied approaches to literary response (the historical, the moral, the analytic, etc.) affect the response of readers, but no one really knows how extensively these approaches are used in our classrooms and what may be their effect. To understand what really is happening in literary education requires observational studies.

Directed and open-ended interviews with teachers, coupled with questionnaire studies, provide useful tools in understanding classroom teaching. Such instruments can describe teacher attitudes and teacher impressions of current classroom conditions, but seldom do they accurately reveal what the teachers do in the classrooms (Squire and Applebee, 1968; Mason and Osborn, 1982). Squire and Applebee report the case of a superb teacher's lecture and platform reading of *Macbeth* being recalled as a satisfying "discussion." For whatever reasons, teachers seldom report accurately on their own behavior. Hence, interviews and questionnaire studies are best paired with actual observations.

But interviews can clearly reveal teacher opinions. Hahn (1968), for example, found that 50 percent of Wisconsin teachers preferred units organized around life experiences, compared with 30 percent around form, and 10 percent around themes. Others have tabulated the interest in individualized reading, or the degree of understanding of a preference for selected instructional techniques.

Forced-choice, Likert scales, rankings, or contrasts based on the semantic differential are useful in assessing attitudes. Stated preferences for one of three descriptions of approaches to teaching a particular short story can indicate attitudes to different kinds of teaching. The possibilities are legion, and the time almost certainly will be limited to not more than 30 minutes. Investigators are urged to prepare interview schedules carefully and to test them under field conditions.

Except for a few "ice breakers" which serve to orient the interviewer and teacher respondent, time is most productively spent on questions aimed at revealing data which can be secured only through personal interview. Where factual information is required, such as on the teacher's background of course work, interviewers are urged to leave a questionnaire with each respondent to be mailed in following the school visit. Such post-observation reports also provide opportunity for afterthoughts, as does the availability of the interviewer in the school for one or two days following the interview.

Where the organizational structure of a school is important, early interviews with the department head or supervisor are important. Where the total curriculum in literature is to be assessed, group interviews with all members of a Department of English should be scheduled. Such interviews can focus on areas of agreement and disagreement not easily ascertained in the meetings with individuals.

- Where does the department take responsibility for teaching about literary form? (Everywhere? Nowhere?)
- What do you do about world literature in translation? (And for what percentage of students?)
- How are literary anthologies selected? How are they used?

Hold group interviews on the first day of a school visit to provide time for subsequent elaboration and correction on the part of individual faculty members.

Independently or separately, studies of teacher attitudes and opinions can reveal much about present conditions in literary education. In concert with classroom study, they yield a comprehensive portrait of what is taught, where, and by whom. They are particularly important in defining the conditions under which literature is taught and the attitude of teachers toward these conditions.

Observations and Student Interviews

Whenever interaction of student or text is critical in an investigation, researchers must plan for actual observation of and interviews with students. In addition to the procedures described by Cooper, Purves, and Applebee elsewhere in this volume, directed and open-ended interviews can yield important findings on student knowledge, preferences, and experiences.

Students have been asked to reveal their reading habits, their viewing habits, and the patterns of their interests. The amount of time they spend reading out of school can be estimated in contrast with the amount observed in school. Differences from grade to grade and school to school can be charted as can the habits of students who deviate from the accepted norm.

Given the affective base on which literary appreciation resides, students' attitudes are especially critical. Scales that measure attitudes, such as a Degree of Liking Scale, as used by Purves and other investigators (see Figure 16-2) are useful in indicating pupil reactions to particular practices or particular selections.

Checklists of literary concepts—those unknown, when taught—were used by Squire and Applebee (1968) and contrasted with similar reports from teachers. The gap between what was taught and what was remembered offers one indication of curricular effectiveness. Smith (1941) used checklists of 50 authors and 35 titles as a way of obtaining an indication of what was taught in the curriculum.

What children write about literature may be influenced as much by what is taught as by the characteristics of individual works. Assessing representative student papers— and the annotations made by teachers—can help to reveal the thrust of the literary education in a school district. Carroll (1960, pp. 283–292), Diederich (1974), and Purves and Rippere (1968) offer useful methods of analyzing written literary responses. Smith (1941) used reading diaries maintained by pupils over a period to time to

Figure 16-2.   Degree of liking scale

Compare the story you have just read to other stories. If you think it is one of the best stories you have read, circle +3 below. If you think it is one of the worst you have read, circle −3

one of the best	good	fairly good	fairly poor	poor	one of the worst
+3	+2	+1	−1	−2	−3

indicate their current reading. Purves and Beach (1973) describe a number of studies based on instruments of this kind.

Contrasting pupil responses secured through interviews has yielded important insights. Squire and Applebee contrasted the responses of adolescents in the United Kingdom to the question, "Which reading experience in school has had the greatest impact on you?" with responses from similarly-aged adolescents in the United States (1969). They reported that culture appears to influence reading response only in selected ways. In contrast to American adolescents who responded favorably to stories about racial relations, British youngsters liked depictions of the working class struggle. But on both sides of the Atlantic the title most preferred by adolescents at that time was William Golding's tumultous tale of peer group relations, the *Lord of the Flies*.

For certain studies, group interviews with selected students can be important. Ask a school to interview a typical twelfth-grade group of academic students or a ninth-grade general class. With only a few pleasantries, students respond well to open-ended questions which engage them in reflecting on their experience. Interpretation of such group responses is difficult, of course, since students are unlikely to reveal sensitive data to an outsider. Still, group approaches have been useful when peer prompting is important. How frequently do you recall having personal conferences with a teacher about the books you have read? Or, what usually happens when your teachers assigns a poem to be read? The answers to such questions of this kind can be exceptionally helpful.

Case studies are also of value, especially in analyzing differences in the reactions of children; so are extensive interviews and observations with a small number of selected individuals observed on several occasions over a period of time. Duffy and Roehler have been using repeated observation of selected students at the Institute for Research on Teaching as one way of assessing the impact of changes in teacher modeling behavior. Studies of individuals can pinpoint differences in reactions created by varying conditions.

Interviews with Administrators and Support Staff

School surveys that do not direct some attention to the context in which English instruction occurs yield a less than complete picture. Interviews with administrators and supervisors are important not only to facilitate arrangements but to reveal the schoolwide climate under which literature is taught; the ways in which the curriculum is organized; the methods used in supervision, curriculum development, and staff development; the extent of schoolwide emphasis on achievement in literature and in reading; and similar concerns. The recent series of teaching effectiveness studies suggest that the role of the principal is critical. Only direct study of ways in which the principal functions as an instructional leader and, in the high school, his or her interaction with the department chairman, provide an adequate picture of schoolwide conditions.

The role of the principal is especially important in determining the free access of children to books. What does the principal do when parents object to a book?

This question, asked in both American and British schools by Squire and Applebee (1968, 1969), revealed important natinal differences in censorship pressures in the two cultures. The most recent report by the Committee on Freedom to Read indicated that objections to student reading are widespread and that most objections are to contemporary literature (1980). What impact does limiting the access to books have on student response to literature?

The school librarian offers important resources for a program in literature, and in any full study of literature in schools, the librarian and the library demand attention. How accessible are books to students? What do records show about the extent of book withdrawals? Is the collection reasonably large and up-to-date in all important areas? Can students interested in poetry or drama find specialized titles to suit their personal needs? Are frequently-challenged titles included with contemporary literature? How closely does the librarian really work with teachers of English? What role do teachers play in book selection? Questions such as these can suggest the extent to which the program in literature permeates the entire school.

Do interviews with selected teachers in other subject fields with respect to their attitudes toward the teaching of literature in the school. Teachers of history are perhaps most sensitive to literary knowledge. School counselors can reveal much about the popularity of courses and teachers, and about the reasons children are programmed into particular offerings. Here, as elsewhere, a multidimensional approach to studying school programs appears to be required.

Curriculum Guidelines, Textbooks, and Tests

According to Purves (1973), programs in literature can be oriented to taste heritage, self-understanding, form, the students themselves, or language. By studying guidelines or courses of study, researchers can identify the public stance of school programs and what programs purport to teach. Jewett's national analysis (1958) reveals the value and the deficiences of investigations limited to an analysis of curriculum guidelines alone. Such guides, committed ultimately to such broad overreaching objectives as "appreciation of literature" and "recognizing worthwhile literature," frequently seem unfocused in detail. What they fail to say, however, can be more interesting than what they specify. Indeed, a lack of attention to the quality of student interaction with texts or to instruction in bedrock literary concepts seems to reveal something on the nature of emphasis within a program.

During the sixties, several investigators independently analyzed the uniqueness of different curricular emphases. Their approaches might well be applied to contemporary programs. (See especially Burton, 1968; Steinberg et al., 1968). Purves and Beach summarize these studies (1971).

Analyses of basal readers and textbooks used in teaching literature also have revealed critical differences. A report on high school anthologies by Lynch and Evans (1963), for example, pinpointed a whole series of questionable practices. Durkin (1981) reported on the lack of instructional support in the teacher manuals that accompany basal readers. And the Crossley secondary school Market Check (1981) reported that high school students only have 0.5 literature texts for every grammar and composition text. Given the fact that published instructional materials are an important influence on instructional practice at every educational level, studies of textbooks can yield persuasive data on the state of today's practice. Among the critical questions which have been addressed through studying the nature of instructional materials are several of continuing importance to the teaching of literature:

1. The adequacy of coverage of literary genre and authors (Lynch and Evans, 1963).
2. The expository patterns and story grammars presented to pupils (Tierney and Mosenthal, 1982).
3. The presentation of such elements as allusion, poetic language, ethnicity, role of females, metaphor, and other discrete elements.
4. The level of challenges of textbooks in readability and concept difficulty (Chall 1978).
5. The nature of questioning and levels of questioning about a literary work.
6. The teaching of poetry or prose or drama or any particular genre in the textbooks.

But if textbooks can reveal the emphasis to which children are exposed in our schools, tests signify what is important. Any investigator seriously concerned with what is taught and what is learned must concern himself or herself with how literature instruction is assessed. The long range impact of objective testing which focuses on multiple choice reactions rather than a personal response to a text has been documented by the National Assessment of Educational Progress (NAEP) (1980). In particular schools, researchers need to study both formal and informal methods of assessment—the periodic survey tests (if any), as well as the week-to-week appraisals. Interviews with teachers and especially students can reveal what each think they are attempting to assess and how the approaches are making an impact the learning of students. By examining selected tests, researchers can compare practice with expressed intent.

SUMMARY

The multiplicity of instruments and assortment of data gathered in most school surveys can be difficult to summarize unless steps are taken in advance to assure that coherent patterns emerge.

Stating basic hypothesis in advance and using them to guide the development of instruments proved useful with the National Study of High School English Programs (Squire and Applebee, 1968).

Although such guiding concepts tend to focus the attention of investigators on particular concerns and thus blind them to other factors, they do help in marshaling and interpreting data.

Impressionistic summaries of individual impressions are useful in encouraging members of visiting teams to summarize their interviews and observations. Such reports are best written immediately after school visits are completed and prior to a final team meeting to share impressions. Such a summarizing evaluation session can be a useful tool in ensuring that the distilled report of the survey does not distort individual experience. Where members of the visiting team experienced different impressions, such reviews provide opportunity to reconcile differences.

Finally, surveys that are evaluative by nature in their attempts to describe the state of teaching in a school are advised to include a summary review of perceived strengths and weaknesses. Such cumulative statements help to represent the complexity of teaching conditions in most school situations.

QUESTIONS THAT NEED RESEARCH

Of all issues in studying response to literature and the teaching of literature, the most amenable to school survey approaches are those which deal with current and changing curriculum and instruction. We need more studies like Applebee's replication of the findings of the National Study fifteen years after the initial selection of schools (1978). Indeed a goodly number of current studies might well attempt to review in today's schools any of several earlier findings on areas of emphasis in content and methods; student preferences; teaching conditions; and changes in instructional materials. A continuing survey of the language education of eleven-year-olds, including preference for and response to literature, was launched in Britain in 1979 and is expected to be continued periodically hereafter (see Gorman et al., 1981).

Clearly the findings of the many recent studies on the effectiveness of schooling need to be applied to the teaching of literature. Is instructional leadership as important in developing literary appreciation as in skill instruction? What about direct instruction? Or time on task?

Recent research in reading comprehension indicate the significance of prior knowledge in determining level of understanding (Anderson, 1977; Langer and Smith-Burke, 1982; Steffensen and Colker, 1982). But where and how in our school curriculum do we develop world knowledge? And where and how do we systematically introduce children to the kinds of rhetorical texts with which they must interact? (See for example, Brown and Smiley, 1977, or Tierney and Mosenthal, 1982.) Only school surveys can provide answers to such questions.

Studies of actual practice in teaching literature have not been extensive, perhaps because researchers lacked adequate controlling hypotheses to guide such investigation. But the rich increase in insights into response to literature developed over the past decade augurs well for surveys that attempt to reveal how, where, and whether teachers and schools are implementing the ideas in tomorrow's classrooms.

APPENDIX A:
SUMMARY OF CLASS VISITATION

The following report, used by Squire and Applebee (1968, 1969), provides for convenient summary of observer impressions and suggests the variety of aspects of teaching which can be observed.

School _____   No. of classes observed _____
Observer _____   Approximate number of minutes _____

I. Indicate by *numbers* the order of emphasis in the following *content areas* (i.e.,
   1 for content receiving *most* emphasis, *2* for content receiving next emphasis,
   etc., using as many as apply).

Literature ____	Speech: formal ____
Composition ____	informal ____
	Mass Media ____
Language ____	No content ____
Reading ____	

Other (Please describe) _____

II. Indicate by *numbers* the order of emphasis in the following methods:

Lecture, demonstration ____	Talk (unplanned by purposeful) ____
Groups ____	Discussion (planned) ____
Silent work ____	Socratic method ____
Recitation ____	Pupil presentation ____
	Teaching operating equipment ____

Other (Please describe) _____

III. Pupil Involvement
    Circle the number below which corresponds to the *average* degree of pupil
    involvement in all classes observed:

        Completely involved   Uninvolved
        1   2   3   4   5   6   7

IV. Methods, Materials and Approaches

	Much in evidence; widespread to constant use in the department	Frequent use by some teachers	Some indication occasional use	Infrequent use suggested	No evidence of any use
(a) Silent reading in class	1 ( )	2 ( )	3 ( )	4 ( )	5 ( )
(b) Writing in class	1 ( )	2 ( )	3 ( )	4 ( )	5 ( )
(c) Individual conferences with teacher	1 ( )	2 ( )	3 ( )	4 ( )	5 ( )

(*Appendix A continued*)

(d) Classroom libraries
    or wide use of
    school libraries
    by classes   1 ( )   2 ( )   3 ( )   4 ( )   5 ( )

(e) Workbooks   1 ( )   2 ( )   3 ( )   4 ( )   5 ( )

(f) Programmed
    instruction   1 ( )   2 ( )   3 ( )   4 ( )   5 ( )

(g) Team teaching   1 ( )   2 ( )   3 ( )   4 ( )   5 ( )

(h) Independent study
    (library)   1 ( )   2 ( )   3 ( )   4 ( )   5 ( )

(i) Use of single
    anthology for
    entire course   1 ( )   2 ( )   3 ( )   4 ( )   5 ( )

(j) Use of grammar texts   1 ( )   2 ( )   3 ( )   4 ( )   5 ( )

(k) Use of multiple sets
    of texts   1 ( )   2 ( )   3 ( )   4 ( )   5 ( )

(l) Remedial reading
    program   1 ( )   2 ( )   3 ( )   4 ( )   5 ( )

(m) Developmental
    reading program   1 ( )   2 ( )   3 ( )   4 ( )   5 ( )

(n) Use of reading
    laboratory   1 ( )   2 ( )   3 ( )   4 ( )   5 ( )

(o) Thematic or idea-
    centered teaching
    of literature   1 ( )   2 ( )   3 ( )   4 ( )   5 ( )

(p) Emphasis on literary
    history   1 ( )   2 ( )   3 ( )   4 ( )   5 ( )

(q) Emphasis on
    literature as social
    documentation   1 ( )   2 ( )   3 ( )   4 ( )   5 ( )

(r) Emphasis on morals
    to be gleaned
    from literature   1 ( )   2 ( )   3 ( )   4 ( )   5 ( )

(s) Emphasis on analysis
    of particular work   1 ( )   2 ( )   3 ( )   4 ( )   5 ( )

Great variety of teaching *methods*   Little variety of teaching *methods*

    1   2   3   4   5   6   7

Great variety of teaching *materials*   Little variety of teaching *materials*

    1   2   3   4   5   6   7

V. Character of class discussion:

Pupils are eager to respond, to forward
opinions—challenge and question

Pupils are generally unresponsive, use stock
replies when questioned, answer in single
words or phrases

    1   2   3   4   5   6   7

(*continued on next page*)

Teachers are catalysts, they prompt discussion but allow pupils much latitude in expressing opinions, drawing conclusions				Teachers dominate discussion; do virtually all of the talking, state unsupported opinions		
1	2	3	4	5	6	7

VI. Literature program:

Ideas evoked from the literature read, not foisted on pupils from teacher's predilections. (Ideas might deal with form and/or content, such as could occur through close textual analysis)				Emphasis on memory work in literature. Names, dates, authors, kinds, periods, rote-learning heavily practiced		
1	2	3	4	5	6	7

VII. Intellectual climate of the school:

Accessible library, well stocked with good books				Meager library, or one inaccessible to pupils		
1	2	3	4	5	6	7

Good general intellectual climate				Poor intellectual climate		
1	2	3	4	5	6	7

VIII. Writing:

Frequent and varied writing experiences in evidence				Infrequent and unimaginative assignments in evidence		
1	2	3	4	5	6	7

IX. Course Content:

Language, literature and composition coordinated				Language, literature and composition taught as separate courses or units—definite demarcation		
1	2	3	4	5	6	7

Language, literature, composition taught in appropriate proportion and sequence				Language, literature, composition taught disproportionately with little thought to sequence		
1	2	3	4	5	6	7

X. Reading:

Effective, coordinated instruction in reading carried on by the English department or reading specialist				No apparent effort or an ineffective attempt to teach reading as a skill by English department or reading specialist		
1	2	3	4	5	6	7

XI. Organization, administration and supervision:

Supervision administered by capable department chairman with time to attend to important details

Only nominal department chairman—or one with inadequate training or time to function

| | 1 | 2 | 3 | 4 | 5 | 6 | 7 |

Ideas, principles and new departures of teachers supported by administration

Ideas, principles and new departures of teachers not supported by administration

| | 1 | 2 | 3 | 4 | . 5 | 6 | 7 |

XII. Unique, dedicated teachers:

Within department are some unique, dedicated teachers who spark department

In general, no especially well qualified or enthusiastic teachers

| | 1 | 2 | 3 | 4 | 5 | 6 | 7 |

XIII. Curriculum:

Special program for non-college bound pupils is effective

No special program for non-college bound pupils or ineffective one

| | 1 | 2 | 3 | 4 | 5 | 6 | 7 |

In general, the curriculum reflects changing conditions and patterns of the times

Curriculum is static, does not change or keep pace with times

| | 1 | 2 | 3 | 4 | 5 | 6 | 7 |

APPENDIX B:
SUMMARY OF REACTION TO SCHOOL
[Each item asks for a single page response]

School _____   Observer _____

Address _____   Dates of Visit _____

                                               Present Date _____

(This summary sheet should be completed soon after the visit before conferring with other members of the team.)

1. What is your dominant impression of the overall educational program which you observed in the school?
2. In what way does the *total* program in English appear to be among the stronger or weaker aspects of the whole school program?
3. Insofar as you can determine, what seemed to be the basic attitude in the school toward the English program? (Include also relevant comments by administrators, teachers of other subjects, and pupils. Note evidence of attempts to support the work of the English program in subjects other than English.)
4. What special strengths of the English program seem worthy of comment? (Here summarize as much as you can your general reactions and your reactions to the comments of those in the school with which you had contact.)
5. What overall weaknesses in the program seemed apparent to you? (Discuss in detail.)
6. Characterize *in as much detail as possible* the overall intellectual atmosphere of the school.

7. *What unusual approaches or methods* were discovered? (Refer to outstanding teachers, indicating what you believe to be the most important reasons for their individual success as English teachers.)

REFERENCES

Anderson, R. C. *Schema-directed processes in language comprehension.* Technical Report Number 50, Center for the Study of Reading, University of Illinois, July 1977.

Anderson, S. *Between the Grimms and the group: Literature in American high schools.* Princeton, NJ: Educational Testing Service, 1964.

Applebee, A. *A survey of teaching conditions in English.* Urbana, IL: National Council of Teachers of English, 1977.

Applebee, A. Teaching high-achieving students: A survey of the winners of the 1977 NCTE achievement awards in writing. *Research in the Teaching of English,* 1978, *12*(4), 339–348.

Applebee, A. *Writing in the secondary school, English and the content areas.* Urbana, IL: National Council of Teachers of English, 1981.

Association for Supervision and Curriculum Development (ASCD). Studies of teaching effectiveness: A videotape with related manual. Alexandria, VA, 1980.

Aw, K. H. & Mason, J. M. *A microethnographic approach to the study of classroom reading instruction: Rationale and procedures.* Center for Study of Reading, Technical Report 237, University of Illinois, March, 1982.

Brophy, J. *Recent research of teaching.* Occasional Paper Number 40, Institute of Research on Teaching, Michigan State University, 1980.

Brown, A. L. & Smiley, S. S. *Rating the importance of structural units of prose passages.* A problem of metacognitive development. *Child Development,* 1977, *48,* 1–8.

Buchmann, M. & Schmidt, W. H. *The school day and content commitments.* Institute for Research on Teaching, Research Series Number 83, Michigan State University, March 1981.

Bullock Report. *A language for life.* London: Her Majesty's Stationery Office, 1975.

Burton, D. L. *The development and teaching of approaches to teaching of English in the junior high school.* Final Report Project Number H-026, Florida State University, 1968.

Campbell, D. T. & Stanley, J. C. Experimental and quasi-experimental designs for research in teaching, in Gage, N. L. (Ed.), *Handbook for research in teaching.* Chicago: Rand McNally, 1963.

Carroll, J. B. Vectors of prose style. In T. A. Sebock, (Ed.), *Style in language.* New York: Technology Press and John Wiley, 1960.

Chall, J. *The relationahip of textbooks to falling SAT scores.* New York: College Entrance Examination Board, 1978.

Coleman, J. S. Campbell, E. Q., Hobson, C. J., McPartland, J., Mood, A. M., Weinfeld, F. D., & York, R. L. *Equality of educational opportunity.* Washington, DC: Government Printing Office, 1966.

Committee on Freedom to Read. *Limiting student access to books.* Washington DC: Association of American Publishers, 1980.

Conner, J. W. *Practices in teaching literature in representatives public four-year high school districts.* Doctoral dissertation, University of Iowa, 1966.

Corbin, R. & Crosby, M. *Language programs for the disadvantaged.* Champaign, IL: National Council of Teachers of English, 1963.

Crossley Surveys. *Secondary school market check.* New York: Crossley Surveys, May 1981.

Diederich, P. B. *Measuring growth in English.* Urbana, IL: National Council of Teachers of English, 1974.

Denham, C. & Lieberman, A. *Time to learn.* Washington, DC: United States Office of Education and National Institute on Education, May 1980.

Department of Education and Science. *Aspects of secondary education in England.* London: Her Majesty's Stationery Office, July 1980.

Duckworth, K. *Linking education policy and management with student achievement.* Eugene, OR: Center for Educational Policy and Management, University of Oregon, 1981 (duplicated).

Duffy, G. G. *Teaching effectiveness research: Implications for the reading profession.* Occasional Paper Number 45. Institute for Research on Teaching, Michigan State University, 1981. (a)

Duffy, G. G., Roehler, L. R. & Reinsmoen, D. *Two styles of direct instruction in teaching second-grade reading and language arts: A descriptive study.* Research Series Number 100, Institute for Research on Teaching, Michigan State University, 1981. (b)

Durkin, D. *What classroom observation reveals about reading comprehension instruction.* Technical Report Number 106, Center for Reading, University of Illinois, October, 1978.

Durkin, D. Reading comprehension instruction in five basal reader series. *Reading Research Quarterly,* 1981, *16*(4), 515–544.

Evertson, C., Anderson, C., Anderson, L., & Brophy, J. Relationships between classroom behaviors and students outcomes in junior high mathematics and English classes. *American Educational Research Journal,* 1980, *17*, 43–60.

Flanders, N. A. *Analyzing teacher behavior.* Reading, MA: Addison-Wesley, 1970.

Filby, N., & Fisher, C. W. Description of patterns of teaching behavior within and across classes during the B-C period. *Beginning teacher evaluation study,* Technical Notes IV 36. San Francisco: Far West Laboratory for Educational Research and Development, October 1977.

Gorman, T. P., White, J., Orchard, L. & Tate, A. *Language performances in schools.* Primary Survey Report Number 1. London: Her Majesty's Stationery Office, 1981.

Hahn, E. C. L. *Critical emphasis revealed in selected practices in literature instruction in public secondary schools.* Doctoral dissertation, University of Connecticut, 1968.

Hosic, J. F. *The reorganization of English in secondary schools.* Bulletin Number 21. Washington DC: Government Printing Office, 1917.

Institutional Tracking Service. *Reading/language arts.* White Plains, New York: ITS, August 1980.

Jencks, C., Smith, M., Acland, H., Bane, M. J., Cohen, D., Gintis, H., Hyns, B., & Michelson, S., *Inequality: A reassessment of the effect of family and schooling in America.* New York: Basic Books, 1972.

Jewett, A. *English language arts in American high schools.* Bulletin 1958, Number 13. Washington DC: United States Department of Education, 1958.

Kinnear, T. C. & Taylor, J. R. *Marketing research, an applied approach.* New York. McGraw-Hill, 1979.

LaBrant, L. L., & Heller, F. M. *An evaluation of free reading in grades seven to twelve inclusive.* Contributions to Education Number 4. Columbus, OH: Ohio State University Press, 1939.

LaBrant, L. L. The use of communication media. In Margaret Willis (Ed.), *The guinea pigs after twenty years.* Columbus, OH: Ohio State University, 1961.

Langer, J. A., & Smith-Burke, M. T. *Reader meets author/bridging the gap.* Newark, DE: International Reading Association, 1982.

Lynch, J. J. & Evans, B. *High school English textbooks.* Boston, MA: Little Brown, 1963.

Mason, J. & Osborn, Jean. *When do children begin "Reading to Learn"? A survey of reading instruction in grades two through five.* Technical Report Number 261, University of Illinois, September 1982.

Medley, D. *Teacher competence and teacher effectiveness: A review of process-product research.* Washington, DC: American Association of Colleges of Teacher Education, 1977.

Medley, D. The effectiveness of teachers. In P. Peterson, & H. Walberg (Eds.), *Research on teaching: Concepts, findings, and implications.* Berkeley: McCutchan Publishing, 1979.

Norvell, G. *The reading interests of young people.* Boston: D. C. Heath, 1950.

Norvell, G. *What boys and girls like to read.* Norristown, NJ: Silver Burdett Company, 1958.

National Assessment of Educational Progress. *Reading, thinking and writing.* Denver: NAEP, 1980.

Pooley, R. C. *The teaching of English in wisconsin.* Madison: University of Wisconsin Press, 1948.

Purves, A. C. *Literature education in ten counties.* New York: John Wiley, 1973.

Purves, A. C. *Literature education in ten counties, an empirical study:* New York: John Wiley, 1977.

Purves, A. C. & Beach, R. *Literature and the reader.* Urbana, IL: National Council of Teachers of English, 1972.

Purves, A. C., & Beach, R. *Reading and literature, American achievement in international perspective.* Urbana, IL: National Council of Teachers of English, 1981.

Purves, A. C., & Kadar-Fulop. Assessing composition: The issue of perspective. Paper prepared for the International Education Assessment, October 1982.

Purves, A. C., & Rippere, V. *Elements of writing about literary work: A study of response to literature.* Urbana, IL: National Council of Teachers of English, 1968.

Rickards, M. H. *A study of newer programs and trends in the teaching of literature in selected Oregon senior high schools.* Doctoral dissertation, University of Oregon, 1967.

Roehler, L., Schmidt, W. & Beckman, M. *How do teachers spend their language arts time?* Institute for Research on Teaching, Research Series Number 66, Michigan State University, 1979.

Rosenshine, B., & Furst, N. *The use of direct observation to study teaching.* In Robert Travers (Ed.), *Second handbook of research on teaching.* Chicago: Rand McNally, 1973.

Rutter, M., Maughan, B., Mortimore, P., & Ouston, J. *Fifteen thousand hours.* Cambridge: Harvard University Press, 1979.

Shavelson, R. Teacher's decision making. In N. Gage (Ed.), *Psychology of teaching methods.* Seventy-fifth yearbook of the National Society for the Study of Education, Part I. Chicago: University of Chicago Press, 1976.

Smith, D. V. *Instruction in English.* Monograph Number 20, National Survey of Secondary Education, Bulletin 17. Washington, DC: Office of Education, 1933.

Smith, D. V. *Evaluating instruction in secondary school English.* Chicago: National Council of Teachers of English, 1941.

Spiro, R. J. *Etiology of reading comprehension style.* Technical Report Number 124, Center for Study of Reading, University of Illinois, May 1979.

Squire, J. R., Applebee, R. K., & Lacampagne, R. J. *High school departments of English: Their organization, administration, and supervision.* Champaign, IL: National Council of Teachers of English, 1965.

Squire, J. R., & Applebee, R. K. *High school English instruction today.* New York: Appleton-Century-Crofts, 1968.

Squire, J. R., & Applebee, R. K. *Teaching English in the United Kingdom.* Champaign, IL: National Council of Teachers of English 1969.

Stallings, J., Cory, R., Fairweather, J. & Needles, M. *A study of basic skills taught in secondary schools.* Phase I Findings. Palo Alto, CA: SIR International, January 1978.

Stallings, J., Needles, M., & Stayrook, N. *How to change the process of teaching basic reading skills in secondary schools.* Final Report, Stanford Research Institute International, Palo Alto, CA February 1980.

Steffensen, M. S., & Colker, L. *The effect of cultural knowledge on memory and language.* Technical Report 248, Center for the Study of Reading. Champaign, IL: University of Illinois, June 1982.

Steinberg, E., Director. *A senior high curriculum in English for able college bound students.* Summary Report. Pittsburgh: Carnegie-Mellon University, 1968.

Thorndike, R. L. & Hogan, E. *Measurement and evaluation of psychology and education.* New York: John Wiley, 1977.

Tierney, R. J., & Mosenthal, J. Discourse comprehension and production. Analyzing text structure and cohension. In J. Langer, et al., *Reader meets author*, 1982.

Tikunoff, W., Berliner, D., & Rist, R. C. *An ethnographic study of the forty classrooms of the beginning teacher evaluation study.* San Francisco: Far West Laboratory, 1975.

Venezky, R. L., & Winfield, L. *Schools that succeed beyond expectations in teaching reading.* Contributions to Education No. 1, Department of Education, University of Delaware, 1979.

Warwick, D. P., & Lininger, C. A. *The sample survey: Theory and practice.* New York: McGraw-Hill, 1975.

Whitworth, R. G. *An appraisal of the problems experienced by and the techniques used by English teachers in Indianapolis, Indiana, in improving student reading tastes.* Doctoral dissertation, Indiana University, 1964.

Chapter 17
Evaluating the Results of Classroom Literary Study

Charles R. Cooper

Department of Literature
University of California, San Diego

INTRODUCTION

This chapter is concerned with the evaluation of the outcomes of literature instruction for students in school and college classrooms. Most of the discussion will consider the possibilities of selected response (multiple-choice) tests, but some attention will also be given to the coding and analysis of expressed response and to holistic scoring of expressed response. The chapter will be of interest primarily to a teacher or curriculum evaluator who wants to test the usefulness of an experimental teaching plan or who must collect evidence that instruction in literature results in some measurable changes in students.

My purpose is not at all to argue against the usefulness of informal and unobtrusive approaches: crucial information for evaluators may come from interviews or from observations, from looking on shrewdly, sensitively, insightfully. I am interested only in illustrating that either standardized or criterion-referenced selected-response tests may be useful to us in limited ways to evaluate some of the short-range outcomes of instruction in literature.

This, then, is a chapter for curriculum evaluators, not for basic researchers. The researcher looking into the basic psycholinguistic process of reading and responding to literature will find no help here. Tests are not research instruments. We can learn little if anything about the actual, temporal, psycholinguistic process of reading and responding to literature by giving people tests, whether we correlate the test scores or analyze the variance from them, whether we "look for relationships" or "test hypotheses." A deep confusion between researching a psycholinguistic process and giving people tests has derailed reading research for decades. Correlational and factor analysis research on reading has taught us so little about the reading process mainly because the tests used in the research have had no basis in a theory of human cognition or of written discourse. For the same reason, reading researchers were naive to think that hypothesis-testing research with norm-referenced reading comprehension tests would teach us anything about what humans are doing when they read and respond to print. Even in the basic sciences, hypothesis-testing has been used only as a partial confirmation of new theoretical insights, not to discover or create new theory (Popper, 1959). Most of the social and psychological sciences have been doing their work over the last few decades with research models, with "patterns of discovery" (Diesing, 1971), quite different from the narrow hypothesis-testing model common in the physical sciences and popular still among some educational psychologists and reading researchers.

The relation of basic research—like that encouraged in most of the chapter in this collection—and curriculum evaluation test-making of the kind encouraged in this chapter is this: basic research informs us about the thing of interest so that any curriculum-evaluation test-making we do will not be trivial.

The pencil-and-paper curriculum evaluation tests I will recommend are useful only for the evaluation of some of the outcomes of literary study. They are one way of obtaining summative evaluations of part of what students are learning from the literature programs in the schools or colleges they attend.

A digression on terminology: Very few of us trained in literature are familiar with current work in curriculum evaluation. Nevertheless, I will use freely the current jargon from evaluation. The concepts are not difficult, and they help sharpen some distinctions that evaluators must observe. A few of these current distinctions are the following:

- diagnostic-formative-summative evaluation
- constructed-selected response
- natural-controlled stimulus situation
- construct-content-predictive-face validity
- content-behavior
- affective-cognitive
- criterion-referenced–domain-referenced–norm-referenced
- internal-external validity of evaluation design

Where the context does not make the meaning of the term clear, I will supply a definition. Several introductions to the concepts in curriculum evaluation are available. My favorite remains W. James Popham's *Educational Evaluation* (Popham, 1975). Perhaps the best known is *Handbook on Formative and Summative Evaluation of Student Learning* (Bloom, Hastings, and Madaus, 1971), and a valuable resource is a comprehensive series of eight guides for evaluators prepared by Lynn Morris and her colleagues at the Center for the Study of Evaluation at UCLA (Morris, 1978).

DEFINITIONS AND LIMITATIONS

At this point, I should offer brief definitions of *evaluate* and *test*.

By *evaluate* I mean to decide whether readers are improving in their ability

- to read works of literature with discrimination and insight,
- to prefer works of merit over prosaic, predictable, or sentimental works,
- to widen and vary the patterns of their expressed responses,
- and to organize and develop their expressed responses in increasingly sophisticated ways.

Such a list enumerates some of the main goals of instruction in literature, but certainly not all of the goals. The above list contains only goals which are measurable in ways so reliable as to satisfy the most conservative psychometrician, as I will demonstrate. That is both its advantage and its great danger. Anytime we concern ourselves with the easily measurable, we run the risk of reducing literature programs only to what is measurable.

Notice that I am using the term *evaluate* to mean only *deciding whether a certain kind of growth has occurred.* I am not concerned here with deciding the worth of the particular amount of growth and of assigning it some public value, and I am certainly not suggesting that the growth implied by goals in the list can or should be forced. A bright sixth grader loves sentimental and predictable works. In my view, this sixth grader must read a great many such works for years in order eventually to persist with works of merit and come to prefer them. My main concern, then, is only with reliable description of change for individuals and groups in school literature programs.

By *test* I mean giving readers literary texts (or portions of them) they have *never seen before* and asking them to respond to them in talk or writing or to choose best answers in a multiple-choice format. The expressed responses (talking or writing) would be scored either by counting the presence of certain features, by categorizing and coding certain elements, or by carefully standardized holistic judgments of trained raters. The multiple-choice answers would either be hand- or machine-scored in the usual ways. The purpose of this chapter is to outline the possibilities of just such testing, and to suggest further work which needs to be undertaken.

Notice the restriction to texts the readers have not seen before. This seems to me an important restriction because it keeps the testing/evaluation focus on the reader's ability to read insightfully, not on his or her ability to recall what was heard in class or read in literary criticism. I am assuming that one goal of any school or college literature program—even one concerned with coverage of the literary heritage—is that the student will come to read more willingly, insightfully, and discriminatingly. The tests I am proposing would be useful partial outcome measures for any program, and would be the most acceptable criterion measures in any comparison-group curriculum evaluation study comparing two or more ways to teach literature.

A current distinction of some importance in evaluation circles is the distinction between norm-referenced testing and criterion-referenced (or domain-referenced or objectives-referenced) testing. Any of the multiple-choice tests I discuss can be used in either form of testing. In norm-referenced testing, the test items are carefully modified and refined through tryouts (following what are now quite conventional psychometric procedures) in order to insure that about half the test-takers will miss each item. These refinements insure a normal distribution of scores, where half the scores are above and half below the mean (or average) of all the scores for those taking the test, assuming the test-takers are very much like the group on which the test was "normed." The purpose of such a test is to spread students out across the distribution of possible scores, insuring that only a few do well, a few do badly, and most are in the middle. Nearly all published tests (intelligence tests, aptitude tests, reading comprehension tests) are norm-referenced. (Some people believe the schools should bring all students up to the average or above on norm-referenced reading comprehension tests. What they do not know and what the schools have failed to communicate is that on any single test administration, half the test-takers will always score below the average. The test is a failure and would need to be recalled like a faulty Ford if any other result was obtained. In a school with students exactly like those in the norming population of a reading comprehension test, half the students at the beginning of Grade 9 will *always* be reading below "grade level," no matter how good the reading program in Grades 7 and 8.)

As outcome measures for the direct comparison of the performance of two or more groups, the use of norm-referenced tests can still be defended. However, I want to recommend strongly that the tests I propose be used in a criterion-referenced framework. A full discussion of the advantages for curriculum evaluation of criterion-referenced tests over norm-referenced tests is not appropriate here (Popham, 1975, has a concise, readable discussion of the advantages), but I will point out that the basic advantage is sensitivity to the effects of instruction. The items in nationally standardized, norm-referenced tests are never congruent with the objectives of local instructional programs. Further, the tests are designed to eliminate items on which most students succeed, those which are most sensitive to what school programs emphasize. By contrast, criterion-referenced tests are designed to test the outcomes of instruction in a specific program and to detect as far as is possible what effect instruction or practice is having on students' performance. Criterion-referenced tests try to be as descriptive as possible; they are not at all concerned with response variance, or with insuring that some students do poorly, even though the students may have just experienced an intensive period of development in the performance being tested. Since they are descriptive and can be designed in clusters to test multiple outcomes of instruction, they tell us more than which horse won the race or which fertilizer produces the most corn.

Popham conjectures that the developers of standardized achievement tests, from their first development and widespread use about sixty years ago, have never had much faith in instruction. They seem to assume that most learners will never learn very much of what they were being taught, no matter how eager the learners or how helpful the teacher. But perhaps they only confused what might be justifiable for aptitude testing (How smart am I right now in comparison to others taking this test with me?) with what was appropriate for achievement testing (How much have I learned of what I am being taught in this course?).

A final limitation of this chapter: Since my concern is limited to tests for curriculum evaluation, I will not say anything about the design of curriculum evaluation studies. There is extensive literature on the subject; in cases where the evaluator compares the outcomes of different kinds of instruction in literature, certain design constraints which insure that the findings from the study cannot be explained away easily, become critical. Almost any text on educational evaluation will have chapters on design. The classic reference for conventional pre- and post-test studies is Campbell and Stanley's (1963) *Experimental and Quasi-Experimental Designs for Research,* but the volume *How to Design a Program Evaluation* (one volume of the set *Program evaluation kit*) in the evaluator's guides developed by Morris (1978) and her colleagues is particularly accessible. Here I must signal the reader that I am quite aware that other models of curriculum evaluation—certainly what is presently called "qualitative evaluation" (Guba and Lincoln, 1981; Patton, 1980)—require none of the instrumentation I describe in this chapter. This is quite unabashedly a chapter about quantitative evaluation and the instrumention and standardized procedures which make it possible. Some evaluations may need to be quantitative, some qualitative. Agnes Webb's chapter in this book illustrates that an evaluation can be both quantitative and qualitative; each teaches us different things, and the two can be nicely complementary.

WHY DEVISE STANDARDIZED PROCEDURES FOR EVALUATION OF LITERATURE PROGRAMS?

After centuries of literary study without standardized tests or scoring procedures of any kind, why, suddenly, should I and others recommend them? Given the energy and dedication good instruction in literature requires, how we can justify encouraging even a few of us in literary studies diverting our efforts to standardized program evaluation? In light of the compelling basic research questions raised by other chapters in this book, is it not frivolous to devote time to evaluation problems at present?

Let me list and discuss briefly a few arguments for concerning ourselves with test-making in one small corner of our field.

1. *To protect the place of literature in school and college programs, especially school programs.* Schools are testing more and more and, increasingly, these tests are not designed by the teachers who will be administering them. Comprehensive centralized evaluation schemes are seen as a basic requirement by those insisting on school accountability. The testing requirements of the new competency-based education movement tend to remove test construction still further from students and teachers. Consequently, teachers who value literature may find themselves under pressure to slight literature in favor of the sort of informational materials that are the focus of general reading comprehension tests (Cooper, 1981). These tests predominate in all standardized competency tests and other tests of the outcomes of schooling. A poem or a piece of prose fiction rarely appears in these tests as the selection on which test items are based. It is a truism in educational practice that the power to test is the power to determine the curriculum. What happens to literature if we tell the test-makers that the outcomes of instruction in literature are altogether too ineffable for any sort of group assessment?

2. *To enable us to carry out more sophisticated studies of perennial instructional questions.* With more varied and more valid tests of the outcomes of literature instruction—joined to recent developments in the design of curriculum evaluation studies, in item-sampling among large groups, and in data analysis—we could all benefit from a sound current study of the effects of intensive and extensive teaching,

for example. One of the few replicated findings in literary studies is that extensive curricula (wide reading, most of it free choice) enables readers to do as well on tests of comprehension and interpretation of literature as intensive curricula (close analysis of a few tests chosen by the teacher) (Coryell, 1927; Norvell, 1950; Hardwick, 1970).

3. *To justify the newer models of instruction implied by the theoretical approaches in several chapters in this book*, especially the "transactional model." The justification would be only partial, of course, because the measures would be directed at only a few of the outcomes of these new programs. Nevertheless, for the people who still decide how much money is to be divided among school programs, we must be able to demonstrate that new teaching approaches—especially those that look radically different from conventional approaches—have measurable outcomes that reflect growth in the way students read literary texts.

4. *To survey achievement in literature for large groups of students*—in school districts, states, or in the nation. Such surveys are already in existence at the national level (National Assessment of Educational Progress) and in many states. My main concern is that those of us in literary studies contribute to these already-existing surveys by high-quality test development work which produces a great variety of tests and test formats that we consider valid and acceptable.

5. *To test for the presence of possible unexpected outcomes of literature instruction suggested by new basic research or by surveys in our field*. One example is a major implication of the IEA international survey of achievement in literature: that the main effect of literature instruction in schools may be to shift the pattern of a student's way of responding, to produce a convergence on an acceptable style of response, which differs among national groups (Purves, 1973). One study (Michalak, 1976) offers tentative evidence of this effect of instruction.

6. *To continue to demonstrate the contribution of literary study to general reading development*. This seems to me crucial since literature is constantly endangered in many places because of a misplaced emphasis on general "reading skills." Reading is a psycholinguistic skill, enhanced by a variety of print-processing strategies (Smith, 1978; Cooper and Petrosky, 1976), to which the reading of fiction contributes as much as other kinds of reading. We need to continue to demonstrate this contribution in straightforward, conventional curriculum evaluation studies.

WRITING ITEMS, ASKING QUESTIONS, CLASSIFYING OR SCORING EXPRESSED RESPONSES: SOME POSSIBILITIES FOR GROUP EVALUATION

With reservations and limitations accounted for and with some tentative arguments to support the usefulness of what I am about to demonstrate, we can look directly at the present state of the art of evaluating how carefully and discriminatingly individual students or groups of students can read unfamiliar literary works. We will look first at multiple-choice items, then at ways to describe and classify expressed responses, and finally at procedures for reliable holistic scoring of expressed responses.

Before I get too far into this section of the chapter I must express my indebtedness to the pioneering work of Alan Purves. He has done more than anyone to extend the possibilities of testing how well people read literature. At the time I joined him in developing an evaluation program for a new secondary school literature series, he had just designed the first national assessment of literature for the National Assessment of Educational Progress. He had also completed a comprehensive survey of ways to evaluate learning in literature (Purves, 1971). His work on the International Educational Achievement literature survey (Purves, 1973, 1981) had produced an array of interesting and novel test instruments. For the secondary school literature series evaluation project (Cooper and Purves, 1973), we attempted to combine some of the results of Purves' work with some new instruments. I have since worked on exercise development for the second national assessment of literature (combined in 1979–80 with the reading assessment) and have made a thorough investigation of the research on evaluation of literature.

What follows demonstrates almost every approach presently available to us. I would be pleased if most readers are surprised by how much we already have available. The purpose of this chapter, of course, is to interest other evaluators in test development and to persuade them that some intensive further development is possible and worthwhile. As we will see, the crucial background comments are these six:

1. Purves'(1971) chapter "Evaluation of Literature."
2. Cooper and Purves' (1973) evaluation program for Ginn literature series, *A Guide to Evaluation* and accompanying tests.
3. The released exercises from the first national assessment of literature (NAEP, 1973) and the third national assessment of reading/literature (NAEP, 1981b).
4. The National Assessment report *Reading, Thinking, and Writing* (1981) based on the third national assessment of reading/literature, but reporting just results from literature exercises.
5. Fagan, Cooper, and Jensen (1975), *Measures for Research and Evaluation in the English Language Arts*, a collection of largely unpublished measures, some of them for evaluation in literature. The authors of this volume are planning a second, supplementary volume for 1985.
6. The criterion-referenced testing program developed for Grades 1–6 in the Montgomery County, Maryland, schools: Criterion-Referenced Reading Tests: Comprehension of Narrative Excerpts (1980).

This article and these documents are points of departure for the work that needs to be done over the next few years.

Text-Centered Tests

The traditional reading comprehension test presents the student with a brief selection followed by several multiple-choice questions. These questions usually range across "levels" of reading or "skills" of reading: word knowledge, literal comprehension, inferential comprehension, following the organization of a selection, recognizing the tone of the selection, and so on. On this pattern, we can present an unfamiliar work of literature and ask several questions which direct the student's attention to linguistic, structural, and content features unique to literature. A set of questions by Purves (1971) based on Keats' "On First Looking Into Chapman's Homer" illustrates the possibilities:

> Much have I traveled in the realms of gold,   5
> And many goodly states and kingdoms seen;
> Round many western islands have I been
> Which bards in fealty to Apollo hold.
> Oft of one wide expanse had I been told
> That deep-browed Homer ruled as his demesne: 10
> Yet did I never breathe its pure serene
> Till I heard Chapman speak out loud and bold;
> Then felt I like some watcher of the skies
> When a new planet swims into his ken;
> Or like stout Cortez when with eagle eyes
> He stared at the Pacific—and all his men
> Looked at each other with a wild surmise—
> Silent, upon a peak in Darien.

Diction: Which of the following best expresses the sense of line 4?

a. Which poets owe in submission to Apollo
b. Which poets use to make fun of Apollo
c. Which poets try to keep from Apollo
d. Which poets chained to Apollo cling to

Connotation: Which of the following words in lines 1 and 2 most clearly intimates that the traveling is a profitable and important occupation for the speaker?

a. realms
b. gold
c. goodly
d. kingdoms

Rhythm: The normal rhythm of this poem consists of an unaccented syllable followed by an accented syllable. At times, however, this rhythm is reversed and the accented syllable comes first. This happens most frequently

a. at the beginning of a line
b. in the middle of a line
c. at the end of a line
d. at no particular point in the line

Syntax: The adjective "Silent" (line 14) modifies

a. "I" (line 9)
b. "watcher" (line 9)

   c. "He" (line 12)
   d. "Men" (line 12)

Imagery: In the first six lines, there is a comparison of travel with

   a. business
   b. reading
   c. chivalry
   d. astronomy

Mood: The mood of the speaker is best described as

   a. wistfully joyous
   b. apprehensive and excited
   c. sardonically amused
   d. awed and exhilarated

Content: The speaker of the poem is primarily describing his

   a. feelings
   b. plans
   c. thoughts
   d. childhood experiences

Relationship between parts: Which of the following best describes the relationship between the first eight lines and the last six lines?

   a. The first eight lines explain the condition of the speaker; the last six give his reaction.
   b. The first eight lines present a problem facing the speaker; the last six lines present his solution.
   c. The first eight lines give the situation of the speaker; the last six lines a symbolic interpretation of the situation.
   d. The first eight lines present the dilemma in which the speaker finds himself; the last six his prayer for deliverance.

Relationship between form and content: The mood of the speaker is made most apparent by

   a. the single-syllable rhymes
   b. the lack of caesuras in twelve of the lines
   c. the contrast between the lonely astronomer and the band of explorers led by Cortez
   d. the two images of vast vision—in the sky and over the ocean

Interpretation: Which of the following is the best interpretation of lines 1 to 4?

   a. I have travelled a great deal in search of the gold that has been sung about by ancient poets.
   b. I have read a good deal of great literature, particularly the classic poets.

c. I have read a great deal of travel literature, particularly in verse by American travelers.

d. I have dreamed of being an immortal poet like the ancient bards who were led by Apollo.

Purves (1971) has suggested a promising refinement on the above procedure. Instead of testing "levels" of reading in some arbitrary order, the question would "attempt to follow the process of reading the text" and would point the student to significant features of the text, possibly even illustrating the features that should be considered in answering a final inference question or in developing an essay answer. Literature teachers will see that the set of questions below is a model inductive-questioning set, which begins small and leads the reader to a general insight about the whole text. Again, the questions are based on the Keats poem. (Note that all the questions could be rewritten as multiple-choice questions.)

Questions on the octave:

• What kind of a land would be a realm of gold?
• Why do bards owe fealty to Apollo?
• In lines 1 to 8, to what is travel being compared? Restate lines 1 to 4, showing what they mean in terms of the implied comparison.
• Chapman was the translator of Homer's poetry. What is the poet saying about Homer and Chapman in lines 5 to 8?
• What is the poet's attitude toward literature as it is made apparent in lines 1 to 8? What words in those lines make that attitude apparent?

Questions on the sestet:

• In lines 9 to 14, what aspect of himself is the poet describing? What sense do the two comparisons of lines 9 and 14 emphasize? What do the watcher of the skies and Cortez have in common? A contrast is established between Cortez and his men. What is that contrast?
• What word does "silent" (line 14) modify?
• Summarize the mood described in lines 9 to 14.

Questions on the poem as a whole:

• What is the relationship between the implied comparison of lines 1 to 8 and the comparison of lines 9 to 14?
• What is the relationship between the attitude described in lines 1 to 8 and the mood established in lines 9 to 14?

An essay task:

• Describe the way in which the structure of the poem reinforces the speaker's mood as it is presented in lines 9 to 14. In your essay show how the attitude in the first part of the poem is related to the mood at the end of the poem.

Perhaps it is better to say that such a set of questions represents the process of close analysis of a text in New Critical fashion, rather than the process of reading the text. Such sequential question sets are difficult to devise but seem to me an improvement over random sets. The sequential sets direct the reader's attention first to the more discrete linguistic and structural features of the text, which are then the base for later decisions requiring the relating of parts and inferences about the whole.

Text-centered literature tests are presently available from two publishers and from one recent research report:

1. The Literature subtest of the *Iowa Tests of Educational Development* (Chicago: Science Research Associates, 1968). For Grades 9–12.
2. *A Look at Literature* (Princeton, New Jersey: Educational Testing Service, 1968). For Grades 4–6.
3. The International Education Achievement report of the international literature survey (Purves, 1973, or Purves, 1981) contains four tests, each based on a different short story. (They seem especially useful to me because two of the tests can be used together as a pretest and the other two as a post-test in a curriculum evaluation study, permitting about forty questions of understanding and interpretation at each test time.)

The three tests recommended above are all norm-referenced tests and have been developed through conventional psychometric procedures. Within that context the main problem with all of the published text-centered tests is that scores on them correlate so highly with general reading comprehension tests: the Iowa Literature subtest, .76 and .77 with two reading tests in the same battery; two forms of *A Look at Literature*, .78 and .79 with a reading test by the same publisher; and the IEA tests, about .60 (in the U.S.) with reading tests developed for another IEA survey. (A correlation of 1.00 would indicate a perfect relation, and 0.00 no relation.) In the case of *A Look at Literature* the correlation with reading (.78 or .79) is so close to the coefficient of reliability of the test (.83) that there is no reason to believe the two tests are measuring anything different, and the test publisher admits as much. This problem has always plagued makers of norm-referenced literature tests, but there has been so little work done on the problem that it seems reasonable to call for considerably more developmental work before we give up. One promising study (Ashley, 1972), using new statistical techniques called convergent-discriminant analysis, concluded that *A Look at Literature* was measuring something that a reading test was not measuring.

The Iowa subtest and *A Look at Literature* may presently be purchased in quantity and used in any evaluation study. The IEA tests may be used with permission of the International Association for the Evaluation of Educational Achievement (University of Stockholm, S–10691, Stockholm, Sweden). One other battery of tests should be mentioned here although there are limitations in their development and constraints on their use: Pretests and Growth Tests from a *Guide to Evaluation* (Cooper and Purves, 1973). What recommends these tests for curriculum evaluation is the size of the test battery: A Pretest and Growth Test for six grade levels (Grades 7–12), with six poems or prose selections and thirty-six test items in each test, for a total of seventy-two literature selections and 432 test items in the complete battery. Evaluators could reassemble this collection in a variety of ways appropriate to local needs. Though field testing, item analysis, and revision of items were carried out before these tests were published, there is no normative or reliability data on them. Since nearly all of the seventy-two literature selections are still under copyright, even public use not-for-profit would involve a time-consuming permission process, though one worth the effort in a large school district where the tests might see widespread use.

The main limitation of text-centered tests is the limitation of all norm-referenced tests: they do not tell us very much about what students are learning, except in the very global sense of something we might call "text-processing ability." Clustering types of questions (diction, inference, etc.) and analyzing the results does not tell us anything useful because there are so few question types within any currently available test. Nevertheless, as long as we need scores of "literature text-processing ability" within a normative context, we will need some energetic developmental work, especially to devise tests which measure something in addition to or different from general reading comprehension. This sort of work does not have a high priority for me, but it may have for others. I have tried here only to illustrate what we presently have available and to identify some of its limitations.

Literary Features Tests

A much more promising approach, in my view, is the literary features tests, which looks in detail at a student's ability to deal with a selected feature of a literary text: diction, metaphor, tone, characterization, or organization, to list some possibilities. A complete test is developed around one of these features. The brief selections or portions of selections are chosen to demonstrate the feature in a particular way, and the questions are tailored specifically to disclose how well the student can identify or anlayze or interpret the feature. These tests lend themselves particularly well to criterion-referenced testing. They are quite descriptive in that they illustrate with such precision just how well a student understands one feature of literary texts.

Here are some possibilities from the Cooper and Purves *Guide to Evaluation* mentioned above:

Diction:

> Thou fair-haired angel of the evening,
> Now, whilst the sun rests on the mountains, light
> Thy bright torch of love; thy radiant crown
> Put on, and smile upon our evening bed!
> Smile on our loves, and while thou drawest the
> Blue curtains of the sky, [1] thy silver dew
> On every flower that shuts its sweet eyes
> In timely sleep. Let the west wind sleep on
> The lake; speak silence with thy [2] eyes,
> And wash the dusk with silver. Soon, full soon,
> Dost thou withdraw; then the wolf rages wide,

And the lion glares through the dun forest:
The fleeces of our flocks are covered with
Thy sacred dew; protect them with thine influence.
            —*To the Evening Star*
            by William Blake

1. (a) anoint
 *(b) scatter
  (c) distribute ·
  (d) bestow
2.*(a) glimmering
  (b) silent
  (c) spectacled
  (d) many

Complete the Poem:

They hold their hands over their mouths
And stare at the stretch of water.
What can be said has been said before:
Strokes of light like herons' legs in the cattails,
Mud underneath, frogs lying even deeper.
Therefore, the poets may keep quiet.
But the corners of their mouths grin past their hands.
            —*The Poets Agree to Be Quiet by the
            Swamp*
            by David Wagoner

 A. They remove their hands and laugh aloud
    And begin again their joyful shaping.
*B. They stick their elbows out into the evening,
    Stoop, and begin the ancient croaking.
 C. They flap their wings and soar over the still water,
    Cry out, and return to their nests.
 D. But the dark stillness changes the grin to a grimace,
    And frowning, they take up again their age-old task.

The correct choice (marked with an asterisk) on Diction or Complete the Poem items is, of course, the poet's own word or lines. These items function in the manner of a cloze reading test in which words are deleted in some pattern (usually a deletion at least every tenth word) and the student tries to guess the original word, using all the semantic and syntactic cues available in the text. To make the right choice students must be sensitive to meaning, diction, tone, rhythm, syntax, and imagery in the full text. It is a guessing game, but a very sophisticated one. Items are relatively easy to construct, but distractors are difficult to write.

Metaphor:

I am as glad as grass would be of rain.
            —from *The Marriage of Sir Gawaine*
            Author Unknown

1. From this line we could conclude that
   (a) the rain would thank the grass.
   *(b) the grass would thank the rain.
   (c) the speaker would thank the rain.
   (d) the speaker would thank both the rain and the grass.

2. How grateful is the speaker?
   (a) As grateful as if someone had done him a small favor.
   (b) As grateful as if someone had helped him solve a difficult problem.
   (c) As grateful as if someone had paid him a compliment.
   *(d) As grateful as if someone had saved his life.

In this two-question set for Metaphor the first question asks about the vehicle of the metaphor, the second its tenor, to use I. A. Richards' terms.

Tone:

> Whenas in silks my Julia goes,
> Then, then, methinks, how sweetly flows
> The liquefaction of her clothes.
>
> Next, when I cast mine eyes, and see
> That brave vibration, each way free,
> O, how that glittering taketh me!
>
> —*Upon Julia's Clothes*
> by Robert Herrick

1. How does the speaker feel about Julia?
   (a) He is angry with her.
   (b) He tolerates her.
   *(c) He is fascinated by her.
   (d) He is attracted to her.

2. Which one of the following statements best supports your answer to Question 1?
   *(a) The speaker's remarks in lines 2, 3, and 6 leave no doubts about his attitude.
   (b) Archaic words like *methinks* (line 2) and *taketh* (line 6) reveal the speaker's feeling.
   (c) The three-line stanzas indicate the speaker's feeling.
   (d) The brevity of the poem indicates the speaker's feeling.

The first question asks about the tone; the second askes for the determinant of the tone. Since the second question is so difficult to devise, an alternative is to ask students to write down what they think determines the tone in the poem. This presents scoring problems in a formal evaluation study, but they are not insurmountable (*Reading, Thinking and Writing*, 1981).

Characterization:

> Because the Bible says, Thou shalt not kill,
> They arrested me for talking on birth control.

But if the stream of life should have its way;
And to loose it and then divert it be a crime,
Why not arrest a few deliberate celibates?
—*William Seaman*
by Edgar Lee Masters

1. As he is presented in this poem, what sort of man was William Seaman?
   a. an intelligent criminal
   *b. a cynical but concerned man
   c. an anti-religious man
   d. a crusading dreamer

2. Why was William Seaman the way he was?
   a. People had always been cruel to him.
   b. He couldn't always think straight.
   *c. Society was out to make an example of him.
   d. He hated children.

The first question asks directly about character; the second asks the student to think about motivation or, another possibility, to imagine what the character might do in a different situation.

Other features besides those illustrated here might very well be the basis for a special test. Any such test would probably need to be based on at least twenty literature selections (forty if both a pre- and post-test are needed), to insure reliability. How might feature tests be used? Let us assume that an evaluator needs to determine the effectiveness of a course on the modern short story. Since characterization and tone (or point of view) are such important features of the short story, the evaluator might use a Characterization Test and a Tone Test, both based on unfamiliar brief prose fiction selections, along with the more conventional tests of understanding and interpreting stories mentioned above from the IEA study (Purves, 1981). Because the abilities assessed by these tests would be only partial short-range outcomes of such a course, the evaluator might use still other measures, some formal, some informal, but almost certainly one based on an expressed response.

All of the examples above are from the Ginn evaluation program *Guide to Evaluation* (Cooper and Purves, 1973). Another source of literary features test items is the released exercises from the National Assessment (NAEP, 1973, 1981b). Still another source, and a very valuable one, is the criterion-referenced reading comprehension tests developed by the Montgomery County Public Schools in Maryland. The new tests serve to evaluate the performance objectives of a new instructional program called Instructional System in Reading/Language Arts. The particular tests of interest to us are titled *Criterion Referenced Reading Tests: Comprehension of Narrative Excerpts* (1980). Like the Ginn tests illustrated above, these tests present a brief prose fiction selection and then ask a single multiple-choice question of the selection, a question concerned with a particular literary feature: characterization, motivation, conflict, events, vocabulary, dialogue, cohesion, and setting. Tests are available for Grades 1–8. Developed as part of a large curriculum project under the direction of Ted Schuder, these tests can be requested from the Board of Education, Montgomery County Public Schools, Rockville, Maryland 20850. But again, as with the Ginn program Pretests and Growth Tests discussed in the previous section, the Montgomery County tests contain copyrighted literary passages for which users must obtain permission to reprint. As big an obstacle as that may seem, I see no alternatives to the permission process. We cannot test literature without using literature. Nearly all publishers or copyright holders will give permission to reprint without charge when the use is not-for-profit, as in school or college program evaluation or in research studies. Publishers' addresses can be located in *Literary Market Place* or behind the "Z" section in the second volume of the current *Books in Print*. Both are available in libraries.

One final test I should mention is not so much a features test as a discourse or genre test. Developed by Alan Purves for the first national literature assessment (NAEP, 1973, pp. 40–51), it works like this in one version: the student is given four brief selections, two of them poem stanzas, one a few sentences from a prose fiction narrative, and one a brief bit of dialogue exchange from a play. The task is to identify the two which are alike. Simple as this may seem to adults, it is not necessarily simple or obvious at all to a young child whose sense of how texts differ develops very slowly during the school years. Recent research in cognitive science makes this sense of text or discourse distinctions seem a critically important educational objective. It seems that discourse competence, both from the reading side and the writing side, is largely a matter of knowing a particular discourse type (recipe, argument, poem, fable) well enough to "represent" it to ourselves in order to make productive predictions as readers and to have a pattern to follow as writer.

In another version of Purves' discourse test, the two selections which are "alike" of the four are stage directions from a play and dialogue from a play, the two unlike being rapid exchange of dialogue in a narrative and a third-person narrative. In still another version the two "alike" are first-person narratives, the two unlike being a third-person narrative and a short section of dialogue from a play. The possibilities for development of this kind of test seem to me particularly promising and important. For example, I could envision in this format a test of the range of points of view in short fiction (Moffett and McElheny, 1966), a refinement which could create a challenging test for an upper secondary or college student.

Discrimination Tests

Tests of "discrimination" or "appreciation" have an interesting history. As early as 1914, a test of prose discrimination was devised (Ballard, 1914) which presented students ages nine to 14 with a short extract from Sir Thomas Malory's *Morte d'Arthur*, along with three different versions (florid, plain, and jocular) of the extract written by the evaluator. The right answer was, of course, the Malory original.

I am not certain how many school and college literature teachers still have the development of taste or appreciation as a major objective. Certainly it is no longer mentioned so prominently in journal articles or published materials, but I suspect it is still a strongly held implicit objective. Some pronouncements from the 1920s and 1930s imply that good teaching of the classics will automatically elevate taste: if children are presented with the best, they will come to prefer the best. We are no longer so naive; now we are uncertain whether taste or discrimination can be "developed" at all; we suspect that it may grow very gradually after encouragement to read all kinds of things, the good and the not-so-good, and we need not force young readers to read texts which are too complex or sophisticated. Yet most of us remain convinced that knowing the best at the appropriate time will insure that at least some students will come to prefer the best; or, as I put it in the list of objectives at the beginning of this article, they will come to prefer works of merit over prosaic, predictable, or sentimental works.

If that is a course objective—or, more realistically, a school literature program objective over several years' time—a curriculum evaluator can collect evidence of growth in the student's ability to recognize or prefer works of merit by using a discrimination test. I have reviewed elsewhere all such tests available in reports and publications (Cooper, 1971, 1972). In addition to the approach used by Ballard above, let me note here just a few other approaches, to give some indication of the possibilities.

Williams, Winter, and Woods (1938) devised a variety of tests. In one, students sorted, in the manner of a Q-sort, short prose extracts of quite different quality. In another, they chose the best from among three short prose extracts: the best from the *Oxford Book of Prose*, the intermediate from "an author of an intermediate type," and the worst from popular magazines. In still another, students chose the best of three sentences, with the criteria for the best sentence being its sound, construction, and diction. Abbott and Trabue (1921) presented a well-known poem of quality with three inferior versions of it (sentimental, prosaic, metrical) which they wrote themselves. Rigg (1942) chose forty short extracts of poetry (from two to six lines) from poets of "established reputation" and paired them with versions "purposely made inferior in some respect."

Response Preference Tests
There is some research evidence from aesthetics and from response to literature that readers have different response styles. Purves (1973) reports in the IEA study that there are national response styles, but not individual styles, and conjectures that the way literature is taught in a country results in a convergence by the end of secondary school on a preferred way of responding. Where a literature program had the specific objective of changing or broadening response style, measures are available, all of which need further development and tryouts. In the IEA study, Purves asked students to choose questions they thought important to ask about stories they had just read. The twenty questions were based on Purves' content analysis of expressed responses, to be discussed in the next section.

Here are the questions as they were phrased for the short story *The Man by the Fountain* by the Belgian writer Georges Hebbelinck:

Directions: Answer the following questions as carefully and as honestly as you can.

Here are a number of questions that might be asked about "The Man by the Fountain." Some of these are more important than others. Read the list carefully and choose the five (5) questions that you think are the most important to ask about "The Man by the Fountain" and blacken the appropriate spaces on your answer card.

1. What is the writer's opinion of or attitude toward the people in "The Man by the Fountain"?
2. Is there any one part of "The Man by the Fountain" that explains the whole story?
3. What emotions does "The Man by the Fountain" arouse in me?
4. What does "The Man by the Fountain" tell us about people I know?
5. Does "The Man by the Fountain" succeed in getting me involved in the situation?
6. What metaphors (or comparisons), images (or references to things outside the story), or other writer's devices are used in "The Man by the Fountain"?
7. When was "The Man by the Fountain" written? What is the historical background of the story and the writer? Does the fact that the author is Belgian tell me anything about the story?
8. Is there anything in "The Man by the Fountain" that has a hidden meaning?
9. Is this a proper subject for a story?
10. How is the way of telling the story related to what "The Man by the Fountain" is about?
11. Is there a lesson to be learned from "The Man by the Fountain"?
12. Is "The Man by the Fountain" well written?
13. How does the story build up? How is it organized?
14. What type of story is "The Man by the Fountain"? Is it like any other story I know?
15. How can we explain the way people behave in "The Man by the Fountain"?
16. Are any of the characters in "The Man by the Fountain" like people I know?
17. Has the writer used words or sentences differently from the way people usually write?
18. What happens in "The Man by the Fountain"?
19. Is "The Man by the Fountain" about important things? Is it a trivial or serious work?
20. Does the story tell me anything about people or ideas in general?

Michalak (1976) has suggested revisions in the Purves list, and Cooper and Michalak (1981) have argued that the most valid way to assess response style—within the context of the Purves content analysis system—is to classify an entire free response essay in a holistic way.

In the different context of ego psychology, one's response style reflects one's ego structure and would not be amenable to change by instruction of any kind (Holland, 1975, and this volume). This theoretical challenge to the notion that response styles can be learned and changes in them measured indicates a need for basic research on that question. Such research would enable us to refine our measures of response style—or perhaps persuade us to give them up.

A quite different sort of response preference measure is one developed at the Carnegie Curriculum Study Center (available in ERIC: ED-011-966). Students read a story and then choose among four descriptions which emphasize (1) facts about setting, characterization, or plot; (2) entertainment value; (3) literary techniques; and (4) theme. Here is a question set based on Akutagawa's "The Dragon":

> Which of the following descriptions of the story "The Dragon" seems most appropriate to you?
>
> a. (Technique) In "The Dragon" the author has used a story about medieval times to make ironic comments about modern behavior. Modern readers may find belief in dragons fanciful and the language of the story strange, but the portrayal of human behavior seems "true."
> b. (Theme) The main theme of "The Dragon" concerns the way human beings come to believe things. The author seems to be saying that it is hard to distinguish between what is true and what is thought to be true.
> c. (Facts) "The Dragon" is a story set in medieval Japan. It tells of a Buddhist priest who started a rumor that a dragon would ascend from a pond, and then came to believe the rumor himself.
> d. (Entertainment) "The Dragon" is a funny story that makes fun of people who take themselves seriously. The language, the character descriptions, and the incidents that are related contribute to the story's humor.

Tests of Sophistication of Reading Preferences

I mention two available tests in this category with some hesitation because they are so crude, a conclusion about them which I am certain their developers would accept. These tests do, nevertheless, suggest interesting possibilities for further development, not so much as criterion measures in a curriculum evaluation study as survey instruments to gather information about trends in large groups.

Reich (1973) developed a simple instrument which asks students in a survey to name the one novel they have read recently that they enjoyed most. From a list of twenty-three topics "that frequently appear in novels" students then checked those that appeared in their most-enjoyed novel. Number of topics is equated here with thematic complexity. The instrument is surprisingly reliable in one sense: students agree with each other about topics in novels read in common. Further, teachers and students agree very closely on the number and kind of topics in a novel.

Zais (1969) wrote brief book synopses at three levels of "sophistication" and then presented these to students in dyads: least sophisticated-moderately sophisticated; least-most; and moderately-most. Scoring is three points for choosing correctly the *most* sophisticated choice where it appears in a dyad, two points for a *moderately* sophisticated choice, and one point for a *least* sophisticated choice.

These humble beginnings seem to me worth our attention because of the importance in school literature programs of developing maturity or sophistication or, perhaps better, catholicity of reading choices. Like discrimination or taste, sophistication of reading preferences is something we claim we are developing. If we are developing it, why shouldn't we attempt to demonstrate it, particularly if some of us can develop simple, efficient survey instruments to demonstrate it for groups of students, perhaps by comparing the results for incoming ninth graders and outgoing twelfth graders? The Reich instrument might produce quite dramatic results in such an instance. The results would hold only for groups, not for individuals: what a student would say about the number of topics in a single novel is not a reliable index of maturity for that student.

Before moving on to a consideration of constructed-response measures, let me restate the main point of the just-completed brief summary of selected response measures: some interesting and useful work has been done, but we have barely begun the developmental effort that will provide us with an array of tests for use in literature curriculum evaluation studies. What we need is not so much refinement of the possibilities I have listed above—although even that would be challenging and important work—but creative new item types and formats. Those new developments must be grounded in the best current theory and research about the way people read literature.

I must reiterate that I am not recommending norm-referenced standardized testing of the outcomes of literature instruction. I am quite specifically exhorting us to do our test development work within a criterion-referenced framework. That way we will learn about the effects of instruction in a way useful to ourselves and our students, and we will avoid a simple-minded rank-ordering of students on the basis of a single global score occurring somewhere within a normal distribution of scores. We will be able to describe part of what students can do when they examine literary texts, and we will be able to make general statements about certain outcomes — certain benefits—of literature instruction.

We move now to a brief look at two approaches to reliable group assessment by constructed-response procedures.

Content Analysis of Expressed Responses

Elsewhere I have reviewed the development of content-analysis schemes for classifying and analyzing expressed responses, beginning with I. A. Richards' landmark *Practical Criticism* (Cooper, 1972). The work I reviewed had culminated in the now widely known content analysis scheme developed by Alan Purves (1968). It permits a precise classification of each written or recorded statement a responder makes, using either an exhaustively comprehensive list of 120 "elements" of response derived from the responses of a great many students and published critics, a set of twenty subcategories abstracted from the 120 elements, or a group of four "stances" a responder can take toward a work. These four stances or categories organize the entire scheme. With all its limitations—for example, the four categories were too general and needed their own subcategories (Purves and Beach, 1972); it does not permit clear enough distinctions among statements made about the work, the author, and the speaker or narrator (Beardsley, 1969); it looks only at the surface structure of the expressed response—it was a brilliant achievement which touched off a flurry of studies (reviewed by Applebee, 1977).

With some refinements and extensions for specialized uses (for example, Odell and Cooper, 1976), this scheme is useful right now for curriculum evaluation studies. It is highly descriptive and gives us a clear sense of the elements and the patterns of students' expressed responses. We can learn from it whether the content or pattern of a student's expressed response changes as a result of instruction. The scheme has been the basis for selected-response measures (the Response Preference Measure from the IEA study reviewed above).

Some recent developments suggest other possibilities for content-analysis—for the planned, systematic analysis of a reader's expressed response. Following I. A. Richards' procedures, Paula Johnson (1975) asked her Yale freshmen to write out their first response to a group of unidentified poems (by Lawrence, Plath, Stevens, Veitch, Carew). Her insightful analysis of the students' respones led her to classify them as *decoding* (paraphrasing, analyzing, describing), the most common response; *valuing*; and four kinds of *situating*: finding literary context, interpreting the "message," making social conjectures, and adducing private associations. I can imagine a college literature program with the primary objective of increasing students' reliance on "literary contexts" when they are faced with the problem of "situating" themselves with a new poem. A content-analysis like Johnson's of written responses to two poems early in the course and two late in the course would determine whether students were learning what the program was designed to teach them. I want to emphasize that such a test—following widely accepted procedures which I note in the next section to ensure reliability of the content-analysis—is completely appropriate in every way for the most formal curriculum evaluation study.

Another recent development is the scoring guides devised for the "open-ended exercises" (written responses) to literature selections in the 1979–80 Reading/ Literature assessment of the National Assessment of Educational Progress (NAEP, 1981b; *Reading, Thinking and Writing*, 1981). They were devised by Kay Barrow, Ina Mullis, and Mike Noe of the NAEP staff, Arthur Applebee, Anthony Petrosky, and me. I mention them because they are a very natural extension of primary-trait description and scoring (identifying the primary or essential rhetorical traits in a piece of writing) developed by Carl Klaus and Richard Lloyd-Jones for the second and third national assessments of writing (see the Lloyd-Jones chapter in Cooper and Odell [1977] and the released exercises from the second and third national writing assessment [NAEP, 1978, and 1981a]). Such scoring guides simply list the features of interest, and these features then focus the content-analysis of written responses. Responses can be analyzed for the presence or absence of certain features or for qualitative levels of a feature. After considerable refinement and collection of examples, raters can be trained to describe or score papers quite reliably.

Even though content analysis procedures are quite time-consuming, they are worth careful consideration by curriculum evaluators. They are criterion-referenced in that the content analysis itself can always reflect important objectives in the teaching program, and they are generally more acceptable to literature teachers than selected response (multiple-choice) tests. However, even though the student constructs the response, a careful content-analysis like those I have reviewed, can be as objective and reliable (in the psychometric sense) as selected-response testing.

Holistic Scoring of Expressed Response

The Purves, Johnson, and National Assessment content-analysis schemes permit a neutral description of an expressed response. Where we need to sort, rank, or score responses to literature or essays about literature in a normative way, we can do so quite reliably with holistic scoring procedures.

Recent developments in the evaluation of writing (see Cooper and Odell, 1977) informs much of what I want to say on this topic. Perhaps the most significant thing we have learned recently is the importance of the way we state the topic for an essay task (when we assign a specific task, rather than asking the student for a free response). Roberts (1977) suggests one range of possible topics for essays of literature, and Purves (1971, pp. 276–728) has contributed a thoughtful discussion of the level of explicitness appropriate in setting the task. In addition, discourse theorists (see the Lloyd-Jones chapter in Cooper and Odell, 1977) have stressed the importance of presenting the task in a full rhetorical context so that the writer has a clear sense of his or her purpose, audience, and persona. I should add that my own preference is to base the task on a fresh new work or works so that we can learn what the students can do on their own with new works like those they may have been studying in the course or program. In summary, for evaluation purposes—in order to be fair to the student—the response task should be precise, explicit, and rhetorically complete. This turns out to be a great advantage when devising the scoring guide or rubric.

We also have tentative evidence that we get the best sample of a student's ability to write about literature by permitting the student to know the topic in advance in order to rehearse, research, or outline and then to give the student a chance a few days after the first draft for a complete revision. Of course, both the draft and the revision are written under the supervision of the teacher or evaluator. In addition, we know that in order to be completely fair to the student we need at least two essays at each test-time. Finally, we know that each of these two essays at each test-time must be scored independently by at least two raters who have been trained carefully to use a scoring guide developed from close analysis of a small set of papers to be scored. There are several authoritative guides to planning and organizing such testing sessions and to scoring the essays (Davis, Scriven, and Thomas, 1981; Meyers, 1980; Odell, 1981).

These constraints may make essay scoring so complicated and time-consuming that it seems unusable for evaluation purposes with large groups, just as proponents of multiple-choice, machine-scorable tests argue. However, the great advantage of the essay test is that it permits individual expressiveness, giving writers the opportunity to organize what they know and to make further discoveries during drafting and revising.

Of course, rather than set a topic, we can ask students to write whatever they like about a work and then use criteria of judgment appropriate to the type of response they have chosen to make. Purves outlines some procedures for this alternative (Cooper and Purves, 1973).

CONCLUSION

In the introduction to this chapter I spent much time saying what I was *not* doing—and for very good reasons. I do not want to be misunderstood. I am making only the smallest and most limited claims for the proposals in this chapter. The measures I have outlined might interest school and college classroom teachers of literature and perhaps inform their decisions about the ways they will evaluate students in their own courses, but experienced teachers who are informed by the theories expounded elsewhere in this collection will have their own informal ways to evaluate student response and growth. They may talk to their students, for example. The measures reviewed here, and newer measures which I hope will be developed, are of concern mainly to the curriculum evaluator interested in status studies or surveys of achievement in literature or in growth measurement over long periods of time for students in particular programs. Such an evaluator could also be a classroom teacher, of course.

And I have insisted that the curriculum evaluator must recognize that the best procedures we presently have available let us look at only a very few of the outcomes of literary study.

What we know now is only a point of departure for future work. My purpose in writing this chapter has been to suggest starting points for the test development work which needs to be done in the years ahead.

REFERENCES

Abbott, A., & Trabue, M. R. A measure of ability to judge poetry. *Teachers College Record*, 1921, *22*, 101–126.

Applebee, A. N. ERIC/RCS report: The elements of response to a literary work: What we have learned. *Research in the Teaching of English*, 1977, *11*, 255–271.

Ashley, H. C. A study of the relationships of several measures of interpretive skill in literature and achievement in reading. Unpublished doctoral dissertation, State University of New York at Buffalo, 1972.

Ballard, P. B. Prose preferences of school children. *Journal of Educational Psychology*, 1914, *5*, 10–21.

Beardsley, M. C., Review of *Elements of writing about a work of literature*. *Journal of Aesthetic Education*, 1969, *3*, 165–167.

Bloom, B. S., Hastings, J. T., & Madaus, G. F. *Handbook on formative and summative evaluation of student learning*. New York: McGraw-Hill, 1971.

Campbell, D. T., & Stanley, J. C. *Experimental and quasi-experimental designs for research*. Chicago: Rand and McNally, 1963.

Cooper, C. R. Measuring appreciation of literature: a review of attempts. *Research in the Teaching of English*, 1971, *5*, 5–23.

Cooper, C. R. *Measuring growth in appreciation of literature*. Newark, DE: International Reading Association, 1972.

Cooper, C. R. (Ed.). *The nature and measurement of competency in English.* Urbana, IL: National Council of Teachers of English, 1981.

Cooper, C. R., & Michalak, D. A. A note on determining response styles in research on response to literature. *Research in the Teaching of English*, 1981, *15*, 163–169.

Cooper, C. R., & Odell, L. *Evaluating writing: Describing, measuring, judging.* Urbana, IL: National Council of Teachers of English, 1977.

Cooper, C. R., & Petrosky, A. R. A psycholinguistic view of the fluent reading process. *Journal of Reading*, 1976, *20*, 184–205.

Cooper, C. R., & Purves, A. *A guide to evaluation for responding.* Lexington, MA: Ginn, 1973. (The *Guide* is available from ERIC Document Reproduction Service No. ED 155 691. The tests themselves are now out of print along with the literature series they accompanied, but they may be borrowed for the cost of mailing from Charles R. Cooper, Department of Literature, D-007, University of California at San Diego, La Jolla, CA 92093).

Coryell, N. G. *An evaluation of extensive and intensive teaching of literature.* New York: Teachers College, Columbia University, 1927.

Criterion-referenced reading tests: Comprehension of narrative excerpts. Rockville, MD: Board of Education of Montgomery County, 1980.

Davis, B. G., Scriven, M., & Thomas, S. *The evaluation of composition instruction.* Inverness, CA: Edgepress, 1981.

Diesing, P. *Patterns of discovery in the social sciences.* New York: Aldine-Atherton, 1971.

Fagan, W. T., Cooper, C. R., & Jensen, J. M. *Measures for research and evaluation in the English language arts.* Urbana, IL: National Council of Teachers of English, 1975.

Guba, E. G., & Lincoln, Y. S. *Effective evaluation.* San Francisco: Jossey-Bass, 1981.

Hardwick, L. The effects of a personalized reading program on the reading skills, attitudes, study habits, and self-concepts of seventh grade students. Unpublished doctoral disserrtation, University of California at Los Angeles, 1970.

Holland, N. *5 readers reading.* New Haven: Yale University Press, 1975.

Johnson, P. Getting acquainted with a poem. *College English*, 1975, *37*, 358–367.

Meyers, M. *A procedure for writing assessment and holistic scoring.* Urbana, IL: National Council of Teachers of English, 1980.

Michalak, D. A. The effect of instruction in literature on high school students' preferred way of responding to literature. Unpublished doctoral dissertation, State University of New York at Buffalo, 1976.

Moffett, J., & McElheny, K. R. *Points of view: An anthology of short stories.* New York: Mentor, 1966.

Morris, L. L. *Program evaluation kit.* Beverly Hills: Sage Publications, 1978. (Ordering information can be obtained from Sage Publications, 275 South Beverly Drive, Beverly Hills, CA 90212.)

National Assessment of Educational Progress. *Literature: Released exercises* (1970-71 Assessment). Denver: NAEP, 1973.

National Assessment of Educational Progress. *The second national assessment of writing: New and reassessed exercises with technical information and data.* Denver: NAEP, 1978. (Available in ERIC: ED-155-728).

National Assessment of Educational Progress. *The third assessment of writing: 1978-79 released exercise set.* Denver: NAEP, 1981. (Available from ERIC Document Reproduction Service No. ED-205-583.) (a).

National Assessment of Educational Progress. *Reading/literature released exercise set, 1979-80 assessment.* Denver: NAEP, 1981. (Available in ERIC Document Reproduction Service No.: ED 205 589.) (b).

Norvell, G. W. *The reading interests of young people.* Boston: D. C. Heath, 1950.

Odell, L. Defining and assessing competence in writing. In C. R. Cooper (Ed.), *The nature and measurement of competency in English.* Urbana, IL: National Council of Teachers of English, 1981.

Odell, L., & Cooper, C. R. Describing responses to works of fiction. *Research in the teaching of English*, 1976, *10*, 203–225.

Patton, M. Q. *Qualitative evaluation methods.* Beverly Hills: Sage, 1980.

Popham, W. J. *Educational evaluation*. Englewood Cliffs, NJ: Prentice-Hall, 1975.

Popper, K. R. *The logic of scientific discovery*. New York: Basic Books, 1959.

Purves, A. *Elements of writing about a literary work: a study of response to literature*. Urbana, IL: National Council of Teachers of English Research Monograph, 1968.

Purves, A. Evaluation of learning in literature. In B. Bloom, J. T. Hastings, & G. F. Madaus (Eds.), *Handbook on formative and summative evaluation of student learning*. New York: McGraw-Hill, 1971.

Purves, A. *Literature education in ten countries*. New York: John Wiley, 1973.

Purves, A. *Reading and literature: American achievement in international perspective*. Urbana, IL: National Council of Teachers of English, 1981.

Purves, A., & Beach, R. *Literature and the reader*. Urbana, IL: National Council of Teachers of English, 1972.

Reading, thinking, and writing. Denver: National Assessment of Educational Progress, 1981.

Reich, C. A scale to assess reading maturity. *Journal of Reading*, 1973, *17*, 220–223.

Rigg, M. D. *The Rigg poetry judgment test*. Iowa City: Bureau of Educational Research and Services, State University of Iowa, 1942.

Roberts, E. V. *Writing themes about literature*. 4th ed. Englewood Cliffs, NJ: Prentice-Hall, 1977.

Smith, F. *Understanding reading* (2nd ed.). New York: Holt, Rinehart & Winston, 1978.

Williams, E. D., Winter, L., & Woods, I. M. Tests of literary appreciation. *British Journal of Educational Psychology*, 1938, *8*, 265–283.

Zais, R. A scale to measure sophistication of reading interests. *Journal of Reading*, 1969, *12*, 273–276, 326–335.

Author Index

Italic page numbers indicate bibliographic citations.

A

Aaronson, D., 213, *231*
Abbott, A., 323, *329*
Abbott, V., 201, *210*
Abelson, R. P., 60*n*, *69*, 196, 199, 201, 205, 206, *210*, *211*
Acland, H., *305*
Ames, A., 35, *51*
Anderson, C., *305*
Anderson, L., *305*
Anderson, R. C., 106, *125*, 157, *168*, 299, *304*
Anderson, S., *304*
Antos, S. J., 162, 164, *168*
Applebee, A. N., 5, 72, 75, *81*, 92, 93, 96, 99, 100, *101*, 170, *188*, 289, 299, *304*, 326, 327, *329*
Applebee, R. K., 288, 291–299, *306*
Arnold, W., 142, *149*
Arter, J. A., 151, 154, 159, *168*
Asch, S., 152, 159, *167*
Ashley, H. C., 317, *329*
Austin, J. L., 107, *125*
Aw, K. H., *304*

B

Bach, K., 107, *125*
Ballard, P. B., 322, *329*
Bane, M. J., *305*
Barnes, D., 284, *285*
Barrow, K., 75, *81*, 327
Bartlett, F. C., 195, 196, *210*
Bates, E., 41, *51*, 105, *125*
Bateson, G., 35, *51*
Bauer, W., 222, *232*
Beach, R., 34, 44, 46, *52*, 67, *69*, 110, 120, 124, *125*, *126*, 128, *150*, 272, 297, *305*, *306*, 326, *331*
Beardsley, M. C., 326, *329*
Beck, I. L., 75, *81*
Beckman, M., *306*
Benedict, R., 34
Bentley, A. F., 34, *52*
Berliner, D., *306*
Bettelheim, B., *188*
Bever, T. G., 137, *149*
Billow, R. M., 162, *167*
Black, J. B., 171, 193–196, 198, 199, 201, 203, 205, 206, *210*, *211*

Black, M., 154, *167*
Bleich, D., 22, 25, 26, 28, *32*, 36, *51*, 75, *81*, 253, 272, 274, 284, *285*
Bloom, B. S., 308, *329*
Boas, F., 34
Bobrow, D., 106, *126*
Bohr, N., 40, *51*
Boldrick, D., *210*
Bolgar, H., 77, *81*
Bower, G. H., 170, *188*, 193–195, 198, 199, 201, 203, *210*
Bower, T. G. R., 13, *19*
Brainerd, C. J., 162, *167*
Bransford, J., 106, *126*
Brewer, W. F., 104, *127*, 156, *168*, 208, *210*
Britton, J., 27, *32*, 37, 38*n*, *51*, 57, 68, *69*, 87, 90, *101*, 105, *126*
Brooks, C., 34, *51*
Brophy, J., 287, *304*, *305*
Broudy, H., 105, *126*
Brown, A. L., 162, *167*, 170, *188*, 299, *304*
Brown, J. S., 60, *69*
Brown, P., 108, *126*
Brown, R., 75, *81*, 104, 106, 107, *126*, *127*
Bruce, B. C., 104, 106, 113, *126*, *127*, 156, *168*
Bruner, J. S., 97, *101*
Buchler, J., 239, *249*
Buchmann, M., *304*
Burgess, T., 90, *101*
Burke, K., 229
Burkes, A. M., 75, *81*
Burton, D. L., 297, *304*

C

Campbell, D. T., 289, *304*, 311, *329*
Campbell, E. Q., *304*
Cantril, H., 35, *51*
Carew, T., 327
Carey, R. F., 42, *52*
Carroll, J. B., 295, *304*
Carroll, L., 42, 152
Chall, J., 298, *304*
Chamberlain, A. F., 166, *167*
Chamberlain, J. C., 166, *167*
Chapman, A., 185, *189*
Chi, M. T. H., 165, *167*
Chomsky, N., 13, 15, 88, *101*, 272
Churley, P., 284, *285*

Subject Index